Mar
Debbie Law

Tomcat

KICK START

SAMS

800 East 96th Street, Indianapolis, Indiana 46240

Tomcat Kick Start

International Standard Book Number: 0-672-32439-3

Library of Congress Catalog Card Number: 2002105435

Printed in the United States of America

First Printing: November 2002

05 04 03 4 3 2

Trademarks

Warning and Disclaimer

Bulk Sales

Sams Publishing offers excellent discounts on this book when ordered in quantity for bulk purchases or special sales. For more information, please contact

U.S. Corporate and Government Sales
1-800-382-3419
corpsales@pearsontechgroup.com

For sales outside of the U.S., please contact

International Sales
1-317-428-3341
international@pearsontechgroup.com

Executive Editor
Michael Stephens

Acquisitions Editor
Todd Green

Development Editor
Tiffany Taylor

Managing Editor
Charlotte Clapp

Project Editor
Andy Beaster

Copy Editors
Mike Dietsch
Matt Wynalda

Indexer
Tom Dinse

Proofreader
Kevin Ober

Technical Editors
Lowell Thomas
Robert Brunner

Expert Reviewer
Robert Herrman

Team Coordinator
Lynne Williams

Interior Designer
Gary Adair

Cover Designer
Aren Howell

Page Layout
Michelle Mitchell

Graphics
Oliver Jackson
Tammy Graham

Contents at a Glance

Table of Contents

Part II Development and Administration

About the Authors

The authors of this book work for Content Master Ltd., a technical authoring company in the United Kingdom specializing in the production of training and educational materials. For more information on Content Master, see its Web site at `www.contentmaster.com`. Previously, the authors contributed to *Sams Teach Yourself J2EE in 21 Days* (Sams, 2002).

Martin Bond, B.Sc., M.Sc., C.Eng., M.B.C.S., was born in Blackburn, England, in 1958, has honours and master's degrees in computer science, is a European Chartered Engineer, and has been working as a senior technologist for Content Master Ltd. for more than a year. After leaving university, Martin led an R&D team developing parallel processing compilers for the occam language, later moving into open systems software design and development working with Unix, C, C++, Oracle, and Windows NT. Since 1995, he has worked primarily as a trainer, course writer, and technical author specialising in Unix, C, C++, Java, and software design. He has written training courses on Unix, XML, Java, and Solaris Security and coauthored a book on J2EE. Martin currently lives on a smallholding in Cornwall, England.

Debbie Law, B.Sc., was born in Romsey, England, in 1959. Debbie started her career working on compiler development for parallel processing systems and later worked on the design and development of client/server applications. Debbie, also a senior technologist for Content Master Ltd., writes books, training material, and technical papers to pay the bills and maintains part of the Web site of a major UK charity for fun. She has an honours degree in computer science from Southampton University, England and currently lives on a smallholding in Cornwall, England.

Dedications

To my parents, Bob and Dorothy Bond—Martin

To our nine cats, without whose help this book would have been written much, much, quicker—Debbie

Acknowledgments

Content Master would like to thank Sams Publishing for giving us the opportunity to write about this exciting technology. Special thanks go to Todd Green, Andy Beaster, and the rest of the editing team at Sams. I would also like to thank the authors, Martin Bond and Debbie Law, for hitting all their deadlines and making my job as project manager so stress-free.

Beverly Mullock—Project Manager, Content Master

We Want to Hear from You!

As the reader of this book, *you* are our most important critic and commentator. We value your opinion and want to know what we're doing right, what we could do better, what areas you'd like to see us publish in, and any other words of wisdom you're willing to pass our way.

As an executive editor for Sams, I welcome your comments. You can email or write me directly to let me know what you did or didn't like about this book—as well as what we can do to make our books better.

Please note that I cannot help you with technical problems related to the *topic* of this book. We do have a User Services group, however, where I will forward specific technical questions related to the book.

When you write, please be sure to include this book's title and author as well as your name, email address, and phone number. I will carefully review your comments and share them with the authors and editors who worked on the book.

Email: `feedback@samspublishing.com`

Mail: Michael Stephens, Executive Editor
Sams
800 East 96th Street
Indianapolis, IN 46240 USA

For more information about this book or another Sams title, visit our Web site at `www.samspublishing.com`. Type the ISBN (excluding hyphens) or the title of a book in the Search field to find the page you're looking for.

Introduction

Over the past few years, the Internet has become the lingua franca of the business and information technology world. The World Wide Web has become the primary source of information for many people, and the simple static Web pages that once dominated the Internet landscape have for a long time now been augmented with dynamic content and Web applications delivering online shopping and similar functionality.

Jakarta Tomcat is an open source Web server from the Apache Software Foundation. Tomcat, like other open source software, is provided free of charge to all users and no restrictions are placed on the end user or the specific field of use. This book is an introduction to using and administering Jakarta Tomcat and to developing dynamic Web applications written in Java.

How This Book Is Organized

The chapters in this book are organized into three parts that guide you through different aspects of developing Java Web applications using Tomcat.

Part I, "Basic Principles," provides a basic grounding in using Tomcat and developing servlets and JSPs and is intended for developers new to Java Web technologies. The chapters in this part are as follows:

- Chapter 1, "Overview of Jakarta Tomcat, Servlets, and JSP," provides an introduction to the Tomcat Web server and to servlet and JSP technologies.
- Chapter 2, "Installing Jakarta Tomcat," shows you how to install Tomcat as a development server and as a live Web server.
- Chapter 3, "Basic Principles of Web Servers," gives an overview of the Hypertext Transfer Protocol (HTTP), which underlies all Web services.
- Chapter 4, "Basic Principles of Servlets," teaches the key concepts required for developing simple Java servlets.
- Chapter 5, "Basic Principles of JSPs," introduces the basic information required for developing simple JSPs.
- Chapter 6, "Troubleshooting Servlets and JSPs," offers a quick guide to common problems encountered when developing and deploying Web resources.

Part II, "Development and Administration," assumes a basic grasp of the principles of Java Web technologies and explores different areas of application development and Tomcat administration required to develop robust, real-world Web applications. This part includes the following chapters:

- Chapter 7, "The Web Application Environment," is a comprehensive study of the various objects and APIs used to develop Web resources.
- Chapter 8, "Session Tracking," serves as a guide to managing and maintaining client sessions involving sequential requests to multiple Web pages.
- Chapter 9, "Databases and Tomcat," demonstrates the concepts of configuring and using JDBC databases and J2EE data sources.
- Chapter 10, "Custom Tags and TagLibs," covers writing and developing custom tags to simplify the development of JSPs.
- Chapter 11, " JSP Expression Language and JSTL," discusses the expression language (EL) and custom tags in the JavaServer Pages Standard Tag Library (JSTL).
- Chapter 12, "Error Handling," offers a guide to best practices and facilities for incorporating error handling into Web applications.
- Chapter 13, "Logging Using Tomcat," shows how to add logging capabilities provided by Tomcat, Java 1.4, and Jakarta log4j to Web applications.
- Chapter 14, "Access Control," deals with protecting access to Web resources by requiring the user to log in to a security realm. Topics include configuring and using security realms based on JDBC, JNDI, and XML repositories.
- Chapter 15, "Administering Tomcat in a Live Environment," is a quick guide to starting and stopping Tomcat and managing Web applications for administrators.
- Chapter 16, "Configuring Tomcat," gives a detailed look at the Tomcat configuration files intended for administrators who need to change the default Tomcat configuration (such as HTTP port numbers).

Part III, "Advanced Topics," is intended for developers who are building medium- to large-scale Web applications. The chapters that make up this part look at techniques and technologies that supplement the basic servlet and JSP functionality:

- Chapter 17, "Architectures," serves as a guide to the basic architectures used when designing Web applications, including the Model 1, Model 2, and MVC patterns.
- Chapter 18, "Servlet Filters," covers using filters to add common functionality to new or existing Web resources.

- Chapter 19, "Tomcat Valves," explains how to incorporate features provided by Tomcat valves into Web applications.
- Chapter 20, "Frameworks and Jakarta Struts," deals with writing Web applications incorporating the open source Jakarta Struts framework to improve functional compartmentalization and shorten development times.
- Chapter 21, "Testing with Jakarta Cactus," offers an introduction to Jakarta Cactus, which is useful for implementing server-side unit testing strategies.
- Chapter 22, "Integrating Tomcat with a Web Server," discusses the process of integrating Tomcat into an existing Apache or Microsoft IIS Web server.
- Chapter 23, "Securing Web Applications Under Tomcat," shows how to add support for secure connections to Web applications using HTTPS (HTTP over SSL connections).
- Chapter 24, "Tomcat and J2EE," explores the role of Tomcat within the J2EE specification.
- Chapter 25, "Web Services and Axis," provides an introduction to developing Web services using the Jakarta Axis Web server.

The appendixes include information that supplements the content of the book's chapters. They cover the following topics:

- Appendix A, "Apache Software License, Version 1.1," reproduces the standard Apache license describing the conditions under which Tomcat can be used.
- Appendix B, "Template `web.xml` File," contains a Web application deployment descriptor showing the nested structure of all elements discussed in this book.

About This Book

This book's primary purpose is to enable you to quickly learn to write and deploy Web applications under Tomcat. As such, each chapter studies one aspect of Web application development or Tomcat administration and introduces the key concepts for that topic, but does not go into exhaustive detail concerning the configuration files and APIs used. The aim is to get you started with the technology by using simple examples that illustrate the fundamental principles you need to comprehend. The book avoids going into unnecessary detail, as this often detracts from the key points of the technology. Nor does this book reproduce the Java API and Tomcat documentation, which is readily accessible to developers and administrators.

Each chapter focuses on a key topic and uses examples to illustrate the key points of the relevant technology. As far as possible, the examples in each chapter show only the features under discussion and don't cover extraneous capabilities. This means that the examples on their own often don't demonstrate best practices for features other than those discussed in the chapter. By combining the different technologies from each chapter together, you will be able to build Web applications using the best-of-breed features of all the Java Web technologies discussed.

By the time you finish reading this book, you should have the confidence to design, develop, and test your own Web applications using the latest versions of the Tomcat Web server and other open source technologies. You will also be able to configure and administer Tomcat in a live or development environment.

Who Should Read This Book?

This book in intended for two categories of reader:

- Experienced developers who have been involved with Web-based development for at least one year and Java for at least three months
- Administrators who have basic administration skills for their host operating systems but have not necessarily installed or administered Tomcat or any other Web servers

As a Java developer, you should be confident writing Java code and familiar with the commonly used Java 2 APIs, such as string handling, collections, iterators, and JDBC. As a Web developer, you should understand the role of HTTP and be able to write Web pages using HTML.

As an administrator, you should be able to install software for your platform and be comfortable editing XML configuration files.

How This Book Is Structured

This book is intended to be an introduction to developing Java servlets and JSPs using Jakarta Tomcat and other open source technologies: It is not intended as a complete reference guide. You must use the documentation supplied with the different products under discussion to supplement the information presented in this book.

Care has been taken to ensure that concepts and technologies are introduced in an appropriate order, so it is best to read the early chapters (up to Chapter 14) sequentially. Later chapters, which examine specific aspects of various technologies, can be read in any order.

Software Discussed in the Book

Tomcat Kick Start covers versions 4.0 and 4.1 of the Jakarta Tomcat Web server. Java Servlet and JSP technologies are constantly changing and new drafts of the relevant specifications became available while this book was being written. This book covers Servlets 2.3 and JSP 1.2, and incorporates the known changes and new features of Servlets 2.4 and JSP 2.0 where appropriate. See the "Java Servlet Technology and JavaServer Pages" section in Chapter 1 for full details of what is covered.

Although this book is primarily about Tomcat, several related software products are also discussed. All the software used is freely available and can be downloaded from the Web sites indicated in Table I.1.

You can install this software now—following the instructions provided with the downloads—or wait until you read the appropriate chapter in this book. You must also have a Java development environment installed on your workstation in order to compile the Java examples presented in this book.

TABLE I.1 Software Used in This Book

Product	Download Site	Relevant Chapter
J2SDK1.4	`java.sun.com/j2se`	all
Tomcat 4.1	`jakarta.apache.org/tomcat`	2
JSTL	`jakarta.apache.org/taglibs`	11
Log4j	`jakarta.apache.org/log4j`	13
Struts	`jakarta.apache.org/struts`	20
Apache	`httpd.apache.org`	22
Axis	`xml.apache.org/axis`	25
Cactus	`jakarta.apache.org/cactus`	21

The software examples shown in this book are available online at the Sams Publishing Web site. Go to `http://www.samspublishing.com` and search for this book's ISBN (0672324393).

Typographic Conventions

NOTE

A Note presents interesting, sometimes technical, pieces of information related to the surrounding discussion.

TIP

A Tip offers advice or suggests an easier way of doing something.

CAUTION

A Caution advises you of potential problems or highlights performance or security issues that you should be aware of.

The names of Java classes or methods, filenames and directories, and URLs are presented in `monospace` type. Text that you type appears in **`bold monospace`** type.

When command-line instructions or file locations are presented in the text, the Unix style forward slash (/) is used to separate directories. Windows users should replace the forward slash with a backslash (\).

Operating system environment variables are shown in angle brackets, like this: `<CATALINA_HOME>`. Unix users should use the Unix variable replacement syntax of `${CATALINA_HOME}` or `$CATALINA_HOME`, and Windows users should use `%CATALINA_HOME%`.

Command-line commands are shown with a leading angle bracket (>) followed by a space. This represents the command-line prompt and is not part of the command you have to enter.

PART I
Basic Principles

IN THIS PART

1

Overview of Jakarta Tomcat, Servlets, and JSPs

IN THIS CHAPTER

- Why Have Server-Side Java?
- Introducing Jakarta Tomcat
- Java Servlet Technology and JavaServer Pages
- Tomcat and Static HTML Pages
- Tomcat and J2EE

Web servers have come a long way since Tim Berners-Lee proposed a document-sharing system that used hypertext links for navigation. Modern Web users expect functionality such as online banking, stock and share brokering, and shopping to be accessible though a Web browser or other Web client such as a mobile phone or personal digital assistant (PDA). Traditional fixed Web pages contain what is referred to as *static content*. The more modern functionality is known as *dynamic content*, reflecting the fact that Web pages have to be constructed on demand when the user browses the page's URL.

Jakarta Tomcat is a Web server that supports the provision of dynamic content using the Java programming language. The Java Servlet Technology and JavaServer Pages (JSP) APIs define a feature-rich environment for developing dynamic Web pages written in Java.

This chapter presents an overview of the Tomcat Web server and a summary of the servlet and JSP specifications.

Why Have Server-Side Java?

Today's World Wide Web users expect more information and better functionality from a Web site than users did in the past. Long gone are the days when the novelty of being able to access static Web pages containing hypertext links to related information was sufficient to satisfy most users.

The modern Web user not only expects to browse pages containing text, graphical information and dynamic content, but also wants to use the Web as a front end to any information service. The modern use of Web pages for shopping, banking, brokering, and other online services is a logical progression from the original concept of the Web as a repository for online information.

In order to support user expectations, the Web server has had to evolve and support the ability to access databases and run server-side programs on behalf of the client. Initial proprietary solutions were soon superseded by the introduction of Common Gateway Interface (CGI) scripting. CGI scripts soon became the de facto mechanism for implementing server-side functionality accessible via a Web-based client.

Although CGI provided (and still does provide) the required server-side functionality, in its early days it suffered from some obvious problems:

- Performance was slow because of the way the CGI scripts were run as external processes to the Web server.
- There was, and still is, no standard scripting language; while the majority of CGI developers use Perl, other languages such as PHP are also popular.
- Differences between versions of the scripting environment reduced portability of the server-side scripts, often forcing developers to use old versions of Web servers or script engines and thus denying them access to the benefits of the latest software.

These early CGI problems have been addressed in several ways:

- Fast-CGI was developed to remove some of the performance problems; however, performance is still affected by the CGI scripting language used.
- The Perl community has developed a wide range of standard libraries that can improve the portability of Perl scripts.
- On Microsoft platforms, Active Server Pages (ASP) has superseded CGI as the standard server-side technology for Microsoft's Internet Information Server (IIS).
- Sun Microsystems has specified Java Servlet Technology and JSP as an alternative to CGI scripts for platforms that support Java.

Of all these options, Java servlets and JSPs offer the most scalable, open solution to providing server-side Web functionality. Microsoft's ASP is proprietary to Microsoft Windows platforms and Fast-CGI has not removed the performance and scalability issues associated with the scripting language itself.

Sun Microsystems, in conjunction with the Java user community under the auspices of the Java Community Process (JCP) program, develops and refines the servlet and JSP specifications to meet end user and developer requirements. The actual implementation of these specifications is left to individual manufacturers. The open source Apache Software Foundation's Jakarta Tomcat Web server is Sun's reference implementation for the servlet and JSP specifications.

NOTE

You can find out more about Sun Microsystems' Java initiative from the company's Web site at `http://java.sun.com`.

The Java Community Process Web site can be found at `http://www.jcp.org`.

Introducing Jakarta Tomcat

Although Sun Microsystems controls the servlet and JSP specifications, it no longer provides its own reference implementation of the technology. That honor has been awarded to the open source Jakarta Tomcat project. (For brevity *Jakarta Tomcat* will be referred to as *Tomcat* throughout the rest of this book.)

Tomcat is a Web server that provides a service on TCP/IP port 8080 (by default). Tomcat uses port 8080 because it does not require root privileges, and this has the added benefit of not clashing with any existing Web server using the default HTTP port (80).

But Tomcat is more than just a Web server; it is also a Java servlet container. As a servlet container, Tomcat provides the environment for running Web applications built from Java servlets and JSPs. Java Web application pages can also be seamlessly integrated into the Web server, so Tomcat can provide a single interface for static Web pages as well as servlets and JSPs.

Tomcat is a robust and scalable Web server designed for use in a production environment. It is also well suited for developing and testing servlets and JSPs because of its small footprint and straightforward administration.

As a developer, you have many good reasons for using Tomcat to develop your Web applications:

- It implements the latest servlet and JSP specifications.
- It is free to use under the Apache software license (see Appendix A, "Apache Software License, Version 1.1").
- It integrates with the leading Web servers, including Apache, Netscape, and IIS.
- It has a large user community.

As a production-quality Web server and servlet container, Tomcat can be used to host servlets and JSPs on a "live" Web site. As an open source product from the same stable as the popular Apache Web server, Tomcat is an obvious choice if you prefer to use open source software or are constrained by costs.

You can obtain a copy of Tomcat from `http://jakarta.apache.org/tomcat`. Chapter 2, "Installing Jakarta Tomcat," will show you how to download and install the latest version of Tomcat for Windows NT and Unix platforms.

Sun Microsystems includes a version of Tomcat in the J2EE reference implementation (J2EESDK version 1.3 from `http://java.sun.com/j2ee`) and in the Java Web Services Developer Pack (Java WSDP) (`http://java.sun.com/webservices`), but this is not necessarily the latest Tomcat version.

Apache and Jakarta Projects

Essentially, the Apache Software Foundation (`http://www.apache.org`) is an open source community that develops a wide range of software products. Open source software is provided free of charge to all users and no restrictions are placed on the end user or the specific field of use. In other words, the open source community will not discriminate against a person or group of people of a specific field of endeavor. Open source software must be available in source form, as well as a compiled version, and can be modified and redistributed provided the redistribution is also distributed under the same open source license. More information on open source software can be found at `http://www.opensource.org`. You can download the binary versions of the software produced by the Apache team and run them on your system free of charge. You can also download the source files and modify or enhance the products to customize them for your own use.

The first of the Apache projects was the Apache HTTP Server (`http://httpd.apache.org`). Now there are numerous other open source Apache projects. With the introduction of Java as a development language, many members of the Apache community started to write projects in Java; previously C and C++ had been the primary development languages. Eventually, there were enough Java-based products for a separate subcommunity to evolve purely for products written in Java. Hence the creation of the Jakarta project (`http://jakarta.apache.org`) which is a collaboration between Sun Microsystems, IBM, Oracle, and the Apache server-side Java development community.

NOTE

Besides Tomcat, another well-known Jakarta product is Jakarta Ant, used to automate the software development process. Ant is a modern Java equivalent of the Unix `make` and Windows `NMake` tools known to many developers. Ant is not covered in this book, but you might like to check out `http://jakarta.apache.org/ant` for more information.

Inside Tomcat

Tomcat 4 is a complete rewrite of the previous version (Tomcat 3), and there are significant changes in the internal workings. If you have a look inside Tomcat 4, you will find two distinct components:

Catalina—the servlet container that provides support for servlet applications

Jasper—the container that provides support for JavaServer Pages

As a developer or administrator, you do not have to worry overmuch about the distinction between the two components of Tomcat. However, you will occasionally come across specific references to Tomcat's constituent parts. For example, when you install Tomcat version 4 (see Chapter 2) you will define an environment variable called `CATALINA_HOME` rather than one called `TOMCAT_HOME`.

NOTE

If you have used an older version of Tomcat, you will be accustomed to defining the `TOMCAT_HOME` environment variable to specify the installation, or home, directory of the Tomcat server. In version 4 of Tomcat, this variable has been superseded by the `CATALINA_HOME` variable.

The Catalina Web server can provide multiple services, and by default provides a standalone Tomcat service and a Tomcat-Apache connector service for use with an Apache Web server. These services can be enabled, disabled, and modified using an XML configuration file.

A Catalina service comprises a hierarchical structure of XML elements as follows:

```
Service
  Engine
    Host
      Context
```

Each `Service` element contains a single `Engine` that defines the service being provided. An `Engine` can have one or more `Host` elements that, in the case of the standalone Tomcat service, represent the hostname (or names) of the machine running the service and therefore the client URLs that are used to access the Web resources. A `Host` can contain multiple `Context` elements that represent the different Web applications that are available. A Web application contains the actual Web resources such as HTML files, Java servlets, and JSPs. Given the URL `http://localhost:8080/examples/index.html`, you can see the hierarchical nature of the Catalina structure:

`8080` is the `Service` running on port 8080 (Tomcat standalone).

`localhost` is the `Host`.

`examples` is the `Context`.

`index.html` is the Web resource.

When configuring Catalina, any values defined at the service level apply to all lower engine, host, and context levels unless explicitly overridden. Similarly, values defined at the engine level apply to hosts and contexts unless overridden at a lower level, and so on.

The hierarchical nature of the Catalina configuration file is reflected in the fact that you can define many configuration parameters at several different levels according to the desired effect. An understanding of the roles of services, engines, hosts, and contexts is essential to the correct configuration of Catalina.

Java Servlet Technology and JavaServer Pages

As discussed earlier, Java servlets and JSPs provide the server-side functionality necessary to support the features required by the latest Web-based applications. Applications such as online shopping carts need access to databases as well as other programs and additional network services in order to support end user requirements. Servlets and JSPs are Java applications running within a Web server container that are invoked via a Web client (usually a browser).

Java servlets and JSPs are in direct competition with other Web server technologies such as CGI scripts (Perl) and ASPs. Java has a number of advantages over these other technologies:

- Java is portable and is not tied to any one manufacturer or platform.
- Although Java is an interpreted environment, modern Java Virtual Machine (JVM) technologies such as Sun's HotSpot compiler ensure that Java program performance can rival that of native machine code under typical server application conditions.
- The comprehensive range of Java standard library APIs (2,738 classes and interfaces in Java 1.4) gives the developer unrivaled access to functionality and portability when developing Java server-side applications.
- By using the same language and APIs to develop client-side Applets, server-side servlets, and standalone applications, you can easily switch between developing programs for the different components of modern software architectures and reuse custom class libraries across applications.

No other programming language and environment can rival Java as a portable, scalable, feature-rich development environment.

Servlets

Servlets are Java programs running inside a Web server. They are accessed via a URL and return information to a Web client, typically in the form of an HTML page for display by a browser. However, servlets can output data in any format, as you will discover as you work through the rest of this book.

A standalone Java program invoked from a command line uses command-line arguments to determine its behavior, but a servlet's behavior is determined by the client using the parameter passing mechanism of the Hypertext Transfer Protocol (HTTP) (see Chapter 3, "Basic Principles of Web Servers").

Novice developers sometimes cannot appreciate the difference between a servlet and an Applet. A servlet runs on the Web server and has access to the enterprise resources available to the Web server. A servlet can only return data to the browser for display; it cannot utilize the processing power of the client or interact directly with the end user. An Applet is a Java program that is downloaded to the client and runs within the browser environment, where security restrictions typically prevent it from accessing enterprise resources directly.

The common criticism of servlets is that they make it difficult to write complex HTML pages. Servlets are Java programs and the entire HTML page must be encoded and printed using an output stream (like using `System.out` to write to the console). Servlets have been described as short snatches of Java interspersed with large amounts of tedious `println()` statements.

JavaServer Pages were developed to address this main criticism of servlets. Although JSPs are simpler to use than servlets when working with HTML formatting, they do have their downsides, as discussed in the next section.

Servlet Technology 2.3

The Servlet 2.3 specification (available from `http://java.sun.com/servlets`) specifies what functionality a Web server extension needs to support dynamic Web page content from a Java program. It does not specify how this functionality is actually implemented.

The servlet specification defines

- The container (or environment) in which a servlet will execute
- An API for accessing the HTTP request object
- An API for creating the HTTP response object
- An API for interfacing with the Web server
- Life cycle methods for servlet object construction and disposal
- The structure of an XML deployment descriptor that defines the servlet and its context (such as any URLs it is associated with) within the Web server
- The concept of a Web application resource (WAR) file that can contain several servlets (and other things) that form a single Web application

For developers already familiar with previous versions of the specification, version 2.3 has added

- Application events allowing a servlet to listen and respond to events (see Chapter 7, "The Web Application Environment")
- Servlet filters allowing servlets to intercept and perhaps modify the HTTP request and response objects (see Chapter 18, "Servlet Filters")
- A requirement that J2SE 1.2 or later be used as the underlying platform for Web containers

JavaServer Pages

JSPs are still servlets, but they are written as HTML with embedded Java. A JSP is transformed into a servlet as part of the process of deploying it to the Web server. (This is covered in detail in Chapter 5, "Basic Principles of JSPs.")

With JSPs, the developer's primary focus is on the structure of the HTML page. Java is included in the page when necessary and in a controlled manner similar to server-side includes (SSIs) or scriptlets. The downside of JSPs is that pages with large amounts of embedded Java can become difficult to understand and maintain.

JSPs focus on the presentation of the page information whereas servlets focus on the functionality. This theme is explored further in Chapter 17, "Architectures," which looks at designing Web applications using both servlets and JSPs to realize the relative strengths of each technology.

JSP 1.2

The JSP 1.2 specification (available from `http://java.sun.com/jsp`) defines the functionality that has to be supplied for a Web server to support JSPs in addition to servlets.

The JSP specification defines

- The syntax for including Java declarations, directives, scriptlets, and expressions on an HTML page
- The environment, in terms of implicit variables, available to Java embedded in a JSP
- Life cycle methods for interacting with JSP object construction and disposal
- JSP syntax elements for supporting the use of JavaBeans
- APIs for developing custom tags and tag libraries (TagLibs) for extending the JSP syntax

- JSP syntax elements for supporting the use of custom tags on a page
- Life cycle methods for custom tags supporting interaction with JSP page processing

For developers already familiar with previous versions of the JSP specification, version 1.2 has added

- Required use of J2SE 1.2 or later
- Use of Servlet 2.3 as the foundation for JSP semantics
- Definition of the XML syntax for JSP pages
- Translation-time validation of JSP pages
- Refinements of tag library runtime support

Tag library developers should check Chapter 10, which details the differences between JSP 1.1 and JSP 1.2 that affect existing tag libraries.

Tomcat 4

Tomcat 4 implements the servlet 2.3 and JSP 1.2 specifications.

If you have used previous versions of Tomcat, the major change you will see is support for Web applications (see Chapter 4, "Basic Principles of Servlets"). This support has necessitated a change in the directory structure for storing servlets and JSPs. As mentioned previously, Tomcat 4 is a rewrite of Tomcat 3 and has separated servlet and JSP functionality into the Catalina and Jasper containers (refer back to the section titled "Inside Tomcat"). If you are used to defining the environment variable `TOMCAT_HOME`, you will need to replace this with `CATALINA_HOME`.

If you are a Tomcat 3 user, you should find the upgrade to Tomcat 4 straightforward, as long as you bear in mind these changes. Existing servlets and JSPs should migrate without any modifications. However, some custom JSP tags may need to be amended, as discussed in Chapter 10.

Future Changes

The servlet technology and JSP specifications are not static. Like most Java product specifications, they are continuously under review and new versions are released every 12–18 months. Even as a specification is finalized, a group of experts will be starting to discuss the requirements and features for the next version.

The JSP 2.0 and servlet 2.4 specifications only became available as this book was finalized.

The Java Community Process (JCP) defines several stages for the development of a new product specification. Early expert discussion yields an expert draft, which is made available to interested parties and peer groups, who develop the community draft. Only when the community is satisfied with the draft specification is it made available to all users as a public draft. A proposed final draft and eventually the actual final draft complete the process. Full details of the specification development process are available at `http://www.jcp.org`.

Tomcat undergoes a less formal development process in which new versions are issued to resolve bugs, improve existing features, or add new features. By the time the servlet or JSP specifications reach the public draft stage, a version of Tomcat implementing some or all of the specification will be available, usually as a beta version.

The newest servlet specification (2.4) contains several additions that make small improvements to servlet functionality and provide additional information about the servlet environment. The larger changes include

- The ability to extend the Web application deployment descriptor to include custom features. This allows the same XML document to be used to represent application-specific information as well as servlet container information. The Web application deployment descriptor is discussed throughout this book and a pro forma deployment descriptor is included as Appendix B.
- The addition of event listeners for request and response events. (Chapter 7 discusses current event listeners.)
- Support of filters for request dispatching and forwarding. (Filters are described in Chapter 18.)
- Enhancements to internationalization support.

The next JSP specification (2.0) contains clarifications and minor enhancements to the previous specification and includes one new feature. JSP 2.0 includes support for the expression language in custom tags, which is currently part of the JavaServer Pages Standard Tag Library (JSTL). The JSTL expression language is discussed in Chapter 11, "JSP Expression Language and JSTL."

Tomcat and Static HTML Pages

Besides being a servlet and JSP container, Tomcat can also be used to serve simple HTML pages. Tomcat is therefore a complete Web server and can be used in production as well as development environments.

However, Tomcat is not as sophisticated as a specialized Web server such as Apache, iPlanet, or IIS. Specialized Web servers are designed for performance and configurability when handling large numbers of static Web pages or concurrent client connections.

If you need to support a large number of concurrent clients accessing mainly static Web pages, you should consider using Tomcat solely as the servlet container alongside your specialized Web server. Chapter 22, "Integrating Tomcat with a Web Server," discusses how to do this in detail.

If you only have a small number of concurrent client requests or have a large number of servlets and relatively few static pages, you can use Tomcat as your Web server and avoid the complications of integrating Tomcat with another Web server. You can always begin by using Tomcat as the Web server and refactor your solution to use a Web server such as Apache for the static pages if performance proves to be a problem.

Tomcat and J2EE

Sun's J2EE specification is a comprehensive suite of protocols and APIs required for large-scale enterprise applications. Java servlets and JSPs are a small part of the J2EE technology that must be provided by any J2EE-compliant server.

Tomcat is a servlet and JSP container designed to provide Web applications without the overhead of a full J2EE server. However, you can use Tomcat in conjunction with some or all of the other J2EE technologies where appropriate. Chapter 24, "Tomcat and J2EE," discusses how Tomcat fits into the larger picture of a J2EE server.

Summary

The emergence of the Internet and the World Wide Web has changed the way software applications are developed. The current trend is toward centralized computing accessed via a Web client that does little more than process user input and present information from the server application to the user.

The main Web protocol is HTTP, and Web servers have developed from simply presenting static HTML pages to providing access to databases and other network services.

To support the modern requirement for dynamic content, three key technologies have emerged:

- CGI scripts
- Microsoft ASP
- Java servlets and JSPs

Of these technologies, only Java servlets and JSPs are open and scalable. They are the technologies discussed in this book.

Jakarta Tomcat is a Web server and servlet container that implements the latest Java servlet and JSP specifications. Sun Microsystems uses Tomcat as its reference implementation. Tomcat is provided under the Apache Software Foundation license and is free to use for development and commercial purposes.

In the next few chapters of this book, you will learn the basic principles of Web servers, servlets, JSPs, and Tomcat. Subsequently, you will study different aspects of developing Web applications, administering Tomcat, and integrating Tomcat servlets into the wider enterprise computing environment.

2 Installing Jakarta Tomcat

IN THIS CHAPTER

- Before Downloading Tomcat 4
- Downloading Tomcat 4
- Installing Tomcat
- Checking the Installation
- Stopping Tomcat
- Running Tomcat with Multiple Instances

Chapter 1, "Overview of Jakarta Tomcat, Servlets, and JSP," has given you a brief taste of Tomcat, summarizing how servlets and JSPs can be integrated into enterprise environments. Before moving on to develop your own Web applications, you must ensure that you have an up-to-date version of Tomcat installed and working. In this chapter, you will download and install the latest version of Tomcat and optionally configure Tomcat for multiple instances when using a shared server instead of a dedicated workstation.

If you are lucky enough to have Tomcat installed already on your machine, you may still need to check that the version you have is Tomcat 4.0 or later. Tomcat 4 is needed because this version implements the latest Servlet and JavaServer Pages specifications that are used for examples throughout this book.

TIP

The Tomcat version number is displayed in the command window when Tomcat is started as a standalone server. How to start up Tomcat is covered in the section titled "Checking the Installation," later in this chapter.

Even if you have already installed Tomcat 4 on your system, you might like to check out the sections that cover the Tomcat 4 directory structure and Tomcat environment variables, as these provide important background information for understanding the Tomcat installation.

At the time of writing (mid-2002), Tomcat 4.0.4 is the latest production release available as a standalone Web server, and Tomcat 4.1 is available as a beta release.

NOTE

Tomcat 4 is also bundled in Sun's Java Web Services Developer Pack (JWSDP) early access release 1.0 (available from `http://java.sun.com/webservices`).

Before Downloading Tomcat 4

In order for Tomcat to run successfully, you will need a Java Software Development Kit (SDK) installed on the system.

If you are developing Web applications with Tomcat, you can use the JRE incorporated into Sun Microsystems's Java 2 Standard Development Kit (J2SDK), or a compatible Java Integrated Development Environment (IDE) from one of the many Java tool vendors. Although the servlet specification only requires J2SE 1.2, it is recommended that you use the latest J2SDK available (1.4 at the time of writing).

NOTE

J2SDK was previously referred to as JDK.

CAUTION

The authors have used J2SDK 1.4 as the development platform for all the examples in this book. Where the examples use any J2SE 1.4–specific features, this will be noted in the text. If you have J2SDK 1.3 installed, you may use this to develop your own servlets but you will not be able to run some of the examples in this book.

The authors have encountered problems using Tomcat 4 with JDK 1.2 on certain platforms and therefore do not recommend using this combination.

Installing a JRE or SDK is not covered in detail here, but the following list outlines the steps you need to take to obtain and install a J2SDK from the Sun Microsystems Web site:

1. Download a J2SE or J2SDK release (version 1.4 or later preferred) from `http://java.sun.com/j2se/`.

2. Install the software according to the instructions included with the release.
3. Set an environment variable `JAVA_HOME` to the pathname of the installation directory.

CAUTION

Setting the `JAVA_HOME` variable is a standard requirement in a Java environment. Although some Java tools will work if `JAVA_HOME` is not set, Tomcat will not.

Downloading Tomcat 4

The latest release of Tomcat 4 can be obtained from the Jakarta Project Web site by following the download link at `http://jakarta.apache.org/tomcat`.

The Jakarta Project provides Tomcat in both binary and source-code versions. The only good reason for obtaining the source code would be if you want to customize a Tomcat servlet engine for your own purposes. How to do this is beyond the scope of this book and will not be covered here. In this chapter, you will be shown how to download and install the Tomcat binaries.

The Jakarta Project team categorizes software releases by their stability and the intended user as shown here.

Build Category	Product Stability
Release	Stable production release
Milestone	Probably stable but only use if you need a specific new feature
Nightly	Very unstable; should only be used if you are an experienced developer who likes to live on the edge—and you like to debug other developers' code
Demo	Packaged demos of the products

As the Jakarta Project team put it, the release builds are about "as good as it gets," and unless you have a very good reason to do otherwise, you should always use the latest release build. Tomcat 4.0 is available as a release build but at the time of writing, Tomcat 4.1 is only available as a milestone build described as "buggy" and for advanced users only. The instructions in the rest of this section apply to both Tomcat 4.0 and Tomcat 4.1 with the differences between the two products described where appropriate.

Tomcat 4 Binaries

Before you get to actually download Tomcat, you must make one more decision. Apache Tomcat 4 is available in two different packaging options:

- **Standard**: This is the full binary distribution including all the necessary and optional libraries to allow Tomcat 4 to be run as a standalone server with J2SDK 1.2 and later versions.
- **JDK 1.4 LE**: This is a lightweight binary distribution of Tomcat 4 to use if you have J2SDK 1.4 installed. The version of Tomcat in this distribution utilizes several standard Java libraries (such as XML support) included with J2SDK 1.4 but not available with earlier versions of J2SE.

If you are using J2SDK 1.4, you should download the JDK 1.4 LE version of Tomcat so as to benefit from using the Java 1.4 standard libraries, and to save a bit of disk space, not to mention download time if you have a slow modem.

The installation process is the same for both versions.

Downloading the Binaries

The Tomcat binaries are available in the following formats: self-extracting Windows archive or `exe` file, a WinZip `zip` file, and a GNU zip `gzip` file containing a `tar` archive. With the exception of the Windows `exe` (which can only be used if you are on a Windows platform), the formats can be downloaded for either a Unix or Windows platform (all the tools are able to cope with each other's file formats). The gzip utility has the best compression algorithm so, if download time is an issue, go for this format.

NOTE

Throughout this chapter the term *Windows* refers to any of these platforms: Windows 95, 98, ME, 2000, XP, or NT.

You will need up to 7MB of space to store the compressed download and up to 40MB for the uncompressed files, of which about 16MB is taken up by the documentation. By not installing the documentation locally, you will save some disk space; you can always view the Tomcat documentation online at the Jakarta Web site.

NOTE

If you download a beta release of Tomcat 4.1, you will require an extra 10MB of disk space for the source files. Source files are not included in the release level builds.

When you download the Tomcat archive it is recommended that you choose to save the download file locally so you can easily re-install the software should there be any problems with the installation.

Installing Tomcat

The installation is very similar—and very straightforward—for both Windows and Unix. All the Tomcat downloads include scripts for both the Windows and Unix platforms. The full installation process is explained in the following sections, but briefly you will

1. Extract the Tomcat files to a directory on disk
2. Set the environment variable `CATALINA_HOME` to point to this directory

Installing on Windows Using the Self-Extracting `exe`

If you are installing on a Windows platform, by far the easiest option is to use the download containing the self-extracting `exe`. This will install Tomcat and set up the start-menu shortcuts, shown in the following table, for you.

Shortcut	What It Does
Configuration	Edits Tomcat configuration files
Start Tomcat	Starts the Tomcat server
Stop Tomcat	Stops the Tomcat server
Tomcat 4 Program Directory	Points to the Tomcat installation directory
Tomcat Documentation	Brings up installed Tomcat documentation
Tomcat Home Page	Links to `jakarta.apache.org/tomcat`
Uninstall Tomcat 4	Runs a program to uninstall Tomcat

After you have downloaded the self-extracting archive for Windows, simply follow these steps to install Tomcat:

1. Double-click the self-extracting archive file to start the installation.
2. The installation program will attempt to detect which version of J2SE you are using and display a message box. Click OK to confirm the J2SE. If you do not think the J2SE version is correct, you have probably not set the `JAVA_HOME` environment variable correctly.
3. Read the license and click the I Agree button. If you don't accept the license terms, Tomcat will not be installed.

4. Tomcat 4.1: On the next window, check those product options you want to install. The default selections will be suitable for developers. If you are an administrator, you should select the NT Service (NT/2k/XP) option if you want to run Tomcat as a standard NT Service. You should probably deselect the Tomcat Documentation and Example Web Applications options if you intend to run Tomcat as a production server because these features are primarily of interest to developers. Click Next to move to the next installation option.

   Tomcat 4.0: Select Normal for the type of install (requires 22MB). If space is limited or you are installing a production server, you can select Minimal, which does not install the documentation or example Web applications. Click Next to move to the next installation option.

5. Select the folder where you wish to install Tomcat and click Install.

   If you are installing Tomcat 4.0, there are no additional steps required.

6. Tomcat 4.1: Enter a password for the Tomcat Administration Tool User (see Chapter 15, "Administering Tomcat in a Live Environment"). On this screen you can also change the Web server `HTTP/1.1 Connector Port` from its default value of 8080 (production servers normally use port 80).

CAUTION

Do not change the name of the Administration Tool user from its default value of `admin` because the installation process does not create the user with the required privileges if a different name is used.

TIP

If you forget (or mistype) the administration user password, you can always modify the `conf/tomcat-users.xml` file in the Tomcat installation directory to enter a new password.

7. Click Close to complete the installation.

CAUTION

These instructions are based on the Tomcat 4.1.8 beta release and may not reflect the installation process of the final Tomcat 4.1 release.

Using the WinZip or Gzip Files on Windows or Unix

If you have chosen to download one of the plain archives (either WinZip or gzip), extract the files to a disk with at least 40MB of space. It is not important where the files reside, but the following table defines some conventional places to store new applications that may make it easier for others (and yourself) to find them later.

Operating System	Default Location for Applications
Windows	`Program Files` directory
Solaris	`/opt`
Linux	`/usr/local`

TIP

To improve server performance you should install Tomcat on a separate physical disk or partition from the main system disk. This will help distribute the disk I/O load and avoid some of the bottlenecks that can occur if all the software is installed in the same location.

Setting Tomcat Environment Variables

Tomcat uses a number of environment variables, many of which are optional, but two must be configured before stating up Tomcat for the first time. These variables are `JAVA_HOME` and `CATALINA_HOME`.

Where possible the environment variables should be set on a systemwide basis, but where you do not have sufficient user privileges, or where this will cause problems for other users, it is sufficient to set the variables on a per-user basis.

The `JAVA_HOME` Variable

`JAVA_HOME` should be set to the directory path where the J2SE runtime or J2SDK is installed.

The `CATALINA_HOME` Variable

You need to set an environment variable called `CATALINA_HOME` to the path of the directory into which you have installed Tomcat.

TIP

On Windows 2000, XP, or NT, environment variables are set via the System Properties window. Access this window either by right-clicking the My Computer icon on the desktop and selecting Properties, or by using the System option in Control Panel. In the System Properties window, select the Advanced tab followed by the Environment Variables button. In the System variables section click the New button to add the `JAVA_HOME` and `CATALINA_HOME` variables.

On Windows 9x or ME, set the `JAVA_HOME` and `CATALINA_HOME` variables in `AUTOEXEC.BAT`. For example, if Tomcat was installed in a directory called Tomcat4 on the C drive, you would add

```
set CATALINA_HOME=C:\Tomcat4
```

to the `AUTOEXEC.BAT` file.

On a Unix system, set the JAVA_HOME and CATALINA_HOME variables in either a systemwide login file or in your local profile. For example, if you use the Bourne shell (or one of its derivatives such as ksh or bash) and have installed Tomcat in /usr/local/Tomcat4, add the following line to either /etc/profile or $HOME/.profile:

```
CATALINA_HOME=/usr/local/Tomcat4; export CATALINA_HOME
```

If you are a csh or tcsh user, add the following to $HOME/.login (or a systemwide login file if one is supported for your shell):

```
setenv CATALINA_HOME /usr/local/Tomcat4
```

NOTE

On a Windows platform, it is possible to run Tomcat without setting CATALINA_HOME by double-clicking the Startup.bat file using the Windows Explorer utility.

Tomcat Directory Structure

The Tomcat 4 release contains the files and directories shown in Table 2.1. As there are some minor directory changes between Tomcat 4.0 and Tomcat 4.1, Table 2.1 lists the directories for Tomcat 4.1 with a note indicating the previous location used by Tomcat 4.0.

If you are a Tomcat administrator, you will be primarily concerned with various configuration files stored in the conf directory. As a developer, you will focus on what goes in the webapps and other directories.

TABLE 2.1 Tomcat 4.1 Release Files and Directories

File or Directory	Contents
LICENSE	Apache Software License for this release—reproduced in Appendix A
bin/	All the binary executables and scripts (both Windows .bat and Unix .sh) to run Tomcat and various utilities
common/classes/	Unpacked classes available to both Catalina internal classes and Web applications
common/lib/	JAR files available to both Catalina internal classes and Web applications
conf/	Tomcat configuration files
jasper/	JAR files visible only in the Jasper class loader
logs/	Destination directory for Tomcat log files
server/classes/	Unpacked classes internal to Catalina
server/lib/	Internal Catalina classes in JAR files
server/webapps/	Directory for Web applications supplied with Tomcat (Tomcat 4.0 stored all its applications under the webapps/ directory)
server/webapps/ROOT	Root directory for static Web pages

TABLE 2.1 Continued

File or Directory	Contents
shared/classes/	Unpacked classes global to Web applications (Tomcat 4.0 uses classes/)
shared/lib/	Classes in JAR files global to Web applications (Tomcat 4.0 uses lib/)
webapps/	Directory containing Web applications and WAR files
webapps/tomcat-docs/	HTML documentation for Tomcat
work/	Used by Tomcat for holding temporary files and directories and the servlets generated from JSPs

After installation, some of these directories will be empty—particularity the `logs` directory and those that contain unpacked class files.

Checking the Installation

To check out the installation, you will need to perform the following steps:

1. Start the Tomcat server.
2. Access the default Tomcat server page in your favorite browser.

Starting Tomcat

Using whichever method you prefer, run the startup command file that is in the `<CATALINA_HOME>/bin` directory. On Unix, this file is `startup.sh`, and on Windows, it is `startup.bat`.

NOTE

Wherever you see a variable in angle brackets, such as `<CATALINA_HOME>`, this means replace the variable with the actual value (in this case the home directory where Tomcat is installed).

CAUTION

In the standard installation of a Win 9X/ME–based operating system, the default amount of environment space provided to MS-DOS windows is too small for Tomcat's batch files to run.

If you are running on a Win9X/ME–based operating system and see the message "out of environment space" when running `startup.bat`, you need to change the properties of the program so it runs with more memory. Right-click the `startup.bat` file. Click Properties and then the Memory tab. For the Initial Environment field, enter **`4096`**. Repeat for the `shutdown.bat` file.

It is not recommended that you run a Tomcat production environment server on Win9x/ME platforms; however, these platforms are acceptable for development purposes.

After starting Tomcat, you should see several startup messages in the window in which you started Tomcat. You should see messages similar to the following at the end of the startup:

```
Starting service Tomcat-Standalone
Apache Tomcat/4.1.8-LE-jdk14
15-Jul-2002 11:50:01 org.apache.coyote.http11.Http11Protocol start
INFO: Starting Coyote HTTP/1.1 on port 8080
```

If you don't see these messages and have set your environment variables correctly, skip ahead to the section titled "Troubleshooting the Installation" later in this chapter.

If everything looks okay so far, the final thing is to connect to the Tomcat server using a client browser.

Using the browser of your choice, browse the following URL: `http://localhost:8080/`.

NOTE

If you have had to change the default Tomcat port number as discussed in the upcoming section "Troubleshooting the Installation," replace 8080 in this URL with your new port number.

CAUTION

If your browser is configured to use a proxy Web server, you must add `localhost` to the list of domains excluded from the proxy server.

If everything is working fine, you will see the Tomcat home page as shown in Figure 2.1. If the Tomcat home page does not display, perform the checks outlined the next section, "Troubleshooting the Installation."

The Jakarta project team has provided some example servlets and JSPs as part of the Tomcat distribution. These examples demonstrate the usage of different parts of the Servlet and JSP specifications and can be accessed using the following URLs:

```
http://localhost:8080/examples/servlets/index.html
http://localhost:8080/examples/jsp/index.html
```

Troubleshooting the Installation

Only a few things can go wrong with the installation.

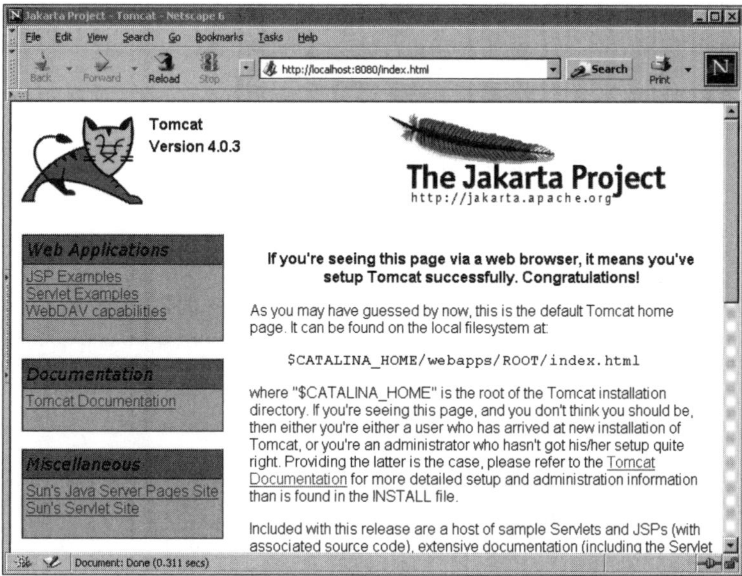

FIGURE 2.1 Tomcat default home page viewed in Netscape 6.2.

If Tomcat fails to start up, the most likely reason is a clash with TCP/IP port numbers.

If Tomcat starts but the browser is unable to access the default home page, go to the section titled "Browser Problems."

Checking Tomcat Port Numbers

Tomcat uses several TCP/IP port services for its communication with other applications. If Tomcat fails to start up, you should check that all ports used by Tomcat are available. If any are used by other services, you will have to change the Tomcat configuration to avoid these port clashes.

The TCP/IP port numbers Tomcat uses are defined in a file called `server.xml` in the <CATALINA_HOME>/conf directory. By default Tomcat 4.1 starts up services on the following ports:

Port Number	Service
8005	Shutdown
8080	HTTP/1.1 Connector (this is the default HTTP port that Tomcat attempts to bind to at startup)

If you are using Tomcat 4.0, it will also start the following additional services used for integrating Tomcat with a Web server (see Chapter 22, "Integrating Tomcat with a Web Server"):

Port Number	Service
8008	Apache Warp Connector
8009	AJP 1.3 Connector

TIP

To run Tomcat 4.0 as a standalone server, you only need the ports 8005 and 8080. If you have clashes on the other ports, you can simply comment out the associated connectors in the `server.xml` file.

These ports are probably free but you can use the command `netstat -a` (on both Windows and Unix platforms) to check that the ports are not in use. The output of `netstat` shown below indicates that two well known service ports (`emap` and `microsoft-ds`) and two other ports (1025 and 1027) are currently in use:

```
D:\>netstat -a
Active Connections
  Proto  Local Address          Foreign Address        State
  TCP    myhost:epmap          myhost:0               LISTENING
  TCP    myhost:microsoft-ds   myhost:0               LISTENING
  TCP    myhost:1025           myhost:0               LISTENING
  TCP    myhost:1027           myhost:0               LISTENING
```

TIP

You will need to run the `netstat -a` command in a DOS Command window or a Unix terminal window.

If any of the four Tomcat ports are currently in use on your host, you will have to change them in the Tomcat `server.xml` file. To do this, you should perform the following steps:

1. Make a backup copy of file `<CATALINA_HOME>/conf/server.xml`.
2. Edit the file `<CATALINA_HOME>/conf/server.xml`. Search for the port number that is being used, making sure that you find the actual configuration line and not just an XML comment.

3. Change the port number to one that isn't currently being used or comment out the service if it is not required. It is normal practice to use a number that is greater than 1024, as ports less than or equal to 1024 require system administrator privileges to access and may be allocated to well-known services (such as HTTP on port 80).

4. Repeat steps 2 and 3 for each port that needs to be changed.

5. Restart Tomcat. If this doesn't fix the problem, you almost certainly have a problem with the J2SE installation. Check that `JAVA_HOME` is defined correctly and that you are running the right version of J2SE version. You can test your J2SE version by running the command

   ```
   java -version
   ```

CAUTION

If you are using a Microsoft Windows platform, you may have several different J2SE runtimes installed because many software applications supporting Java will install their own JRE. Ensure your PATH variable starts with `%JAVA_HOME%\bin` before any Windows directories (such as `%SystemRoot%` on Windows 2000, XP, or NT).

Browser Problems

If your browser shows a "Page cannot be displayed" or equivalent error message and you are certain that Tomcat is running, check the following:

1. Have you typed the correct port number in the URL?

2. Are you working behind a proxy? If this is the case, make sure the proxy configuration for your browser knows that you shouldn't be going through the proxy to access the `localhost` machine.

TIP

You can use the `netstat -a` command as previously discussed to verify that a server is running on the Tomcat HTTP port (8080).

In the unlikely event that you are still experiencing problems, you may find a solution by subscribing to the Tomcat User mailing list available at `http://jakarta.apache.org/site/mail.html` and posting your problem there.

If you still have a problem, you can identify the cause, and you are certain you have found a genuine bug in Tomcat, report it via the Apache bug database at `http://jakarta.apache.org/site/bugs.html`.

Stopping Tomcat

Although Tomcat will normally be left running on the system, there are occasions when you will need to shut Tomcat down. These include

- When changes are required to the Tomcat configuration
- Under certain circumstances when installing new applications
- When you want to shut the whole system down

A script is provided in the `bin` directory to shutdown Tomcat cleanly. For Unix systems this script is called `shutdown.sh` and for Windows `shutdown.bat`.

TIP

Remember to add the Tomcat shutdown to your standard system shutdown scripts or procedures.

Although it is possible to stop Tomcat using Ctrl-C or to allow the process to be killed when the system shuts down, these are bad practices to get in to. If Tomcat is not shut down cleanly, any applications that must save state (such as session information) will fail to work correctly. It is also possible for applications to leave external data sources in an inconsistent state.

Running Tomcat with Multiple Instances

On multiuser systems (typically a Unix system with developers working on a shared server), it is often useful to set up Tomcat so that each developer runs a separate instance of Tomcat. Each Tomcat instance shares the Tomcat binaries and class files but has separate configuration files and directories to store Web applications.

Another reason to have multiple Tomcat instances might be to have different Tomcat configurations—perhaps for testing purposes or version control. For example, one instance could be running Tomcat as a standalone server and a second instance could be running it connected to an Apache server.

To install Tomcat for multiple instances, you need to define a variable called `CATALINA_BASE` for each instance. If `CATALINA_BASE` is not set, Tomcat will simply set it to the same value as `CATALINA_HOME`, in this case all users will share the same directories and configuration files.

If you are a Web developer on your own workstation, it is unlikely that you will want to do run multiple instances and you can safely skip the rest of this section.

Configuring Tomcat for Multiple Instances

Before embarking on the following steps to configure multiple instances, you should ensure that the Tomcat server is working with only one instance configured. Go through the steps shown earlier in the "Checking the Installation" section if you have not already done so.

For each separate instance of Tomcat you will (in brief)

1. Create a new root directory to contain the instance dependent files and directories and set the `CATALINA_BASE` environment variable to point to this directory
2. Copy configuration files from `CATALINA_HOME` into the `CATALINA_BASE` directory
3. Edit the configuration as required and change the port services used by Tomcat

Creating the `CATALINA_BASE` Directory

You should now create a directory to hold instance-dependent directories and files and set the environment variable `CATALINA_BASE` to the pathname of this directory. Under `CATALINA_BASE` create the subdirectories shown in the following table.

Directory	Used to Store Instance
`conf`	Configuration files
`logs`	Log files
`webapps`	Web application files
`work`	Temporary files

Tomcat 4 will now calculate all references for files in these directories based on the value for `CATALINA_BASE` instead of `CATALINA_HOME`.

Copying the Tomcat Configuration Files

Copy the following files from the `conf` directory in `CATALINA_HOME` directory to the `conf` directory in the new `CATALINA_BASE` directory:

```
server.xml

catalina.policy

web.xml
```

TIP

You should set the environment variable CATALINA_BASE in each user's local configuration or profile. Also change the ownership or access permissions of the CATALINA_BASE directories and files so the appropriate user has read and write access.

Editing the Tomcat Configuration

Edit the server.xml file in CATALINA_BASE and change the port service numbers being used so they are unique for each instance. You will need to change the shutdown port (default 8005) and standalone server port (default 8080) in the server.xml file. If you are using Tomcat 4.0 and do not require Tomcat to work with another Web server (such as Apache or IIS), you should comment out the connectors listening on ports 8008 and 8009. You will not need to change the other two files, web.xml and catalina.policy, at this time.

Running a Tomcat Instance

Having created a CATALINA_BASE directory and copied and edited the server.xml configuration file, you are now in a position to start up your instance. As long as CATALINA_BASE has been set to point to the required instance directory, you can use the startup files in CATALINA_HOME to start the new instance.

Remember to use the new port number you have assigned for the Tomcat instance in the URL used to access your Web applications. As you have not yet created your own Web applications, you can check that the instance has started correctly by copying an existing HTML page and storing it in a file called index.html in the /webapps/ROOT/ directory in CATALINA_BASE.

Edit this page so it can be uniquely identified with your instance. Say you have changed the Tomcat standalone port service number to 8181; then, if CATALINA_BASE is set correctly, typing the URL

```
http://localhost:8181/
```

will bring up your new index.html page as the default home page for the instance.

Summary

This chapter has shown how to install Tomcat 4 and how to start and stop the Tomcat server. If necessary you will have edited the server.xml file to change the default TCP/IP port services. Configuring Tomcat for multiple instances on the same platform was also described.

Further administration and configuration of Tomcat is covered throughout this book, which will help you build effective and dynamic Web applications. If administration of Tomcat, rather than servlet and JSP development, is your main interest, you might like to pay particular attention to Chapter 14, "Access Control"; Chapter 15, "Administering Tomcat in a Live Environment"; Chapter 16, "Configuring Tomcat"; Chapter 22, "Integrating Tomcat with a Web Server"; and Chapter 23, "Securing Web Applications Under Tomcat."

At this point you should have J2SE and Tomcat successfully installed. In the next chapter you will use these to develop a simple Web application under Tomcat.

3

Basic Principles of Web Servers

IN THIS CHAPTER

- Hypertext Transfer Protocol
- The Structure of an HTTP Message
- The Structure of an HTTP Request
- The Structure of an HTTP Response
- Testing an HTTP Connection
- Passing Request Parameters
- Client Page Caching
- URI Redirection and Page Refresh
- Persistent Connections
- Using HTTP from Within a Java Program

Web servers and clients communicate using the Hypertext Transfer Protocol (HTTP). To design and develop effective Web applications, you have to be able to write servlets and JSPs that access and configure the underlying HTTP communication. This chapter will discuss the general structure of HTTP requests and responses used to exchange information between the Web client and server.

This chapter is a quick overview of HTTP containing sufficient detail for you to work with servlets and JSPs. For detailed information about HTTP, you should study the relevant RFCs available from `http://www.ietf.org`. The two HTTP RFCs and an RFC defining a URI encoding mechanism are shown here:

RFC	Description
RFC 1945	Hypertext Transfer Protocol—HTTP/1.0
RFC 2277	IETF Policy on Character Sets and Languages
RFC 2616	Hypertext Transfer Protocol—HTTP/1.1

Hypertext Transfer Protocol

The Hypertext Transfer Protocol (HTTP) is the underlying TCP/IP network protocol used by Web servers. HTTP is a synchronous protocol, which in this case means that after a client sends a request to a server, it waits for a single response. The server can only respond to requests. It cannot initiate a connection to the client.

HTTP is also a stateless protocol. Every request must therefore contain all the information required by the Web server to process the request. When, as is often the case, it is necessary for several HTTP requests to maintain state information, the client and server must use a session management technique (discussed in Chapter 8, "Session Tracking") to ensure that information can be traced to a particular client session.

As you will see in Chapter 4, "Basic Principles of Servlets," the supporting APIs for servlets hide many of the details on HTTP headers and responses presented in the following sections. However, you still need to know how HTTP works in order to write servlets that make the best use of the protocol.

The Structure of an HTTP Message

HTTP requests and responses are text-based, and both have a similar four-part structure:

- A single line used to denote whether the message is a request or a response
- A variable number of header fields terminated
- A blank line
- The message body (if applicable)

As you will see, not every message type will have a body. The structure of requests and responses is discussed in more detail in the following sections.

NOTE

HTTP is a generic protocol and refers to a uniform resource indicator (URI). A URI is a more general term than the familiar uniform resource locator (URL). Every URL is a URI, but a not all URIs are URLs. In addition to page locations, a URI can be a uniform resource name (URN) such as the `mailto:` prefix that can be used as a hypertext link on an HTML page.

The Structure of an HTTP Request

The first line of an HTTP request has three space-separated components:

```
<methods> <request-URI> <HTTP-version>
```

`<method>` specifies the type of the request as defined in Table 3.1. `<request-URI>` can be a full URI, but is typically the path component (such as `/` or `/index.html`). `<HTTP-version>` is the version of HTTP used. This component can only take the values `HTTP/1.0` and `HTTP/1.1`.

The defined request methods are shown in Table 3.1 (the method request names are case sensitive).

TABLE 3.1 Common HTTP Request Types

Request	Description
`GET`	Requests a page from the server. This is the normal request used when browsing Web pages.
`HEAD`	Like `GET`, but only returns the response header information, and not the page itself. This can be used to obtain information about a page, such as when it was last modified.
`POST`	This request is used to pass information to the server. Its most common use is with HTML forms where the form data is too long to encode in a `GET` request (see the later section "Passing Request Parameters").
`PUT`	Used to put a new Web page on a server. This request is not normally used because of the security implications of allowing a client to change a Web page.
`DELETE`	Used to delete a Web page from the server. This request is not normally used because of the security implications of permitting a client to change a Web page.
`CONNECT`	Intended for use with proxy servers and not applicable to servlets and JSPs.
`OPTIONS`	Intended for use with the Web server itself and not applicable to servlets and JSPs.
`TRACE`	This is used to request that the server send back the request header to the client in the body of the response, and to check that a connection can be made to the server. The `<request-URI>` is set to `*` in this message type.

A typical `GET` or `POST` request issued by a Web browser will include header fields containing supplementary information that can be accessed by a servlet. The following is a sample `GET` request issued to `www.samspublishing.com` by the Netscape 6.2 browser. There might be minor differences in the header fields if the request is issued from a different browser:

```
GET / HTTP/1.1
Host: www.samspublishing.com
User-Agent: Mozilla/5.0 (Windows; U; Windows NT 5.0; en-GB; rv:0.9.4)
➥ Gecko/20011128 Netscape6/6.2.1
```

```
Accept: text/xml, application/xml, application/xhtml+xml,
➥ text/html;q=0.9, image/png, image/jpeg, image/gif;q=0.2,
➥ text/plain;q=0.8, text/css, */*;q=0.1
Accept-Language: en-gb
Accept-Encoding: gzip, deflate, compress;q=0.9
Keep-Alive: 300
Connection: keep-alive
```

Without going into too much detail, you can see that each header line consists of a field name that is not case sensitive, a colon, and an arbitrary string value. The popular browsers commonly pass the following headers:

Header	Description
`Host`	Defines the hostname used in the request URL.
`User-Agent`	Defines the client browser version.
`Accept`	Defines a list of response body types that the client will accept. The server should not return a response whose MIME type is not in this list.
`Connection`	Used for connection persistence as described in the later section "Persistent Connections."

The Structure of an HTTP Response

An HTTP response, like a request, has a three-part structure:

```
<HTTP-version> <status-code> <reason-phrase>
```

The `<HTTP-version>` component reports the HTTP version used. It can only take the values `HTTP/1.0` and `HTTP/1.1`. The `<status-code>` component contains a response status code. This is a three-digit number whose first digit defines the general response category:

100–199 are informational

200–299 show successful page access

300–399 redirect the request

400–499 are client errors

500–599 are server errors

The `<reason-phrase>` component provides a textual description of the response code.

The following example shows the successful response header from a request to browse the URI `http://localhost:8080/index.html` issued by a Tomcat server:

```
HTTP/1.1 200 OK
Content-Type: text/html
Content-Length: 6827
Connection: close
Date: Tue, 02 Apr 2002 13:30:12 GMT
ETag: "6827-1013538288000"
Server: Apache Tomcat/4.0.2 (HTTP/1.1 Connector)
Last-Modified: Tue, 12 Feb 2002 18:24:48 GMT

... <body omitted>
```

This example shows that a response includes header fields used to pass additional information back to the client. A servlet can define most of the header fields in a response. When Tomcat returns a static HTML page, the following header fields are defined:

Header Field	Description
`Content-Type`	Defines the MIME type of the response body
`Content-Length`	Defines the number of bytes in the body
`Connection`	Used for connection persistence, as described in the later section "Persistent Connections"
`Date`	Defines the date and time when the server issued the response
`ETag`	Defines a unique `Entity Tag` for this page, which can be used to improve the local caching of Web pages (see the later section "Client Page Caching")
`Server`	Defines the server type and version
`Last-Modified`	Defines the date when the HTML was last modified (from the time stamp on the HTML file)

Setting the `Content-Type`, `Content-Length`, `Last-Modified`, and `ETag` header fields within a servlet is discussed in Chapter 7, "The Web Application Environment."

A list of commonly occurring HTTP response codes is shown in Table 3.2. Knowledge of these response codes will assist you in debugging any problems with your Web applications. Note that a 500 series response often occurs if you have a problem with the configuration for your servlets, or if the servlet fails to run correctly (such as might occur when an uncaught exception is thrown).

TABLE 3.2 Common HTTP Response Codes

Response	Description
`200 OK`	Standard response for the successful request of a page.
`301 Moved Permanently`	The requested resource has been moved to a new location. The `Location` header indicates the URI of the new location. The client should request the page from this new URI.
`304 Not Modified`	This is returned when a client requests a page and specifies the `If-modified-since` header in the request. The server will return code 304 rather than 200 if the page has not changed since the indicated modification date. This protocol is used to improve efficiency when a browser is caching local copies of Web pages.
`307 Temporary Redirect`	The requested resource has been temporarily moved to a new location. The `Location` header indicates the URI of the new location. The client should request the page from this new URI. If you request the URI `http://localhost:8080/` from Tomcat, you will get this response code, together with the header `Location=http://localhost:8080/index.html`.
`401 Unauthorized`	Used when a client is not authorized to access a resource. This response is covered in more detail in Chapter 14, "Access Control."
`403 Forbidden`	Access to the resource is denied, and the server might supply further information in the response body.
`404 Not Found`	The requested URI was not found on the server. This response might also be used to deny access without giving further information.
`414 Request-URI Too Long`	This is returned when a `GET` URI is too long for the server to process.
`500 Internal Server Error`	Unknown internal error. In Tomcat, this is often a result of errors in the XML configuration files for a Web application (see Chapter 4, "Basic Principles of Servlets" and Appendix B, "Template `web.xml` File").
`503 Service Unavailable`	This can be used by a servlet to show that an external resource (perhaps a database) is not available. The client can retry the request at a later time.

Setting the response code from within a servlet is also discussed in Chapter 7.

Testing an HTTP Connection

You can use the humble Telnet command-line utility to test out an HTTP connection by specifying the required HTTP port number after the hostname on the command line. The default port number for an HTTP server is 80, but Tomcat uses 8080 to avoid a clash with any existing Web server running on the same host. The following command shows how to trace a connection to a local Tomcat Web server:

```
> telnet localhost 8080
TRACE * HTTP/1.0

HTTP/1.1 200 OK
Content-Type: message/http
Content-Length: 19
Date: Tue, 02 Apr 2002 10:21:36 GMT
Server: Apache Tomcat/4.0.3 (HTTP/1.1 Connector)

TRACE * HTTP/1.0
```

The first three lines in this example are the ones you type in: the first is the Telnet command, and the next two lines are the HTTP request. The rest of the listing is the response from Tomcat, which includes the request as the body of the message.

TIP

When you start up Telnet to connect to an HTTP server, you will not receive a prompt. Simply type in your HTTP request and press the Enter key twice; once to end the request line, and once to enter the blank line that marks the end of the request header fields. You might need to switch local echo on for your Telnet utility in order to see the HTTP request line you type in. You can do this by typing **`CTRL-]`** after starting Telnet to get to the Telnet prompt, and then entering the command **`set local_echo`**. Entering a blank line to the Telnet prompt will enable you to resume the Telnet session to the HTTP server.

Passing Request Parameters

Information you enter on an HTML form is passed as parameters with the HTTP `GET` or `POST` request, defined in the `METHOD` parameter to the `FORM` tag. With `GET` requests, the parameters are encoded with the request URI, but `POST` requests use the request body for the parameters.

The following example shows a simple form that can be used to register a name and email address with a servlet path of `SAMS/Register` (this example uses a `GET` request):

```
<HTML><BODY>
<FORM METHOD="get" ACTION="http://localhost:8080/SAMS/Register">
Name: <INPUT TYPE="text" NAME="name"><P>
Email: <INPUT TYPE="text" NAME="email"><P>
<INPUT TYPE="submit">
</FORM>
</BODY></HTML>
```

CAUTION

This example is fictitious, and you should not use this form or try to access the URI using Telnet.

Using this form to specify a name of `Martin Bond` and a fictitious email address of `martin@samspublishing` results in the following request:

```
GET /SAMS/Register?name=Martin+Bond&email=martin%40samspublishing HTTP/1.1
Host: localhost:8080
User-Agent: Mozilla/5.0 (Windows; U; Windows NT 5.0; en-GB; rv:0.9.4)
➥ Gecko/20011128 Netscape6/6.2.1
Accept: text/xml, application/xml, application/xhtml+xml,
➥ text/html;q=0.9, image/png, image/jpeg, image/gif;q=0.2,
➥ text/plain;q=0.8, text/css, */*;q=0.1
Accept-Language: en-gb
Accept-Encoding: gzip, deflate, compress;q=0.9
Keep-Alive: 300
Connection: keep-alive
```

As you can see, the `GET` header line has the form parameters encoded with the request URI. The form parameters are appended to the URI after the question mark (?), and each parameter is defined by a name and value pair, such as

```
name=Martin+Bond
```

HTTP only permits certain characters in a URI (letters, digits, and a few related characters such as the underscore); other character values must be encoded using a scheme defined in RFC 2277, "IETF Policy on Character Sets and Languages" (available from `http://www.ietf.org`). RFC 2277 defines character encoding as a percent sign and the two-digit hexadecimal value for that character (using the UTF-8 character set); a space is a special case and may be encoded using a plus sign (+) instead of its hex value of `%20`.

Although the HTTP specification does not impose a limit on the length of the request URI, an individual Web server is permitted to reject requests that contain a URI that is considered too long. In practical terms, you should avoid generating a request URI that contains more than 255 characters, as older browsers, Web servers, and proxy servers might not properly support longer URIs.

When using large HTML forms that might create `GET` requests of more than 255 characters, you should use the `POST` request instead. Here's the same form data passed as a `POST` request:

```
GET /SAMS/Register HTTP/1.1
Host: localhost:8080
User-Agent: Mozilla/5.0 (Windows; U; Windows NT 5.0; en-GB; rv:0.9.4)
➥ Gecko/20011128 Netscape6/6.2.1
Accept: text/xml, application/xml, application/xhtml+xml,
➥ text/html;q=0.9, image/png, image/jpeg, image/gif;q=0.2,
➥ text/plain;q=0.8, text/css, */*;q=0.1
Accept-Language: en-gb
Accept-Encoding: gzip, deflate, compress;q=0.9
Keep-Alive: 300
Connection: keep-alive
Content-length: 50
Content-type: application/x-www-form-urlencoded

name=Martin+Bond&email=martin%40samspublishing.com
```

The form data is passed in the body of the request rather than encoded on the request URI. The length of the request body is specified in the `Content-length` header. The `Content-type` header shows that the body type is `application/x-www-form-urlencoded`, which indicates that the form parameters are encoded using the RFC 2277 scheme.

One other difference between `GET` and `POST` requests shows up when you bookmark them within your browser. If a `GET` request is bookmarked, the parameters are included with the bookmark. However, if a `POST` request is bookmarked, no parameters are included, so you will not be able to successfully bookmark a `POST` request with form data.

Client Page Caching

A common mechanism for improving Web client and server performance is for the client to cache Web pages locally and only reload the Web page if the local cached copy is out of date. There are two mechanisms used for caching:

- Store the Web page `Last-Modified` date with the page contents.
- Store the `ETag` header value (if provided) with the page contents.

The `Last-Modified` and `ETag` values are supplied by the server as response header fields; HTTP 1.1–compliant servers should return both fields if at all possible. The Web server takes care of these values for static HTML pages, but you should attempt to provide them for any servlets you develop (see Chapter 7). If neither of these header fields are defined in the response, the client cannot keep a local cache copy of the page, and must always retrieve the page from the server. For many servlets, this will be a necessary requirement, as the servlet page contents will be dynamic and unsuitable for caching by the Web client.

A browser can request that a page only be provided if it isn't in the local cache using the following headers:

Header Field	Description
`If-Modified-Since`	Defines the date of the cached copy of the page.
`If-None-Match`	Defines the `Entity` Tag for the cached copy of the page.

If the date or `ETag` in the request matches the server's copy of the page, a server might return a response of 304 "Not Modified" rather than return the page body. Usually only one of these fields will be specified, but if both are defined in a request, both values must be unchanged for the server to reply with the 304 response.

The `ETag` value is generated by a server to enable more reliable validation of cached Web pages in cases where it is inconvenient to store modification dates, or where the server wants to avoid problems that might arise from using the modification date.

URI Redirection and Page Refresh

Two common techniques for improving the Web browsing experience for users are

- URI redirection—This enables one Web page to send a response asking the browser to automatically fetch a page from a different URI.
- Page refresh—This is used to ask a browser to load a Web page after a specified delay period (this might be the same or a different URI).

URI Redirection

In Table 3.2 you saw that response error codes of 301 and 307 indicate a page request should be redirected to another URI. Most browsers will resubmit the request using the URI specified in the `Location` header field of the response.

The URI redirect response is used to permit multiple URIs to refer to the same document without duplicating the document. This can be useful when reorganizing a Web site to ensure that old hypertext links are still valid. Tomcat uses page redirection to map the default root document (/) onto `/index.html`, as shown in the highlighted lines in this example:

```
HTTP/1.1 302 Moved Temporarily
Content-Type: text/html
Connection: close
```

```
Date: Tue, 02 Apr 2002 14:55:16 GMT
Location: http://localhost:8080/index.html
Server: Apache Tomcat/4.0.2 (HTTP/1.1 Connector)

<html><head><title>Apache Tomcat/4.0.2 - Error report</title>
<STYLE><!---
H1{font-family : sans-serif,Arial,Tahoma;color : white;
   background-color : #0086b2;}
BODY{font-family : sans-serif,Arial,Tahoma;color : black;
   background-color : white;}
B{color : white;background-color : #0086b2;} HR{color : #0086b2;}
--></STYLE> </head><body>
<h1>Apache Tomcat/4.0.2 - HTTP Status 302 - Moved Temporarily</h1>
<HR size="1" noshade><p><b>type</b> Status report</p>
<p><b>message</b> <u>Moved Temporarily</u></p>
<p><b>description</b>
<u>The requested resource (Moved Temporarily) has moved temporarily
to a new location.</u></p>
<HR size="1" noshade>
</body></html>
```

The page body includes a simple notice containing the required redirection URI. If the browser doesn't perform the automatic redirect, the user will see the notice and can manually follow the link to the new URI.

Page Refresh

An alternative technique for asking the browser to load a different URI is an HTML-related feature rather than a standard HTTP feature.

A Web page containing a `META` tag with the `HTTP-EQUIV="refresh"` attribute is used to ask a Web browser to load a page after a specified time period. The following HTML tag refreshes the current page after five minutes:

```
<meta http-equiv="refresh" content="300">
```

The same effect is obtained using the following HTTP response header:

```
Refresh: 300
```

The `Refresh` header is not part of the official HTTP specification, but is recognized by most Web browsers.

Both forms of refreshing can specify a URI to reload after the refresh interval has expired, effectively providing another means of redirecting a client to another URI.

This technique can be used to briefly display one page before moving on to another—something the redirect response cannot do because the redirection cannot have a time delay. The following HTTP header shows how to display the current page for 15 seconds before reloading the Web server home page (the new URL is separated from the refresh time by a semicolon):

```
Refresh: 15;/index.html
```

This technique of requesting the client to refresh a page after a time delay is known as *client pull*. Client pull can be a useful technique for ensuring that a Web page maintains up-to-date information, such as that required for stock and share prices provided by an online trading page.

CAUTION

Web pages with short refresh cycles can cause excessive amounts of network traffic and overload a Web server.

Persistent Connections

Every page request and response requires a new network connection to be set up and torn down. This is a large overhead, especially when requesting lots of small files, such as might occur on a Web page with several embedded images.

HTTP enables a client and server to negotiate to keep a single network connection alive to handle multiple requests and responses. HTTP 1.0 requires the client to explicitly ask to keep a connection alive, whereas HTTP 1.1 assumes the connection is persistent unless the client or server indicates otherwise. The `Connection` header field is used to negotiate connection persistence:

- An HTTP 1.1 client or server can close a persistent connection by sending the `Connection: close` header with the request or response.
- An HTTP 1.0 client can ask the server to keep the connection alive using the `Connection: Keep-Alive` header.

Persistent connections will only stay open for a specified period of time. A server will close a connection after the timeout expires to prevent clients from hogging a network connection and reducing server throughput. Tomcat defines the connection timeout in the `server.xml` file, discussed in Chapter 16, "Configuring Tomcat."

The only constraint on a persistent connection is ensuring that every request and response message indicates the size of the message body using the `Content-Length` header field. If the content length is not specified, the client or server can only determine the end of the body when the network connection is closed. If the request or response does not have a body, the `Content-Length` header can be omitted.

Persistent connections are a good technique for improving Web server performance, and can be supported when developing servlets by ensuring that the servlet specifies the length of the content it's returning to the client. This is discussed in greater detail in Chapter 7.

Using HTTP from Within a Java Program

Before leaving the world of HTTP to look at the basic principles of servlets and JSPs, you might find it useful to know how to retrieve pages from a Web server using a Java client. You can use this technique to pull information from an existing Web site.

A simple example would be a Java program that needs a current exchange rate for a particular currency. The Java program could connect to a Web site that is known to display currency exchange rates (many news and financial sites display this information). The resultant response body can be examined and the exchange rate extracted from the other data (including the HTML formatting) on the Web page.

The complexity of writing a data extraction program such as this currency exchange rate example is in finding the required information within the plethora of HTML elements and other data on the page.

NOTE

With the trend toward writing Web pages in HTML that are also well-formed XML documents, or even using XML or XHTML, you can use the SAX and DOM XML support classes in JAXP and Java 1.4 (and later) to simplify extracting page data from the HTML elements.

Handling HTTP is very simple, as the `java.net.URL` class encapsulates the functionality you need. Listing 3.1 shows a simple program that uses `GET` to request a page from the URL given as the command-line parameter and display it on `System.out`.

LISTING 3.1 `URLGet.java`

```
import java.io.*;
import java.net.*;

public class URLGet
{
    public static void main(String[] args) {
        BufferedReader in=null;
        if (args.length == 1) {
```

LISTING 3.1 Continued

```
            try {
                URL url = new URL(args[0]);
                in = new BufferedReader(
➥ new InputStreamReader(url.openStream()));
                String line=null;
                while ((line=in.readLine()) != null)
                    System.out.println(line);
            }
            catch (MalformedURLException ex) {
                System.err.println(ex);
            }
            catch (FileNotFoundException ex) {
                System.err.println("Failed to open stream to URL: "+ex);
            }
            catch (IOException ex) {
                System.err.println("Error reading URL content: "+ex);
            }
            if (in != null)
                try {in.close();} catch (IOException ex) {}
        }
        else
            System.err.println ("Usage: URLGet URL");
    }
}
```

The URL object created from the first command-line argument defines the required page. When the `URL.openStream()` method is called, the HTTP request is sent to the server and the response body is made available as an `InputStream`.

As an example of a more sophisticated request, the program in Listing 3.2 will accept a command-line URL and an optional list of HTML form parameters. If any form parameters are specified, a `POST` request is issued; otherwise, a `GET` request is used.

LISTING 3.2 `URLRequest.java`

```
import java.io.*;
import java.net.*;
import java.util.*;

public class URLRequest
{
    public static void main(String[] args) {
```

LISTING 3.2 Continued

```
        BufferedReader in = null;
        if (args.length>0) {
            try {
                URL url = new URL(args[0]);
                URLConnection connection = url.openConnection();
                connection.setRequestProperty(
➥"User-Agent","Mozilla/4.0 (compatible; MSIE 5.01; Windows NT 5.0)");
                if (args.length > 1) {
                    connection.setDoOutput(true);
                    Writer post = new OutputStreamWriter(
➥connection.getOutputStream());
                    for (int i=1; i<args.length; i++) {
                        if (i > 1)
                            post.write('&');
                        post.write(encodeParameter(args[i]));
                    }
                    post.write("\r\n");
                    post.close();
                }
                connection.connect();
                Map headers = connection.getHeaderFields();
                Iterator it = headers.keySet().iterator();
                while (it.hasNext()) {
                    String key = (String)it.next();
                    System.out.println(key+": "+headers.get(key));
                }
                System.out.println();
                in = new BufferedReader(new InputStreamReader(
➥connection.getInputStream()));
                String line=null;
                while ((line=in.readLine()) != null)
                    System.out.println(line);
            }
            catch (MalformedURLException ex) {
                System.err.println(ex);
            }
            catch (FileNotFoundException ex) {
                System.err.println("Failed to open stream to URL: "+ex);
            }
            catch (IOException ex) {
                System.err.println("Error reading URL content: "+ex);
            }
```

LISTING 3.2 Continued

```
            if (in != null)
                try {in.close();} catch (IOException ex) {}
        }
        else {
            System.err.println ("Usage: URLRequest URL (uses GET)");
            System.err.println (
                "       URLRequest URL parameters... (uses POST)");
        }
    }

    private static String encodeParameter(String parameter)
    {
        StringBuffer result = new StringBuffer();
        try {
            String name = null;
            String value = "";
            int ix = parameter.indexOf('=');
            if (ix == -1)
                name = parameter;
            else {
                name = parameter.substring(0,ix);
                value = parameter.substring(ix+1);
            }
            result.append(name);
            result.append('=');
            result.append(URLEncoder.encode(value,"UTF-8"));
        }
        catch (UnsupportedEncodingException ex) {
            System.err.println(ex);
        }
        return result.toString();
    }
}
```

Listing 3.2 shows most of the salient features of the `java.net.URL` and `java.net.URLConnection` classes that are used to access a Web server. The method `encodedParameter()` encodes the request parameters using the RFC 2277 scheme; the `java.net.URLEncoder` and `java.net.URLDecoder` classes support this encoding scheme.

Listing 3.2 also shows how to define header fields in the request by setting the `User-Agent` field to masquerade as Internet Explorer Version 6. The header fields in the response are displayed with the response body.

Summary

This chapter has supplied you with the information required to work with HTTP requests and responses. You have seen that HTTP is the synchronous and stateless TCP/IP protocol that underpins Web servers. Web servers respond to Web client requests and return information in the body of the HTTP response. The two most common forms of requests are `GET` and `POST`. `GET` requests are used for simple Web pages, or Web forms containing a small amount of data. `POST` requests are used for Web forms that can send a lot of data (typically more than 255 characters).

HTTP requests and responses contain header fields that are used to pass additional information between the client and server. The HTTP body is used in a request to pass additional information to the server (such as the parameters in a `POST` request), and in the server response to return the requested Web page data.

You have also learned how the `java.net.URL` and `java.net.URLConnection` classes can be used within a Java application to send an HTTP request to a server and read the response.

4

Basic Principles of Servlets

IN THIS CHAPTER

In this chapter you will write a simple Web application that consists of a single servlet and a static HTML form. It is assumed that you know how to code a simple HTML form, therefore, this chapter will only cover the basic principles of servlets. Chapter 5, "Basic Principles of JSPs," will extend your servlet knowledge to cover JavaServer Pages, and Chapter 7, "The Web Application Environment," will tackle more advanced servlet topics. This chapter covers writing Web applications using the Java servlet APIs and deploying Web applications to the Tomcat server (including the syntax of the deployment descriptor XML file).

Introduction to Servlets

Servlets, as you know from Chapter 1, "Overview of Jakarta Tomcat, Servlets, and JSPs," are simply Java programs that are run inside a Web server (strictly the servlet container). Tomcat's servlet container is called Catalina. Servlets are accessed from a Web client and usually return information in the form of an HTTP response for display by a browser. The response normally includes an HTML page for display, but this is not a requirement. Servlets can also be used to support mobile phone clients using Wireless Application Protocol (WAP) and other forms of clients using proprietary data formats or XML.

Departing from tradition, you will not start by studying the ubiquitous "Hello World" servlet because it is really too trivial (an example "Hello World" is included on the Tomcat distribution for you to run if this leaves you feeling deprived). Instead, you will develop a very dumb currency converter application that simply takes an amount in U.S.

dollars and converts it to U.K. sterling. This example improves on "Hello World" in three important respects:

- The servlet is dynamic—that is, the response returned by the servlet varies according to data in the request.
- It shows how to access a servlet and pass parameters from a static HTML page.
- It introduces the concept of writing internationalized servlets to ensure that your code will display data in the correct format according to local conventions.

NOTE

For the sake of simplicity, the examples use text strings rather than Java resource bundles. A truly internationalized servlet should use resource bundles to allow all strings to be mapped into the local language used by the server.

To make a servlet accessible to the Web client, it has to be deployed to the Tomcat servlet container. In this chapter you will be shown how to manually deploy servlets. In Chapter 15, "Administering Tomcat in a Live Environment," you will be introduced to the Tomcat Manager Application, which you can use to deploy applications. If you are familiar with Jakarta Ant (available from `http://jakarta.apache.org/ant`), you can automate the deployment process with Ant scripts.

As you work through the book, the Currency Converter will be used to illustrate different aspects of servlet programming. You are strongly encouraged to either type the code yourself or download it from the Sams Publishing Web site (go to `www.samspublishing.com` and enter this book's ISBN, 0672324393, in the search box) and follow the deployment process. This will make the text more relevant.

CAUTION

Many of the code samples have been written to illustrate a particular feature, and although some error handling is included, more would be required if this application were to be deployed in a live situation.

Creating the Development Directory Structure

Before writing the servlet, you will need to create a work area for Web application development. You are advised to set up the directory structure described in the next section to organize your Web applications in a logical manner.

For servlets to be deployed, they need to be placed in the Tomcat webapps directory. This will either be under CATALINA_HOME or CATALINA_BASE depending on your setup. You should not store your development files in this directory because of the risk of accidentally damaging your production environment or losing the source code if the Web application is removed from the Tomcat server. Always create a separate directory structure and use it for your development files. If you create the directory structure shown in the following table, it will simplify packaging and distributing your Web applications.

Create your development directory and underneath it create the following subdirectories:

Directory	Usage
docs	Documentation to accompany your application
src	Java source files for servlets and other helper or utility classes
web	The *document root* directory used to store static HTML files, JSPs, and other non-Java files used by the application
web/images	GIF and JPEG images
web/WEB-INF	Resource and configuration files
web/WEB-INF/classes	Servlet and utility classes
web/WEB-INF/lib	JAR files used in the application

TIP

You will need to add <CATALINA_HOME>/common/lib/servlet.jar to your CLASSPATH.

To simplify compilation of the many classes that make up your application, you should add the web/WEB-INF/classes directory to your Java CLASSPATH as well.

Creating the Currency Converter Servlet

The Currency Converter (Listings 4.1 and 4.2) uses a static HTML form and a servlet. The end-user types an amount in U.S. dollars into the form and this value is passed in an HTTP request to the servlet. The servlet then applies a fixed (for now) exchange rate to convert dollars to U.K. pounds and returns an HTTP response containing the resulting value imbedded in an HTML page.

Currency Converter HTML Input Form

The input form is deliberately kept very simple. The whole form is shown in Listing 4.1.

LISTING 4.1 Currency Converter Input Form

```
<HTML>
  <HEAD><TITLE>Currency Form</TITLE></HEAD>
  <BODY>
    <FORM METHOD=GET ACTION="servlet/CurrencyConverter">
      <H1>Simple Currency Converter</H1>
      <P>Use this form to convert U.S. Dollars to U.K. Pounds Sterling</P>
      Type in the amount to be converted in the box
      <INPUT TYPE=TEXT NAME="amount">
      <INPUT TYPE=SUBMIT>
    </FORM>
  </BODY>
</HTML>
```

The `FORM` element has two attributes: The `METHOD` defines the use of an HTTP `GET` request, whereas the `ACTION` attribute specifies the URL of the servlet to invoke.

The servlet URL pathname can be relative to either the Web application name, as on the form, or the full pathname including the Web application name, as shown here:

```
http://localhost:8080/basic-servlet/servlet/CurrencyConverter
```

You need to add `servlet` qualifier to the path for the servlet to be invoked by the Tomcat "invoker" servlet. Later, you will see an alternative method of mapping the servlet URL in the deployment descriptor file that avoids having to add `servlet` to the path.

If you have placed your servlet in a package, you will have to change the URL to prefix the servlet class with the package name. For example, if `CurrencyConverter` is in package `first`, the URL is `servlet/first.CurrencyConverter`.

The number of dollars entered on the form is passed to the servlet in a parameter called `amount`.

Save this form in a file called `currency-form.html` in your development `web` directory.

Currency Converter Servlet

The converter servlet is shown in Listing 4.2. The servlet obtains the dollar amount from the HTTP request and uses a constant exchange rate to calculate the new value in U.K. pounds sterling. Most of the complex parts of this servlet are concerned with ensuring that the two currencies display correctly.

LISTING 4.2 Currency Converter Servlet

```
import java.io.*;
import java.util.*;
import java.text.*;
import javax.servlet.*;
import javax.servlet.http.*;

public class CurrencyConverter extends HttpServlet {
    private static final double EXCHANGE_RATE = 0.613;
    public void doGet(HttpServletRequest req, HttpServletResponse res)
                throws ServletException, IOException {
        res.setContentType ("text/html");
        PrintWriter out = res.getWriter();
        out.println ("<HTML>");
        out.println ("<HEAD><TITLE>Currency Conversion</TITLE></HEAD>");
        out.println ("<BODY>");
        Currency dollars = Currency.getInstance(Locale.U.S.);
        Currency pounds = Currency.getInstance(Locale.U.K.);
        String amount = req.getParameter("amount");
        try {
            NumberFormat nf = NumberFormat.getInstance();
            double poundValue = nf.parse(amount).doubleValue();
            poundValue *= EXCHANGE_RATE;
            nf.setMaximumFractionDigits(pounds.getDefaultFractionDigits());
            nf.setMinimumFractionDigits(pounds.getDefaultFractionDigits());
            out.println ("<BIG>"+dollars.getSymbol(Locale.U.S.)+amount+" = "
                + pounds.getSymbol(Locale.U.K.)+nf.format(poundValue)+"</BIG>");
        }
        catch (ParseException e) {
            out.println ("Bad number format");
        }
        out.println ("</BODY>");
        out.println ("</HTML>");
    }
}
```

The servlet API is encapsulated in two packages: `javax.servlet` and `javax.servlet.http`. Although it is possible to write a servlet to implement the `javax.servlet.Servlet` interface, in a Web application it is more usual to extend the `javax.servlet.http.HttpServlet` class, which implements the `Servlet` interface. The `HttpServlet` class provides a lot of functionality that simplifies the process of serving HTTP requests.

The `HttpServlet` class defines a `doGet()` method, which is overridden in this servlet to handle HTTP `GET` requests sent to this servlet. The HTTP requests and responses are encapsulated in the `HttpServletRequest` and `HttpServletResponse` objects passed as parameters to `doGet()`.

The `CurrencyConverter` servlet uses a `PrintWriter` object to send the response back to the client. For the character encoding to take effect, it is important to set the MIME type and character set header field in the response (with the `setContentType()` method) before obtaining the `PrintWriter` object. After the `PrintWriter` object is created, you will not be able to modify the MIME type or character encoding of the response. In `CurrencyConverter` the `PrintWriter` object is used to send HTML back to the client for display. (MIME types are covered in more detail in Chapter 7.)

The `amount` parameter is obtained using the `HttpServletRequest.getParameter()` method. In this case the parameter is accessed by its name, but other methods enable you to access parameters and values when the name is not known.

Methods from the `Currency` class are used to ensure that the currency symbols and denominations are correct for the appropriate server locale.

NOTE

The `Currency` class is new in J2SDK 1.4.

The new currency value in U.K. pounds sterling is calculated and returned in the HTML response.

You should save this code in a file called `CurrencyConverter.java` in your development `src` directory. Put the compiled class in the `web/WEB-INF/classes` directory.

TIP

At this point, make sure you have added `<CATALINA_HOME>/common/lib/servlet.jar` to your `CLASSPATH`.

Before moving on to how to deploy this application, here is a short discussion on one of the disadvantages of using a servlet to produce HTML.

CODING HTML IN A SERVLET

Listing 4.2 is a servlet that produces very simple HTML. If you extract the HTML from the `out.println` statements, it consists of the following:

```
<HTML>
    <HEAD><TITLE>Currency Conversion</TITLE></HEAD>
    <BODY>
        <BIG>   </BIG>
    </BODY>
</HTML>
```

However, even with this small amount of HTML, it is not at all easy to see the structure because of all the other things going on in the servlet. More of an issue is diagnosing where the problem lies when the page does not display correctly. Coding complex HTML in servlets can be troublesome. In Chapter 5, you will see an alternative way of coding a servlet as a JavaServer Page that considerably simplifies producing complex HTML.

Deploying the Currency Converter to Tomcat

There are a number of ways to deploy applications to Tomcat. For this first example, you will deploy manually, which involves the following steps:

1. Copy the application files to Tomcat's `webapps` directory.
2. Stop and restart Tomcat.

Creating the Web Application Directory

Create a directory called `basic-servlet` in the Tomcat `webapps` directory and copy the HTML form and servlet class file into the following directory structure:

```
<CATALINA_HOME>/webapps/basic-servlet/currency-form.html
<CATALINA_HOME>/webapps/basic-servlet/WEB-INF/classes/CurrencyConverter.class
```

After copying in the files, you will need to stop and restart Tomcat so that it recognizes the new Web application (called `basic-servlet`). That is all there is to it.

When Tomcat is restarted, it adds your Web application directory to its `CLASSPATH` so it can find the compiled servlet classes. When the servlet is first accessed, Tomcat uses the `invoker` servlet to create an instance of the servlet to process the HTTP request.

NOTE

Chapter 15 will introduce the Tomcat Manager Application, which can be used to deploy new Web applications without the inconvenience of having to stop and restart Tomcat.

Testing the Currency Converter

Access the input form in the browser of your choice with the following URL:

```
http://localhost:8080/basic-servlet/currency-form.html
```

You should now see the page shown in Figure 4.1.

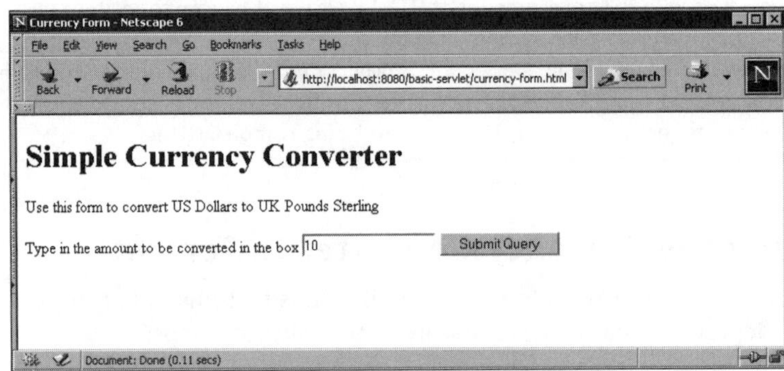

FIGURE 4.1 Currency converter application input form.

Type any numeric value in the input box and click Submit Query. If everything is working correctly, this will open the page shown in Figure 4.2.

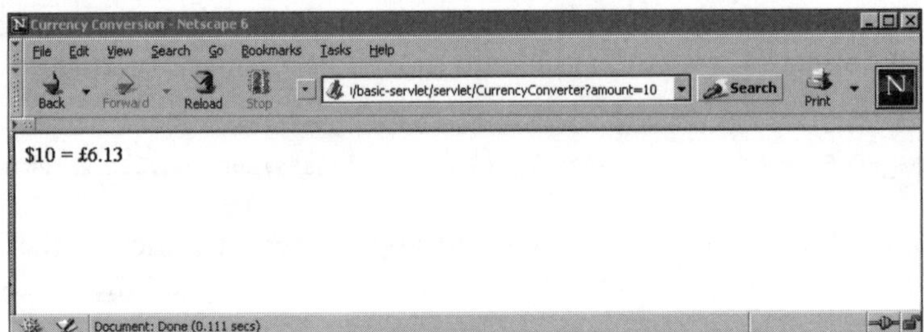

FIGURE 4.2 Currency converter servlet page.

CAUTION

If you receive an error after clicking on the Submit Query button, this might be due to your Tomcat configuration not enabling the Invoker servlet (see Chapter 16, "Configuring Tomcat"). Some later versions of Tomcat 4.1 have disabled the Invoker servlet. You can re-enable the Invoker servlet by editing the file <CATALINA_HOME>/conf/web.xml and uncommenting the following element:

```
<!-- The mapping for the invoker servlet -->
 <servlet-mapping>
     <servlet-name>invoker</servlet-name>
```

```
        <url-patter>/servlet/*</url-pattern>
    </servlet-mapping>
```

You will need to stop and restart Tomcat for this change to take effect.

TIP

Notice that the URL used to access the servlet is

```
http://localhost:8080/basic-servlet/servlet/CurrencyConverter?amount=10
```

where the actual value for `amount` corresponds to the value you typed into the form.

You can use this URL to directly access and test the servlet without using the intervening HTML form.

If the servlet is not working, or you don't get the expected screens, check out Chapter 6, "Troubleshooting Servlets and JSPs," for hints on solving your problem.

Configuring a Web Application Using a Deployment Descriptor

Web applications normally have a deployment descriptor, which contains configuration information. This configuration information is stored in a file named `web.xml` stored in the Web application's `WEB-INF` directory. The contents of this file are defined in the servlet specification (also see Appendix B, "Template `web.xml` File").

Although, as you have seen, Tomcat does not require an application to have a deployment descriptor, there are a number of reasons why your application should have one:

- To ensure that your application is portable to other Web servers
- To use more advanced features such as error pages, welcome pages, event listeners, and servlet filters

Tomcat has a default deployment descriptor in the `<CATALINA_HOME>/conf/web.xml` file that defines certain default values for every Web application loaded into Tomcat. As each Web application is deployed, this document is processed first, followed by the deployment descriptor defined for the Web application. You should edit this file if you want to make changes that affect every servlet. For example, you would edit this file to change the default session timeout or to add a new MIME type.

Creating the Deployment Descriptor

For our simple `CurrencyConverter` servlet you need a minimal `web.xml` file as shown in Listing 4.3.

LISTING 4.3 Deployment Descriptor (`web.xml`) for the Currency Converter

```
<!DOCTYPE web-app
    PUBLIC "-//Sun Microsystems, Inc.//DTD Web Application 2.3//EN"
    "http://java.sun.com/dtd/web-app_2_3.dtd">
<web-app>
    <display-name>Currency Converter</display-name>
    <description>
        This is a simple web application with an HTML form passing
        a single parameter (amount of dollars) to a servlet for conversion.
    </description>
    <servlet>
        <servlet-name>Currency Converter</servlet-name>
        <servlet-class>CurrencyConverter</servlet-class>
    </servlet>
</web-app>
```

The root element of this XML file `<web-app>` represents a single Web application, which in this case has a single servlet. Within the `<servlet>` element, the `<servlet-name>` identifies the servlet (it must be unique within the Web application) and the `<servlet-class>` is used to specify the Java class.

If there are errors in the deployment descriptor, Tomcat will display them in its startup window and in the log file for the `localhost` (`<CATALINA_HOME>/logs/localhost_log.`*`<date>`*`.txt`). Tomcat will startup, but the offending application will not be available.

TIP

You can avoid syntax errors in your deployment descriptor by utilizing an XML validator to check your XML file.

First save this deployment descriptor in the `/WEB-INF/` directory in your development area, then copy the deployment descriptor to Tomcat's `webapps` directory (`webapps/basic-servlet/WEB-INF/web.xml`). You must stop and restart Tomcat after changing a `web.xml` file. Otherwise, Tomcat will not recognize the changes you have made.

This simple deployment descriptor has not told Tomcat anything it couldn't already work out from the files in your Web application. Therefore, the Currency Converter application should run as before. Now you can start adding extra information about your application such as mapping it onto a different URL.

Adding URL Mapping to the Deployment Descriptor

The general form of a URL to access a servlet is

```
<Protocol>//<Host>:port/<Context Root>/<Servlet Path>[?<Query String>]
```

The elements in the `CurrencyConverter` servlet URL are shown in the following table.

URL Element	Corresponding Currency Converter Element
Protocol	`http:`
Host:port	`localhost:8080`
Context Root	`basic-servlet`
Servlet path	`servlet/CurrencyConverter`
Query string	`amount=1`

So far the servlet path element has been prefixed with `servlet` to allow it to be invoked by Tomcat's invoker servlet. Also, the actual classname has been used for the servlet.

This has three major disadvantages:

- Any change made to the servlet classname will necessitate a change to the HTML form or any other clients that accesses this servlet.
- You are exposing the real classname, making it easier for malicious individuals to hack into the application.
- The use of `servlet` in the URL exposes Tomcat implementation–specific details and makes the application less portable.

The solution for this is to map a servlet's actual name to a URL pattern, also known as a servlet alias. In the application's `web.xml` document add an element called `<servlet-mapping>` as shown here.

```
<web-app>
    <!-- ... existing servlet definition -->
    <servlet-mapping>
        <servlet-name>Currency Converter</servlet-name>
        <url-pattern>/convert</url-pattern>
    </servlet-mapping>
</web-app>
```

NOTE

The `<servlet-name>` must match the name defined in the `<servlet>` element. Any `<servlet-mapping>` element must be defined after all the `<servlet>` elements you use to define the servlets in your Web application.

With the `/convert` URL mapping added to the deployment descriptor, the currency converter servlet can now be accessed using the following URL:

```
http:/localhost:8080/basic-servlet/convert?amount=1
```

The `FORM` tag in `currency-form.html` should also be changed to

```
<FORM METHOD=GET ACTION="convert">
```

Using a Wildcard Character in URL Patterns

Wildcards can be used in the URL pattern to address all requests with a particular suffix to a servlet. For example, the following servlet mapping will direct all requests with a .con suffix (such as `basic-servlet/anything.con`) to the currency converter servlet.

```
<servlet-mapping>
    <servlet-name>Currency Converter</servlet-name>
    <url-pattern>*.con </url-pattern>
</servlet-mapping>
```

Where potential mapping conflicts exist, Tomcat will always attempt to find an exact match between the request URL and the alias for the servlet. If an exact match fails, Tomcat will try to match the longest path-prefix by parsing the alias one directory at a time. The longest match determines which servlet is selected, which enables extra path information (see Chapter 8, "Session Tracking") to be added to the servlet URL.

Changing the Servlet Context Path

By default, Tomcat uses the `webapps` subdirectory name as the context name for your Web application. You can create an alias for a Web application context path by adding a new `Context` element to Tomcat's `server.xml` file.

NOTE

You only need to add a `Context` element for your application if you want to change the URL to access it or need to override the default actions defined for all servlets.

There are a number of attributes for the `Context` element, some of which are shown in Table 4.1 (refer to the Tomcat documentation for a full list). The minimal required attributes are `path` and `docBase`.

TABLE 4.1 Some Common Context Element Attributes

Attribute Name	Description
`path`	The context path of this Web application, which is matched against the beginning of each request URL to select the appropriate Web application for processing. All the path attributes must be unique for a particular host.

TABLE 4.1 Continued

Attribute Name	Description
`docBase`	This is the name of the directory where this Web application is actually stored. Either an absolute path or one that is relative to the `webapps` directory can be specified.
`reloadable`	(Optional) Set to `true` if the Web application is to be automatically reloaded when Tomcat detects a change. Default is `false`.
`debug`	(Optional) Level of debugging required. The default level is no debugging defined as zero (0), whereas `debug="9"` will produce lots of debugging info.
`workdir`	(Optional) Pathname of a temporary directory for this context. Default is `<CATALINA_HOME>/work`.
`override`	(Optional) Set to `true` if settings in this context override corresponding settings in the `DefaultContext` component. Default is `false`.

To create a new `Context` for the currency converter, add the following element to Tomcat's `server.xml` file inside the `localhost Host` element for the `Tomcat-Standalone service`.

```
<Host name="localhost" appBase="webapps" unpackWARs="true">
...

   <Context path="/my-servlets" docBase="basic-servlet" />
   ...
</Host>
```

You can now access the application using the path defined in the `Context` element.

```
http://localhost:8080/my-servlets/currency-form.html
```

Automatically Reloading Servlets

For reasons of efficiency, the default configuration of Tomcat doesn't reload servlets when class files are replaced. Servlets are only reloaded when Tomcat is restarted. For a live system, this saves the considerable processing needed for Tomcat to continuously check if an application's class files have changed. During development it is somewhat tedious to stop and restart Tomcat every time a servlet is changed, so most developers enable automatic reloading of servlet class files.

To reload an individual Web application's class files, edit the `server.xml` file and add the `reloadable` attribute to the `Context` element for that servlet. For example:

```
<Context path="/my-servlets" docbase="basic-servlet" reloadable="true" />
```

Tomcat can also be configured so that it monitors all applications and reloads classes in the /WEB-INF/classes directory whenever a change is detected. To do this, add a DefaultContext element in the localhost Host element. Edit the server.xml file and add the following XML element inside the <Host name="localhost"> element as described for a Context element:

```
<DefaultContext reloadable="true"/>
```

Tomcat will need to be restarted for this change to take effect.

Web Application Resource (WAR) Files

So far, to deploy the Web application, you have copied individual files to the Tomcat webapps directory. In this section you will see how you can use a Web Application Resource (WAR) file to simplify this process.

A WAR file is simply a Java archive (JAR) file. On startup, Tomcat searches for WAR files in the webapps directory and extracts any it finds.

To create your own WAR file execute the following steps:

1. cd to the Web directory in your application development area.
2. Run the command jar cvf basic-servlet.war.
3. Copy the basic-servlet.war you have just created to Tomcat's webapps directory.
4. Stop and restart Tomcat.

If Tomcat is not restarted, you will have to expand the WAR file manually. Remember that new applications are not recognized unless Tomcat is restarted.

Adding Servlet Initialization Parameters

In the currency converter application, the dollar-sterling exchange rate was hard-coded into the servlet (obviously a nonsense thing to do in a real application). A slight improvement on hard-coding the exchange rate is to pass the value to the servlet as an initialization parameter. This will allow an administrator to change the value without having to have access to the Java source.

NOTE

This is not a particularly realistic approach, but there are situations where you might need to code a value that changes infrequently and is constant for the lifetime of the servlet. A copyright notice or the name of the company where the Web application is deployed is a good candidate for an initialization parameter.

The web.xml document is used to define initialization parameters for a servlet. Any number of initialization parameters can be defined using the <init-param> element. The <init-param> element must be defined inside the <servlet> element for your servlet:

```
<init-param>
    <param-name>RATE</param-name>
    <param-value>0.65</param-value>
</init-param>
```

Listing 4.4 shows the final Currency Converter web.xml file, which as well as the initialization parameter, includes the servlet URL mappings.

LISTING 4.4 Full Text of the basic-servlet web.xml File

```
<!DOCTYPE web-app
    PUBLIC "-//Sun Microsystems, Inc.//DTD Web Application 2.3//EN"
    "http://java.sun.com/dtd/web-app_2_3.dtd">

<web-app>
    <display-name>Currency Converter</display-name>
    <description>
        This is a simple web application with an HTML form passing
        a single parameter (amount of dollars) to a servlet for conversion.
    </description>
    <servlet>
        <servlet-name>Currency Converter</servlet-name>
        <servlet-class>CurrencyConverter</servlet-class>
        <init-param>
            <param-name>RATE</param-name>
            <param-value>0.65</param-value>
        </init-param>
    </servlet>
    <servlet-mapping>
        <servlet-name>Currency Converter</servlet-name>
        <url-pattern>/convert</url-pattern>
    </servlet-mapping>
    <servlet-mapping>
        <servlet-name>Currency Converter</servlet-name>
        <url-pattern>*.con </url-pattern>
    </servlet-mapping>
</web-app>
```

An initialization parameter is accessed in a servlet using the convenience method `javax.servlet.GenericServlet.getInitParameter()` as shown in the following code fragment:

```
try {
    NumberFormat nf = NumberFormat.getInstance();
    double poundValue = nf.parse(amount).doubleValue();
    String rate = getInitParameter("RATE");
    poundValue *= rate;
```

So far, you have learned how to create simple servlets and deploy them to Tomcat. To conclude this chapter, you will now look at the different stages of a servlet life cycle.

Servlet Life Cycle

The servlet specification defines a number of responsibilities for the servlet container for managing the servlet life cycle. These responsibilities include loading, instantiating, initializing, and removing servlets. What the specification does not define is when these events take place. Therefore, for code to remain portable, you shouldn't rely on the timing of life cycle events or on any specifics of Tomcat's implementation as described here.

Figure 4.3 shows a servlet's life cycle.

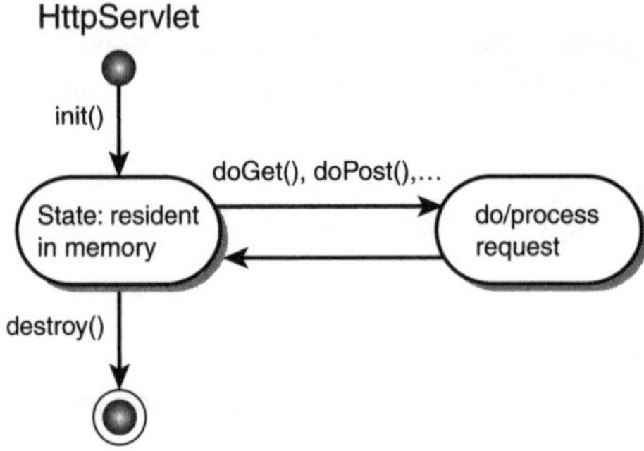

FIGURE 4.3 Servlet life cycle.

Initialization—The `init()` Method

When a servlet is instantiated, Tomcat calls the servlet's `init()` method. As part of the initialization, Tomcat provides the servlet with its `ServletConfig` object, which the servlet can use to obtain

- The initialization parameters
- A reference to the context (`ServletContext`) in which this servlet is running (more on this in Chapter 7)
- The name of this servlet instance (the name assigned in the Web application deployment descriptor, or the classname if there is no deployment descriptor)

It is guaranteed that the `init()` method is called only once for the life of the servlet. It should, therefore, be used to set up servlet resources and initialize servlet instance variables that will exist for the entire life of the servlet.

The `init()` method must complete before the servlet can service any requests. Tomcat will not pass requests to the servlet if the `init()` method fails to complete successfully or throws a `ServletException`.

NOTE

The `init()` method is provided as a convenience method. You only need to define this method if you need to do some initialization for the servlet, and if you do, there is no requirement to call `super.init()`.

Servicing Requests

To handle requests, Tomcat calls the `service()` method in the `HttpServlet` interface. This `service()` method in turn simply passes requests to an appropriate `do`*`XXX`*`()` method, as defined in Table 4.2. Unless you have some peculiar requirements, you do not want to override this `service()` method.

TABLE 4.2 `HttpServlet` Handler Methods for HTTP Requests

HTTP Request Type	`HttpServlet` Handler Method
`DELETE`	`doDelete()`
`GET`	`doGet()`
`HEAD`	`doHead()`
`OPTIONS`	`doOptions()`
`POST`	`doPost()`
`PUT`	`doPut()`
`TRACE`	`doTrace()`

NOTE

The default `doHead()`, `doOptions()`, and `doTrace()` methods defined in the `HTTPServlet` interface will construct an appropriate response for the required request. They do not need to be overridden unless you want to take special actions for these requests.

As you have seen previously, the `doGet()` method was used in the Currency Converter application to handle HTTP `GET` requests. Although you only need to code handler methods for those requests the servlet is expected to receive, it is good programming practice to have both a `doGet()` and a `doPost()` method. This ensures that a change of the request type on the form (which might be required because the parameter string has become too long) does not require the servlet to be rewritten.

Normally, `GET` and `POST` requests are handled in exactly the same way. You can do this very easily by coding the `doPost()` method to call your `doGet()` method (or vice versa) like this:

```
public void doPost (HttpServlet Request req, HttpServletResponse res)
            throws ServletException, IOException {
    doGet(req, res);
}
```

NOTE

Typically, servlets run inside multithreaded servlet containers that can handle multiple requests concurrently. Therefore, you must synchronize access to any shared resources, such as files and network connections, as well as the servlet's class and instance variables in your handler methods. (Multithreading is covered in more detail in Chapter 7.)

If a request is received that is not handled by your servlet, Tomcat will generate an HTTP 405 "Method not supported" error.

Removing a Servlet—The `destroy()` Method

When a servlet is removed from service, Tomcat calls the `destroy()` method. Because Tomcat is free to remove a servlet at any time, it should be used not only to free resources, but also to save any data or state information that might be required when a new servlet instance is instantiated. Tomcat calls a servlet's `destroy()` method when it is shutdown and when a servlet class file is replaced.

Life Cycle Event Listeners

Application event listeners are new in version 2.3 of the servlet specification. These are special classes that implement one or more of the servlet event listener interfaces. You can code event listeners that are triggered when the following servlet life cycle events take place:

- Instance has just been created and is available to service its first request
- The servlet is about to be shut down

There are circumstances where it might be more appropriate to use event listeners to set up to manage resources rather than use the `init()` and `destroy()` methods. Event listeners are covered in more detail in Chapter 7.

Summary

This chapter has covered the basics of creating and deploying a simple servlet in a Web application. The deployment descriptor was introduced and configuration of the servlet was achieved by adding servlet mapping and initialization parameters to this XML document.

Some Tomcat configuration was also performed when a servlet `Context` was added to the `server.xml` file. Similarly, a `DefaultContext` was added to reconfigure Tomcat to automatically reload servlets.

WAR files were introduced as a way of packaging and deploying Web applications. However, you still need to stop and restart Tomcat to get these applications recognized.

The `init()-service()-destroy()` servlet life cycle was discussed, along with the handler methods `doGet()` and `doPost()`, which are used to handle most Web page requests. The use of event listeners was briefly mentioned as an alternative to the `init()` and `destroy()` methods.

This chapter has been an introduction. Servlets will be covered in more detail in Chapter 7. Chapter 5 will show you how JavaServer Pages (JSPs) provide an alternative to servlets. JSPs greatly simplify coding most HTML pages.

5

Basic Principles of JSPs

IN THIS CHAPTER

Chapter 4, "Basic Principles of Servlets," introduced you to simple Web applications using servlets. Although very useful for writing dynamic server-side code, servlets suffer from some disadvantages. In particular, coding complex HTML pages is somewhat tedious and error prone (due to the need to pepper the code with `out.println()` statements), and a servlet developer has to take on the dual roles of developer of application logic and designer of Web pages. JavaServer Pages (JSPs) were designed to address these disadvantages.

In this chapter, you will study the JSP syntax and the translate-compile life cycle used to generate a servlet that services the HTTP request using the information in the JSP Web page.

What Is a JSP?

A JSP is "just a servlet by another name" and is used in the same way to generate dynamic HTML pages. Unlike a servlet, which you deploy as a Java class, a JSP is deployed in a textual form similar to a simple HTML page. When the JSP is first accessed, it is translated into a Java class and compiled. The JSP then services HTTP requests like any other servlet.

A JSP consists of a mix of HTML elements and special JSP elements. You use the JSP elements, among other things, to embed Java code in the HTML. For example, Listing 5.1 shows a simple JSP that prints out the current date. The special JSP scripting element `<%= ... %>` is used to introduce the Java code.

LISTING 5.1 A Simple JSP

```
<HTML>
    <HEAD>
       <TITLE>Date JSP</TITLE>
    </HEAD>
    <BODY>
        <BIG>
            Today's date is <%= new java.util.Date() %>
        </BIG>
    </BODY>
</HTML>
```

Before examining JSP elements in more detail, you will see what Tomcat does when this JSP is deployed.

Deploying a JSP in Tomcat

Deploying a JSP is very simple. There are only a couple of rules:

- JSPs are stored in their textual form in the application directory.
- A JSP must have a `.jsp` suffix.

So, to deploy the JSP in Listing 5.1:

1. Create a new Web application directory in Tomcat's `webapps` directory; call it `basic-jsp`.
2. Create a subdirectory called `WEB-INF` in the `basic-jsp` directory.
3. Copy Listing 5.1 into a file called `date.jsp` in this application directory.
4. Stop and restart Tomcat so it recognizes the new Web application.

Access the JSP using the URL `http://localhost:8080/basic-jsp/date.jsp`. If there are no errors, you will see a screen similar to the one in Figure 5.1.

For this simple example, it is unlikely that you experienced any problems, but a more complex JSP might have generated some errors. The next section on the JSP translate-compile cycle will explain how to handle these errors. If you do not find the answer to your problem there, Chapter 6, "Troubleshooting Servlets and JSPs," covers the subject in far greater detail.

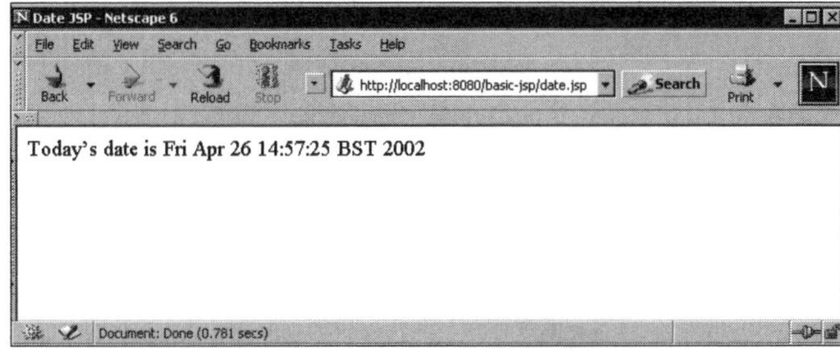

FIGURE 5.1 `date.jsp` displayed using Netscape 6.

JSP Translate—Compile Cycle

Unlike the servlets covered in Chapter 4, JSPs are not compiled before deployment.

NOTE

Actually, it is possible to compile JSPs and deploy them in exactly the same way as servlets, but this is not normally done and will not be covered.

The JSP file is stored in its textual form in the Web application. When a client first requests the page, Tomcat (or more correctly the Jasper JSP container) automatically initiates the translate-compile cycle illustrated in Figure 5.2. This diagram assumes the translation and compilations are both successful. Later in this chapter we discuss how to fix any failures in this cycle.

The JSP is first translated into Java source code, and if there are no translation errors, it is then compiled into a servlet class file.

The translation and compilation obviously causes an initial delay for the first access. If all is well, the JSP will be displayed, but if the translation or compilation fails, the client will be presented with an HTTP 500 "Internal Server Error" accompanied by an error message from Jasper and a Java compiler stack trace. To prevent end users from seeing this, you should always force the translation and compilation of your JSP by making the first page request yourself.

Tomcat implements a mechanism for performing the translate-compile cycle without displaying the JSP. This is achieved by appending the special query string `?jsp_precompile=true` to the URL. This parameter is not passed to the JSP. Instead, it is taken as an instruction for Jasper to translate and compile the JSP. Even if the compilation is successful the JSP is not displayed. This has several advantages:

- In complex applications, you do not need to set up the environment for the JSP.
- Page parameters do not have to be passed to the JSP.
- It simplifies the creation of automatic JSP compilation scripts.

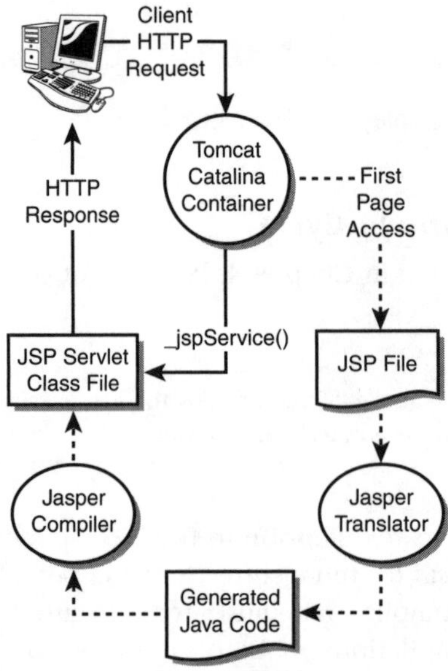

FIGURE 5.2 The Tomcat JSP translate-compile cycle.

If the translate-compile cycle fails, the client will receive the Tomcat error as normal. Figure 5.3 shows the how errors are handled in the translate-compile cycle.

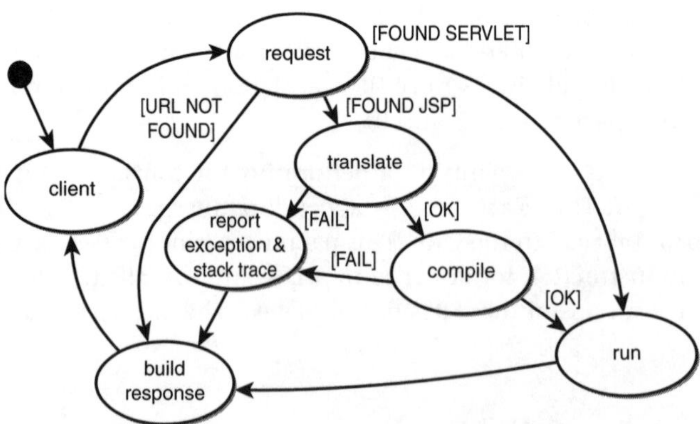

FIGURE 5.3 Error handling during the JSP translate-compile cycle.

Fixing JSP Errors

If the translation fails, Tomcat will report the error in the browser window with a reference to the line in the original JSP where the error occurred. It should then be a simple matter to correct the error and redeploy the JSP.

If there are no translation errors, Tomcat generates a Java source code file for the JSP. The default location for this file is in a Web application directory under `<CATALINA_HOME>/work/<host>/`.

Tomcat then compiles this Java file. If an error occurs during compilation, the error message might be more vague. For example:

```
An error occurred between lines: 7 and 17 in the jsp file: /example.jsp
```

Fortunately, this is always followed by a reference to the translated source code file. Here the error is on line 77 of the translated file:

```
Generated servlet error:
D:\Apache Tomcat 4.0\work\localhost\basic-jsp\example$jsp.java:77:
➥ Class org.apache.jsp. Currency not found.
    Currency dollars = Currency.getInstance(Locale.US);
    ^
1 error, 1 warning
```

From this you will often be able to identify the Java problem, but if not, you can view the generated Java file to get a more complete picture. Listing 5.2 shows the file generated for the simple `date.jsp` in Listing 5.1. As you can see, lines from the original JSP are included as comments.

LISTING 5.2 Generated Servlet Code for `date.jsp`

```
package org.apache.jsp;

import javax.servlet.*;
import javax.servlet.http.*;
import javax.servlet.jsp.*;
import org.apache.jasper.runtime.*;

public class date$jsp extends HttpJspBase {

    static {
    }
    public date$jsp( ) {
    }

    private static boolean _jspx_inited = false;
```

LISTING 5.2 Continued

```
    public final void _jspx_init()
➥throws org.apache.jasper.runtime.JspException {
    }

    public void _jspService(HttpServletRequest request,
➥ HttpServletResponse  response)
        throws java.io.IOException, ServletException {

        JspFactory _jspxFactory = null;
        PageContext pageContext = null;
        HttpSession session = null;
        ServletContext application = null;
        ServletConfig config = null;
        JspWriter out = null;
        Object page = this;
        String  _value = null;
        try {

            if (_jspx_inited == false) {
                synchronized (this) {
                    if (_jspx_inited == false) {
                        _jspx_init();
                        _jspx_inited = true;
                    }
                }
            }
            _jspxFactory = JspFactory.getDefaultFactory();
            response.setContentType("text/html;charset=ISO-8859-1");
            pageContext = _jspxFactory.getPageContext(this, request, response,
                        "", true, 8192, true);

            application = pageContext.getServletContext();
            config = pageContext.getServletConfig();
            session = pageContext.getSession();
            out = pageContext.getOut();

            // HTML // begin [file="/date.jsp";from=(0,0);to=(6,28)]
                out.write("<HTML>\r\n    <HEAD>\r\n
➥ <TITLE>Date JSP</TITLE>\r\n    </HEAD>\r\n
➥ <BODY>\r\n        <BIG>\r\n            Today's date is ");
```

LISTING 5.2 Continued

```
            // end
            // begin [file="/date.jsp";from=(6,31);to=(6,53)]
                out.print( new java.util.Date() );
            // end
            // HTML // begin [file="/date.jsp";from=(6,55);to=(10,0)]
                out.write("\r\n        </BIG>\r\n    </BODY>\r\n</HTML>\r\n");

            // end

        } catch (Throwable t) {
            if (out != null && out.getBufferSize() != 0)
                out.clearBuffer();
            if (pageContext != null) pageContext.handlePageException(t);
        } finally {
            if (_jspxFactory != null) _
                jspxFactory.releasePageContext(pageContext);
        }
    }
}
```

CAUTION

This generated file will be overwritten when the JSP is next accessed, so fix the error in the original JSP and not in this generated file.

The Compiled JSP Class

The Java code you write in your JSP is placed in a Java class with a name supplied by Tomcat. The majority of the code is placed in a method called `_jspService()`, which has the following signature:

```
public void _jspService(HttpServletRequest request,
                        HttpServletResponse response)
                 throws ServletException, java.io.IOException;
```

Tomcat imports the following packages into the translated Java class, so there is no need to include these in your JSP:

```
javax.servlet.*
javax.servlet.http.*
javax.servlet.jsp.*
org.apache.jasper.runtime.*
```

There are also a number of implicitly declared objects that are available for use in JSPs. These are listed in Table 5.1.

TABLE 5.1 JSP Implicit Objects

JSP Name	Java Servlet Object
`request`	`javax.servlet.http.HttpServletRequest`
`response`	`javax.servlet.http.HttpServletResponse`
`config`	`javax.servlet.ServletConfig`
`pageContext`	`javax.servlet.jsp.PageContext`
`session`	`javax.servlet.http.HttpSession`
`application`	`javax.servlet.ServletContext`
`out`	`javax.servlet.jsp.JspWriter`
`page`	`java.lang.Object` (in the Java code on the JSP, this is a synonym for the `this` object)
`exception`	`java.lang.Throwable` (available only if the JSP is designated an error page)

NOTE

We will discuss the use of each of these objects in some detail in Chapter 7, "The Web Application Environment."

Let's now turn our attention to the elements that make up a JSP page.

Elements of a JSP Page

As you saw in Listing 5.1, a JSP element is embedded in otherwise static HTML. Similar to HTML all JSP elements are enclosed in open and close angle brackets (< >). Unlike HTML (but like XML), all JSP elements are case sensitive. JSP elements are distinguished from HTML tags by beginning with either `<%` or `<jsp:`.

NOTE

Although the standard JSP syntax is similar to XML, it does not completely conform to the XML syntax rules. The JSP 1.2 specification defines an alternative XML syntax for JSPs and uses the term *JSP document* to refer to a JSP that is a well-formed XML document. A JSP document has a number of advantages, but as yet it is not in common use. This book uses the standard JSP syntax.

There are three basic JSP element types:

- Directives
- Scripting elements
- Action elements

Each of these elements is discussed in turn in the following sections.

JSP Directives

Directives have the following syntax:

```
<%@ directive { attr="value" }* %>
```

They provide information used to control the translation of the JSP into Java code. There are three directives:

- `include`
- `taglib`
- `page`

The `include` Directive

The `include` directive is used, as the name suggests, to bring in static content from another file. The following example shows how to add a copyright notice to the JSP:

```
<%@ include file="copyright.html" %>
```

This directive is acted on at translate time, and the file is subjected to the Tomcat translate-compile cycle.

The `taglib` Directive

The `taglib` directive is used to introduce a tag library to the JSP. Tag libraries are a convenient way of encapsulating code and extending the functionality of JSP tags. Tag libraries are covered in detail in Chapter 10, "Custom Tags and TagLibs," and Chapter 11, "JSP Expression Language and JSTL"

Page Directives

Page directives are used to define properties for the page together with any files incorporated via the `include` directive. Table 5.2 provides a list of the common page directives (for others see the JSP specification) with examples of how they are used.

TABLE 5.2 Common JSP Page Directives

Directive	Example	Effect
`buffer`	`<%@ page buffer="8kb" %>`	Set the output buffer size. A value of `none` indicates that the output is not buffered. The default is `buffered`.
`autoFlush`	`<%@ page autoflush="false" %>`	Specifies whether the output buffer should be automatically flushed when it is full. The default is `true`.
`contentType`	`<%@ page contentType="text/ plain;ISO-8859-1"`	Defines the MIME type and char acter encoding for the response. MIME type `text/html` and character encoding `ISO-8859-1` are the defaults.
`errorPage`	`<%@ page errorPage="/error/messedup.jsp"`	The client will be redirected to the specified URL when an exception occurs that is not caught by the current page.
`isErrorPage`	`<%@ page isErrorPage="true" %>`	Indicates whether this page is the target URL for an `errorPage` directive. If `true`, an implicit scripting `java.lang.Exception` object called `exception` is defined.

`import`	`<%@ page import=" java.math.*"`	A comma-separated list of package names to be imported for this JSP. The following are imported by default and do not need to be specified in the JSP:
		`java.lang.*`
		`javax.servlet.*`
		`javax.servlet.jsp.*`
		`javax.servlet.http.*`
		`org.apache.jasper.runtime.*`

`isThreadSafe`	`<%@ page isThreadSafe="false" %>`	If set to `true`, this page can be run multithreaded. This is the default, so you should ensure access to shared objects is synchronized.
`session`	`<%@ page session="false" %>`	Set to `true` if the page is to participate in an HTTP session . This is the default.

Listing 5.3 shows the `date.jsp` with page directives to import the `java.util` package and construct the response using a Central European character set. (The use of page directives is covered in greater detail in Chapter 7.)

LISTING 5.3 `date.jsp` with Page Directives

```
<%@ page import="java.util.*" contentType="text/html;iso-8859-2" %>
<HTML>
    <HEAD>
        <TITLE>Date JSP</TITLE>
    </HEAD>
    <BODY>
        <BIG>
            Today's date is <%= new Date() %>
        </BIG>
    </BODY>
</HTML>
```

JSP Scripting Elements

Scripting elements come in the three forms described in Table 5.3.

TABLE 5.3 JSP Scripting Elements

Scripting Element	Example	Description
Declarations	`<%! String msg="Hello"; %>`	Declarations of variables or methods, each one separated by semicolons. Variables declared this way are declared in the class itself and not inside the `_jspService()` method.
Scriptlets	`<% int i = 42;` `answer = select[i];%>`	Elements that contain Java code fragments. These are added to the `_jspService()` method.
Expressions	`<%= msg %>`	JSP expressions are statements that are evaluated, the result cast into a `String` and placed on the JSP page.

CAUTION

Declarations and scriptlets contain normal Java code and require semicolons. Expressions are embedded in `out.print()` statements and should not be terminated with a semicolon. Misplacing semicolons is a common source of JSP compilation errors.

We will cover the use of each of these scripting elements later in this chapter.

JSP Action Elements

The final JSP element type is an action element. The JSP specification defines some standard actions, three of which are concerned with support for JavaBeans. You can also create your own custom actions with the use of tag libraries.

Action elements conform to XML/Namespace syntax with a start tag, an optional body, and an end tag. The JSP specification reserves the special `<jsp:` suffix for standard actions.

Action elements associated with JavaBeans are covered later in this chapter, whereas the other remaining action elements are covered in Chapter 7.

You will now rewrite the Currency Converter example as a JSP.

Currency Converter JSP

Listing 5.4 shows the Currency Converter servlet from Chapter 4, rewritten as a JSP.

LISTING 5.4 `currency-converter.jsp`

```
<%@ page import="java.io.*" %>
<%@ page import="java.util.*" %>
<%@ page import="java.text.*" %>

<%! private static final double EXCHANGE_RATE = 0.613; %>

<%
    Currency dollars = Currency.getInstance(Locale.US);
    Currency pounds = Currency.getInstance(Locale.UK);
    String amount = request.getParameter("amount");
    try {
        NumberFormat nf = NumberFormat.getInstance();
        double newValue = nf.parse(amount).doubleValue();
        poundValue *= EXCHANGE_RATE ;
        nf.setMaximumFractionDigits(pounds.getDefaultFractionDigits());
        nf.setMinimumFractionDigits(pounds.getDefaultFractionDigits());
%>

<HTML>
  <HEAD><TITLE>Currency Conversion JSP</TITLE></HEAD>
  <BODY>
    <BIG>
        <%= dollars.getSymbol(Locale.US) %> <%= amount %> =
➥ <%= pounds.getSymbol(Locale.UK) %> <%= nf.format(poundValue) %>
```

LISTING 5.4 Continued

```
    </BIG>
  </BODY>
</HTML>

<%
    }
    catch (ParseException e) {
        out.println ("Bad number format");
    }
%>
```

As you can see, the majority of the code is encapsulated in two scriptlets, and the HTML formatting is both more obvious and more concise. JSP expressions have been used to output the dollar amount and the converted pound value.

Deploy (copy) this JSP to the `webapps/basic-jsp` directory. Either call this JSP directly, providing the amount as a parameter to the URL, like this:

```
http://localhost:8080/basic-jsp/currency-converter.jsp?amount=3
```

Or edit the `currency-form.html` file from Chapter 4 to call the new JSP as shown in Listing 5.5. Copy this form to `webapps/basic-jsp` directory.

LISTING 5.5 Currency Converter HTML Form Accessing a JSP

```
<HTML>
  <HEAD><TITLE>Currency Form</TITLE></HEAD>
  <BODY>
    <FORM METHOD=GET ACTION="currency-converter.jsp">
      <H1>Simple Currency Converter</H1>
      <P>Use this form to convert US Dollars to UK Pounds Sterling</P>
      Type in the amount to be converted in the box
      <INPUT TYPE=TEXT NAME="amount">
      <INPUT TYPE=SUBMIT>
    </FORM>
  </BODY>
</HTML>
```

From the simple currency converter example shown in Listing 5.4 you can start to see how, with JSPs, it is possible to separate the roles of HTML designer from Java programmer. With the use of JavaBeans, this separation can be made greater as discussed in the next section.

Using JavaBeans in a JSP

The use of implicit object declarations, JSP expressions, and scripting elements goes a long way to simplify and encapsulate the Java code, but the amount of code in a JSP can be reduced further using JavaBeans.

JavaBeans are self-contained, reusable software components that must be written to conform to a particular design convention (called an idiom). The convention is

- A JavaBean class must have a no argument constructor (this is what you get by default).
- A JavaBean can provide properties that allow customization of the bean.
- For each property, you should define a *getter* method to retrieve the property and a *setter* method to modify it.
- A getter method cannot have any parameters and must return an object of the type of the property.
- A setter method must take a single parameter of the type of the property and return a void.

Let's look at a JavaBean written for the Currency Converter application.

Currency Converter Using a JavaBean

Adding a JavaBean to the Currency Converter application involves the following steps:

1. Create a `CurrencyConverterBean` class.
2. Add methods to set and get the US dollar amount.
3. Add a method to get the converted UK pound value.

Listing 5.6 shows the code for the `CurrencyConverterBean` class.

NOTE

For the sake of simplicity, the code to output the currency symbols is included in the getter methods. You might want to split this out into discrete methods.

LISTING 5.6 `CurrencyConverterBean`

```
package converters;

import java.util.*;
import java.text.*;

public class CurrencyConverterBean {

    private static final double EXCHANGE_RATE = 0.613;
    private Currency dollars = Currency.getInstance(Locale.US);
    private Currency pounds = Currency.getInstance(Locale.UK);
    private NumberFormat nf = NumberFormat.getInstance();
    private String amount;

public void setAmount (String amount){
        this.amount = amount;
    }

    public String getAmount () {
        return dollars.getSymbol(Locale.US) + amount;
    }

    public String getPoundValue(){
        try {
            double newValue = nf.parse(amount).doubleValue();
            newValue *= EXCHANGE_RATE ;
            nf.setMaximumFractionDigits(pounds.getDefaultFractionDigits());
            nf.setMinimumFractionDigits(pounds.getDefaultFractionDigits());
            return pounds.getSymbol(Locale.UK) + nf.format(newValue);
             }
        catch (ParseException e) {
            return ("Bad number format");
        }
    }
}
```

NOTE

Because the default no argument JavaBean constructor is not used, it has been omitted.

Support for JavaBeans is provided in JSPs with the use of the three standard action elements `<jsp:useBean>`, `<jsp:setProperty>`, and `<jsp:getProperty>`. Each of these will now be covered in turn.

Using a JavaBean

JavaBeans are defined in a JSP using the standard action element `<jsp:useBean>`, as follows:

```
<jsp:useBean id="<bean name>" class="<bean class>" scope="<scope>">
```

An example is

```
<jsp:useBean id="converter" class="converters.CurrencyConverterBean"
➥ scope="page" />
```

This tag creates an instance of the `CurrencyConverterBean` class and associates it with the `id` attribute `converter` for use in the entire JSP page, as defined by the scope attribute.

Other values for the scope attribute are as follows:

`<jsp:useBean>` **Scope Attribute**	**JavaBean Is in Scope For...**
`page`	Only this page
`request`	This page and any page the request is forwarded to
`session`	The duration of the session
`application`	All components in the Web application

NOTE

Because the scope of JavaBeans can extend beyond the page, they are a useful way of passing information between requests.

Getting and Setting Bean Properties

You retrieve JavaBean properties using the standard element `<jsp:getProperty>`, as shown in the following example:

```
<jsp:getProperty name="converter" property="amount" />
```

The name attribute corresponds to the id attribute defined in the <jsp:useBean> element. The value of the property is converted to a string and placed in the output stream.

NOTE

Alternatively, you can access a JavaBean property inside a scriptlet using its getter method. For example:

```
<%= converter.getAmount() %>
```

You set a JavaBean Property using the <jsp:setProperty> element.

For example, use the following to set the amount in the CurrencyConverterBean to the value 3:

```
<jsp:setProperty name="converter" property="amount" value="3"/>
```

An alternative form of the <jsp:setProperty> element can be used to set a JavaBean property to the value of a request parameter. The following sets the property amount to the value passed as a parameter also called amount:

```
<jsp:setProperty name="date" property="amount" param="amount" />
```

Using this form you can omit the param attribute when the request parameter name is the same as the property name. The following also sets the property amount to the value passed as the parameter called amount:

```
<jsp:setProperty name="date" property="amount" />
```

Initializing JavaBeans

It is usual to set a bean's properties inside the body of the <jsp:useBean> element as follows:

```
<jsp:useBean id="date" class="Date" scope="page" >
    <jsp:setProperty name="date" property="timeZone" value="GMT" />
</jsp:useBean>
```

This idiom reinforces the fact that the bean must be initialized before it is used.

The Currency Converter JSP Using a JavaBean

Listing 5.7 shows the new Currency Converter JSP using the JavaBean standard actions. As you can see the JSP is now extremely straightforward. All the Java code has been transferred to the JavaBean. Although this is obviously a very simple example it still demonstrates the principle of role separation very well. The Java programmer writes the JavaBean that encapsulates all the business logic. The HTML designer then uses the JSP actions to display the JavaBean properties at the appropriate place on the JSP page.

LISTING 5.7 `date.jsp` Utilizing a JavaBean

```
<jsp:useBean id="converter"
➥class="converters.CurrencyConverterBean" scope="page" >
    <jsp:setProperty name="converter" property="amount" />
</jsp:useBean>

<HTML>
  <HEAD><TITLE>Currency Conversion JSP</TITLE></HEAD>
  <BODY>
    <BIG>
         <jsp:getProperty name="converter" property="amount" /> =
➥ <jsp:getProperty name="converter" property="poundValue" />
    </BIG>
  </BODY>
</HTML>
```

Before completing this introduction to JSPs, you need to briefly cover two more topics: the JSP life cycle and the use of the deployment descriptor file with JSPs.

The JSP Life Cycle

JSPs have the same `init-service-destroy` life cycle as servlets. The only difference is that you should use the `jspInit()` and `jspDestroy()` methods from the JSP interface instead of `init()` and `destroy()` from the servlet interface.

When the first request is delivered to a JSP page, Tomcat calls the `jspInit()` method, if there is one, to initialize resources. Similarly, Tomcat invokes the `jspDestroy()` method to reclaim these resources when Tomcat is shut down or the JSP is replaced.

TIP

Put the `jspInit()` and `jspDestroy()` methods in a JSP declaration.

JSPs and the Deployment Descriptor File

So far in this chapter, we have not discussed the deployment descriptor because none of the examples have needed one. Because JSPs are just servlets, there are no special deployment descriptor elements for them; the only difference lies in how you map a servlet name to a JSP.

In Chapter 4, you saw that a `<servlet>` element in the `web.xml` file associates a name with a servlet class using the `<servlet-class>` element. A JSP uses the `<jsp-file>` element instead of the `<servlet-class>` element as follows:

```
<servlet-name>Currency Converter</servlet-name>
<jsp-file>/currency-converter.jsp</jsp-file >
```

As with ordinary servlets, you can hide the implementation details of your Web application by using `<servlet-mapping>` elements for your JSPs. You can use the `web.xml` file shown in Listing 5.8 to ensure that the `date.jsp` JSP can be accessed via a wide range of URLs.

LISTING 5.8 Deployment Descriptor for a JSP

```
<!DOCTYPE web-app
    PUBLIC "-//Sun Microsystems, Inc.//DTD Web Application 2.3//EN"
    "http://java.sun.com/dtd/web-app_2_3.dtd">

<web-app>

<display-name>Currency Converter</display-name>
    <description>
        This is a simple web application with an HTML form passing
        a single parameter to a JSP.
    </description>
    <servlet>
        <servlet-name>Currency Converter</servlet-name>
        <jsp-file>/currency-converter.jsp </jsp-file>
    </servlet>

    <servlet-mapping>
        <servlet-name>Currency Converter</servlet-name>
        <url-pattern>/convert</url-pattern>
    </servlet-mapping>

    <servlet-mapping>
        <servlet-name>Currency Converter</servlet-name>
```

LISTING 5.8 Continued

```
        <url-pattern>*.jsp</url-pattern>
    </servlet-mapping>

</web-app>
```

If this JSP is deployed in an application called `basic-jsp`, it can be accessed using any of the following URLs:

```
http://localhost:8080/basic-jsp/currency-converter.jsp
http://localhost:8080/basic-jsp/convert
http://localhost:8080/basic-jsp/fred.jsp
```

NOTE

Servlet mapping was discussed in Chapter 4. Return to the appropriate section in Chapter 4 if you need to refresh your memory on how servlet mapping works.

Other `web.xml` elements, such as initialization parameters, can be accessed from within JSP scriptlets either using the normal servlet API objects or one of the implicit JSP variables shown in Table 5.1.

Summary

This chapter has provided an introduction to JSPs. You now know that a JSP is a servlet written using HTML and special JSP elements. JSPs have several advantages over servlets: Not only do JSPs simplify the coding of complex HTML documents, but they also allow the roles of Java programmer and HTML designer to be separated.

Servlets and JSPs are not only written differently, but there are also differences in the way they are deployed. Unlike servlets that you compile and deploy as a Java class, a JSP is deployed in its original textual-document form. When the JSP is accessed for the first time, Tomcat detects this fact and subjects the JSP to a translation and compilation cycle. The time taken for this translate-compile cycle causes a significant delay in the display of the JSP for the first access. Precompiling the JSP as it is deployed can eliminate this delay.

The use of JavaBeans to encapsulate the Java code in an accompanying bean class helps simplify JSPs even further by moving most if not all of the Java code into the JavaBean class.

This concludes the introduction to JSPs. Chapter 6 covers troubleshooting your applications. Chapter 7 tackles more advanced servlet and JSP topics.

6 Troubleshooting Servlets and JSPs

IN THIS CHAPTER

- Frequent Servlet and JSP Problems
- Tomcat Not Responding
- Mistyped URL
- JSP Translation Errors
- Java Compilation Errors
- Invalid Deployment Descriptor
- Java Logic/Algorithm Faults
- Uncaught Java Exception
- Invalid HTML
- Tomcat Isn't Reloading Changed Applications Correctly

Now that you have a grasp of the basic principles of Web servers, servlets, and JSPs, you are in a position to start developing your own applications. Before studying the Tomcat servlet and JSP technologies in more detail, you should spend a little time considering what can go wrong.

This chapter will look at the mistakes and errors that you might make when developing and deploying Web applications. The symptom of the problem will be used as the starting point and the underlying errors that can cause the symptom are discussed and explained.

Frequent Servlet and JSP Problems

If you have typed in and deployed the example programs shown so far, you may have come across some of the problems that are outlined in this chapter. You might even be reading this chapter now because your first examples have failed in some way. If you have gotten this far without encountering a problem, well done, but be advised that you will undoubtedly encounter problems eventually. This chapter will give you some general guidelines for troubleshooting the problems that can occur.

As Tomcat is not an Integrated Development Environment (IDE), it does not provide support for source-level symbolic debugging. All you have available are

- Log files for various messages
- Stack traces from uncaught exceptions
- A good understanding of how to identify the cause of an error from the symptoms

Sensible use of logging facilities such as the `Logger` class in Java 1.4 and Jakarta log4j are an invaluable aid to troubleshooting problems in all Java programs. Chapter 13, "Logging Using Tomcat," discusses these logging facilities in detail. You should also study Chapter 12, "Error Handling," which discusses strategies for error handling and recovery within a Web application.

The most general approach to troubleshooting is, "if at first you don't succeed then try something simpler." If a JSP doesn't translate or compile, try stripping it down and adding little bits back in. If a servlet doesn't work as expected remove functionality until you have a servlet that does work as expected and then add functionality back in. In general, start with something simple and prove that it works, then add in additional capabilities in small steps ensuring each new step works before adding another one. Apply the motto "divide and conquer" when troubleshooting problems.

Tomcat servlet problems can be categorized as

- Simple Java syntax errors preventing a program from compiling
- Deployment descriptor errors preventing an application from deploying or causing it to deploy incorrectly
- Invalid HTML causing incorrect display of the servlet page
- Bad Java logic or algorithms causing incorrect behavior
- Uncaught exceptions causing a servlet to fail when servicing a request

JSPs are subject to all of these problems plus some of their own:

- Invalid JSP syntax preventing a JSP from translating correctly
- Invalid Java elements on the JSP causing compilation failure
- Errors with TagLibs (these are discussed in detail in Chapter 10, "Custom Tags and TagLibs")

Table 6.1 shows typical error symptoms and which section or sections of this chapter you should reference to find the most likely cause of, and solution for, the error.

TABLE 6.1 Identifying Web Application Problems

Symptom	Relevant Chapter Section(s)
No response from Tomcat	"Tomcat Not Responding"
URL not found (HTTP response code 404)	"Mistyped URL" "Invalid Deployment Descriptor"

TABLE 6.1 Continued

Symptom	Relevant Chapter Section(s)
Servlet or JSP displays a stack trace	"Uncaught Java Exception" "JSP Translation Errors" "Java Compilation Errors"
Missing data from page	"Invalid HTML" "Java Logic/Algorithm Faults"
No output to browser	"Uncaught Java Exception" (before any page data is written)
Partially complete page	"Invalid HTML" "Uncaught Java Exception" (after partial page generation)
Page does not match latest changes to servlet/JSP	"Tomcat Isn't Reloading Changed Applications Correctly"

The following sections cover each of these problem areas in turn.

Tomcat Not Responding

If Tomcat is not responding, first verify that you have started Tomcat and that there are no configuration problems.

If Tomcat fails to start as expected, you should examine the log files in `<CATALINA_HOME>/logs/<host>` to determine the cause of the problem.

If Tomcat has started up successfully, Table 6.2 lists some likely causes for a lack of response when browsing your Web application.

TABLE 6.2 Causes for Tomcat Not Responding

Cause	Solution
You have forgotten to include the Tomcat port number at the end of the URL.	Append the port number to the URL (for example, `http://localhost:8080`).
You have used the wrong Tomcat port number.	Check `<CATALINA_HOME>/conf/server.xml` for the correct port number.
You have used the wrong hostname.	Validate which host is running Tomcat.
You are using `localhost` behind a proxy server.	Make sure that you have switched off proxy settings for `localhost` in your browser.
You are out of environment space using Tomcat Windows 9x/Me.	Increase your environment space for the `startup.bat` file to at least 4096.

TABLE 6.2 Causes for Tomcat Not Responding

Cause	Solution
You have a syntax error in Tomcat's `server.xml` file.	Revert to a copy of this file that you know is good, and carefully reapply any edits.

If you have not found a solution to your problem in this table, you should next read one of the following sections of the chapter:

- "Mistyped URL"
- "Invalid HTML"
- "Uncaught Java Exception"

Mistyped URL

A mistyped URL normally manifests itself as a lack of response from Tomcat (discussed in the previous section) or an HTTP response 404. If you have a 404 error, check out the hints in Table 6.3.

TABLE 6.3 Causes for HTTP Response 404

Hint	Solution
URL pathnames are case sensitive.	Verify that your URL exactly matches the classname for your servlet or URL mapping entry in the deployment descriptor.
Are you using the `servlet/classname` style URL?	Make sure that `servlet` is lowercase and the classname is spelled correctly.
Are you using Java packages?	Prefix the classname with the package name in the `web.xml` file (or on the URL if you are not using URL mappings).
Are you using a Web application context?	Check the `<context>` element in `<CATALINA_HOME>/conf/server.xml`.
Have you updated the deployment descriptor or created a new Web application?	Stop and restart Tomcat or use the Manager Application for deployment.

NOTE

If you have defined an error page to trap 404 errors (see Chapter 12), your error page will be shown instead of the standard Tomcat error page. If you have incorrectly defined the error page, you may see a blank response from Tomcat rather than the 404 error.

If none of these hints has solved your problem, verify that Tomcat is running and responding to simple HTTP requests (such as `http://localhost:8080/`). If you browse your Web application directory (for example, `http://localhost:8080/basic-servlet`) and have not set up any welcome files (see Chapter 7, "The Web Application Environment"), you will normally see a directory listing for your Web application, which proves that Tomcat has recognized your Web application.

TIP

A new Web application is only recognized when you start up Tomcat or use the Manager Application (see Chapter 15, "Administering Tomcat in a Live Environment"). In order for the Web application to be valid, a Web application directory under `<CATALINA_HOME>/webapps` must include a `WEB-INF` subdirectory. You might forget to create the `WEB-INF` directory if you are devloping JSPs and are not using the `web.xml` file.

If you know that Tomcat is running and is only responding to some URL requests, you should study the following sections:

- "Invalid HTML"
- "Uncaught Java Exception"
- "JSP Translation Errors"
- "Java Compilation Errors"

JSP Translation Errors

A badly written JSP can fail at translation time. If the Jasper container detects an error in the JSP, it will return a stack trace to the client identifying the error and the source line number on the original JSP. From this you should be able to identify the JSP error.

Tomcat does not regard the following as JSP errors:

- Invalid HTML.
- Unrecognized tags, including those that start with `jsp:`. A common error is to use `<jsp:usebean>` rather than `<jsp:useBean>`; Jasper ignores the unrecognized tag and treats it as an HTML tag.

The most common translation errors are

- Forgetting to use `%>` to terminate a JSP element
- Not using quotes around a parameter of a JSP action element (such as a custom tag)

When deploying a JSP to a live site, you should always access the JSP URL with the parameter `?jsp_precompile=true` to ensure that the page translates and compiles successfully.

Java Compilation Errors

Java compilation errors can occur when

- You compile servlets prior to deploying them to Tomcat
- The Jasper container translates and compiles JSPs on first access

Servlet Compilation Problems

Servlet compilation problems can be categorized as follows:

- Java syntax or semantic errors
- Missing class files

Java syntax and semantic errors are not specific to Tomcat and you should be able to resolve them in the same manner as other Java programs.

You can prevent errors due to missing Java classes by setting up your environment correctly. If you are compiling a servlet for deployment to Tomcat, make sure your `CLASSPATH` contains all the necessary JAR files. To compile a servlet, you will need the following archive for the servlet and JSP packages:

```
<CATALINA_HOME>/common/lib/servlet.jar
```

Either include this archive in your `CLASSPATH` or copy it to the Java Extensions directory.

Also, if you are using XML in your servlet, you will need to do one of the following:

- Use J2SDK 1.4.
- Include the XML parser supplied with Tomcat (`<CATALINA_HOME>/common/lib/xerces.jar`) in your `CLASSPATH`.
- Download JAXP from `http://java.sun.com/xml/jaxp` to use with J2SDK 1.3.

When you deploy a servlet, you need to make sure that Tomcat has access to all the class files needed by the servlet:

- Ensure that you include the class files in the Web application `WEB-INF/classes` directory.

- Place any supporting JAR files in the WEB-INF/lib directory.
- If you want to use the same JAR file in all of your Web applications, you can place the JAR file in <CATALINA_HOME>/shared/lib rather than copying it for every Web application.

TIP

JAR files are only recognized when Tomcat starts up. You will need to restart Tomcat if you add a JAR file to <CATALINA_HOME>/shared/lib or the WEB-INF/lib directory in the Web application.

JSP-Specific Errors

A JSP compilation error is displayed as an error message and a stack trace returned to the browser in lieu of the failed JSP. Only one compilation error at a time is reported, as shown in Figure 6.1.

The example in Figure 6.1 has identified an error at line 7 in the JSP:

```
An error occurred at line: 7 in the jsp file: /date.jsp
```

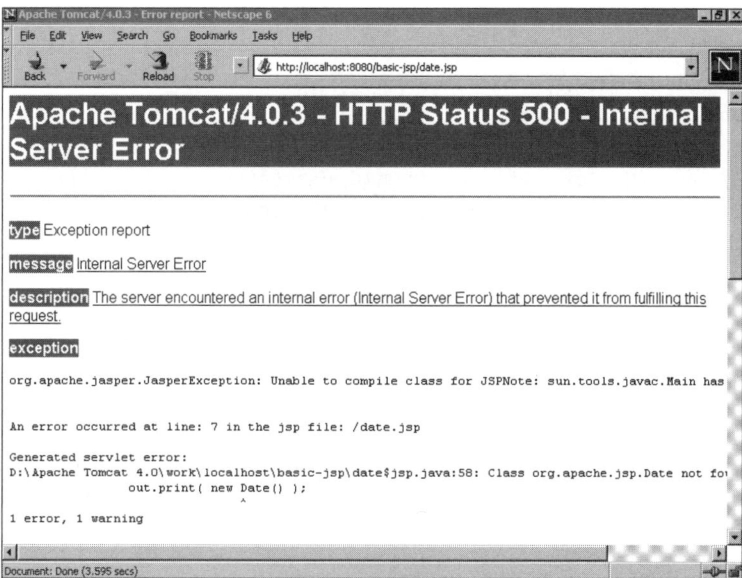

FIGURE 6.1 Tomcat displaying a JSP compilation error.

This corresponds to an error on line 58 in the generated Java file:

```
D:\Apache Tomcat 4\work\localhost\basic-jsp\date$jsp.java:58:
Class org.apache.jsp.Date not found.
```

This simple example uses the simple name `Date` rather than the qualified name `java.util.Date`, and the compiler has not been told to import the package `java.util`.

The information provided by Tomcat should be sufficient for you to trace the error in most situations. If the problem is hard to identify using the JSP source, you can examine the generated Java file that is stored in `<CATALINA_HOME>/work/<hostname>/<application>`. The generated filename reflects the original JSP name. This example using `basic-jsp/date.jsp` was stored in `<CATALINA_HOME>/work/localhost/basic-jsp/date$jsp.java`. The extract in Listing 6.1 consists of lines 53–63 of the generated Java file and shows how the file includes comments, which you can use to relate the generated code back to the original JSP.

LISTING 6.1 An Extract from a Generated JSP Java File

```
// HTML // begin [file="/date.jsp";from=(0,0);to=(6,28)]
out.write("<HTML>\r\n    <HEAD>\r\n        <TITLE>Date JSP</TITLE>\r\n
➥     </HEAD>\r\n    <BODY>\r\n        <BIG>\r\n
➥             Today's date is ");

// end
// begin [file="/date.jsp";from=(6,31);to=(6,43)]
    out.print( new Date() );
// end
// HTML // begin [file="/date.jsp";from=(6,45);to=(14,0)]
    out.write("\r\n        </BIG>\r\n    </BODY>\r\n
➥ </HTML>\r\n\r\n\r\n\r\n\r\n");

// end
```

You will find it tedious to fix large numbers of Java errors on a JSP. Use JavaBeans and custom tags to remove as much Java code from the JSP as possible.

Tomcat must have access to all the class files needed by the JSP. Ensure that you include the necessary class files and JAR files, as discussed at the end of the section titled "Java Compilation Errors."

TIP

The Java compiler leaks memory each time Jasper compiles a class. Out of memory errors may occur once a significant number of pages have been recompiled. You must stop and restart Tomcat to recover from this problem.

Invalid Deployment Descriptor

Tomcat reports an invalid deployment descriptor on the console and in the <CATALINA_HOME>/logs/<host>_log.<date>.txt log file. Unlike the log file error message, the error message written to the screen does not identify the source of the problem as the web.xml file. This can be confusing because the error message may not obviously relate to the deployment descriptor.

TIP

A common error in the deployment descriptor is the inclusion of a <servlet-mapping> element with a <url-pattern> value that does not start with a forward slash (/). Suppose you mistype the example <servlet-mapping> shown in Chapter 5, "Basic Principles of JSPs," as follows:

```
<servlet-mapping>
   <servlet-name>Date JSP</servlet-name>
   <url-pattern>date</url-pattern>
</servlet-mapping>
```

You will get the following unhelpful error message:

```
ERROR reading java.io.ByteArrayInputStream@359c1b
At Line 18 /web-app/servlet-mapping/
```

If you do not understand a Tomcat error message on the console, examine the log file for further information.

The deployment descriptor is only parsed when you start up Tomcat or use the Manager Application (see Chapter 15). The Tomcat Manager Application also reports deployment problems back to your browser Web page.

Use the error message reported by Tomcat to identify the deployment descriptor problem in the web.xml file. Be aware the entries in the <web-app> elements must be defined in the specific order dictated by the DTD:

```
<!ELEMENT web-app (icon?, display-name?, description?,
distributable?, context-param*, filter*, filter-mapping*,
listener*, servlet*, servlet-mapping*, session-config?, mimemapping*,
welcome-file-list?, error-page*, taglib*, resourceenv-
ref*, resource-ref*, security-constraint*, login-config?,
security-role*, env-entry*, ejb-ref*, ejb-local-ref*)>
```

A pro forma DTD is included in Appendix B, "Template web.xml File," as a simple guide to the order and structure of elements in the web.xml file.

Other deployment problems include missing Java class files or JARs, as discussed in the "Java Compilation Errors" section.

Java Logic/Algorithm Faults

These can be the hardest problems to identify. If you rely on the symbolic debuggers provided with many Java IDEs to help resolve program errors, then you have three choices when working with Tomcat:

- Temporarily use your favorite IDE to identify the servlet or JSP problem with the IDE debug environment and then revert to using Tomcat when you've fixed the problem.
- Use debug-level logging statements (see Chapter 13) to trace the execution paths of your code.
- Apply the "divide and conquer" maxim and comment out functionality from your web component until you get something that works correctly, then replace the missing functionality in small, easily debugged stages.

A symbolic debugger is a poor substitute for effective logging statements in your application. Good use of logging statements will help identify a problem on a live Web application server, whereas a symbolic debugger only helps during development.

TIP

You can use multiple Tomcat `<Context>` elements in the `<CATALINA_HOME>/conf/server.xml` file to refer to the same Web application using a different context name (URL path component). If you define multiple Web application contexts, each with a different logging level (see Chapter 13), you can change the logging level simply by using a different URL to access the Web resources.

An apparent Java logic error might in reality be a problem discussed in one of the following sections:

- "Invalid HTML"
- "Tomcat Not Reloading Changed Applications Correctly"

Uncaught Java Exception

Uncaught Java exceptions can manifest themselves in three ways:

- An HTTP 500 response
- A nonsensical or blank Web page
- An incomplete HTML page

If a servlet throws an uncaught exception, Tomcat will delete the servlet instance without calling the `servlet.destroy()` method. Tomcat will then complete the HTTP request on behalf of the deleted servlet instance.

If an errant servlet has produced enough data so that the response output buffer has been flushed and data has been returned to the client, Tomcat simply terminates the HTTP response and the browser is likely to display an incomplete Web page.

If the servlet has not produced sufficient data to flush the output buffer before the uncaught exception is thrown, Tomcat will return an HTTP Internal Server Error 500 response with a stack trace of the exception to the client.

If you have defined an error page (see Chapter 12), it will be shown instead of Tomcat's error page. However, if you refer to an error page that doesn't exist, Tomcat will not report this as an error. Instead, you will probably see a blank Web page.

> **NOTE**
>
> Netscape 6.2 may display the page source `<html><body></body></html>` when a Web application error page is not defined correctly.

A log of the uncaught exception is written to `<CATALINA_HOME>/logs/<host>_log.<date>.txt` regardless of how Tomcat processes the exception.

Missing Java class files will also result in an HTTP 500 response and a stack trace being returned to the browser. Missing class files are discussed in the "Java Compilation Errors" section.

Invalid HTML

Invalid HTML can be difficult to identify. Most browsers will interpret what was intended when displaying a badly structured HTML page and will attempt some sort of formatting that can often render the page correctly (or very nearly correctly). However, later changes to a page may cause the original error to be exposed. When looking for HTML errors, consider all changes, not just your latest changes.

Use the browser's View Source option to study the HTML data in the response rather than viewing the browser's interpretation of the response on the screen. You can save this response to a file for analysis if the error is not readily apparent.

HTML errors are easily created in servlets and can be difficult to identify. You should consider using a JSP when you have complex HTML to write. Most editors use colored syntax highlighting that might help you avoid some HTML errors when editing a JSP page.

Invalid HTML can be the result of other errors, as discussed in the section titled "Uncaught Java Exception."

Tomcat Isn't Reloading Changed Applications Correctly

If you have made changes to your Web application and browsed the application pages only to discover that the browser display is incorrect, Tomcat has probably not recognized the changes you have made. Tomcat's failure to recognize an updated Web application can usually be traced to one of the problems listed in Table 6.4.

TABLE 6.4 Causes for Tomcat Not Reloading a Changed Application

Hint	Solution
Did you successfully recompile the source code?	Recompile and check for compilation errors.
Did your JSP translate and compile successfully?	Use the `?jsp_precompile=true` parameter with the JSP URL and verify that you don't get a stack trace from Jasper.
Did you copy all the required class files into the Web application?	Copy the files into the Web application (put class files into the `WEB-INF/classes` subdirectory).
Is the deployment descriptor correct?	Check the Tomcat output window of the `<CATALINA_HOME>/logs/<host>_log.<date>.txt` file to ensure that Tomcat has parsed the deployment descriptor successfully.
Have you changed the deployment descriptor?	Stop and restart Tomcat or use the Manager Application.
Have you enabled automatic class reloading?	Check the `<CATALINA_HOME>/conf/server.xml` file and add the `<DefaultContext reloadable="true"/>` element or add a `<Context>` element for your application with the `reloadable="true"` parameter. You should also allow time for Tomcat to check that the class files have changed. Monitor the Tomcat console window for the diagnostic message confirming that Tomcat has reloaded the changed class file.
Have you disabled automatic class reloading?	Use the Tomcat Manager Application to manage the deployment or stop and restart Tomcat.

Automatic class reloading was discussed in Chapter 4, "Basic Principles of Servlets." Note that Tomcat will not reload the deployment descriptor unless you use the Manager Application (see Chapter 15) or stop and restart the server.

TIP

A useful technique to identify class version problems is to use logging to display a version number of a servlet or JSP from the `servlet.init()` or `JspPage.JspInit()` as an informational log message. You will need to be sure to maintain the version number accurately, either manually or in conjunction with any facilities provided by your source code control system.

If you cannot diagnose the problem from the hints in Table 6.4, the ultimate solution is to stop Tomcat, delete the Web application directory, copy in a new version of your Web application, and restart Tomcat. If this does not fix the problem then you need to have another look at the application, as the error is almost certainly in your application logic.

Summary

There are lots of reasons for Tomcat Web applications not working as expected. To solve an error, you will need to study the problem you can see (the symptom) and relate this back to the original error.

The errors that you are most likely to make are

- JSP or Java syntax errors
- HTML syntax errors (easily done inside a servlet)
- Missing class files or JAR files preventing servlets or JSPs from compiling or running
- Using the wrong URL (often omitting the Tomcat port number 8080 from the host)
- Using a browser with proxy settings that do not exclude `localhost`

Troubleshooting a problem Web application requires good detective work and a lot of patience. If all else fails, try taking a break and coming back to the problem after thinking about something else for a while. More often than not, you will then solve the problem almost immediately.

PART II

Development and Administration

IN THIS PART

7

The Web Application Environment

IN THIS CHAPTER

- The Servlet Context Object
- Forwarding HTTP Requests
- The Request Object
- The Response Object
- Last Modified Times
- Persistent Connections
- JSP Implicit Objects
- JSP Standard Actions
- Servlet Listeners
- Servlet Threading Issues
- Welcome Files

Chapters 1–6 of this book have given you an introduction to writing Tomcat Web applications using simple servlets and JSPs. Here you will see how to write Web applications that are more robust and that can interact with their environments. This chapter will explore several topics that are commonly required to develop fully functional Web applications under Tomcat.

The Servlet Context Object

In Chapter 4, "Basic Principles of Servlets," you learned about a Web application context path. You learned that it is associated by default with the Tomcat application directory and that you can change it by creating a new `Context` element in Tomcat's `server.xml` file. Here you will look at how you can access and manipulate objects associated with the Web application context.

Every servlet has access to a `javax.servlet.ServletContext` object. There is only one `ServletContext` object per Web application. You can think of it as defining the servlet's view of the Web application.

The `ServletContext` interface defines a set of methods that your servlet can use to communicate with Tomcat in order to (among other things)

- Get application initialization parameters
- Get and set attributes that other servlets in this context can access

- Obtain static resources
- Log events (this process is discussed in Chapter 13, "Logging Using Tomcat")

The following subsections describe what you can do with the servlet context object.

Getting Context Initialization Parameters

In Chapter 4, you used the convenience `getInitParameter()` method to obtain a servlet's initialization parameters. Now, using the context object, you can obtain initialization parameters that are set up for the entire Web application and accessible by all servlets. This method is also called `getInitParameter()`:

```
ServletContext context = getServletContext();
out.println("Contact the Web Master: " + context.getInitParameter("WebMaster"));
```

Web application initialization parameters are defined in the deployment descriptor using the `<context-param>` element.

A sample use for a `ServletContext` initialization parameter is to store the Webmaster's email address:

```
<web-app>
    <display-name>Currency Converter</display-name>
    <context-param>
        <param-name>WebMaster</param-name>
        <param-value>martin@samspublishing</param-value>
    </context-param>
...
</web-app>
```

Getting and Setting Web Application Context Attributes

Context initialization parameters are useful for communicating static information between servlets, but they are read-only. Attributes provide an alternative mechanism for binding mutable objects that are available to all other servlets in the same context. The following methods are available to manipulate attributes:

Method	Return Type	Description
`setAttribute(name, object)`	`void`	Binds an object to an attribute name
`getAttribute(name)`	`Object`	Returns the attribute with the given name
`getAttributeNames()`	`Enumeration`	Returns all the attribute names in this `ServletContext`
`removeAttribute(name)`	`void`	Removes the attribute with the given name

The following code sample shows how you might list all the attributes in a context:

```
ServletContext context = getServletContext();
for (Enumeration e = context.getAttributeNames(); e.hasMoreElements();) {
    String attribute = (String)e.nextElement();
    out.println (attribute + ":" + context.getAttribute(attribute));
}
```

Attributes have a number of defining characteristics. They are

- Local to the Tomcat JVM
- Shared by all servlet instances in the same Web application
- Nonpersistent

Attributes are often used as a local data cache. For example, a more sophisticated version of the currency converter application could include a servlet whose function it is to periodically obtain the current exchange rate (from some external source), store it in a database, and cache it in an attribute. When a servlet processes a client request, it can simply use the attribute, thereby avoiding the overhead of a database access.

While multithreading issues are covered later in this chapter, it is worth mentioning here that Tomcat does not synchronize access to attributes. Therefore, if simultaneous changes to the attribute would damage data integrity, you should synchronize all `setAttribute()` method calls. As the attribute is shared by all servlets in the context, you must synchronize on the `ServletContext` object, not on the servlet's `this` object. The following code sample shows how to set a `context` attribute in a thread-safe manner:

```
ServletContext context = getServletContext();
synchronized (context) {
    context.setAttribute("Counter", new Integer(1));
}
```

Getting Static Resources

You can use the `ServletContext` object to provide access to static documents in the Web application (such as the HTML, XML, JSP, GIF, and JPEG files). Access is provided via the following methods:

Method	Return Type	Returns
`getResource(URL_path)`	`java.net.URL`	A URL to the resource
`getResourceAsStream(URL_path)`	`java.io.InputStream`	The static content of the resource
`getResourcePaths(URL_path)`	`java.util.Set`	Directory listing of *URL_path*

The *URL_path* parameter is specified relative to the context. For example, you could use the following to obtain a directory-like listing of the images in a subdirectory of a hypothetical Web application:

```
Set paths = context.getResourcePaths("/images");
Iterator i = paths.iterator();
while (i.hasNext()) {
    out.println("<br>" + (String) i.next());
}
```

Possibly the most useful of these methods is `getResourceAsStream()`, which returns the resource as an `InputStream` object. You could use this functionality, for example, to input an XSLT style sheet to transform an XML document into HTML before returning to the client.

Forwarding HTTP Requests

Sometimes you may want one servlet to forward a request to another servlet for processing. For example, a servlet may do some initial processing to validate parameters before passing the request either to another servlet for final processing or to an error page if validation fails. Or, if you are using a Model-View-Controller (MVC) architecture, you will want to separate out the data manipulation before forwarding the request to another servlet for presentation back to the client. These and other architecture issues are discussed in Chapter 17, "Architectures."

The `RequestDispatcher` interface provides a mechanism to forward requests. A `RequestDispatcher` object is obtained using the `HttpServletRequest.getRequestDispatcher()` method, and the `RequestDispatcher.forward()` method is used to forward the request, as the following example illustrates:

```
RequestDispatcher rd = request.getRequestDispatcher("/process.jsp");
if (rd != null)
    rd.forward(request, response);
```

CAUTION

The URL path is relative to the Web application, and the forward cannot extend beyond the current servlet context.

The cool thing about this method is that the request forwarding is done entirely by Tomcat without the client's intervention (unlike the HTTP redirect response). This can be useful for hiding the architecture of your Web site from hackers.

The request forward is an all-or-nothing operation. If a servlet calls `forward()`, it must not send a response to the client. If some or all of the response has been sent before `forward()` is called, the method will throw an `IllegalStateException`.

The Request Object

In Chapter 4, you used the `HttpServletRequest` object solely to access a form parameter, but there is much more that you can do with the request object. You can use the request object to access

- Any or all of the HTTP request headers
- Any cookie objects sent with the request
- The `HTTPSession` object associated with the request
- The preferred locale associated with the client
- Any extra path information included in the URL

Cookies, sessions, and extra path information are all covered in Chapter 8, "Session Tracking."

The HTTP request headers are available to the servlet via the following `HttpServletRequest` methods:

Method	Return Type	Returns
`getHeader()`	`String`	A comma-separated list of request header values
`getHeaders(`*`name`*`)`	`Enumeration`	The value of the request header with name indicated by the `String` literal or variable *`name`*
`getHeaderNames()`	`Enumeration`	The names of all the headers in this request

As an example, the following piece of code prints the request headers to the Web page:

```
for (Enumeration e = request.getHeaderNames(); e.hasMoreElements();) {
    String header = (String)e.nextElement();
    out.println ("<br><b>" + header + "</b>:" );
    for (Enumeration h = request.getHeaders(header); h.hasMoreElements();) {
        out.println(h.nextElement());
    }
}
```

Localization

The `ServletRequest.getLocale()` method can be used to obtain a `Locale` object corresponding to the preferred locale for the client. This is determined from the `Accept-Language` header in the request.

NOTE

If the client request doesn't provide an `Accept-Language` header, this method will return the default locale for the server.

This method enables you to generate responses tailored to the client's locale. For example, in the currency converter you can use the following code to produce appropriate currency symbols according to the location of the client:

```
Locale client = request.getLocale();
String result = dollars.getSymbol(client) +
    format(dollars, oldValue) + " = " +
    pounds.getSymbol(client) + format(pounds, newValue);
```

The Response Object

In Chapter 4, you saw how to set the `ContentType` for the response and send data back to the client using a `PrintWriter` object. You can also use an `HttpServletResponse` object to

- Set values for the other HTTP headers
- Add extra HTTP headers to the response
- Redirect the client to a different URL
- Set the HTTP status code
- Send an error response for display by the client
- Add a cookie to the response

Cookies are covered in Chapter 8. The other uses are covered in the following subsections.

Setting/Adding Headers to the Response

You can add arbitrary headers to the response using the `HttpServletResponse.addHeader()` method. This method adds a header with a `String` value. Other methods are available that add headers with `int` and `Date` values. Typically, you will only add extra headers if you have unusual client requirements. The common operations, such as adding cookies and headers associated with the body content, have specific methods in the response object.

Returning an HTTP Status Code

You can set an arbitrary HTTP response code using the `HttpServletResponse.setStatus()` method, which takes as a single parameter the value of the status code to be returned.

A number of final static constants that correspond to the common HTTP status codes are defined in the `HttpServletResponse` interface, and these should be used instead of numeric values.

If you use this method, you are responsible for ensuring that both the content type and the response body are constructed to correspond with the HTTP status being returned. Where possible, you should use the convenience methods `sendRedirect()` and `sendError()` (discussed next), which construct the appropriate response for you.

Temporarily Redirecting the Client Request

The `HttpServletResponse.sendRedirect()` method will set the appropriate headers and body content to redirect the client to a different URL. This method sets an HTTP 302 status code indicating that this is a temporary redirect and that future requests should reference the original URL.

NOTE

The only way to send a permanent redirect is to construct the response yourself and set the HTTP status code to 301—"Moved Permanently."

You should use `sendRedirect()` in situations where the servlet is unable to handle the request for some transient reason. For example, if the servlet is unable to obtain a database connection because the maximum number of connections has been exceeded, you can use the `sendRedirect()` method to present the client with an appropriate page displaying a "Try again later" message, as shown here:

```
response.sendRedirect("try-again.jsp");
```

CAUTION

For `sendRedirect()`, a URL with a leading slash (/) is interpreted relative to the Tomcat container root. Omit the leading / to obtain a URL relative to the Web application context.

The `sendRedirect()` method completes the current response. All uncommitted data in the output buffer is immediately flushed and any data written to the response by the servlet after the `sendRedirect()` method is silently ignored.

Returning an HTTP Error

In some error situations all you want to do is set an appropriate HTTP status error code and let the client deal with the error. This is achieved using the `HttpServletResponse.sendError()` method.

As with `sendStatus()`, you should use one of the final static HTTP status code constants as a parameter to this method.

For example, a servlet could send a 400 error to indicate that there is a syntax error somewhere in the request:

```
response.sendError(HttpServletResponse.SC_BAD_REQUEST);
```

Like `sendRedirect()`, `sendError()` terminates the response.

Setting Content Type

When Tomcat services a static Web page, it will automatically generate a `Content-Type` header based on the resource's filename extension.

NOTE

The correlation between an extension and a MIME type is based on a set of mappings in Tomcat's `web.xml` file. You can add any new mappings there or in your Web application `web.xml` file. This is covered in more detail in Chapter 16, "Configuring Tomcat."

For a dynamic servlet, you need to set the content type explicitly with the `HttpServletResponse.setContentType()` method. So far in this book, you have only seen servlets that return the MIME type `text/html`, but a servlet can just as easily return graphics or other data if you set the appropriate MIME type. The following example shows how to return data in plain text rather than HTML:

```
response.setContentType("text/plain");
```

The content type setting may also include the character encoding after the MIME type as follows:

```
text/html; charset=UTF-8
```

NOTE

UTF-8 (UCS Transformation Format, 8-bit) is a variable-length Unicode character set that is useful for servlets that need to generate Web pages containing text in multiple languages.

Last Modified Times

It may seem odd to set a last modified time in a dynamic servlet, but there are circumstances where a servlet can determine the time at which the dynamic data last changed. Setting the last modified time for a servlet will make browser and proxy caches more effective and may reduce Tomcat's workload.

You can set the last modified time in cases where the data is updated at specific times. For example, if a servlet receives an external data feed every 20 minutes or recalculates some value on a daily basis, it can set the last modified time appropriately.

If the servlet can easily determine its last modified time then it should override the `HttpServlet.getLastModified()` method. Use this method to return the time the data was last modified, in milliseconds since midnight January 1, 1970 GMT. The `java.util.Date.getTime()` method provides a suitable `long` value that this method can use.

In the following code sample, an attribute has been used to store a `Date` object with the time that data last changed in this Web application. If the last modified time is not known, the `getLastModified()` method should return a negative number:

```
public long getLastModified(HttpServletRequest request) {
    ServletContext context = getServletContext();
    Date timestamp = (Date) context.getAttribute("timestamp");
    if (timestamp == null)
        return -1;
    else
        return timestamp.getTime();
    }
}
```

Tomcat uses the value returned by this method to support the `if-modified-since` HTTP header field.

Persistent Connections

As you saw in Chapter 3, "Basic Principles of Web Servers," persistent connections are a good thing because they reduce the number of TCP connections that have to be established. This in turn

- Reduces the overhead in opening and closing TCP connections in servers and clients (not to mention routers, gateways, firewalls, and proxies)
- Reduces overall network traffic
- Increases response speed

In order to maintain a persistent connection, the client and Tomcat have to concur on when the response ends. The way this works is that Tomcat simply tells the client how big the response is by setting the `Content-Length` response header.

Tomcat sets the content length automatically if the entire response fits inside the response buffer, so one way of ensuring a persistent connection is to set a big enough buffer to hold the entire response.

You can use `HttpServletResponse.setBufferSize()` to set your preferred buffer size for the body of the response. Tomcat is then obliged to provide a buffer at least as large as the size requested. You can find the actual buffer size using the `ServletResponse.getBufferSize()` method.

NOTE

Tomcat's default buffer size is 2048. You can obtain a different buffer size using the `ServletResponse.setBufferSize()` method. If used, this method must be called before any response body content is written.

Obviously, this only works when you know in advance how big the response will be. An alternative approach to setting an explicit buffer size and hoping it is big enough is to replace the `PrintWriter` object returned by `getWriter()` with one that uses a `ByteArrayOutputStream`. This effectively provides a buffer that grows to accommodate the response.

NOTE

As the normal output `PrintWriter` object returned by `getWriter()` can only be used for character text, you should use a `ServletOutputStream` obtained with the `HttpResponse.getOutputStream()` method for sending binary data in the response.

Now your servlet can determine the length of the response and set the `Content-Length` header using the `ServletResponse.setContentLength()` method.

There are two requirements when using the `setContentLength()` method:

- It must be called prior to sending the response body.
- The size given must be accurate.

Listing 7.1 shows a `doGet()` method that uses this approach to ensure that a persistent connection is maintained.

LISTING 7.1 A Servlet Written to Use an Internal Buffer to Support Persistent Connections

```
import java.io.*;
import javax.servlet.*;
import javax.servlet.http.*;

public class PersistentConnection extends HttpServlet {
    public void doGet(HttpServletRequest request, HttpServletResponse response)
             throws ServletException, IOException {

    response.setContentType ("text/html");
    ByteArrayOutputStream buffer = new ByteArrayOutputStream(2048);
    PrintWriter out = new PrintWriter(buffer, true);

    out.println ("<HTML>");
    out.println ("<HEAD><TITLE>Persistent Connection</TITLE></HEAD>");
    out.println ("<BODY>");
    out.println ("<BIG>Persistent Connection</BIG>");
    out.println ("</BODY>");
    out.println ("</HTML>");

    response.setContentLength(buffer.size());
    buffer.writeTo(response.getOutputStream());
    }
}
```

CAUTION

Buffering a large amount of output and sending it in one go will place a strain on Tomcat resources. It will also cause a delay on the client receiving the response, which may negate any gains from using the persistent connection.

JSP Implicit Objects

Implicit objects on a JSP were introduced in Chapter 5, "Basic Principles of JSPs," where they were used in JSP scripting elements. In each case, the object represents an instance of a Java servlet class or interface. These implicit objects provide a convenient shorthand notation that you can use without having to include definitions for the objects in the JSP. When the page is translated, The Jasper container inserts the appropriate definition for each object. Table 7.1 lists and describes the JSP implicit objects.

TABLE 7.1 JSP Implicit Objects

Object	Description
`application`	This object is provided as a convenient means of accessing the Web application context (`javax.servlet.ServletContext`). It is commonly used to share information in the form of context attributes between servlets and JSPs in the same Web application.
`config`	The `config` object provides access to the `javax.servlet.ServletConfig` object, which provides information about the container in which the Web application is running.
`out`	The `out` object represents a `javax.servlet.jsp.JspWriter` object, which provides access to the `print()` and `println()` methods.
`page`	This object contains a reference to the current JSP instance and you use it as you would use the `this` object in Java code.
`pageContext`	The `pageContext` object is used to access namespaces associated with a JSP. It represents a `javax.servlet.jsp.PageContext` class.
`request`	This object represents the `javax.servlet.http.HttpServletRequest` interface. A common use of this object is to access request headers, parameters, attributes, or cookies: `<% String rate = request.getParameter("rate"); %>`
`response`	This object represents the `javax.servlet.http.HttpServletResponse` interface. Use a `response` object to set response headers, content type, and so on: `<% response.setStatus(SC_BAD_REQUEST); %>`
`session`	Sessions are used to store state between client requests—see Chapter 8 for more information on how to use a `session` object.
`exception`	This object is only available to a JSP that has been defined in a JSP page directive as a JSP error page. JSP error pages are covered in Chapter 12, "Error Handling."

JSP Standard Actions

Chapter 5 covered the JSP standard actions involved with JavaBeans. There are four more standard actions defined in the JSP specification that you may use:

<jsp:include>, <jsp:forward>, <jsp:param>, and <jsp:plugin>. The following sections describe these actions.

<jsp:include>

A <jsp:include> element is used to include both static and dynamic resources into a JSP. A <jsp:include> action element differs from the include directive (<%@ include ...>) in several respects. With an include action

- The include is done at runtime, which means the included input from the resource is not parsed as if it were part of the JSP.
- The request object is available to the included resource.
- The included resource only has access to the JspWriter out object.

For example, you could use the following include to output a copyright notice that is tailored to a particular client locale:

```
<jsp:include page="copyright.jsp" />
```

You can send additional parameters to the included file with the <jsp:param> action (described in an upcoming section).

<jsp:forward>

This action element forwards the request to another URL. This forward is done entirely by Tomcat and is transparent to the client:

```
<jsp:forward page="process-request.jsp" />
```

The forwarded page has access to the original request object, but it can also have additional parameters defined with a <jsp:param> action (described in the next section).

<jsp:param>

If you need to add additional parameters to a <jsp:include> or <jsp:forward> or override existing ones, you must use the <jsp:param> action. Adding parameters in the form of a query string appended to the URL does not work, as these are simply ignored.

To override the value of an existing request parameter, you simply use the same name. The <jsp:param> parameter takes precedence over a request parameter.

The following defines a new parameter called id to be sent to a forwarded page:

```
<jsp:forward page="process-request.jsp" >
    <jsp:param name="id" value="02052002:1" />
</jsp:forward>
```

<jsp:plugin>

With a `<jsp:plugin>` action, you indicate to Jasper, or any other JSP-compatible container, that it should generate the appropriate HTML that instructs the browser to download a Java plug-in (if required) for the subsequent execution of an Applet.

Servlet Listeners

Up to now, all the servlets you have seen have been called by Tomcat to handle an HTTP request. There are two other uses for servlets. They can act as

- A servlet filter or Tomcat valve that preprocesses requests or responses (valves and filters are covered in Chapter 18, "Servlet Filters," and Chapter 19, "Tomcat Valves")
- A servlet event listener that is notified when some external event or change has taken place

There are six listener interfaces that you can implement in your servlet; two are connected to application life cycle events, two to session life cycle events, and two involve events affecting session attributes. All the listener interfaces extend the `java.util.EventListener` interface.

Table 7.2 provides a list of the servlet event listeners.

TABLE 7.2 Servlet Event Listener Interfaces

Listener Interface	Servlet Is Notified...
`ServletContextAttributeListener`	When a servlet context attribute is added, removed, or replaced
`ServletContextListener`	About changes to servlet context, such as context initialization or shutdown
`HttpSessionActivationListener`	When a session is activated or deactivated
`HttpSessionListener`	When a session is created or destroyed
`HttpSessionAttributeListener`	When a session attribute is added, removed, or replaced
`HttpSessionBindingListener`	When an object is bound to or unbound from a session

Session listeners are used as a way of tracking sessions within a Web application and are discussed in Chapter 8.

Context life cycle listeners can be used to correctly initialize resources or save servlet data before the application is shut down. This use is similar to that of the `init()` and `destroy()` methods, but these events are connected to the life cycle of the Web application, not an individual servlet, and can be used to support requirements that are common to many servlets.

The following two methods are provided in the `ServletContextListener` class:

Method	Description
`contextInitialized()`	This method receives notification that the application is ready to process requests.
`contextDestroyed()`	This method is notified that the context is about to be shut down.

Listing 7.2 shows a servlet listener using these methods to initialize a context attribute and save the value to Tomcat's log file.

LISTING 7.2 Example Servlet Listener

```
import javax.servlet.*;
import javax.servlet.http.*;

public class AppListener implements ServletContextListener {

    private ServletContext context = null;

    public void contextInitialized(ServletContextEvent event) {
       context = event.getServletContext();
       context.setAttribute("Counter", new Integer(0));
    }

    public void contextDestroyed(ServletContextEvent event) {
       context = event.getServletContext();
       context.log ((String)context.getAttribute("Counter"));
       context.removeAttribute("Counter");
   }
}
```

You should package your listener classes in the WAR file just like any other servlet, either under the `WEB-INF/classes` directory or inside a JAR in the `WEB-INF/lib` directory.

To register a listener class, you will have to add a `<listener>` entry in the application's deployment descriptor `web.xml` file as follows:

```
<listener>
    <listener-class>AppListener</listener-class>
</listener>
```

If you have many listener servlets waiting on the same event, Tomcat will invoke them in the order in which they are defined in the deployment descriptor.

To maintain the integrity of the deployment descriptor, listener servlets must be defined after filter servlets (see Chapter 18) and before ordinary servlets.

Servlet Threading Issues

By default, Tomcat assumes that your servlet code is thread-safe and therefore runs servlets multithreaded. If you need to ensure that your servlet is single-threaded, your servlet should implement the `javax.servlet.SingleThreadModel` interface. When it does, Tomcat will not create multiple instance threads on the servlet instance. For example:

```
public class HTMLPage extends HttpServlet implements SingleThreadModel {...}
```

For a JSP, you can achieve the same effect by setting the `IsThreadSafe` page directive:

```
<%@ page isThreadSafe="false" %>
```

The servlet specification states that a server *may* create a pool of single-threaded servlet instances to handle multiple requests, but the current Tomcat implementation does not do this. Instead, Tomcat creates one instance of your servlet and serializes all requests to it. This could cause clients to experience delays if a large part of your application implements the `SingleThreadModel`.

CAUTION

Tomcat will reject incoming client connections if the backlog of current requests gets too large.

Because Tomcat does not create a servlet pool, you should consider using synchronized blocks to protect shared data and resources rather than forcing your servlets to be single-threaded. To minimize the amount of time requests are blocked, you should synchronize the smallest amount of code possible.

CAUTION

Do not synchronize the servlet's service methods (`doGet()` or `doPost()`)—if you do, access to your servlet will be serialized regardless of whether Tomcat implements a servlet pool.

Wherever possible, you should write your servlets and JSPs to avoid threading issues. You should avoid using nonfinal instance variables and use `HTTPSession` objects instead because these are bound to a particular client session (see Chapter 8).

Database access is another common cause of concurrency issues, as most databases allow only a limited number of concurrent connections (sometimes only one). You should therefore make use of datasources and resource pooling as described in detail in Chapter 9, "Databases and Tomcat."

Welcome Files

You may have noticed that when Tomcat is running and you type `http://localhost:8080/` into your browser window, you are redirected to `http://localhost:8080/index.html`. As you have guessed, this does not happen by magic. Instead, configured in Tomcat's deployment descriptor (`<CATALINA_HOME>/conf/web.xml`) is a list of what are called welcome files:

```
<welcome-file-list>
    <welcome-file>index.html</welcome-file>
    <welcome-file>index.htm</welcome-file>
    <welcome-file>index.jsp</welcome-file>
</welcome-file-list>
```

When a request URL references a directory rather than an individual document, Tomcat will look for a welcome file in that directory. If one is present, it will redirect the client to the welcome file.

If you do not define a welcome file list, or do not include any welcome files, Tomcat will display a directory listing of your Web application content. This presents a security risk and you should always add a welcome file for your application to display as a default page because it prevents clients from browsing your Web application directories.

CAUTION

Providing users with a directory listing is an aid to hackers. Unless you have a good reason to do otherwise, you should turn this feature off. You configure Tomcat to not display directory listings by setting listings to `false` for the default servlet in `<CATALINA_HOME>/conf/web.xml`:

```
<servlet>
    <servlet-name>default</servlet-name>
    <servlet-class>
        org.apache.catalina.servlets.DefaultServlet
    </servlet-class>
    <init-param>
        <param-name>debug</param-name>
        <param-value>0</param-value>
    </init-param>
    <init-param>
        <param-name>listings</param-name>
        <param-value>false</param-value>
    </init-param>
    <load-on-startup>1</load-on-startup>
</servlet>
```

Welcome files are not a cure-all for the ubiquitous HTTP 404 error. They only come into play when a URL is provided that maps to a directory. If users explicitly request a document that does not exist, they will still see the error page.

Summary

This chapter has given you a quick overview of the various servlet and JSP objects, methods, and directives that will enable you to write superior Web applications. You have found out how to

- Send different HTTP response codes to the client
- Forward a request to a different Web page
- Return different types of documents (not just HTML)
- Support persistent HTTP sessions by setting the content length of your response
- Support client browsing caches by providing the date of last modification for your servlets
- Use attributes to share data between servlets in a Web application

- Avoid using shared data that can adversely affect the multithreading behavior of servlets
- Use welcome files to give your Web applications a more professional look

In the next chapter, you will see how servlets can store and retrieve information about individual users using sessions.

8 Session Tracking

IN THIS CHAPTER

- Managing Session Data
- Cookies
- The Servlet Session Object
- Hidden Fields
- URL Rewriting

So far, you have seen how to develop Web applications consisting of standalone Web pages. Applications made up of discrete Web pages are only sufficient for simple sites. In most situations a Web application must be able to track users as they browse from one page to another and revisit pages. Often, information required by one page is provided by another. An online shopping system, for example, requires users to add items to a virtual shopping cart and then to complete the purchase using some form of electronic checkout. All the pages in the application must have access to the items in the shopping cart. Such information sharing is made possible with the use of sessions.

In this chapter you will learn how to track sessions using the servlet session object, URL rewriting, HTML form fields, and cookies.

Managing Session Data

HTTP is a stateless protocol; consequently, implementing the request and response approach is simple. But it also means that an application using HTTP will have to provide its own solution to passing state (or information) from one HTTP request to another. The state information maintained across multiple HTTP requests is known as a *session.* A session is usually associated with a single user browsing one or more pages within a single Web application.

Session Tracking in Servlets and JSPs

Java servlets and JSPs have a number of techniques available to track sessions, as shown in Table 8.1.

TABLE 8.1 Session Tracking Techniques

Technique	Description
Cookies	Originally used by CGI scripts to maintain session information and currently supported by most browsers and servers
The servlet session object	Servlet container support for session data (implemented by Tomcat using cookies and URL rewriting)
Hidden form fields	Data returned with a Web form but not displayed by the browser
URL rewriting	Extra data included with a URL

Each technique has advantages and disadvantages; the relative merits of each are discussed in this chapter. Regardless of which technique is used, you must take care to ensure session tracking information remains secure.

Security Issues

There are three basic approaches to storing session data:

- Store all the data on the client
- Store all the data on the server accessed via a unique key and store the key on the client
- A combination of the other two approaches

Any data stored on the client can potentially be accessed and modified by the end user or a malicious user with access to the client system. Similarly, any data exchanged between the client and server can potentially be accessed by an unknown or unauthorized party.

CAUTION

Because you cannot control how a client will store session information, you must assume the session information is accessible to all users of the client system. It is imperative that you never store confidential information on the client.

Purely from the security viewpoint, you should keep all session information on the server and store a session key on the client. Because session information can become potentially quite large, you will also reduce the volume of network traffic by keeping all session data on the server.

In order to keep the session key secure, you should study Chapter 23, "Securing Web Applications Under Tomcat," which discusses encrypting network traffic using Secure Sockets (SSL).

Storing Session Data

Having ruled out keeping session data on the client, you must therefore keep it on the server. How you do this is up to you. The most popular approaches are listed in the following sections.

Using the Servlet Session Object

By using the servlet session object, you can let Tomcat manage the session data for you, using an appropriate method (in fact Tomcat uses cookies or URL rewriting).

Tomcat manages the session data and ensures all servlets in the Web application have access to the data. Tomcat will also expire the session should the client connection remain idle for a specified period of time.

The downside of using this approach is that you cannot use the session object when different Web applications must share the same session data. If your clients do not support cookies, you will also need to use URL rewriting to support Tomcat sessions.

Managing the Session Data Manually

By managing your session data manually, you can share it among different Web applications. You will have to store the data on an individual client basis and you will need a unique key to identify the data for each client.

You need to choose the key carefully: An apparently unique value for a client is the client's domain name or IP address (you can obtain these from `HttpRequest` object). However, with the increasing use of shared client machines (as typified by an Internet café), you will have no way of telling when the end user changes. Also, a malicious user can easily spoof (falsify) this data in an attempt to break your application's security. This approach is inherently insecure.

> **CAUTION**
>
> Do not use the remote client hostname or IP address as a session key when managing session data manually. This value will not change when one user logs off and another logs on and can easily be spoofed by a hacker.

If you are managing the session data manually, you should apply access controls to your Web application as described in Chapter 14, "Access Control." After users have authenticated themselves, you can use their unique Tomcat user ID (their security principal name) as the key to access their session data.

If you manage the session data manually, you should also consider the expected lifetime of the data and apply an expiry timeout unless the data should be retained indefinitely.

How you actually store the data is up to you, but Table 8.2 lists some solutions you might consider.

TABLE 8.2 Manual Session Data Storage Locations

Location	Pros and Cons
JDBC database	Easy to use and well understood. Ensures session data is persistent across server restarts. Some runtime overhead in accessing the database and potential access problems if a client sends multiple concurrent requests.
Java collection	Easy to use and faster than a database but data is transient. Care must be taken to ensure concurrent access to the collection is thread safe.
External repository	This can be any form of external data store such as a JNDI server (typically LDAP), or a custom network service (perhaps RMI or CORBA) providing data storage and retrieval. Not as widely understood as a database and probably has similar performance penalties.

Unless the session data needs to be persistent, you can use a Java Collection class to store session data and take advantage of the simple fast interface. A database is a good option for making the data persistent.

Cookies

Cookies were developed to allow CGI scripts to store information on the client. Although cookies are not part of the HTTP specification, they are widely supported by Web browsers and servers. Cookies can be used to support session tracking by storing session information on the client. Cookies are implicitly connected with a session and can be used to store any information on the client.

Due to their lack of security and abuse by some Web site developers, cookies have earned a poor reputation. Most Web browsers have configuration options to allow the user to do some or all of the following:

- Disable all cookies
- Enable or disable cookies from specified sites
- Be warned whenever a site attempts to create a cookie
- Be able to view and delete the cookies stored on the client

Some organizations now have security policy statements that specify that Web browsers should disable all cookies. Obviously, using cookies to support sessions for clients that have disabled cookies will not work and you will have to use a different technique, such as hidden fields or URL rewriting, as an alternative to cookies.

Cookie HTTP Header Fields

Cookies are name and value data objects that are associated with the domain name and path name of a URL. A Web server can send one or more cookies back to the client using the `Set-Cookie` header in the HTTP response message (see Chapter 3, "Basic Principles of Web Servers," for more information on HTTP). The following example shows the start of the HTTP response from the Sams Publishing Web site at the time that this book was written:

```
HTTP/1.1 200 OK
Server: Microsoft-IIS/5.0
Date: Wed, 03 Apr 2002 12:26:13 GMT
Connection: Keep-Alive
Content-Length: 19018
Content-Type: text/html
Expires: Wed, 03 Apr 2002 12:25:14 GMT
Set-Cookie: session%5Fid=%7BE2097965%2D1352%2D4E2F%2DB2F0%2DACD988334242%7D; path=/
Cache-control: private
```

This example returns a single cookie with the name `session%5Fid` and the value `%7BE2097965%2D1352%2D4E2F%2DB2F0%2DACD988334242%7D`. This cookie is explicitly associated with the path `/` and implicitly associated with the domain `www.samspublishing.com`. The Web client stores this cookie locally against the given domain and path.

Every time a Web client requests a page it checks the local cookie repository for all cookies matching the domain name and document path name of the URI. All matched cookies are added to the request URI as `Cookie` header fields. The next shows a subsequent request to `http://www.samspublishing.com/` made from the same client with the cookie passed as the last header field:

```
GET / HTTP/1.1
Host: www.samspublishing.com
User-Agent: Mozilla/5.0 (Windows; U; Windows NT 5.0; en-GB; rv:0.9.4)
➥Gecko/20011128 Netscape6/6.2.1
Accept: text/xml, application/xml, application/xhtml+xml, text/html;q=0.9,
➥image/png, image/jpeg, image/gif;q=0.2, text/plain;q=0.8, text/css, */*;q=0.1
Accept-Language: en-gb
Accept-Encoding: gzip, deflate, compress;q=0.9
Keep-Alive: 300
Connection: keep-alive
Cookie: session%5Fid=%7BE2097965%2D1352%2D4E2F%2DB2F0%2DACD988334242%7D
```

Because the cookie used in this example is associated with the root document (`/`), it is always sent with any request for `www.samspublishing.com`. If the cookie had been associated with `/SAMS`, it would only have been sent if the requested path name started with `/SAMS`. Similar rules apply to matching the cookie domain name against the domain name in the URI.

Cookies also have an expiration date. By default cookies exist only for the duration of the browser session (as seen in the examples in Listings 8.1 and 8.2). A cookie can be defined to have an explicit expiration date, and the browser will continue to send the cookie until that date is reached. An infinite date can be specified ensuring the cookie is kept permanently.

Servlet Support for Cookies

The `javax.servlet.http` package provides simple support for cookies. Unless you specifically want to use cookies for purposes other than session management, you should always use one of the other session management techniques instead of cookies because of the inherent insecurity of cookies and the fact that clients can disable cookies.

Use cookies only if all of the following are true:

- You are not storing confidential information on the client.
- You want to utilize the persistent nature of cookies allowing them to live across browser startup and shutdown.
- You are aware that the end user can disable cookies, effectively negating your use of cookies.

CAUTION

Do not write Web applications that will only work if cookies are enabled unless you can guarantee that no client will disable cookie support.

The `HttpRequest` object for a servlet has a `getCookie()` method that returns an array of `javax.servlet.http.Cookie` objects representing the cookie header fields in the HTTP request. If no cookie headers were sent then `getCookies()` returns null and not an empty array.

You can create new `Cookie` objects and add them to the `HttpResponse` object using the `addCookie()` method. Listing 8.1 shows a JSP that defines a simple form to allow users to add cookies to their session.

LISTING 8.1 JSP Using Cookies: `cookie-list.jsp`

```
<%@ page import="java.util.*" %>
<%
    Cookie[] cookies = request.getCookies();
    if (cookies == null)
        cookies = new Cookie[0];
    Date thisVisit = new Date();
    // add data cookie to session
    Cookie c = new Cookie("lastVisit",""+thisVisit);
    response.addCookie(c);
    // add cookie to session
    String name = request.getParameter("name");
    String value = request.getParameter("value");
    Cookie added = null;
    if (name!=null && value!=null && name.length()>0) {
        added = new Cookie(name,value);
        response.addCookie(added);
    }
%>
<HTML>
    <HEAD>
        <TITLE>Cookie List</TITLE>
    </HEAD>
    <BODY>
        <H1>Cookie List</H1>
        This visit: <%= thisVisit %><BR>
        Number of cookies: <%= cookies.length %><BR>
        <H2>Cookies</H2>
        <%
        for (int i=0; i<cookies.length; i++) {
            out.println(cookies[i].getName()+":\t"+
                cookies[i].getValue()+"<BR>");
            // check if added cookie already present
            if (added!=null && added.getName().equals(cookies[i].getName()))
                added = null;
        }
        if (added != null)
            out.println("New cookie "+added.getName()+":\t"+
                added.getValue()+"<BR>");
        %>
        <H2>New cookie</H2>
        <FORM>
```

LISTING 8.1 Continued

```
            <P>Name: <INPUT TYPE='TEXT' NAME='name'></P>
            <P>Value: <INPUT TYPE='TEXT' NAME='value'></P>
            <INPUT TYPE='SUBMIT' VALUE='Add new value'>
        </FORM>
    </BODY>
</HTML>
```

In Listing 8.1, the `lastVisit` cookie is created to store the date the user last visited this servlet, and it is always added to the response object. If the user supplied a cookie name and value, this is also added to the response.

TIP

Always add your cookies before sending any output to the client. The cookies are written to the client as part of the HTTP response header, and the header fields are written out the first time the output buffer is flushed. If you add new cookies (or create any other header field) after the output buffer has been flushed, your changes to the header fields will be silently ignored.

In Listing 8.1, the JSP does not need to copy the cookies from the request to the response object because the client will retain a copy of all cookies sent with the request.

The `Cookie` objects used in Listing 8.1 also have methods for getting and setting other cookie properties such as

- The cookie's value
- The associated domain
- The associated pathname
- The maximum age of the cookie in seconds

Newly created cookies in Listing 8.1 will only last for the lifetime of the browser session and are associated with the servlet URL's domain name and pathname. To change the default values for a cookie, you have to create the cookie and then change the required values using the appropriate setter methods. The following code fragment will create a cookie with a one-week timeout (specified in seconds) that is associated with all pages in the `myapplication` Web application:

```
c = new Cookie(name,value);
c.setMaxAge(604800);
c.setPath("/myapplication");
response.addCookie(c);
```

TIP

You can delete a cookie from the client by defining a cookie header field to have a maximum age of 0 (zero) seconds. When the browser receives the new header defining the zero maximum age, it will delete any existing cookie with the same name.

Cookies are often used to store user preference information allowing a Web site to be customized for each individual user.

The Servlet Session Object

The good news is that if you use the servlet session object, Tomcat does all the hard work for managing the session data for you. The bad news is that Tomcat uses a cookie (called `JSESSIONID`) to store the session key on the client. If your clients do not support cookies, you will need to use URL rewriting to use Tomcat sessions.

The servlet session object is of class `javax.servlet.http.HttpSession` and is obtained via the `getSession()` method of the `HttpServletRequest` object. The `getSession()` method will automatically create a new session if one does not already exist. The overloaded `getSession(boolean)` method lets you specify a false parameter to return only an existing session object (or null if one has not been created).

The `HttpSession` object manages a collection of attributes. Each attribute is a name/value pair—the value being any Java object. The `getAttribute()` and `setAttribute()` methods can retrieve and store name/value pairs and the `getAttributeNames()` method returns an `Enumeration` of all the defined attributes in the session. Attributes can be removed using the `removeAttribute()` method (this is the same idiom as used for `Context` attributes).

Listing 8.2 shows a simple form that allows the user to define parameters to add to the session object.

LISTING 8.2 JSP Using Session Data: `session-list.jsp`

```
<%@ page import="java.util.*" %>
<%
    // add parameter to session
    String name = request.getParameter("name");
    String value = request.getParameter("value");
    if (name!=null && value!=null && name.length()>0) {
        session.setAttribute(name,value);
    }
    Date lastVisit = (Date)session.getAttribute("lastVisit");
    Date thisVisit = new Date();
```

LISTING 8.2 Continued

```
%>
<HTML>
    <HEAD>
        <TITLE>Session List</TITLE>
    </HEAD>
    <BODY>
        <H1>Session List</H1>
        Last visit: <%= lastVisit %><BR>
        This visit: <%= thisVisit %><BR>
        Session ID: <%= session.getId() %><BR>
        Session max interval: <%= session.getMaxInactiveInterval() %><BR>

        <H2>Session parameters</H2>
        <%
            Enumeration enum = session.getAttributeNames();
            while (enum.hasMoreElements()) {
                String attribute = (String) enum.nextElement();
                out.println(""+attribute+"="+
                    session.getAttribute(attribute)+"<BR>");
            }
            session.setAttribute("lastVisit",thisVisit);
        %>

        <H2>New session parameter</H2>
        <FORM>
            <P>Name: <INPUT TYPE='TEXT' NAME='name'></P>
            <P>Value: <INPUT TYPE='TEXT' NAME='value'></P>
            <INPUT TYPE='SUBMIT' VALUE='Add new value'>
        </FORM>
    </BODY>
</HTML>
```

Listing 8.2 has many features in common with the `CookieList` class shown in Listing 8.1. In Listing 8.2 the `lastVisit` Data object is used to store the date the user last visited this servlet. If the user supplied a new parameter name and value, this is added to the session. The servlet sends back the following information for display by the client: current date, date of the last visit to this page, session identifier, session timeout value (in seconds), as well as all the parameters defined by the user in the session.

Session Duration

Session data will be deleted automatically if Tomcat does not receive any HTTP requests from the client for a specified timeout period (Tomcat sets the default session timeout to 30 minutes).

The `HttpSession.invalidate()` method can be used to discard all the session data and render the session invalid. Potentially, this will allow the garbage collector to reclaim the memory used by the session sooner than if the session had been allowed to timeout. Tomcat will create a new session object if future client requests require session data.

The session timeout value can be read using `HttpSession.getMaxInactiveInterval()` and the value can be set dynamically using `HttpSession.setMaxInactiveInterval()`; both methods define the timeout in seconds.

Tomcat defines the default session timeout for all Web applications in the `<CATALINA_HOME>/conf/web.xml` file. The timeout is set in the `<web-app>/<session-config>/<session-timeout>` element in this file. The `<session-timeout>` element somewhat perversely specifies the timeout in minutes. The `<session-timeout>` element must be defined immediately after any `<servlet-mapping>` elements. A default timeout of 30 minutes is defined for all applications.

The default session timeout for an individual application can be added to the `WEB-INF/web.xml` file. The default timeout is set in the `<web-app>/<session-config>/<session-timeout>` element.

Choosing the right session timeout is not straightforward. The Tomcat 30-minute default set in `<CATALINA_HOME>/conf/web.xml` is a good compromise. Ideally the session should persist as long as the end user requires it and no longer.

TIP

Calling the `HttpSession.invalidate()` method to remove a session when it is no longer required for a client will improve memory utilization and potentially improve overall server performance.

If a session is allowed to exist after a client has finished using the session data (such as after completing an online purchase), the session data remains unused in memory for at least 30 minutes and potentially much longer. The session data will remain valid as long as the client continues to browse Web application pages even if those pages do not use the session data.

When supporting a large number of clients, the memory allocated to redundant session data could become significant. Reducing the session timeout will help reduce memory usage if this is perceived to be a problem but at the expense of disenchanting users who take a long time to browse from page to page. For many applications setting the timeout to be less than 10 minutes is counterproductive.

More Session Configuration

A number of other attributes can be configured in the `<Manager>` section of an application's `<Context>` element in the `<CATALINA_HOME>/conf/server.xml` file.

Perhaps the most useful `<Manager>` attribute is `checkInterval`, which can be used to set the polling interval for checking for expired sessions. The default interval is 60 seconds. Making the interval larger will improve server performance by reducing the amount of time spent on checking for expired sessions. The interval can be set to 5 minutes with

```
checkInterval='300'
```

The downside of longer intervals is that unused sessions will live longer. Using a 30-minute session timeout and a check interval of 5 minutes means that session will live for between 30 and 35 minutes. Extending the check interval is a good idea if your servlets and JSPs invalidate session data whenever possible, as the longer check interval will not extend the life of invalidated session objects.

A second `<Context>` attribute associated with sessions that may be overridden is `maxActiveSessions`; this can be used to limit the number of sessions created by Tomcat. Restricting the number of sessions can be useful to stop Tomcat gobbling up memory to support large numbers of concurrent users. The default value is to allow an unlimited number of sessions (represented by the value –1).

If the number of sessions exceeds `maxActiveSessions`, Tomcat will not create any more sessions but instead will generate an HTTP 500, internal server error. This is returned to the client browser along with a stack trace showing the error. On a live server, this is not desirable and you should use an error page (see Chapter 12, "Error Handling") to display an appropriate message when an error occurs.

Unfortunately, you cannot trap 500 errors originating from Tomcat, which means you will have to catch the Java `java.lang.IllegalStateException` thrown when Tomcat refuses to create a new session. For completeness, the following `<error-page>` element will do what is required, but you should read Chapter 12 for more information on how to use error pages:

```
<error-page>
    <exception-type>java.lang.IllegalStateException</exception-type>
    <location>/tooManySessions.html</location>
</error-page>
```

Multithreading Issues

The session object is not thread safe; so, unless your servlet implements the `SingleThreadModel`, it is your responsibility to synchronize access to the session object. The use of the `SingleThreadModel` and synchronization is described in Chapter 7, "The Web Application Environment."

Persistent Sessions

Tomcat provides support for persistent sessions. Whenever a Web application is reloaded or Tomcat is stopped and restarted, all the session data is saved to a file. This allows client sessions to persist across application upgrades and server restarts. By default the saved session data is stored in the file

```
<CATALINA_HOME>/work/<host>/<webApplication>/SESSIONS.ser
```

CAUTION

If you are a developer in the habit of shutting down Tomcat by closing down the Tomcat server window (or typing Ctrl+C in this window), Tomcat will not save the session data on closedown. You must use the `shutdown` script provided in `<CATALINA_HOME>/bin` to shut down Tomcat in order to save the session data.

Session persistence uses serialization to store the session data. In order to be able to save a session object, it must be serializable: The object class must implement the `Serializable` interface. Any object in the session that is not serializable will not be saved. The standard Java classes such as `String`, `Date`, the primitive wrapper classes, and so on are all serializable. If you write your own classes and store objects of these classes in the session, you must make sure these objects are serializable.

CAUTION

You will not receive any indication that a non-serializable session object has not been saved as part of the persistent session. Even worse, any session after the first session with a non-serializable object will not be restored. Tomcat throws an exception on encountering a non-serializable object and then stops restoring sessions. It is possible that Tomcat will not restore any sessions at all (if a non-serializable object is in the stream).

As a side effect of setting the parameter `distributable='true'` in the `<Context>/<Manager>` element in `<CATALINA_HOME>/conf/server.xml`, Tomcat will check that all objects added to a session are serializable. With this parameter defined, any attempt to add a non-serializable object to the session will cause Tomcat to generate an HTTP 500 error.

Alternatively, you can also add the empty element `<distributable/>` to the `<web-app>` element in the Web application `web.xml` file to prevent non-serializable elements from being added to the session.

If you want to change the name of the location of the session serialization data file, you can use the `pathname` attribute of the `<Context>/<Manager>` element. A pathname is relative to the `<CATALINA_HOME>/work/<host>/<webApplication>/` directory unless an absolute pathname is used.

If not required, you can disable persistent sessions by defining the `saveOnRestart='false'` parameter to the `<Context>/<Manager>` element.

Tomcat 4 has a new session manager called the Persistent Manager that is still considered experimental. It provides more comprehensive session management than the basic session manager.

The persistent session manager can swap out idle session data, potentially freeing up memory. Additional attributes of the `<Context>/<Manager>` element, described in the Tomcat documentation, are used to define the parameters for swapping idle sessions.

The persistent session can save session data to a database as well as a serialized file. Session data saved to a database is saved as a BLOB (Binary Large Object).

CAUTION

Not all databases support BLOB data, so you may not be able to use the persistent manager to store the session data to your preferred database.

For more information on the persistent manager and configuration of the basic session manager, you should study the online Tomcat documentation for the manager component of the server configuration.

Session Listeners

Chapter 7 showed how to set up servlets that listen for life cycle events associated with the servlet context. You can set up session listeners in a similar manner. You can listen for the session events listed in Table 8.3.

TABLE 8.3 HTTP Session Events

Type	Description	Interface
Life cycle	An `HttpSession` has been created, invalidated, or timed out.	`javax.servlet.http.HttpSessionListener`
Attribute changes	Attributes have been added, removed, or replaced in an `HttpSession`.	`javax.servlet.HttpSessionAttributeListener`
Attribute binding	Attributes have been bound or unbound from an `HttpSession`.	`javax.servlet.HttpSessionBindingListener`
Activation changes	An `HttpSession` has been activated or passivated	`javax.servlet.HttpSessionActivation`

A session listener is a servlet that implements the appropriate listener interface. The following example servlet listens for a session being timed out or invalidated, and closes down any database connection objects it finds in the session:

```
import java.sql.*;
import java.util.*;
import javax.servlet.*;
import javax.servlet.http.*;

public class SessionListener extends HttpServlet
    implements HttpSessionListener {

    public void sessionCreated(HttpSessionEvent event) {
    }

    public void sessionDestroyed(HttpSessionEvent event) {
        HttpSession session = event.getSession();
        Enumeration enum = session.getAttributeNames();
        while (enum.hasMoreElements()) {
            Object attribute = enum.nextElement();
            if (attribute instanceof Connection) {
                try {
                    ((Connection)attribute).close();
                }
                catch (SQLException ex) {}
            }
        }
    }
}
```

To register this listener, you must add a `<listener>` element to the `<web-app>` entry in the deployment descriptor:

```
<listener>
    <listener-class>SessionListener</listener-class>
</listener>
```

Any `<listener>` servlets must be defined after filter servlets (see Chapter 18, "Servlet Filters") and before ordinary `<servlet>` elements in the `web.xml` file. You will need to stop and restart Tomcat before this session listener servlet is recognized.

Disabling Tomcat Sessions

Tomcat uses cookies to support servlet session objects. The `<Context>` element in `<CATALINA_HOME>/conf/server.xml` can be used to disable support for servlet sessions. If you set the attribute `cookies='false'` in the `<Context>` tag, this will disable sessions for a specific Web application. Setting `cookies='false'` in the `<DefaultContext>` tag will disable sessions for all servlets. If cookies are disabled, you will not be able to use Tomcat for URL rewriting but will have to do so manually (see the section "URL Rewriting").

Hidden Fields

Hidden fields on an HTML form are a convenient way of passing information from one Web request to another. They can only be used with HTML forms and are therefore not applicable when you want to use hypertext links to move from one page to another (you would use URL rewriting when passing information in a hypertext link).

To show the use of hidden fields consider the simple `CurrencyConverterBean` developed in Chapter 5, "Basic Principles of JSPs." For simplicity, this bean used a fixed exchange rate. A more realistic example would treat the exchange rate as an attribute of the bean and initialize this attribute from an external source such as a database.

If the exchange rate is constantly changing throughout the day, this could be confusing for the end user when his converted values (perhaps the prices of goods in the shopping cart) change from one Web page to another. Setting the exchange rate once at the start of the session would lead to consistent price comparisons.

Assuming the bean has an attribute called `exchangeRate`, this can be used to capture the exchange rate on a form in a hidden field and pass this to subsequent pages as a form parameter.

As a simple example consider the currency converter JSP in Listing 8.3.

LISTING 8.3 The `currency-converter.jsp` Using a Hidden Field for Session Data

```
<jsp:useBean id="converter"
    class="converters.CurrencyConverterBean" scope="page"/>
<% if (request.getParameter("exchangeRate")!=null ) { %>
    <jsp:setProperty name="converter" property="exchangeRate" />
<% } %>
<HTML>
  <HEAD><TITLE>Currency Form</TITLE></HEAD>
  <BODY>
    <H1>Simple Currency Converter</H1>
    <% String amount = request.getParameter("amount"); %>
    <% if (amount!=null && amount.length()>0) { %>
      <P><BIG>
        <jsp:setProperty name="converter" property="amount" />
        Requested Conversion:
            <jsp:getProperty name="converter" property="amount" /> =
            <jsp:getProperty name="converter" property="poundValue" />
      </BIG></P>
    <% } %>
    <FORM>
      <INPUT TYPE="HIDDEN" NAME="exchangeRate"
          VALUE="<%=converter.getExchangeRate()%>">
      <P>Use this form to convert US Dollars to UK Pounds Sterling</P>
      Type in the amount to be converted in the box
      <INPUT TYPE="TEXT" NAME="amount">
      <INPUT TYPE="SUBMIT">
    </FORM>
  </BODY>
</HTML>
```

The JSP in Listing 8.3 fulfills two functions:

- Displaying the conversion of a previously supplied value
- Displaying a form for entering a new value

The first time the JSP is displayed, there will be no form parameters provided. The Java scripting code at the top of the form will use the default exchange rate rather than the one supplied on the form as a hidden field. The `if` statement in the Java scriptlet after the `<H1>` heading suppresses the display of a converted value passed as a request parameter.

The currency conversion form at the bottom of the page is always displayed, and the hidden field called amount is initialized with the exchange rate from the `CurrencyConverterBean`.

When the user submits this form, the two form parameters define the exchange rate and the amount to convert. The Java scripting code will set the converter bean's exchange rate to the value provided with the request and then display the converted value using this defined exchange rate.

In this example, the hidden form parameter ensures the same conversion rate is applied for all conversions until the conversion pages are accessed once again without the `exchangeRate` parameter.

Several hidden fields can be used to track different items of information. Be aware that the recommended size limit of an HTTP `GET` request is 255 characters so the `POST` request should be used when large numbers of form parameters are used.

As a general policy, you should consider using the `POST` method for returning form data with hidden fields, as this prevents the user from bookmarking the page and its data. When the user returns to a bookmarked page there will be no `POST` parameters and your application can

- Generate a new form with appropriate hidden fields
- Forward the request to a suitable "starting" page that will take the user through the appropriate Web pages to reach the one that was bookmarked
- Display an error page indicating that the page cannot be bookmarked

CAUTION

Malicious users can and will examine and modify the values of hidden fields, so you should be careful about how they are used. A suggested approach is to store the data on the server in a Java collection such as a map or in a database, and use the hidden field to keep a key for accessing the relevant data from the map.

URL Rewriting

URL rewriting is used to pass additional information with a page request or to implement servlet session tracking when the client disables cookies. Manual URL rewriting can be used in the same manner as with hidden fields but is not just restricted to HTML forms.

There are three common forms of URL rewriting:

- Using Tomcat to add the session ID to a URL on a Web page
- Appending parameters to the `GET` request
- Appending extra path information to the URL

Tracking Servlet Sessions with URL Rewriting

The usual meaning of URL rewriting is to support servlet sessions for clients that do not support cookies. The servlet `HttpServletResponse` object supports URL rewriting via the `encodeURL()` method. A string representing the target URL is passed to the `encodeURL()` method, which will add session information to the URL if required. If the client supports cookies or sessions are disabled, the `encodeURL()` returns the URL unchanged.

If the client has disabled cookies, the string returned from `encodeURL()` includes the session ID information at the end of the URL. The following example shows how the URL `/session/session-rewrite` is rewritten to include the Tomcat session ID:

```
/session/session-rewrite;jsessionid=2815652F930426EC91B351970C43F304
```

For robust session tracking, all URLs used on a servlet or JSP Web page should be generated using `encodeURL()`. Otherwise, the servlet session object cannot be used with browsers that do not support cookies.

There is an equivalent `encodeRedirectURL()` that should be used when redirecting HTTP requests to another page (such as using the `HttpServletResponse.sendRedirect()` method).

Listing 8.4 shows how the JSP presented in Listing 8.2 should have been written to support URL rewriting. The form's `action` attribute is encoded to ensure this page supports sessions when the client does not support cookies.

LISTING 8.4 URL Rewriting on the `session-rewrite.jsp`

```
<%@ page import="java.util.*" %>
<%
    // add parameter to session
    String name = request.getParameter("name");
    String value = request.getParameter("value");
    if (name!=null && value!=null && name.length()>0) {
        session.setAttribute(name,value);
```

LISTING 8.4 Continued

```
    }
    Date lastVisit = (Date)session.getAttribute("lastVisit");
    Date thisVisit = new Date();
%>
<HTML>
    <HEAD>
        <TITLE>Session List</TITLE>
    </HEAD>
    <BODY>
        <H1>Session List</H1>
        Last visit: <%= lastVisit %><BR>
        This visit: <%= thisVisit %><BR>
        Session ID: <%= session.getId() %><BR>
        Session max interval: <%= session.getMaxInactiveInterval() %><BR>

        <H2>Session parameters</H2>
        <%
            Enumeration enum = session.getAttributeNames();
            while (enum.hasMoreElements()) {
                String attribute = (String) enum.nextElement();
                out.println(""+attribute+"="+
                    session.getAttribute(attribute)+"<BR>");
            }
            session.setAttribute("lastVisit",thisVisit);
        %>

        <H2>New session parameter</H2>
        <% String url = response.encodeURL("session-rewrite"); %>
        <P>Form URL '<%= url %>'</P>
        <FORM ACTION='<%= url %>'>
            <P>Name: <INPUT TYPE='TEXT' NAME='name'></P>
            <P>Value: <INPUT TYPE='TEXT' NAME='value'></P>
            <INPUT TYPE='SUBMIT' VALUE='Add new value'>
        </FORM>
    </BODY>
</HTML>
```

The example in Listing 8.4 displays the form URL on the Web page so that you can see the generated URL without resorting to the browser's view source functionality.

TIP

All URLs in a servlet or JSP should be passed through `response.encodeURL()` to ensure your application will work with clients that do not support cookies.

Adding Data Using URL Parameters

The first form of manual URL rewriting simply adds arbitrary request parameters into the `HREF` attribute of a hypertext link (the `<A>` element). The following code fragment shows how an HTML page could call the `currency-converter.jsp` page shown in Listing 8.3 with a number of preset exchange rates:

```
<P><A HREF="currency-converter.jsp?">
    Conversion using current rates</A></P>
<P><A HREF="currency-converter.jsp?exchangeRate=0.632">
    Conversion using previous weeks average rate</A></P>
<P><A HREF="currency-converter.jsp?exchangeRate=0.690">
    Conversion using previous months average rate</A></P>
<P><A HREF="currency-converter.jsp?exchangeRate=0.702">
    Conversion using previous years average rate</A></P>
```

Obviously, in a real application the conversion rates would be obtained from a data source such as a database (see Chapter 9, "Databases and Tomcat") or a Web service (see Chapter 25, "Web Services and Axis") rather than use simple hard-coded values as shown here.

When using URL parameters you must ensure they conform to the RFC2277 encoding scheme (discussed in Chapter 3). You should use the `java.net.URLEncoder.encode()` method to encode your URL parameters within your servlet or JSP.

Adding Data Using URL Extra Path Information

A second form of manual URL rewriting is to include additional information after the servlet pathname. Using the example from the previous section—including the exchange rate with the URL—this can be done using the URL extra path as follows:

```
<P><A HREF="converterPath/0.632">
    Conversion using previous weeks average rate</A></P>
```

In order to use the extra path information, you must use the URL mapping features of servlets and JSPs. To run this example you will have to add the following elements to the `web.xml` file to give the new currency converter the name `converterPath`:

```
<servlet>
  <servlet-name>CurrencyConverter</servlet-name>
```

```
  <jsp-file>/currency-converter-path.jsp</jsp-file>
</servlet>
<servlet-mapping>
  <servlet-name>CurrencyConverter</servlet-name>
  <url-pattern>/converterPath/*</url-pattern>
</servlet-mapping>
```

The JSP matches any URL pattern starting with `/converterPath/` as defined by the pattern `/converterPath/*`.

To complete this example, the JSP must use the extra path information for the exchange rate. The method `HttpRequest.getPathInfo()` returns the variable path-name component of the URL. Listing 8.5 shows how this information can be used to define the exchange rate at the start of the revised JSP.

LISTING 8.5 The Text of `currency-converter-path.jsp`

```
<jsp:useBean id="converter"
    class="converters.CurrencyConverterBean" scope="page"/>
<%
  String info = request.getPathInfo();
  if (info != null) {
    converter.setExchangeRate(Double.parseDouble(info.substring(1)));
  }
%>
<HTML>
  <HEAD><TITLE>Currency Form</TITLE></HEAD>
  <BODY>
    <H1>Simple Currency Converter</H1>
    <% String amount = request.getParameter("amount"); %>
    <% if (amount!=null && amount.length()>0) { %>
      <P><BIG>
        <jsp:setProperty name="converter" property="amount" />
        Requested Conversion:
            <jsp:getProperty name="converter" property="amount" /> =
            <jsp:getProperty name="converter" property="poundValue" />
      </BIG></P>
    <% } %>
    <FORM ACTION="converterPath/<%=converter.getExchangeRate()%>">
      <P>Use this form to convert US Dollars to UK Pounds Sterling</P>
      Type in the amount to be converted in the box
      <INPUT TYPE="TEXT" NAME="amount">
      <INPUT TYPE="SUBMIT">
```

LISTING 8.5 Continued

```
    </FORM>
  </BODY>
</HTML>
```

In Listing 8.5, the form for submitting the conversion value must include the extra path information to define the conversion rate. This is achieved as follows:

```
<FORM ACTION="converterPath/<%=converter.getExchangeRate()%>">
```

Extra path information provides a convenient method of passing data from one Web page to another but requires references to every URL within the Web application to be modified to include the session data.

Summary

Session information is a necessary part of many Web applications. Web pages no longer need to work in isolation but can cooperate to produce a more functional system. A session tracks the activity of a single client accessing several Web pages. Data must be shared across the cooperating Web pages to create the concept of a session.

HTTP is a stateless protocol and does not support session data. Session tracking must be implemented at the Web application level.

The preferred approach to session tracking is to use the `HttpSession` object that is created and managed by Tomcat. The session object is used to store arbitrary objects against names. Separate Web pages can store and retrieve data in the session.

Tomcat uses cookies to store a session ID on the client. This cookie is passed with every Web request and enables Tomcat to associate the session data with each page request from the client. Session data has a limited duration; by default, Tomcat will time-out session data after 30 minutes of client inactivity. If the client disables cookies, Tomcat supports sessions using URL rewriting. To support URL rewriting in your applications, all URLs on a Web page must be generated using the `HttpServletResponse.encodeURL()` method.

Servlet and JSP developers can use cookies to store information on the client. Cookie data is associated with a domain name and pathname (essentially a URL) and is passed with every request to the appropriate URL. Cookies potentially have long lifetimes—typically days or months but this can be indefinite. This makes them useful for storing non-critical information on the client. A common use of cookies is to enable clients to customize a Web site by storing user preference information on the client.

The use of hidden fields on HTML forms, GET request parameters, and URL extra path information are alternative mechanisms for transferring data between one Web page and another.

9

Databases and Tomcat

IN THIS CHAPTER

- Using JDBC and Data Sources
- Direct JDBC Database Access
- Tomcat Data Sources
- Data Access Objects (DAOs)
- Security Considerations

Most Web applications need to store information on a temporary or permanent basis. The most common repository for data storage is the ubiquitous relational database. In this chapter you will be using databases from within Tomcat Web applications using both direct JDBC access and the preferred approach of JNDI data sources. The Data Access Object (DAO) design pattern is shown as a method of encapsulating database access into a reusable component.

Using JDBC and Data Sources

Tomcat servlets and JSPs use JDBC in the same manner as any other Java program. In many Java programs, it is normal to ask the user to provide a username and password for database access. With Web applications, you would typically use a single database account for all users and encode the account name and password within either the servlet or JSP, or encapsulate database access using a data source (see the section "Tomcat Data Sources") or a DAO (see the section "Data Access Objects (DAOs)"). You must then add the business logic of the application to enforce any user security authorization and ensure the data integrity of the database.

The disadvantage to using JDBC from within a servlet is that the JDBC driver class, database connection string, user account name, and password are all hard-coded into the program. The hard-coded database details link the servlet to a specific database, complicating the move from a development environment (with test data) to a production environment (potentially using a different database supplier). Hard-coded details always reduce portability of code and should be avoided if at all possible.

A common approach in reducing coupling of the servlet to the database is to provide the database connection parameters using servlet initialization parameters (see the `<init-params>` element discussion in Chapter 7, "The Web Application Environment"). If in the future you change database vendors, move the database to a new server, move the tables into a new database, change the username, or change the password, you can do so without modifying the Java servlet (or JSP). This is a good technique; but, as you will be shown, there are other performance problems that suggest you shouldn't use direct JDBC access from within a servlet.

A connection pooling data source provides a solution to both the hard coding of database access details and the performance issues inherent in using direct database access. This chapter describes how to use Tomcat data sources after briefly discussing, and rejecting, using direct JDBC access from within a servlet.

Before we describe direct JDBC access and data sources, you need a bit of background information about the database tables and sample data used for the examples.

The Sample Database

Continuing with the currency converter example application, the code examples in this chapter use a currency definition table called `Currency` and a database exchange rate table called `Exchange`. The `Currency` table has columns for the ISO 4217 currency `name` as well as the currency's ISO `country` name and ISO `language`. The `Exchange` table has columns that define the three-character ISO 4217 code for the currency to convert from (`src`) and to (`dst`). The `rate` column defines the appropriate exchange rate. The two tables can be created in any SQL database with the following SQL:

```
create table Currency(
    language varchar(2),
    country varchar(2),
    name varchar(3)
);
create table Exchange(
    src varchar(3),
    dst varchar(3),
    rate double
);
```

You will need to create this table in your database and add some sample data in order to use the examples presented in this chapter. The following SQL will populate the table with suitable data:

```
insert into Currency values ('en','CA', 'CAD');
insert into Currency values ('de','DE', 'EUR');
insert into Currency values ('en','GB', 'GBP');
insert into Currency values ('en','US', 'USD');
```

```
insert into Exchange values ('CAD','EUR', 0.6955);
insert into Exchange values ('CAD','USD', 0.6376);
insert into Exchange values ('CAD','GBP', 0.4344);
insert into Exchange values ('EUR','CAD', 1.4376);
insert into Exchange values ('EUR','GBP', 0.6246);
insert into Exchange values ('EUR','USD', 0.9166);
insert into Exchange values ('GBP','CAD', 2.3019);
insert into Exchange values ('GBP','EUR', 1.6011);
insert into Exchange values ('GBP','USD', 1.4676);
insert into Exchange values ('USD','CAD', 1.5685);
insert into Exchange values ('USD','EUR', 1.0909);
insert into Exchange values ('USD','GBP', 0.6813);
```

TIP

The `CreateDB.java` program available from the accompanying Web site for this book (browse to `http://www.samspublishing.com` and search for the ISBN 0-672-32439-3) can be used to create and populate the sample database tables.

NOTE

The examples in this chapter use the MySQL database available from `http://www.mysql.com`. MySQL is a popular, open source, SQL database available under the GNU General Public License (`http://www.gnu.org/`). Several JDBC drivers are available for MySQL. This chapter uses the MM.MySQL JDBC driver that is also provided under the GNU General Public License and is downloadable from the MySQL Web site. The MM.MySQL JDBC driver class name is `org.gjt.mm.mysql.Driver`. The examples use a JDBC connect string of `jdbc:mysql://localhost/test` to access the MySQL `test` database, which has been configured with a user account called `root`, password `secret`.

Now that you've finished the database configuration, let's take a closer look at using databases with Tomcat.

Direct JDBC Database Access

Any JDBC-compliant database can be used with Tomcat provided the necessary supporting classes are available. If the JDBC driver for a database is provided as a JAR file, this JAR file must be added to the `<CATALINA_HOME>/common/lib` directory; otherwise, the Tomcat 4.1 class loader will not be able to load the driver.

NOTE

The restriction of placing JDBC driver JAR files in `<CATALINA_HOME>/common/lib` applies to the Tomcat 4.1 beta release. Under Tomcat 4.0, you may also store the JAR files in the `WEB-INF/lib` or `<CATALINA_HOME>/lib` directory.

A Simple Database Servlet

The first example program shown in Listing 9.1 is a simple servlet that uses a database to display the exchange rate for converting UK pounds sterling (GBP) to US dollars (USD).

LISTING 9.1 The Simple Database Program `DatabaseRates.java`

```
import java.io.*;
import java.sql.*;
import javax.sql.*;
import javax.servlet.*;
import javax.servlet.http.*;
import java.util.*;

public class DatabaseRates extends HttpServlet
{
    public void doGet(HttpServletRequest request,
➥ HttpServletResponse response)
    throws ServletException, IOException
    {
        response.setContentType("text/html");
        PrintWriter out = response.getWriter();
        Connection con = null;
        out.println ("<HTML><HEAD><TITLE>Conversion Rates");
        out.println ("</TITLE></HEAD><BODY>");
        out.println("<H1>Conversion Rates</H1>");

        try {
            Class.forName("org.gjt.mm.mysql.Driver");
            con = DriverManager.getConnection(
➥ "jdbc:mysql://localhost/test","root","secret");
            PreparedStatement pstmt = con.prepareStatement(
➥ "SELECT rate FROM Exchange WHERE src = ? and dst = ?");
            pstmt.setString(1,"GBP");
            pstmt.setString(2,"USD");
            ResultSet results = pstmt.executeQuery();
            if (!results.next())
                throw new SQLException("Missing Exchange rate data row");
            double rate = results.getDouble(1);
            out.println("GBP to USD rate = "+rate+"<BR>");
            pstmt.setString(1,"EUR");
            pstmt.setString(2,"USD");
```

LISTING 9.1 Continued

```
            results = pstmt.executeQuery();
            if (!results.next())
                throw new SQLException("Missing Exchange rate data row");
            rate = results.getDouble(1);
            out.println("EUR to USD rate = "+rate+"<BR>");
        }
        catch (Exception ex)
        {
            out.println("<H2>Exception Occurred</H2>");
            out.println(ex);
            if (ex instanceof SQLException) {
                SQLException sqlex = (SQLException) ex;
                out.println("SQL state: "+sqlex.getSQLState()+"<BR>");
                out.println("Error code: "+sqlex.getErrorCode()+"<BR>");
            }
        }
        finally {
            try { con.close(); } catch (Exception ex) {}
        }
        out.println ("</BODY></HTML>");
    }
}
```

NOTE

The error handling in Listing 9.1 and all other examples in this chapter is designed to aid development and debugging. Chapter 12, "Error Handling," discusses techniques for incorporating user-friendly error handling for a live application.

Although the example in Listing 9.1 works and is thread-safe, there are a large number of problems:

- The JDBC driver, database, username, and password are hard-coded into the program.
- Every HTTP request must open a new connection to the database.
- The database access code and the HTML presentation code are inextricably intermixed within the servlet.

As previously discussed, hard-coded database details always reduce portability of code and should be avoided if at all possible.

Opening a database connection for every request will result in slower performance and may overload the database server because creating new client connections is a resource-intensive operation. In addition, as you have already been shown, the mixing of business logic and data presentation in a single class is a sign of poor system design and makes code maintenance a nightmare. Each of the problems just identified can be resolved using standard tools and design techniques as discussed later in this chapter.

A Bad Example Servlet

Before studying the correct approach to database access using data sources, a common technique suggested by some online tutorials and textbooks will be examined and rejected due to the complications inherent in the approach.

In order to improve performance, you might think of moving the database connection code into the `HttpServlet.init()` method as follows:

```
public class DatabaseRates extends HttpServlet
    implements SingleThreadModel
{
    Connection con;
    PreparedStatement pstmt ;
    public void init() throws ServletException
    {
        try {
            Class.forName("org.gjt.mm.mysql.Driver");
            con = DriverManager.getConnection(
➥ "jdbc:mysql://localhost/test","root","secret");
            pstmt = con.prepareStatement(
➥ "SELECT rate FROM Exchange WHERE src = ? and dst = ?");
        }
        catch (SQLException ex) {
            throw new ServletException(
➥ "Cannot create database connection",ex);
        }
    }
...
```

This is a technique you should not adopt. By attempting to improve performance in this manner, you create a whole range of other potential problems:

- The `Connection` and `PreparedStatement` instance variables are not multi-thread–safe, and the servlet must now implement the `SingleThreadModel`, which will degrade servlet performance and scalability.
- The database connection is kept open for the lifetime of the servlet instance and this may affect database performance and scalability. If you adopt the same approach for many servlets, you will use up large numbers of database connections for servlets that are idle for a lot of the time. You may even have to reconfigure your database to support an unusually large number of connections.
- A database may time out a connection that is kept open for too long or one that remains idle for specified period of time. If this happens, you will have to add code to your servlet to deal with a closed connection, further complicating the logic of your servlet.

You can address these problems by using the servlet `init()` method to cache the exchange rate in an instance variable when the servlet is first accessed. All subsequent accesses will use the cached rate rather than access the database. But this approach cannot handle the real-world situation where the exchange rate varies over time. To solve this problem, the servlet must periodically update the cached exchange rate from the master value stored in the database. You then have the problem of deciding on a suitable algorithm for updating the cached exchange rate and adding additional database access code. This adds complications to the servlet that can be avoided simply by using connection pooling.

Connection Pooling

To improve database performance, you should use a technique known as *connection pooling*. This approach involves implementing a broker class that encapsulates access to the database. Typically the connection broker class has a `getConnection()` method that returns a proxy object that can partake in connection pooling. In other words, the connections do not connect directly to the database but will share a pool of available connections. New connections are added to the pool if demand exceeds current capacity, and excess connections can be closed down during idle periods.

As far as your written code is concerned, the connection behaves like a normal JDBC connection but the connection broker manages the pool of actual connections to the database.

Connection pooling is a well-understood technique, and many JDBC driver suppliers provide connection pooling implementations with their drivers. The J2EE specification has extended the JDBC support to include the `DataSource` class that may be used to support connection pooling in a portable manner.

Tomcat has adopted the J2EE specification and uses the `javax.sql.DataSource` class to provide connection pooling as discussed in the next section, "Tomcat Data Sources."

NOTE

If you want to use connection pooling outside of Tomcat, or do not want to use the Tomcat data source implementation, then there are several open-source connection pooling implementations available from the Internet. A popular, freely available broker that works with any JDBC driver is `DbConnectionBroker`, which is available from `http://www.javaexchange.com`.

Tomcat Data Sources

The recommended approach for accessing databases from Tomcat is to use the Database Connection Pool (DBCP) connection broker incorporated into Tomcat. DBCP is part of the Jakarta commons subproject that can be found at `http://jakarta.apache.org/commons`. DBCP has many advantages for Web application developers:

- It supports connection pooling.
- It manages the database driver and connection URL information.
- It is J2EE compliant.
- It is a standard component of Tomcat.

Not all beta releases of the Tomcat 4.1 archive included the DBCP package. If the DBCP package is not included in your Tomcat 4.1 archive, you will need to download and install DBCP yourself. If your Tomcat archive contains the file `<CATALINA_HOME>/common/lib/commons-dbcp.jar`, DBCP is included with Tomcat.

If DBCP is not included with your Tomcat archive, download it from `http://jakarta.apache.org/builds/jakarta-commons`. At the time of writing this book (mid-2002), DBCP had not yet reached the release milestone build and must be downloaded from the latest nightly build at `http://jakarta.apache.org/builds/jakarta-commons/nightly/commons-dbcp/`. If a release version is available from `http://jakarta.apache.org/builds/jakarta-commons/release/commons-dbcp/`, you should use it in preference to a nightly build.

Download and extract the `commons-dbcp.tar` archive and copy the `commons-dbcp.jar` to `<CATALINA_HOME>/common/lib`.

DBCP uses the Jakarta Commons Pool package. At the time of this writing, the commons-pool package was at release 1.0, if a later release is available you should use it.

The `commons-pool-1.0.tar` archive must be downloaded from `http://builds/jakarta-commons/release/commons-pool/`. Move the `commons-pool.jar` from the extracted archive to `<CATALINA_HOME>/common/lib`.

After the `commons-dbcp.jar` and `commons-pool.jar` files are stored in `<CATALINA_HOME>/common/lib`, you can use the Tomcat data sources as described in the rest of this section. If the DBCP classes are not included with Tomcat, you will receive a "`javax.naming.NamingException`: Cannot create resource instance" error when accessing the data source.

> **NOTE**
>
> Tomcat 4.0 uses a third-party connection broker called Tyrex (see `http://www.tyrex.com`) which has been replaced by the DBCP connection broker. Tyrex has the same functionality and advantages as DBCP and is included with the Tomcat 4.0 download.

A minor complexity to using DBCP is that it uses the Java Naming Directory Interface (JNDI), and you have to configure the JNDI data source before you can use it. Here you will be shown how to define a JDBC data source without any unnecessary background information about JNDI.

To use a Tomcat data source you will have to

- Define a JNDI resource reference in your Web application deployment descriptor
- Map the JNDI resource reference onto a real resource (database connection) in the context of your application
- Look up the JNDI data source resource reference in your code to obtain a pooled database connection

Defining a Resource Reference

First, you will need a JNDI name for your database connection; conventionally it should begin with `jdbc/`. The example uses the name `jdbc/conversion`. Now add a `<resource-ref>` element to the `web.xml` file for your Web application to define the data source as follows:

```
<resource-ref>
  <res-ref-name>jdbc/conversion</res-ref-name>
  <res-type>javax.sql.DataSource</res-type>
  <res-auth>Container</res-auth>
</resource-ref>
```

The <res-ref-name> element identifies the resource reference name, the <res-type> entry defines the reference as a JDBC data source, and the <res-auth> specifies that resource authentication is applied by the Container. The <resource-ref> element must be added after any <servlet-mapping> elements in the deployment descriptor.

Defining the Resource

Second, you must add an entry for the database resource to the <CATALINA_HOME>/conf/server.xml file by adding a <ResourceParams> element to define the database connection information. The <ResourceParams> can be defined inside the <DefaultContext> tag to be available to all Web applications, or it can be defined inside the <Context> element for a specific application.

A suitable Tomcat 4.1 <ResourceParams> element for the example database is shown in the following listing (Tomcat 4.0 uses different attribute names as explained in the notes):

```
<Context path="/database" docBase="database" debug="0"
         reloadable="true" >
  <ResourceParams name="jdbc/conversion">
    <parameter>
      <name>username</name>
      <value>root</value>
    </parameter>
    <parameter>
      <name>password</name>
      <value>secret</value>
    </parameter>
    <parameter>
      <name>driverClassName</name>
      <value>org.gjt.mm.mysql.Driver</value>
    </parameter>
    <parameter>
      <name>url</name>
      <value>jdbc:mysql://localhost/test</value>
    </parameter>
  </ResourceParams>
</Context>
```

In the <ResourceParams> element example, the name attribute must exactly match the <res-ref-name> value you defined in the <resource-ref> element of the web.xml file.

NOTE

As an alternative to using resource references in an application's `web.xml` file, you can define the resource using a `<Resource>` element in the `server.xml` file. You can add a `<resource>` element to the `<Context>` element for an individual application or to the `<DefaultContext>` element to define the resource for all Web applications. The `<Resource>` definition for the example JDBC data source is

```
<Resource name="jdbc/conversion"
          auth="Container"
          type="javax.sql.DataSource"/>
```

The various `<ResourceParams>` components define the database connection parameters as follows:

Parameter	Value
`username`	Username for the database (`root`); under Tomcat 4.0 this attribute is called `user`
`password`	Password for the user root (`secret`)
`driverClassName`	Driver class for the database connection (`org.gjt.mm.mysql.Driver`)
`url`	JDBC connection string for the database (`jdbc:mysql://localhost/test`); under Tomcat 4.0 this attribute is called `driverName`

CAUTION

The `server.xml` file contains the unencrypted password for accessing the database. This file should be secured so that unauthorized users cannot read it.

The `<ResourceParams>` element in the `server.xml` file encapsulates all the information required to access the database. When moving your application from a development environment to a live environment, you need only change the values for the parameters in the `server.xml` file. Neither the Java code nor the `web.xml` resource reference entry need to be modified.

Using Tomcat data sources decouples the database vendor connection details from the servlet code and gives you the performance benefits gained from using a connection pool. Put simply, always use Tomcat's data sources when accessing a database.

CAUTION

When using data sources with both Tomcat 4.1 and Tomcat 4.0, you must place the JDBC JAR file for your database driver in the `<CATALINA_HOME>/common/lib` directory; otherwise, Tomcat will not be able to load the JDBC driver.

Obtaining the Data Source Connection

When you are using resource references in your application, you must use JNDI to look up and access the resource. You will have to import the `javax.naming` package to use JNDI. Note that the JNDI methods shown below can throw a `javax.naming.NamingException` error.

The name you defined in the `<res-ref-name>` element is the JNDI name you must use in your code. In order to resolve the resource associated with this name, you must obtain the JNDI context for your Web application. Use the `javax.naming.Context.lookup()` method to look up the data source and obtain a database connection as shown in the following code:

```
Context init = new InitialContext();
Context ctx = (Context) init.lookup("java:comp/env");
DataSource ds = (DataSource) ctx.lookup("jdbc/conversion");
Connection con = ds.getConnection();
```

Use this `Connection` object just like a normal JDBC connection. Listing 9.2 shows the simple database example rewritten to use the JNDI data source shown in the previous examples.

LISTING 9.2 Using a `DataSource` Object in `DataSourceRates.java`

```
import java.io.*;
import java.sql.*;
import javax.naming.*;
import javax.sql.*;
import javax.servlet.*;
import javax.servlet.http.*;
import java.util.*;

public class DataSourceRates extends HttpServlet
{
    private DataSource dataSource;
```

LISTING 9.2 Continued

```
public void init(ServletConfig config) throws ServletException {
    try {
        Context init = new InitialContext();
        Context ctx = (Context) init.lookup("java:comp/env");
        dataSource = (DataSource) ctx.lookup("jdbc/conversion");
    }
    catch (NamingException ex) {
        throw new ServletException(
            "Cannot retrieve java:comp/env/jdbc/conversion",ex);
    }
}

public void doGet(HttpServletRequest request, HttpServletResponse response)
throws ServletException, IOException
{
    response.setContentType("text/html");
    PrintWriter out = response.getWriter();
    Connection con = null;
    out.println ("<HTML><HEAD><TITLE>Conversion Rates</TITLE></HEAD><BODY>");
    out.println("<H1>Conversion Rates</H1>");

    try {
        synchronized (dataSource) {
            con = dataSource.getConnection();
        }
        PreparedStatement pstmt = con.prepareStatement(
            "SELECT rate FROM Exchange WHERE src = ? and dst = ?");
        pstmt.setString(1,"GBP");
        pstmt.setString(2,"USD");
        ResultSet results = pstmt.executeQuery();
        if (!results.next())
            throw new SQLException("Missing Exchange rate data row");
        double rate = results.getDouble(1);
        out.println("GBP to USD rate = "+rate+"<BR>");
        pstmt.setString(1,"EUR");
        pstmt.setString(2,"USD");
        results = pstmt.executeQuery();
        if (!results.next())
            throw new SQLException("Missing Exchange rate data row");
        rate = results.getDouble(1);
        out.println("EUR to USD rate = "+rate+"<BR>");
    }
```

LISTING 9.2 Continued

```
        catch (Exception ex)
        {
            out.println("<H2>Exception Occurred</H2>");
            out.println(ex);
            if (ex instanceof SQLException) {
                SQLException sqlex = (SQLException) ex;
                out.println("SQL state: "+sqlex.getSQLState()+"<BR>");
                out.println("Error code: "+sqlex.getErrorCode()+"<BR>");
            }
        }
        finally {
            try { con.close(); } catch (Exception ex) {}
        }
        out.println ("</BODY></HTML>");
    }
}
```

NOTE

To recap, to run the example in Listing 9.2, you must have defined the `<resource-ref>` element in `WEB-INF/web.xml` and the `<ResourceParams>` element in `<CATALINA_HOME>/conf/server.xml`. Furthermore, you must place your JDBC JAR file in the directory `<CATALINA_HOME>/common/lib` so the Tomcat class loader can load the driver correctly. You will need to stop and restart Tomcat in order for your changes to the `server.xml` file to be recognized.

In Listing 9.2, all the data source lookup code is added to the `init()` method to avoid the costly JNDI operations for every HTTP request. Because the `dataSource` instance variable is potentially shared across multiple threads, access to the variable must be from within a synchronized block.

The example in Listing 9.2 is an improvement over Listing 9.1, but it still has problems. The intermingling of HTML presentation code and database access code is less than ideal. You will now be shown how to refactor the example by using the Java design pattern (or idiom) called a Data Access Object.

Data Access Objects (DAOs)

A Data Access Object (DAO) encapsulates access to a database so that data manipulation code can be separated out from other business logic and data presentation code.

Good use of DAOs will simplify the design and development of Web applications and reduce the cost of ongoing maintenance and upgrades.

DAOs are a Java design pattern where all the database access code is encapsulated in supporting Java classes. Changes to the database details such as the table schema (column names and types) will usually only affect the DAO and not the Java code using the DAO. Combining the DAO with a Tomcat data source provides a good solution to using a database with Tomcat.

Listing 9.3 shows a JSP that uses a Java Bean DAO to display a table of currency exchange rates.

LISTING 9.3 The `rates.jsp` Page Using a DAO

```
<jsp:useBean id="dao" class="converters.ConversionDAO" scope="page" >
    <jsp:setProperty name="dao" property='*'/>
</jsp:useBean>
<% dao.updateRate(); %>
<HTML>
  <HEAD><TITLE>Currency Conversion Rates</TITLE></HEAD>
  <BODY>
    <H1>Conversion Rates</H1>
    GBP to USD rate = <%= dao.selectRate("GBP","USD") %><BR>
    EUR to USD rate = <%= dao.selectRate("EUR","USD") %><BR>
    EUR to GBP rate = <%= dao.selectRate("EUR","GBP") %><BR>
    <H1>Update Rate</H1>
    <FORM>
        <TABLE>
            <TR>
                <TD>Convert from:</TD>
                <TD><SELECT NAME='src'>
                    <OPTION>EUR<OPTION>GBP<OPTION>USD
                    </SELECT></TD>
                <TD>to:</TD>
                <TD><SELECT NAME='dst'>
                    <OPTION>EUR<OPTION>GBP<OPTION>USD
                    </SELECT></TD>
            </TR>
            <TR>
                <TD>Rate:</TD>
                <TD COLSPAN='3'><INPUT TYPE='text' NAME='rate'></TD>
            </TR>
        </TABLE>
        <P> <INPUT TYPE='submit' VALUE='Set new Rate'> </P>
```

LISTING 9.3 Continued

```
    </FORM>
  </BODY>
</HTML>
```

The first thing that should strike you about Listing 9.3 is the absence of complex Java code and any database access code. The beginning of the page creates the DAO as a Java Bean and sets the properties of the DAO that match the HTTP request parameters by using the element

```
<jsp:setProperty name="dao" property='*'/>
```

The DAO has been designed so that the properties reflect the three columns of the underlying `Exchange` table (`src`, `dst`, and `rate`). If the HTTP request parameters include these three properties, the DAO's `updateRate()` method will update the underlying `Exchange` table with a new exchange rate. The line

```
<% dao.updateRate(); %>
```

will update an existing exchange rate with parameters supplied with the HTTP request.

The main part of the JSP uses the DAO bean to display the exchange rates for three currencies (EUR, GBP, and USD) and displays a simple form for updating a conversion rate. Filling in a new conversion rate and submitting the form will invoke this JSP to update the database (using the `<% dao.updateRate(); %>` action coded at the top of the page).

The DAO is not complicated, as shown in Listing 9.4.

LISTING 9.4 The `ConversionDAO.Java` Data Access Object

```
package converters;

import java.io.*;
import java.sql.*;
import javax.naming.*;
import javax.sql.*;
import java.util.*;

public class ConversionDAO
{
    private Connection con;
    private PreparedStatement select;
```

LISTING 9.4 Continued

```
    private PreparedStatement update;
    private String src;
    private String dst;
    private double rate;

    public ConversionDAO() throws SQLException, NamingException
    {
        Context init = new InitialContext();
        Context ctx = (Context) init.lookup("java:comp/env");
        DataSource ds = (DataSource) ctx.lookup("jdbc/conversion");
        con = ds.getConnection();
        select = con.prepareStatement(
➥ "SELECT rate FROM Exchange WHERE src = ? AND dst = ?");
        update = con.prepareStatement(
➥ "UPDATE Exchange SET rate = ? WHERE src = ? AND dst = ?");
    }

    public String getSrc() { return src;}
    public String getDst() { return dst;}
    public double getRate() { return rate;}
    public void setSrc(String src) { this.src = src;}
    public void setDst(String dst) { this.dst = dst;}
    public void setRate(double rate) { this.rate = rate;}

    public double selectRate(String src, String dst) throws SQLException
    {
        ResultSet results = null;
        try {
            select.setString(1,src);
            select.setString(2,dst);
            results = select.executeQuery();
            if (!results.next())
                throw new SQLException("Missing Exchange rate data row");
            return results.getDouble(1);
        }
        finally {
            try { results.close(); } catch (Exception ex) {}
        }
    }

    public int updateRate() throws SQLException
    {
```

LISTING 9.4 Continued

```
        if (src==null || dst==null)
            return 0;
        update.setDouble(1,rate);
        update.setString(2,src);
        update.setString(3,dst);
        return update.executeUpdate();
    }

    public void close()
    {
        try { select.close(); } catch (Exception ex) {}
        try { update.close(); } catch (Exception ex) {}
        try { con.close(); } catch (Exception ex) {}
    }
}
```

For simplicity, the examples in Listings 9.3 and 9.4 exclude any error-handling code. In Chapter 12, you will be shown how to use Web application error pages and other error-handling techniques that will enable you to enhance the JSP to deal gracefully with any underlying database or JNDI problems.

NOTE

You will need to deploy any DAO classes to the `WEB-INF/classes` directory together with the JSPs in your Web application.

An alternative technique for accessing a database from within a JSP is to use a custom tag to encapsulate the database access (see Chapter 11, "JSP Expression Language and JSTL").

That's it. You now know how to work with DAOs and data sources to access a JDBC database.

Security Considerations

Your main security problem concerns the coding of plain-text passwords in the `server.xml` file. You must ensure that only authorized users (ideally only the Tomcat administrator) can read the `server.xml` file.

One minor headache occurs if you configured Tomcat to use a security manager (see Chapter 14, "Access Control"). If you are accessing a database with a security manager, you will need to add appropriate permission lines to the `<CATALINA_HOME>/conf/catalina.policy` file to allow the Web application to connect to the database. You will need to add the following lines to the `catalina.policy` file (assuming the MySQL database is running on `localhost` using the default 3306 port):

```
grant codeBase "file:${catalina.home}/webapps/database/WEB-INF/classes/- {
    permission java.net.SocketPermission "localhost:3306", "connect";
};
```

If you use a different database, you will need to amend the database hostname and port number specified for the `java.net.SocketPermission` permission to match your database server configuration.

Tomcat does not use a security manager by default, so you will normally not have permission problems with database access.

Summary

Using a database with Tomcat is straightforward so long as you apply the following simple, well-known design criteria:

- Do not access the database directly from the servlet or JSP but encapsulate the database access in a Data Access Object (DAO) helper class. By putting all the database access code into a single class that is separate from the business and presentation logic of your application, you will simplify application maintenance and future feature enhancements.
- To obtain best performance, you should use a connection broker class that implements database connection pooling. Tomcat includes the DBCP connection broker that is compatible with any JDBC driver.

DBCP uses a JNDI resource reference to separate database connection details from database data access. This separation of database administration information is an invaluable aid in managing the deployment of a Web application in different environments. Moving an application from development, to test, to production environments is a simple administrative issue that will not require changes to the Java code of the application.

10

Custom Tags and TagLibs

IN THIS CHAPTER

- Writing a Simple Custom Tag
- Custom Tag Life Cycle
- Changing Custom Tag Behavior
- Iterative Tags
- Using Tag Extra Information Classes
- Exception Handling

Custom tags and tag libraries (TagLibs) together form another tool you can use to simplify the development of Java Server Pages. TagLibs are collections of user-defined tags that can be used within a JSP. A TagLib consists of

- A Tag Library Descriptor file (TLD) that specifies all the tags in the library
- A Java class file for every custom tag

It is possible with custom tags to remove most if not all of the Java code from a JSP, leaving a Web page that can be written and maintained by an HTML developer who does not necessarily have to know Java. For this to work successfully you will, of course, have to document carefully the interface to your custom tags.

Removing the Java code from the JSP greatly speeds up and simplifies development, as you can now resolve Java compilation errors while developing the custom tag rather than when deploying the JSP.

This chapter will examine the life cycle of a custom tag, including how XML attributes are passed into the tag and how the tag interacts with the processing of the JSP. In addition to simple tags that write information to the JSP, more complex tags that form cooperating tag hierarchies and iterative data processing structures will also be discussed.

At the time of this book's writing (mid-2002), a Java Standard Tag Library (JSTL) has just been finalized; this is discussed in Chapter 11, "JSP Expression Language and JSTL."

Writing a Simple Custom Tag

Writing a tag involves several steps:

1. Design the functionality to be encapsulated in the tag.
2. Write the Java class that implements the tag.
3. Define the tag in a Tag Library Definition file.
4. Use the tag on a JSP.

The example shown in the rest of this section is a simple tag called `<rate>` in a `converter` tag library. The `<rate>` tag simply writes the current exchange rate to the JSP and is shown in Listing 10.1.

LISTING 10.1 Custom `<rate>` Tag Used in `rate.jsp`

```
<%@ taglib uri="/converter" prefix="conv" %>
<HTML>
  <HEAD>
    <TITLE>USD to GBP Exchange Rate</TITLE>
  </HEAD>
  <BODY>
    <H1>USD to GBP Exchange Rate</H1>
    Current USD to GBP exchange rate is <conv:rate/>
  </BODY>
</HTML>
```

Whenever a JSP uses a TagLib, it must reference the appropriate Tag Library Definition (TLD) file using a JSP `taglib` directive at the start of the page. In Listing 10.1 the `<%@ taglib %>` directive defines the TLD using the `uri` attribute and the custom tag prefix namespace in the `prefix` attribute. It is usual for the prefix name to be the same as the `<short-name>` tag in the TLD (see the next section, "Creating the TLD"), but this is not strictly necessary.

Once the TagLib has been defined, any or all of the custom tags in the TLD can be used on the JSP. The custom tag names must be specified using the prefix defined in the `taglib` directive.

You must map the `uri` attribute of the JSP `taglib` directive onto the actual TLD file. Conventionally, TLD files are stored in the `WEB-INF` directory of your application.

Creating the TLD

Listing 10.2 shows the TLD file for the example `<rate>` tag. This TLD file provides the mapping between the tag name `rate` and an implementing class `converters.RateTag` shown later in Listing 10.4.

LISTING 10.2 A Simple Tag Library Descriptor (TLD) File: `converter.tld`

```
<?xml version="1.0" encoding="ISO-8859-1" ?>
<!DOCTYPE taglib PUBLIC
        "-//Sun Microsystems, Inc.//DTD JSP Tag Library 1.2//EN"
        "http://java.sun.com/dtd/web-jsptaglibrary_1_2.dtd">
<taglib>
  <tlib-version>1.0</tlib-version>
  <jsp-version>1.2</jsp-version>
  <short-name>conv</short-name>
  <tag>
    <name>rate</name>
    <tag-class>converters.RateTag</tag-class>
    <body-content>empty</body-content>
  </tag>
</taglib>
```

The TLD file in Listing 10.2 is an XML document that conforms to the Tag Library DTD defined on the Sun Microsystems Java Web site (`http://java.sun.com/dtd/web-jsptaglibrary_1_2.dtd`). The `<taglib>` root element of TLD document specifies the version numbers of the Tag Library and JSP specifications that this TLD conforms to. The `<short-name>` element defines the suggested prefix for the custom tags when they are referenced on the JSP page.

The `<taglib>` element is used to define one or more `<tag>` elements where each `<tag>` element describes the tag name, its implementing Java class, and any other relevant tag information. The full list of nested `<tag>` elements is shown by the following DTD extract:

```
<!ELEMENT tag (name, tag-class, tei-class?, body-content?,
  display-name?, small-icon?, large-icon?, description?,
  variable*, attribute*, example?) >
```

As you can see in Listing 10.2, the `<name>` is set to `rate`, the `<tag-class>` is set to `converters.RateTag`, and the `<body-content>` is set to `empty` to indicate that the tag should not have a body. Accidentally putting text between the start and end tags of this custom tag will cause a page translation error. Possible tag `<body-content>` values are

<body-content>	Definition
empty	The tag body must be empty.
JSP	The tag contains JSP data.
tagdependent	The text between the start and end tags will be processed by the Java class and not included on the page.

A TLD file must be included in a `<taglib>` element in the `web.xml` file for your application as shown in Listing 10.3.

LISTING 10.3 `web.xml` File for the Example `rate` Tag

```
<?xml version="1.0" encoding="UTF-8"?>

<!DOCTYPE web-app PUBLIC
  '-//Sun Microsystems, Inc.//DTD Web Application 2.3//EN'
  'http://java.sun.com/dtd/web-app_2_3.dtd'>

<web-app>
  <servlet>
    <servlet-name>Exchange Rate</servlet-name>
    <jsp-file>/rate.jsp</jsp-file>
  </servlet>
  <servlet-mapping>
    <servlet-name>Exchange Rate</servlet-name>
    <url-pattern>/rate</url-pattern>
  </servlet-mapping>
  <taglib>
    <taglib-uri>/converter</taglib-uri>
    <taglib-location>/WEB-INF/converter.tld</taglib-location>
  </taglib>
</web-app>
```

The `<taglib>` directive maps the TagLib URI onto the TLD file using the following elements:

- `<taglib-uri>` defines the `uri` attribute value used in `<%@ taglib %>` directive on the JSP.
- `<taglib-location>` defines the TLD filename.

You will need to include the TLD file with your Web application.

NOTE

On a JSP page, you can refer to a TLD using any URI, not just one within your own application. Doing so allows you to, for example, store one copy of a TLD on a Web server and refer to it from many applications instead of supplying the TLD with each application. The drawback to sharing a TLD file in this way is you must ensure any changes to the TLD do not render existing Web applications invalid. Of course, you can use versioning to circumvent this problem.

Writing the Java Tag Class

The Java class file for a <rate> tag is shown in Listing 10.4.

LISTING 10.4 Exchange Rate Tag Class `RateTag.java`

```
package converters;

import java.io.*;
import javax.servlet.jsp.*;
import javax.servlet.jsp.tagext.*;

public class RateTag extends TagSupport {
    private static final double exchangeRate = 0.613;
    public int doStartTag() throws JspException {
        try {
            pageContext.getOut().print(exchangeRate);
        } catch (IOException ex) {
            throw new JspTagException("RateTag: "+ex);
        }
        return SKIP_BODY;
    }
}
```

Custom tags must implement interfaces from the `java.servlet.jsp.tagext` package to allow them to interact with the JSP processing. To facilitate tag development, two supporting classes (`TagSupport` and `BodyTagSupport`) provide default implementations of these interfaces. A full description of the interfaces and support classes is included in the "Custom Tag Life Cycle" section later in this chapter.

A simple tag such as the `<rate>` example will extend the `TagSupport` class and override the `doStartTag()` method to write data to the JSP.

In Listing 10.4, the tag's `doStartTag()` method simply writes the current exchange rate to the JSP using the `JSPWriter` object from the `PageContext` object.

The pageContext instance variable is declared in the TagSupport super class. Note that the print() method of the JSPWriter can throw an IOException, and this exception must be caught, because it cannot be specified as a throws clause in the doStartTag() method signature.

The doStartTag() method must return a value to the JSP page processing mechanism to indicate how the body of the tag is to be processed. In the case of an empty tag such as the <rate> example, this value must be SKIP_BODY to tell the JSP processing to ignore the body of the tag.

You must include the tag implementation class with your Web application.

TIP

A TagLib can have many custom tags and you may find it more convenient to store the class files in a JAR file and deploy this to the WEB-INF/lib directory.

Figure 10.1 shows a browser accessing the example JSP shown in Listing 10.1.

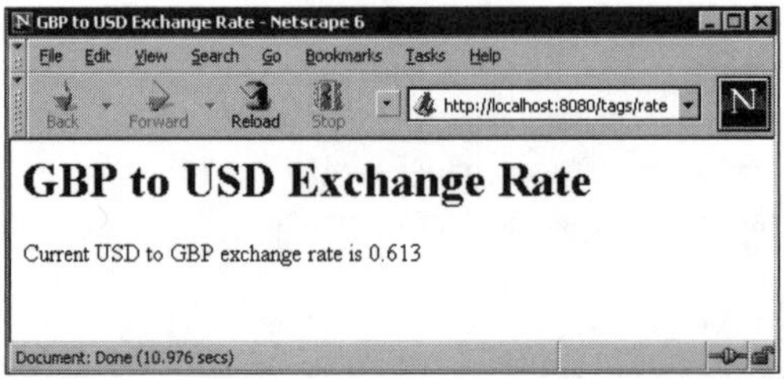

FIGURE 10.1 Browser accessing the rate.jsp Web page.

Custom Tag Life Cycle

The Java class that implements each tag interacts with the JSP page processing in a well-defined life cycle. A custom tag class must implement one or more of the following interfaces:

```
javax.servlet.jsp.tagext.Tag
javax.servlet.jsp.tagext.IterationTag
javax.servlet.jsp.tagext.BodyTag
```

It is usual for a custom class to extend one of the following tag support classes (in the javax.servlet.jsp.tagext package) rather than implement the interfaces directly:

Tag Support Class	Usage
`TagSupport`	Implements `Tag` and `IterationTag` interfaces. Extend this class for tags that do not need to process the tag body.
`BodyTagSupport`	Implements `Tag`, `IterationTag`, and `BodyTag` interfaces. Extend this class for tags that process the tag body.

As you will see, very few tags need to process the tag body in a tag dependent manner, so most custom tags will extend `TagSupport`. These tags will either have empty tag bodies or simple JSP text in the body.

Figure 10.2 shows how the methods defined in the three tag interfaces are called as a custom tag is processed when the JSP processing mechanism builds the response to return to the client. The interaction methods of the life cycle are explained in the following sections.

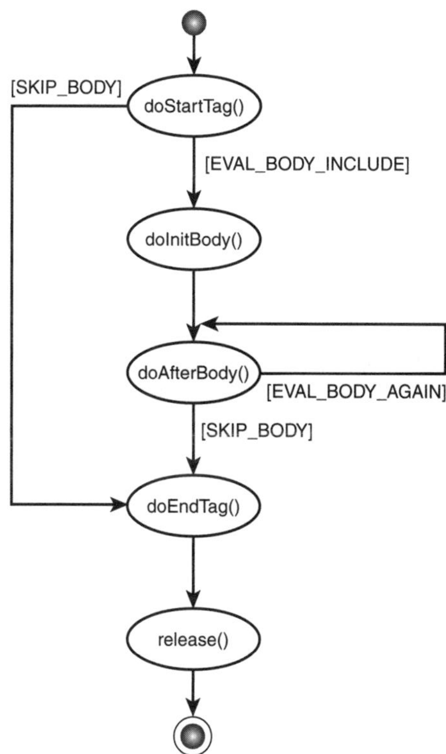

FIGURE 10.2 Custom tag life cycle.

NOTE

The IterationTag interface was introduced with the JSP 1.2 specification. In previous versions the functionality, now refactored into IterationTag, was present in the BodyTag interface. The new class hierarchy allows a custom tag designer to differentiate between simple tags, iterative tags, and tags that have custom body processing.

The doStartTag() Method

The Tag.doStartTag() method is called once when the start tag is processed. This method must return an int value that tells the JSP how to process the tag body. The returned value must be one of

Return Value	Meaning
Tag.SKIP_BODY	The tag body must be empty.
Tag.EVAL_BODY_INCLUDE	The body tag must be evaluated and included in the JSP page.
BodyTag.EVAL_BODY_BUFFERED	The body tag content is written to an in-memory buffer for further processing by the tag.

The return value must be consistent with the <body-content> entry in the TLD. Tags with an empty body must return SKIP_BODY, tags with JSP will normally return EVAL_BODY_INCLUDE, and tags with tagdependent bodies normally return EVAL_BODY_BUFFERED.

The doInitBody() Method

The BodyTag.doInitBody() method is called once after the doStartTag() method but before the tag body is processed and can be used for initialization in addition to, or instead of, the doStartTag() method. The doInitBody() method is only used in tags that implement the BodyTag interface (those that extend BodyTagSupport). This method is not called if the doStartTag() method returns SKIP_BODY. The doInitBody() method returns a void.

The doAfterBody() Method

The IterationTag.doAfterBody() method is called after the tag body has been processed and before the doEndTag() method is called. This method is only called for classes that implement IterationTag. It must return one of the following values to the JSP page indicating how the tag body should be processed:

Return Value	Meaning
IterationTag.EVAL_BODY_AGAIN	Informs the page that the tag body should be processed once more
Tag.SKIP_BODY	Marks the end of the processing of the tag body

If the `doAfterBody()` method returns `EVAL_BODY_AGAIN`, the JSP will read and process the tag body once more and call the `doAfterBody()` method again after the body has been processed.

When returning the `EVAL_BODY_AGAIN` result, `doAfterBody()` will typically change some value so that when the tag body is processed once more, different output is written to the Web page. A simple example of this is a tag that executes a database query in the `doStartTag()` method and reads the next row of the result set in this method returning `EVAL_BODY_AGAIN` until the end of the result set is reached when `SKIP_BODY` is returned.

The `doEndTag()` Method

The `Tag.doEndTag()` method is called once when the end tag is processed. This method must return an `int` value indicating how the remainder of the JSP page should be processed:

Return Value	Meaning
`Tag.EVAL_PAGE`	Evaluate the rest of the page.
`Tag.SKIP_PAGE`	Stop processing the page after this tag.

Most tags will return `EVAL_PAGE` from this method.

Where a tag has an `empty` body, the `doEndTag()` method is still called after the `doStartTag()` method.

The `release()` Method

The `Tag.release()` method is called once when the JSP has finished using the tag. You should use it to release any resources that the tag may have acquired. This method returns `void`.

Defining or Overriding Life Cycle Methods

A custom tag class that implements the tag interfaces directly must provide default implementations of all methods in the interface.

The two tag support classes implement the requisite interfaces and provide default no-operation functionality so that the tag is effectively ignored. The `TagSupport.doStartTag()` method returns `SKIP_BODY`, and the `BodyTagSupport.doStartTag()` returns `EVAL_BODY_BUFFERED`; however, the `BodyTagSupport.doAfterBody()` method ignores the buffered body content.

Custom tags that extend the tag support classes need only override those methods necessary to achieve the tag's required functionality. Typically, simple tags will override `doStartTag()`, and tags that iterate over the body or have tag dependent body content will override `doAfterBody()`.

Once you understand the role of the tag life cycle methods, you can start writing more functional tags.

Changing Custom Tag Behavior

In order to change the behavior of a custom tag, you must pass information from the Web page to the tag. There are three mechanisms for achieving this:

- Passing information in tag attributes
- Passing information via scripting variables
- Passing information in the tag body

All of these mechanisms will be discussed in this section.

Tags with Attributes

Custom tags support attributes using JavaBean properties. Every attribute supported by a tag must be defined both in the TLD file and as a property for the Java class.

Listing 10.5 shows a custom tag class that will convert a U.S. dollar amount into an equivalent U.K. pounds amount.

LISTING 10.5 Currency Converter Tag: `ConvertTag.java`

```
package converters;

import java.io.*;
import java.text.*;
import java.util.*;
import javax.servlet.jsp.*;
import javax.servlet.jsp.tagext.*;

public class ConvertTag extends TagSupport {
    private static final double exchangeRate = 0.613;
    private Currency pounds = Currency.getInstance(Locale.UK);
    private NumberFormat nf = NumberFormat.getInstance();
    private String dollarValue;

    public String getDollarValue() { return dollarValue; }

    public void setDollarValue(String dollarValue)
        { this.dollarValue = dollarValue; }

    public int doStartTag() throws JspException {
        try {
```

LISTING 10.5 Continued

```
            double value = nf.parse(dollarValue).doubleValue();
            nf.setMaximumFractionDigits(pounds.getDefaultFractionDigits());
            nf.setMinimumFractionDigits(pounds.getDefaultFractionDigits());
            pageContext.getOut().print(nf.format(value*exchangeRate));
        } catch (ParseException ex) {
            throw new JspTagException(
                "ConvertTag: illegal dollar value: "+dollarValue);
        } catch (NullPointerException ex) {
            throw new JspTagException(
➥ "ConvertTag: no dollar value specified");
        } catch (IOException ex) {
            throw new JspTagException("ConvertTag: "+ex);
        }
        return SKIP_BODY;
    }
}
```

The `ConvertTag` class in Listing 10.5 defines a `dollarValue` property as a `String`. The TLD file must also include an appropriate `<attribute>` element in the definition of this tag. The TLD elements for an `<attribute>` tag are as follows:

Element	Meaning
`<name>`	Defines the attribute and bean property name
`<required>`	If set to `true`, the attribute must be provided (default `false`)
`<rtexprvalue>`	Set to `true` to allow the attribute; value can be a request-time expression which is a JSP action of the form `<%= %>`, (default `false`)
`<type>`	Defines the class of an attribute (default `java.lang.String`)

An appropriate TLD entry for the `<tag>` element defining the `dollarValue` `<attribute>` of the `convert` custom tag is shown in the following example:

```
<tag>
    <name>convert</name>
    <tag-class>converters.ConvertTag</tag-class>
    <body-content>empty</body-content>
    <attribute>
        <name>dollarValue</name>
        <required>true</required>
        <rtexprvalue>true</rtexprvalue>
        <type>java.lang.String</type>
    </attribute>
</tag>
```

The example tag has an <rtexprvalue> value of true allowing the attribute to be defined with a JSP expression as shown in the following code:

```
<conv:convert dollarValue='<%= request.getParameter("dollar")%>' />
```

TIP

Although the dollarValue property is used as a double value within the class, in the JSP it is treated as a String property. If the property is defined as a java.lang.Double, the generated JSP Java code must convert the String value in the JSP into a Double object. If the value used on the page is not a valid double value (as can easily happen if the user enters the value on an HTML form), an exception is thrown by the generated JSP code. It is better to convert the string value into a Double object within the custom tag as this gives you more control over the error handling. At the very least you can then supply the user with a more appropriate error message than the generic one provided by the Jasper container. Exception handling in tags is discussed in detail in the "Exception Handling" section of this chapter.

Listing 10.6 shows the convert custom tag being used on a JSP that presents the user with the simple currency conversion form you have seen before.

LISTING 10.6 Simple Currency Conversion Form convert.jsp

```
<%@ taglib uri="/converter" prefix="conv" %>
<% String dollar = request.getParameter("dollar"); %>
<HTML>
  <HEAD><TITLE>Currency Converter Using Tags</TITLE></HEAD>
  <BODY>
    <H1>Currency Converter</H1>
    <% if (dollar!=null && dollar.length()>0) {%>
      <BIG>
        USD <%= dollar %> = GBP <conv:convert dollarValue='<%= dollar %>'/>
      </BIG>
    <% } %>
    <FORM>
      <P>Enter dollar value: <INPUT TYPE='text' NAME='dollar'></P>
      <INPUT TYPE='submit' VALUE='Convert'>
    </FORM>
  </BODY>
</HTML>
```

In Listing 10.6, the JSP the value to be converted is obtained from the request parameter and passed using the dollarValue attribute of the tag.

Tags Declaring Scripting Variables

Custom tags can create scripting variables for communicating information to other tags and providing information to the JSP actions.

Custom tags can simplify and improve the use of JavaBean objects on the JSP by encapsulating bean initialization within a custom tag. Consider the very first JavaBean you were shown in Chapter 5, "Basic Principles of JSPs," where a currency converter bean was defined on the JSP as follows:

```
<jsp:useBean id="converter" class="converters.CurrencyConverterBean" scope="page" >
    <jsp:setProperty name="converter" property="amount" />
</jsp:useBean>
```

The currency bean must be initialized with a U.S. dollar value for conversion to U.K. pounds, but this value cannot be captured in the bean class semantics because all JavaBeans must have a no-argument constructor. Ideally the bean would define a single constructor that required a double value to convert. Using custom tags, you can capture the initialization requirements of a bean more succinctly.

The `<conv:currencyBean>` tag in Listing 10.7 creates and initializes the same `CurrencyConverterBean` object shown in Chapter 5. The rest of the JSP uses the bean as though it was created with a `<jsp:useBean>` tag.

LISTING 10.7 `currency-converter.jsp` Using a Custom Tag

```
<%@ taglib uri="/converter" prefix="conv" %>
<conv:currencyBean id="converter"
                   amount='<%= request.getParameter("amount") %>' />
<HTML>
  <HEAD><TITLE>Currency Conversion JSP</TITLE></HEAD>
  <BODY>
    <H1>Currency Converter</H1>
    <BIG>
        <jsp:getProperty name="converter" property="amount" /> =
        <jsp:getProperty name="converter" property="poundValue" />
    </BIG>
    <P><A HREF="currency-form.html">Convert another amount...</A>
  </BODY>
</HTML>
```

The `<conv:currencyBean>` tag uses the `id` attribute to define the name of the bean (scripting variable) and the `amount` attribute to initialize the bean.

The one disadvantage of using a custom tag over the `<jsp:useBean>` tag is that the bean properties must be explicitly initialized from the request parameters: There is no implicit support for mapping request parameters onto custom tag properties.

A custom tag that declares a scripting variable must specify the variable in the TLD file. The `<variable>` tag can contain the following elements:

Element	Meaning
`<name-given>`	Defines the name for the scripting variable as a fixed value (cannot be specified if `<name-from-attribute>` is defined).
`<name-from-attribute>`	Specifies the attribute that is used to define the scripting variable name (cannot be specified if `<name-given>` is defined).
`<variable-class>`	Specifies the class of the scripting variable.
`<declare>`	Specifies if the variable is a new object (default `true`).
`<scope>`	Defines where in the custom tag processing the variable can be accessed. Must be one of `NESTED`, `AT_BEGIN`, or `AT_END`. This is not the scope of the variable itself, which is specified when the variable is created.

The following example shows the TLD entry for the `currencyBean` tag:

```
<tag>
    <name>currencyBean</name>
    <tag-class>converters.CurrencyBeanTag</tag-class>
    <body-content>empty</body-content>
    <variable>
        <name-from-attribute>id</name-from-attribute>
        <variable-class>converters.CurrencyConverterBean</variable-class>
    </variable>
    <attribute>
        <name>id</name>
        <required>true</required>
    </attribute>
    <attribute>
        <name>amount</name>
        <required>true</required>
        <rtexprvalue>true</rtexprvalue>
        <type>java.lang.String</type>
    </attribute>
</tag>
```

Note that all <variable> elements must be defined before the <attribute> elements in the <tag> definition. In this example, the <name-from-attribute> element specifies that the scripting variable name is defined by the id attribute in the tag. If the variable name is specified as an attribute, the attribute must be a static value and not a request-time expression.

NOTE

The TLD entry defines the same information about the scripting variable as the <jsp:useBean> tag: specifically, the variable name and its class. The scope of the bean is defined when the custom tag creates the scripting variable as discussed in the next part of this section.

Listing 10.8 shows the custom class that creates the CurrencyConverterBean object.

LISTING 10.8 Creating a JavaBean Within CurrencyBeanTag.java

```
package converters;

import javax.servlet.jsp.*;
import javax.servlet.jsp.tagext.*;

public class CurrencyBeanTag extends TagSupport {
    private String id;
    public String getId() { return id; }
    public void setId(String id) { this.id = id; }

    private String amount;
    public String getAmount() { return amount; }
    public void setAmount(String amount) { this.amount = amount; }

    public int doStartTag() throws JspException {
        CurrencyConverterBean bean = new CurrencyConverterBean();
        bean.setAmount(amount);
        pageContext.setAttribute(id,bean,PageContext.PAGE_SCOPE);
        return SKIP_BODY;
    }
}
```

In Listing 10.8, the scripting variable is added as an attribute of the JSP page context by the PageContext.setAttribute() method. The setAttribute() method requires three parameters to define the variable name, the variable object, and the scope of the variable (as would have been specified using a <useBean> tag).

The variable name is specified by the `id` property of the custom tag matching the use of the `<name-from-attribute>` entry in the TLD. If the TLD uses the `<name-given>` element to define the variable name, the custom tag must define the name when it adds the attribute to the page context.

Scripting variables can have the following scope:

- `APPLICATION_SCOPE`—Available until the context is reclaimed
- `PAGE_SCOPE`—Available until the current page processing completes
- `REQUEST_SCOPE`—Available until the current request completes
- `SESSION_SCOPE`—Available to all pages in the current session

NOTE

There might appear to be some duplication of effort between the TLD file and the `PageContext.setAttribute()` method when specifying a scripting variable. In practice, the variable is defined by the `setAttribute()` method and not the `<variable>` element in the TLD. The entry in the TLD file is there to allow a JSP container to do some simple translation time validation of the `<jsp:setProperty>` and `<jsp:getProperty>` tags (checking the tag `name` attribute and the tag `property` attribute values).

Currently, Tomcat's Jasper container does not do any translate-time checking of scripting variables defined by custom tags. This means that forgetting to add the TLD `<variable>` element will not stop your JSP from translating correctly. However, this may not be the case in the future, or indeed for other containers, so you should always include the `<variable>` definition in the TLD.

Tags Using Scripting Variables

Custom tags can use scripting variables to obtain information from the JSP page context and potentially change their behavior based on the values of the variables. Variables used to communicate information from one custom tag to another can simplify the use of tags and tag attributes.

A custom tag can use any scripting variable defined in the JSP page context simply by retrieving the required attribute (variable name) from the `PageContext` object. The variable may have been declared by another custom tag or a `<jsp:useBean>` action on the JSP (or by another JSP or servlet if the scope of the bean extends beyond the current page).

Listing 10.9 shows a simple tag that retrieves the `poundValue` property of a `CurrencyConverterBean` stored in the page context.

LISTING 10.9 Using a Scripting Variable in `ConvertPoundValueTag.java`

```
package converters;

import java.io.*;
import javax.servlet.jsp.*;
import javax.servlet.jsp.tagext.*;

public class ConvertPoundValueTag extends TagSupport {
    private String name;
    public String getName() { return name; }
    public void setName(String name) { this.name = name; }

    public int doStartTag() throws JspException {
        try {
            CurrencyConverterBean bean =
                (CurrencyConverterBean)pageContext.getAttribute(name);
            pageContext.getOut().print(bean.getPoundValue());
        }
        catch (IOException ex) {
            throw new JspTagException("ConvertPoundValueTag: "+ex);
        }
        return SKIP_BODY;
    }
}
```

In Listing 10.9, the bean name is defined in the (mandatory) `name` attribute of the tag. The TLD entry for this tag is shown in the following XML element:

```
<tag>
    <name>convertPoundValue</name>
    <tag-class>converters.ConvertPoundValueTag</tag-class>
    <body-content>empty</body-content>
    <variable>
        <name-from-attribute>name</name-from-attribute>
        <variable-class>converters.CurrencyConverterBean</variable-class>
        <declare>false</declare>
    </variable>
    <attribute>
        <name>name</name>
        <required>true</required>
    </attribute>
</tag>
```

The <variable> definition includes the <declare>false</declare> element to show that this tag uses an existing variable instead of declaring a new one.

Listing 10.10 shows how the <convertPoundValue> tag and a similar <convertAmount> tag can be used instead of the <jsp:getProperty> tag.

LISTING 10.10 JSP Reading Scripting Variables: currency-converter-var.jsp

```
<%@ taglib uri="/converter" prefix="conv" %>
<conv:currencyBean id="converter"
                   amount='<%= request.getParameter("amount") %>' />
<HTML>
  <HEAD><TITLE>Currency Conversion JSP</TITLE></HEAD>
  <BODY>
    <H1>Currency Converter</H1>
    <BIG>
      <conv:convertAmount name="converter"/> =
      <conv:convertPoundValue name="converter" />
    </BIG>
    <P><A HREF="currency-form-var.htm">Convert another amount...</A>
  </BODY>
</HTML>
```

The custom tags in Listing 10.10 can be simplified by removing the capability of specifying the variable name and hard-coding this within the tags. The JSP page developer will find the tags easier to use because the code will now look like the following example:

```
<%@ taglib uri="/converter" prefix="conv" %>
<conv:currencyBean amount='<%= request.getParameter("amount") %>' />
<HTML>
  <HEAD><TITLE>Currency Conversion JSP</TITLE></HEAD>
  <BODY>
    <H1>Currency Converter</H1>
    <BIG>
    <conv:convertAmount/> = <conv:convertPoundValue/>
    </BIG>
    <P><A HREF="currency-form-var.htm">Convert another amount...</A>
  </BODY>
</HTML>
```

However, you must be careful to avoid using a variable name that could be used by JSP developers for their own variables.

TIP

When using hard-coded tag names for convenience, adopt a naming convention that requires names unlikely to be used by the JSP developer. A simple approach would be to prefix all variable names with an underscore and the TagLib `prefix` name. The tag used in this example would be named `_convCurrencyConverter`. JSP developers can simply be asked not to use variable names starting with underscore.

Using hard-coded variable names prevents the JSP developer from using the tag more than once on a single page. This may not be appropriate for some types of tags such as a converter tag that can convert between several different currencies rather than just U.K. pounds and U.S. dollars.

Tags with Tag Dependent Body Content

Besides attributes and scripting variables, the body of a tag can also be used to pass information to the implementing Java class. Custom tags with tag-dependent body content can allow any form of data between the start and end tags. The JSP processing will buffer up the tag body data and pass it to the Java object for processing rather than interpret the tag body as normal JSP text.

Tags with a custom body interpret the body of the tag in some specific way. As a simple example consider a `convertRow` tag that will read a comma separated list of U.S. dollar values from the tag body and convert these values to their U.K. pound equivalents. Listing 10.11 shows the JSP that uses this tag within the HTML `<TD>` elements.

LISTING 10.11 Tag with Tag-Dependent Body Content in `currency-table.jsp`

```
<%@ taglib uri="/converter" prefix="conv" %>
<HTML>
  <HEAD><TITLE>Currency Conversion Table</TITLE></HEAD>
  <BODY>
    <H1>Currency Table</H1>
    <TABLE>
      <TR><TH></TH><TH>0</TH><TH>1</TH><TH>2</TH><TH>3</TH><TH>4</TH>
          <TH>5</TH><TH>6</TH><TH>7</TH><TH>8</TH><TH>9</TH></TR>
      <TR>
        <TD ALIGN="right"><B>0</B></TD>
        <conv:convertRow> 0,1,2,3,4,5,6,7,8,9 </conv:convertRow>
      </TR>
      <TR>
        <TD ALIGN="right"><B>10</B></TD>
        <conv:convertRow> 10,11,12,13,14,15,16,17,18,19 </conv:convertRow>
      </TR>
```

LISTING 10.11 Continued

```
        <TR>
          <TD ALIGN="right"><B>20</B></TD>
          <conv:convertRow> 20,21,22,23,24,25,26,27,28,29 </conv:convertRow>
        </TR>
      </TABLE>
    </BODY>
</HTML>
```

Listing 10.12 shows the implementation of the custom `convertRow` tag.

LISTING 10.12 Body Processing Tag: `ConvertRowTag.java`

```
package converters;

import java.io.*;
import java.util.*;
import javax.servlet.jsp.*;
import javax.servlet.jsp.tagext.*;

public class ConvertRowTag extends BodyTagSupport {
    CurrencyConverterBean bean = new CurrencyConverterBean();

    public int doAfterBody() throws JspException {
        try {
            JspWriter out = getPreviousOut();
            StringTokenizer values =
                new StringTokenizer(bodyContent.getString().trim(),",");
            while (values.hasMoreTokens()) {
                String dollar = values.nextToken();
                bean.setAmount(dollar);
                out.print("<TD  ALIGN='right'>");
                out.print(bean.getPoundValue());
                out.println("</TD>");
            }
            bodyContent.clearBody();
        }
        catch (IOException ex) {
            throw new JspTagException("ConvertRowTag: "+ex);
        }
        return SKIP_BODY;
    }
}
```

NOTE

You might like to take a look at the JSP Standard Template library `<sql:query>` tag shown in Chapter 11, for an example of a tag that expects an SQL statement as tag-dependent body content.

As already stated, a custom tag that interacts with the tag body must extend the `BodyTagSupport` class and override the `doAfterBody()` method.

In the example in Listing 10.12, the `doAfterBody()` method obtains the body content text and uses a `StringTokenizer` to extract the comma-separated values for output as `<TD>` elements on the JSP. Access to the tag body data is encapsulated in a `javax.servlet.jsp.tagext.BodyContent` object declared in the `BodyTagSupport` superclass as `bodyContent`. The text of the body can be accessed as a string using the `bodyContent.getString()` method.

The converted currency values are written to a JSP output stream obtained using the `getPreviousOut()` method of the superclass. The `pageContext.getOut()` method returns a stream that writes to the `BodyContent` object rather than the actual JSP page.

The `doAfterBody()` method uses the `clearBody()` method to erase the body text after processing. Although not strictly necessary in this particular case, it is good practice to do this so as to avoid the body content accidentally being included on the JSP.

The example `doAfterBody()` method returns `SKIP_BODY` to stop any further processing of the tag's body. This is slightly misleading because you have not skipped the body processing as such but are stopping further processing of the body.

The final requirement for a tag with a tag-dependent body is to define the tag's entry in the TLD as follows:

```
<tag>
    <name>convertRow</name>
    <tag-class>converters.ConvertRowTag</tag-class>
    <body-content>tagdependent</body-content>
</tag>
```

The `<body-content>` element is set to the value `tagdependent` to prevent the JSP page processing from trying to interpret the tag body as normal JSP text. If you want the body to be interpreted as normal JSP text, use the value `JSP` instead of `tagdependent`.

Iterative Tags

A common requirement for Web pages is to be able to provide a variable number of items to a common format (such as multiple rows in a table populated from a data query). Iterative custom tags can implement this functionality. Typically this is achieved using a nested parent and child hierarchy, where the parent tag controls iteration and the child tag retrieves the data for the current iteration.

Looking back at the `ConvertRowTag` class shown in Listing 10.12, you can see that this tag outputs HTML formatting information around the converted currency value. This tag is poorly designed because it does not separate out presentation from computation. Using iterative tags, you can devise a better solution to produce a currency conversion table as shown in Listing 10.13.

LISTING 10.13 Iterative Tags Used in `currency-table-loop.jsp`

```
<%@ taglib uri="/converter" prefix="conv" %>

<HTML>
  <HEAD><TITLE>Currency Conversion Table (Loop)</TITLE></HEAD>
  <BODY>
    <H1>Currency Table (Loop)</H1>
    <TABLE BORDER="1">
      <TR>
        <TH> </TH>
        <conv:iterateOver from="0" to="9" step="1">
          <TH><conv:currentDollar/></TH>
        </conv:iterateOver>
      <TR>
      <conv:iterateOver from="0" to="90" step="10">
        <TR>
          <TD ALIGN="right"><B><conv:currentDollar/></B></TD>
          <conv:iterateOver from="0" to="9" step="1">
            <TD ALIGN="right"><conv:currentPound/></TD>
          </conv:iterateOver>
        </TR>
      </conv:iterateOver>
    </TABLE>
  </BODY>
</HTML>
```

Figure 10.3 shows this JSP displayed in a browser window.

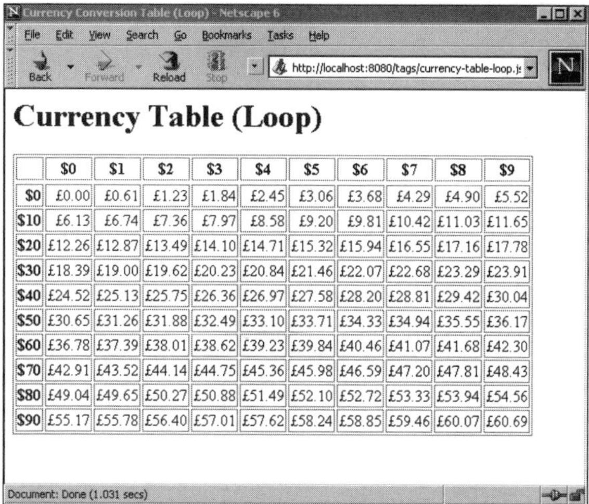

FIGURE 10.3 Conversion table JSP displayed in a browser.

The first thing that should strike you about the JSP in Listing 10.13 is how little JSP code was required to generate the table of converted values. This is the beauty of using iterative tags; they allow you to define how to format a piece of data once and then apply this format to as many blocks of data as required.

In Listing 10.13, the `<iterateOver>` tag is used to iterate over several values in the same manner as a `for` loop does in Java. The tags `<currentDollar>` and `<currentPound>` use the enclosing `<iterateOver>` tag to obtain the current value for the iteration. The `<iterateOver>` tag sets up the current value for each loop and determines when the iteration ends.

TIP

You should use the JSTL `forEach` tag for iteration over a range of values rather than writing your own iteration tag. The JSTL is discussed in Chapter 11.

A tag that has to support iteration should extend the `TagSupport` class and override the `doStartTag()` and `doAfterBody()` methods. The example `<iterateOver>` tag class is shown in Listing 10.14.

LISTING 10.14 The Iterative Tag: `IterateOverTag.java`

```
package converters;

import javax.servlet.jsp.*;
```

LISTING 10.14 Continued

```
import javax.servlet.jsp.tagext.*;

public class IterateOverTag extends TagSupport {
    private double from;
    public Double getFrom() { return new Double(from); }
    public void setFrom(Double from) { this.from = from.doubleValue(); }

    private double to;
    public Double getTo() { return new Double(to); }
    public void setTo(Double to) { this.to = to.doubleValue(); }

    private double step = 1.0;
    public Double getStep() { return new Double(step); }
    public void setStep(Double step) { this.step = step.doubleValue(); }

    private double current;
    public double getCurrent() { return current; }

    public int doStartTag() throws JspException {
        current = from;
        if (current > to)
            return SKIP_BODY;
        return EVAL_BODY_INCLUDE;
    }

    public int doAfterBody() throws JspException {
        current += step;
        if (current > to) {
            return SKIP_BODY;
        }
        return EVAL_BODY_AGAIN;
    }
}
```

This tag uses the three properties `from`, `to`, and `step` to control the iteration. The properties are declared as `Double` values so that the JSP can perform translate time checking to ensure that only numeric values are specified (see the example TLD later in this section). The `current` property of the class allows child tags to access the current iteration value.

The `doStartTag()` method sets up the initial loop value and returns `SKIP_BODY` if the start value is larger then the end value; otherwise, `IterationTag.EVAL_BODY_INCLUDE` is returned to start processing the body of the tag.

The `doAfterBody()` method increments the iteration value and returns `EVAL_BODY_AGAIN` if the iteration has not finished or returns `SKIP_BODY` to stop the iteration.

NOTE

In a previous version of the JSP specification, the value `BodyTag.EVAL_BODY_TAG` was used to reprocess the tag body. The `EVAL_BODY_TAG` value is now deprecated and the `IterationTag.EVAL_BODY_AGAIN` constant should be used in its place.

The `IterateOverTag` class extends `TagSupport` because it does not interact with the body; its body content is normal JSP text. This is shown in the TLD as follows:

```
<tag>
    <name>iterateOver</name>
    <tag-class>converters.IterateOverTag</tag-class>
    <body-content>JSP</body-content>
    <attribute>
      <name>from</name>
      <required>true</required>
      <type>java.lang.Double</type>
    </attribute>
    <attribute>
      <name>to</name>
      <required>true</required>
      <type>java.lang.Double</type>
    </attribute>
    <attribute>
      <name>step</name>
      <type>java.lang.Double</type>
    </attribute>
  </tag>
```

The tag's attributes are defined to be `java.lang.Double` values. The absence of the `<rtexprvalue>` tag means they can only be specified as static values (numbers coded on the JSP page).

In order to access the iteration tag's current value, a nested child tag must have some way of accessing the enclosing parent. The `TagSupport.findAncestorWithClass()` method enables a child tag to find an enclosing tag of a particular class. Listing 10.15 shows a child tag that looks for an immediately enclosing `IterateOverTag` parent tag.

LISTING 10.15 Iteration Child Tag: `CurrentDollarTag.java`

```
package converters;

import java.io.*;
import java.util.*;
import javax.servlet.jsp.*;
import javax.servlet.jsp.tagext.*;

public class CurrentDollarTag extends TagSupport {
    private CurrencyConverterBean bean = new CurrencyConverterBean();

    public int doStartTag() throws JspException {
        try {
            IterateOverTag current = (IterateOverTag)
                    findAncestorWithClass(this,IterateOverTag.class);
            bean.setAmount(current.getCurrent().toString());
            pageContext.getOut().print(bean.getAmount());
            return SKIP_BODY;
        }
        catch (IOException ex) {
            throw new JspTagException("CurrentTag: "+ex);
        }
    }
}
```

The child tag in Listing 10.15 is a simple tag with no attributes and an `empty` tag body. It uses the `findAncestorWithClass()` method to find the immediately enclosing tag of the class `IterateOver`. The parameters to `findAncestorWithClass()` are

- The starting point for the search within the tag hierarchy which is usually the `this` object
- The class of the enclosing parent tag to search for

The method will return a reference to the enclosing parent tag if one is found or null if an enclosing tag of the indicated class is not found. The example tag writes the current iteration value obtained from the parent tag to the JSP.

The child tag in Listing 10.16 is a little more complex because it is designed to convert a currency value for a cell in a table.

LISTING 10.16 Nested Tag Using Multiple Enclosing Tags: `CurrentPoundTag.java`

```
package converters;

import java.io.*;
import javax.servlet.jsp.*;
import javax.servlet.jsp.tagext.*;

public class CurrentPoundTag extends TagSupport {
    private CurrencyConverterBean bean = new CurrencyConverterBean();

    public int doStartTag() throws JspException {
        try {
            double current = 0.0;
            IterateOverTag iter = (IterateOverTag)
                    findAncestorWithClass(this,IterateOverTag.class);
            while (iter != null) {
                current += iter.getCurrent();
                iter = (IterateOverTag)
                        findAncestorWithClass(iter,IterateOverTag.class);
            }
            bean.setAmount(""+current);
            pageContext.getOut().print(bean.getPoundValue());
            return SKIP_BODY;
        }
        catch (IOException ex) {
            throw new JspTagException("ConvertCellTag: "+ex);
        }
    }
}
```

Again, the simple tag in Listing 10.16 has no attributes and no body. However, this tag expects to be used inside multiple `IterateOverTag` tags. The `doStartTag()` method finds the immediately enclosing `IterateOverTag` object in the same manner as the `CurrentTag` in Listing 10.15 but then goes on to look for a parent of this tag, and so on until the tag hierarchy is exhausted. As each enclosing `IterateOverTag` is found, the iteration value of the enclosing tag is added to the accumulated value for all enclosing iterations. The resultant combined value is then converted using the `CurrencyConverterBean` defined in Chapter 5 and printed to the JSP.

The TLD entries for the tags in Listings 10.15 and 10.16 are shown in the following extract:

```
<tag>
    <name>currentDollar</name>
    <tag-class>converters.CurrentDollarTag</tag-class>
    <body-content>empty</body-content>
</tag>
<tag>
    <name>currentPound</name>
    <tag-class>converters.CurrentPoundTag</tag-class>
    <body-content>empty</body-content>
</tag>
```

Well-designed iterative and nested cooperating tags can be used to add dynamic content to your Web pages in a simple and effective manner.

Using Tag Extra Information Classes

Tag Extra Information (TEI) classes are used to provide supplementary information about custom tags. Each custom tag can have an optional TEI class to

- Validate tag attributes at page translation time
- Specify the scripting variables created by the tag

A TEI class extends the `javax.servlet.jsp.tagext.TagExtraInfo` class and optionally provides the following methods:

- `isValid()` checks tag attributes and returns true if all attributes are valid.
- `getVariableInfo()` returns an array of `VariableInfo` objects that define the variables used by the tag.

These methods are discussed in the next two subsections.

A TEI class for a tag is added to the tag's entry in the TLD as a `<tei-class>` element specifying the TEI class name after the tag class name. The following example adds a TEI class called `converters.CurrencyBeanTei` to the `CurrencyBeanTag` entry:

```
<tag>
    <name>currencyBean</name>
    <tag-class>converters.CurrencyBeanTag</tag-class>
    <tei-class>converters.CurrencyBeanTei</tei-class>
    <body-content>empty</body-content>
    <variable>
        <name-from-attribute>id</name-from-attribute>
        <variable-class>converters.CurrencyConverterBean</variable-class>
```

```
    </variable>
    <attribute>
      <name>id</name>
      <required>true</required>
    </attribute>
    <attribute>
      <name>amount</name>
      <required>true</required>
      <rtexprvalue>true</rtexprvalue>
      <type>java.lang.String</type>
    </attribute>
  </tag>
```

Validating Attributes

The standard custom tag attribute validation is fairly basic and only checks the following:

- All mandatory attributes are defined.
- All specified attribute names match entries in the TLD.

A TEI class can be used to supplement this translate time validation. The `TagExtraInfo.isValid()` method is called with a `TagData` parameter, which encapsulates the attributes defined on the JSP. The `isValid()` method can check which attributes are provided and disallow various combinations or validate the values of static attributes.

NOTE

TEI attribute validation can only be applied to static `String` values on the JSP. Attributes that accept request-time values must be validated by the custom tag itself.

As a simple example, consider extending the `ConvertTag` example shown earlier so that it will convert either U.S. dollars to U.K. pounds or U.K. pounds to U.S. dollars but not both. By defining either a `dollarValue` attribute or a `poundValue` attribute, the enhanced tag could do the required conversion. A TEI class could be used to enforce the either/or nature of the two attributes as follows:

```
package converters;

import javax.servlet.jsp.tagext.*;
```

```
public class OptionTagTEI extends TagExtraInfo {
    public boolean isValid(TagData data) {
        Object selected = data.getAttribute("dollarValue");
        Object def = data.getAttribute("poundValue");
        if (def!=null && selected!=null)
          return false;
        else if (def==null && selected==null)
          return false;
        return true;
    }
}
```

A second example shows how to use a TEI class to validate that an attribute can only accept a range of static `String` values (in this case, a list of colors for a traffic light):

```
public class SignalTagTEI extends TagExtraInfo {
   public boolean isValid(Tagdata data) {
      Object o = data.getAttribute("color");
      if (o != null && o != TagData.REQUEST_TIME_VALUE) {
          String color = (String)o;
          if (col.equals("red") ||
             col.equals("amber") || col.equals("green"))
            return true;
          else
            return false;
      }
      else
         return true;
   }
}
```

This example retrieves the color attribute, checks that it is not a request-time expression, and then verifies this value against a list of allowed color values.

Once you have defined the TEI class for your custom tags, the JSP-processing mechanism will create an object of the TEI class when processing a JSP and call the `isValid()` method to validate the attributes of all occurrences of the custom tag on the page.

Defining Scripting Variables

The second use of the Tag Extra Info class is to provide information about the scripting variables used by the tag. This TEI information is not required for deploying a tag that creates scripting variables, but it does provide information that may be used by some manufacturer's JSP design tools.

The following example shows how the CurrencyBeanTag defined in Listing 10.8 can define the CurrencyConverterBean scripting variable:

```
public class DefineTei extends TagExtraInfo {
   public VariableInfo[] getVariableInfo(TagData data) {
      String name = data.getAttributeString("id");
      return new VariableInfo[] {
          new VariableInfo(name, converters.CurrencyConverterBean,
                           true, VariableInfo.AT_BEGIN)
      };
   }
}
```

The VariableInfo object returned from the getVariableInfo() method defines the name of the scripting variable (from the id attribute of the tag), its class (converters.CurrencyConverterBean), whether it is declared (true), and the variable scope within the tag (AT_BEGIN).

After you have defined the TEI class for your custom tags, a JSP design tool will create an object of the TEI class when adding custom tags to its palette of JSP tags. The TEI getVariableInfo() method can be used to augment the design tool's capabilities.

Exception Handling

The JSP 1.2 Specification introduced a new feature for supporting exception handling within a custom tag. Previously, exception handling had to be coded within each life cycle method, which often led to duplicated error-handling code. A new javax.servlet.jsp.tagext.TryCatchFinally interface defines the following methods to support common exception handling for the life cycle methods:

Method	Description
void doCatch(Throwable)	Invoked if a Throwable occurs in doStartTag(), doEndTag(), doAfterBody(), or doInitBody()
void doFinally()	Invoked after doEndTag() unless an exception is thrown by one of the other methods

The doCatch() and doFinally() methods are not called if exceptions occur in the property getter or setter methods of the tag. The pseudocode for the calls to these methods for custom tag processing is

```
t = get a tag handler
// initialize properties from tag attributes
try {
```

```
    doStartTag()
    ...
    doEndTag()
} catch (Throwable t) {
    t.doCatch(t);
}
finally {
    t.doFinally();
}
t.release()
```

For a custom tag implementing the `TryCatchFinally` interface, the `doEndTag()` may not be called; so, any resource cleanup code for the tag should be added to the `doFinally()` or `release()` methods.

The `TagSupport` and `BodyTagSupport` classes do not implement the `TryCatchFinally` interface by default. You will have to explicitly implement this interface in your custom tag if you want to use the `doCatch()` and `doFinally()` methods.

Summary

Tag libraries are collections of custom tags that can be used to simplify the development of a JSP. A custom tag is a Java class that extends either `TagSupport` or `BodyTagSupport` according to the nature of the tag being developed. The custom tag interacts with the JSP page processing using life cycle methods defined in the tag support classes. Custom tags override the life cycle methods to implement the functionality required.

Custom tags can

- Write information to the JSP
- Read the text of the tag body
- Iterate over the body of a tag an arbitrary number of times
- Use tag attributes to configure their behavior

Well-designed TagLibs can be used in multiple applications to enhance code reusability. A Java Standard Tag Library (see Chapter 11) has been specified to support many common requirements for JSP page development.

11

JSP Expression Language and JSTL

IN THIS CHAPTER

Most JSP container vendors supply standard tag libraries to support the development of Web pages. Some supplied libraries are more comprehensive than others; the Jakarta project, for example, provides about 20 standard libraries, each containing several custom tags (the Jakarta libraries can be found at `http://jakarta.apache.org/taglibs`).

There are many common themes in the various manufacturers' TagLibs, and in 2001 the Java Community Process proposed a JSP Standard Tag Library (JSTL) specification to avoid duplication of effort and to increase JSP portability. The JSP 2.0 specification has incorporated the JSTL expression language (EL) into the core JSP functionality. This chapter examines the JSTL custom tags and support for the JSP EL.

JSP Standard Tag Library (JSTL)

The JSP Standard Tag Library (JSTL) is a collection of custom JSP tags and a supporting scripting language that can be used to simplify JSP authors' lives. In order to make JSP tags more akin to HTML and JavaScript (EcmaScript), JSTL provides tags to support programming language features.

NOTE

JSTL was originally known as JSPTL (JavaServer Pages Template Library).

JSTL is specified as JSR52 available from `http://www.jcp.org/aboutJava/communityprocess/review/jsr052/index.htm`. The JSTL EL (see the "Expression Language Support" section) component of the JSTL has been included in the JSP 2.0 specification available from `http://jcp.org/aboutJava/communityprocess/review/jsr152/index.html` or `http://java.sun.com/jsp`.

The JSTL implementation can be downloaded from the Jakarta Web site at `http://jakarta.apache.org/taglibs`, and the latest information on JSTL is available from `http://java.sun.com/products/jsp/taglibraries.html`.

NOTE

The information in this chapter is based on the Public Draft version of the JSTL (JSR52) specification and the Beta 2 implementation of JSTL. By the time you read this book, the specification and implementation will probably have been finalized. You should consult the latest specification and documentation if you find discrepancies or problems when testing the examples shown in this chapter.

One of the problems with JSP development is the necessity to include Java scriptlets and actions on the Web page in order to implement some of the dynamic behavior required. Custom tags and TagLibs can be written to alleviate this problem, but many pages face the same problems, and having each developer write his or her own custom tags is counterproductive.

The JSTL is a collection of tags designed to address many of the common requirements of JSP development. Underpinning the tags is a simple scripting language that can be used instead of JSP request-time expressions.

The JSTL tags are separated into the following libraries:

Library	Usage
Core (`c.tld`)	Tags for supporting expressions, flow control, and URL management
XML (`x.tld`)	Tags for supporting XML
I18n (`fmt.tld`)	Tags for supporting internationalization, and message and number formatting
Database (`sql.tld`)	Support for SQL databases

Two versions of each library are provided: One uses JSP request-time expressions and the other uses the JSTL EL (which is based on EcmaScript syntax). Before you can use JSTL, you will need to update Tomcat to include the JSTL JAR files.

Using JSTL with Tomcat

To use the JSTL, you must download and extract the latest JSTL archive available from `http://jakarta.apache.org/builds/jakarta-taglibs/releases/standard`. You can extract the archive to any location on your workstation.

Inside the `jakarta-taglibs` directory created when you extracted the archive you will find two subdirectories:

Directory	Contents
`lib`	JAR files required to support JSTL
`tld`	TLD files required by your Web applications

If you have a beta version of the JSTL, you will find the `lib` and `tld` directories in a subdirectory for the version of the archive you have obtained (such as `jstl-beta2`).

In the `jakarta-taglibs` directory, you will also find WAR files containing documentation and examples of the use of the JSTL. You can study them to supplement the information in this chapter.

To make the JSTL available to all Web applications, copy the following files to the `<CATALINA_HOME>/lib` directory:

```
jakarta-taglibs/lib/jstl.jar
jakarta-taglibs/lib/standard.jar
```

TIP

If you plan to use JSTL script variables in your custom tags, you should also copy the `standard.jar` file to the Java standard extensions directory to make the JSTL support classes available to your Java compiler. The Java extension directory for J2SDK is `<JAVA_HOME>/jre/lib/ext`.

Stop and restart Tomcat after installing the JSTL JAR files.

You will need to include the TLD files for each JSTL package you use in your Web applications.

Using JSTL with Request-Time Expressions

The JSTL expression language is a major improvement over JSP request-time expressions but may not be applicable to all developers. If you already use a lot of custom tags, you may find the benefits of using the expression language are undermined by having to maintain backward compatibility with the other tags.

This chapter focuses on using the JSTL expression language, but before introducing the expression language a quick look at using the JSTL with request-time expressions is in order.

In Chapter 10, “Custom Tags and TagLibs,” you were shown a currency converter JSP that contained the following Java `if` test:

```
<% if (dollar!=null && dollar.length()>0) {%>
  <BIG>
     USD <%= dollar %> = GBP <conv:convert dollarValue='<%= dollar %>'/>
  </BIG>
<% } %>
```

Using the JSTL with request-time expressions, this test can be replaced by the following:

```
<c-rt:if test='<%= dollar!=null && dollar.length()>0 %>'>
  <BIG>
    USD <%= dollar %> = GBP <conv:convert dollarValue='<%= dollar %>'/>
  </BIG>
</c-rt:if>
```

A refactored JSP using the JSTL is shown in Listing 11.1.

LISTING 11.1 JSTL `if` Tag Used in `convert-rt.jsp`

```
<%@ taglib uri="/converter" prefix="conv" %>
<%@ taglib uri="/jstl-c-rt" prefix="c-rt" %>
<% String dollar = request.getParameter("dollar"); %>
<HTML>
  <HEAD><TITLE>Currency Converter Using Tags</TITLE></HEAD>
  <BODY>
    <H1>Currency Converter</H1>
    <c-rt:if test='<%= dollar!=null && dollar.length()>0 %>'>
      <BIG>
      USD <%= dollar %> = GBP <conv:convert dollarValue='<%= dollar %>'/>
      </BIG>
    </c-rt:if>
    <FORM>
      <P>Enter dollar value: <INPUT TYPE='text' NAME='dollar'></P>
      <INPUT TYPE='submit' VALUE='Convert'>
    </FORM>
  </BODY>
</HTML>
```

The JSTL request time TagLib for the core library is defined with the recommended `uri` of `/jstl-c-rt` and the prefix `c-rt`. You must add a TLD definition for the JSTL to the application’s `WEB-INF/web.xml` file as follows:

```
<taglib>
    <taglib-uri>/jstl-c-rt</taglib-uri>
    <taglib-location>/WEB-INF/c-rt.tld</taglib-location>
</taglib>
```

The actual TLD for the JSTL core package supporting request-time expressions can be found in `jakarta-taglibs/tld/c-rt.tld`. This file must be added to the application's `WEB-INF` directory as dictated by the `<taglib-location>` element in the `web.xml` file.

The JSTL `<if>` tag takes a `test` attribute, which must be set to the value `true` or `false`. In Listing 11.1, the value of the `test` attribute is obtained from a JSP expression. The `if` tag is discussed in more detail in the "Flow Control Tags" section of this chapter after the JSTL expression language is introduced.

NOTE

The `<if>` tag does not have an else component. The `<choose>` tag should be used if a multi-way choice is required.

Although this currency converter doesn't seem to be a big improvement over the original version, it does reduce the amount of Java a JSP developer must learn. Using the JSTL `if` tag, a JSP developer only needs to know the syntax of Java expressions; there is no requirement for understanding the syntax of an `if` statement and those omnipresent braces.

A bigger improvement in JSP development is achieved when the expression language is used instead of request-time expressions (JSP expressions `<%= %>`).

Expression Language Support

The JSTL includes an expression language (EL) that simplifies the management of data on a JSP. Expressions are only recognized within attribute values for custom tags. Tag developers can easily extend their own custom tags to support JSTL expressions.

JSTL expressions are specified using a `${ }` construct inside an attribute value. The EL supports variables, constants, operators, access to the implicit Java objects on a JSP, and the ability to write the value of an expression to the `JSPWriter` object.

Writing Expressions to the JSP

The following example writes the value of the `dollar` request parameter to the Web page:

```
<c:out value='${param.dollar}'/>
```

The core language tag prefix is c, and the out tag takes a value attribute that contains the text to be written to the page. Any expressions in the value attribute will be converted to a Java String representation. The JSTL predefined variable param in the example is used to access the dollar HTTP request parameter.

The EL uses . and [] to access properties of variables. The . operator is used when the property name follows the conventions of Java identifiers, and [] allows for more generalized access, typically using an expression. The following example is equivalent to the previous one but uses a literal string:

```
<c:out value='${param["dollar"]}'/>
```

The same . and [] syntax is used to access properties of JavaBeans. The following example outputs the poundValue property from a CurrencyConverterBean variable called bean (the CurrencyConverterBean class was introduced in Chapter 5, "Basic Principles of JSPs"):

<c:out value='${bean.poundValue}'/> or <c:out value='${bean["poundValue"]}'/>

If a property does not exist, null is returned as the value of the expression.

Defining Variables

EL variables are created as attributes of the JSP PageContext and can therefore reside in any of the four JSP scopes: page, request, session, or application (scopes were discussed in Chapter 7, "The Web Application Environment"). A null value is returned if a variable does not exist in any of the scopes.

Variables are defined using the <set> tag. The var attribute defines the variable name and the variable value can be defined in the value attribute or in the body of the tag if no value attribute is specified. The following example defines a variable called paramName to be the value dollar in the default page scope:

```
<c:set var='paramName' value='dollar'/>
```

The scope attribute can be used to define the scope of the variable. The following example uses the paramName variable to retrieve a request parameter and assign it to a session-scoped variable called paramValue:

```
<c:set var='paramValue' value='${param[paramName]}' scope='session'/>
```

It is also possible to set the value of the variable in the tag body as in

```
<c:set var='paramName'>dollar</c:set>
```

This latter form allows the JSP to process the tag body to generate the value possibly from nested tags within the <set> tag.

You can remove variables using the <remove> tag, defining the variable's name and scope in var and scope attributes.

Expression Operators

Expressions can use the comparison operators ==, !=, <, <=, >, and >= and the arithmetic operators +, -, *, /, and %. To avoid problems with having to use entity values for special XML characters (such as <, which must be represented as <), alternative symbolic names are provided for some of these operators: lt, le, gt, ge, div, and mod. Logical expressions can also use and, or, and not operators. There is no assignment operator nor is there a string concatenation operator. Operator precedence is the same as Java, and parentheses () can be used to change precedence or group subexpressions.

The EL will apply a plethora of conversion rules to convert operands of expressions. The basic rules are as follows:

- null will convert to "", 0, 0.0, or false as required.
- Numbers will narrow or widen silently to match the required data type (int to double and double to int) but will not convert to Boolean values.
- Primitives will convert to the appropriate wrapper classes (for example int to Integer) and vice versa.
- String objects will convert to numbers using the valueOf() method of the appropriate wrapper class.
- All objects will convert to String using the java.lang.toString() method.

This allows the EL to be written very much like a weakly typed language such as JavaScript or Visual Basic.

The following example adds 1 to a counter object in the HTTP session:

```
<c:set var='counter' value='${counter + 1}' scope='session' />
```

The first time this tag is evaluated, the counter does not exist and is a null object; this is coerced to a zero, one is added, and the expression value attribute is therefore 1.

Implicit Variables

Access to the Java objects of a JSP is via implicit variables in the EL. The following variables are defined:

Variable	JSP Object
pageContext	The PageContext object
page	A java.util.Map storing page-scoped attribute names and their values
request	A Map storing request-scoped attribute names and their values
session	A Map storing session-scoped attribute names and their values
application	A Map storing application-scoped attribute names and their values
param	A Map storing parameter names and their String parameter value obtained from ServletRequest.getParameter()
params	A Map storing parameter names and a String[] of all their values obtained by calling ServletRequest.getParameterValues()

The implicit variables that represent java.util.Map objects are accessed using the . or [] operator and the required key value (the attribute name) as shown in the following examples:

```
<c:out value='${session.counter}'/>
```

Typically you would access a variable simply by name; you would only use the page, request, session, and application variables to resolve potential variable name conflicts. The following example is the normal method of outputting the value of the counter session variable:

```
<c:out value='${counter}'/>
```

You can use the <forEach> tag described in the "Flow Control Tags" section to access all objects in a Map or the String[] of values from the params object when this is required.

The pageContext variable is used to access the HttpRequest and HttpResponse objects. The following example writes the remote hostname to the JSP:

```
<c:out value='${pageContext.request.remoteHost}'/>
```

The JSTL expression syntax uses the JavaBean naming mechanism to map the object attributes into the required bean property accessor methods, in this case pageContext.getRequest().getRemoteHost().

Using Expressions

Adding expressions to the currency converter in Listing 11.1 is easy, apart from the need to provide a scripting variable for the <convert> tag. Listing 11.2 shows a solution to updating the currency converter without adding support for the JSTL expression language to the <convert> tag.

LISTING 11.2 Using Expressions in `convert.jsp`

```
<%@ taglib uri="/converter" prefix="conv" %>
<%@ taglib uri="/jstl-c" prefix="c" %>
<c:set var="dollar" value="${param.dollar}"/>
<jsp:useBean id="dollar" type="java.lang.String"/>
<HTML>
  <HEAD><TITLE>Currency Converter Using Tags</TITLE></HEAD>
  <BODY>
    <H1>Currency Converter</H1>
    <c:if test='${dollar != null and dollar != ""}'>
    <BIG>
      USD <c:out value="${dollar}"/> =
      GBP <conv:convert dollarValue='<%= dollar %>'/>
    </BIG>
    </c:if>
    <FORM>
      <P>Enter dollar value: <INPUT TYPE='text' NAME='dollar'></P>
      <INPUT TYPE='submit' VALUE='Convert'>
    </FORM>
  </BODY>
</HTML>
```

In Listing 11.2, the JSTL core package with expression support is specified using `uri='/jstl-c'` and `prefix='c'`. The corresponding <taglib> entry in `web.xml` is

```
<taglib>
    <taglib-uri>/jstl-c</taglib-uri>
    <taglib-location>/WEB-INF/c.tld</taglib-location>
</taglib>
```

The required JSTL core TLD file to be added to the `WEB-INF` directory can be found in `jakarta-taglibs/tld/c.tld`.

The problem with Listing 11.2 is that the <conv:convert> tag does not currently support JSTL expressions and requires its `dollarValue` attribute to use the `dollar` scripting variable. Scripting variables are not the same thing as JSTL expression variables. The following JSP tag from Listing 11.2 generates the code to create a scripting variable that references the EL variable called `dollar`:

```
<jsp:useBean id="dollar" type="java.lang.String"/>
```

The <useBean> tag generates a variable declaration on the translated JSP page that retrieves the dollar attribute from the PageContext object. This allows the generated JSP code to use the dollar scripting variable to access the dollar expression variable. The generated code is similar to the following:

```
java.lang.String dollar = null;
synchronized (pageContext) {
  dollar = (java.lang.String) pageContext.getAttribute(
           "dollar",PageContext.PAGE_SCOPE);
  if (dollar  == null)
    throw new java.lang.InstantiationException (
           "bean dollar not found within scope ");
}
```

Adding the <useBean> tag to access an expression variable is a rather clumsy approach that can be avoided if you are able to update the custom tag. If you cannot update the custom tag to support JSTL expressions, you will have to use <jsp:useBean> to create the scripting variables for all expression language variables needed by custom tags.

Adding support for expressions to a custom tag is simply a matter of calling the org.apache.taglibs.standard.lang.support.ExpressionEvaluatorManager. evaluate() static method to process the attributes of your tag. The code for the custom tag in Listing 11.3 shows how a single dollarValue property can be evaluated for JSTL expressions.

NOTE

The public draft JSP 2.0 specification proposes the official class for expression evaluation as javax.servlet.jsp.el.ExpressionEvaluator. The evaluate() method and parameters remain as described in this chapter; it uses the beta release JSTL package and classnames.

LISTING 11.3 ConvertElTag.java with Support for JSTL Expressions

```
package converters;

import java.io.*;
import java.text.*;
import java.util.*;
import javax.servlet.jsp.*;
import javax.servlet.jsp.tagext.*;
import org.apache.taglibs.standard.lang.support.*;
```

LISTING 11.3 Continued

```
public class ConvertElTag extends TagSupport {
    private static final double exchangeRate = 0.613;
    private Currency pounds = Currency.getInstance(Locale.UK);
    private NumberFormat nf = NumberFormat.getInstance();
    private String dollarValue;

    public String getDollarValue() { return dollarValue; }

    public void setDollarValue(String dollarValue)
        { this.dollarValue = dollarValue; }

    public int doStartTag() throws JspException {
        dollarValue = (String)ExpressionEvaluatorManager.evaluate(
➥ "dollarValue", dollarValue, String.class, this, pageContext);
        try {
            double value = nf.parse(dollarValue).doubleValue();
            nf.setMaximumFractionDigits(pounds.getDefaultFractionDigits());
            nf.setMinimumFractionDigits(pounds.getDefaultFractionDigits());
            pageContext.getOut().print(nf.format(value*exchangeRate));
        } catch (ParseException ex) {
            throw new JspTagException(
                "ConvertTag: illegal dollar value: "+dollarValue);
        } catch (NullPointerException ex) {
            throw new JspTagException(
➥ "ConvertTag: no dollar value specified");
        } catch (IOException ex) {
            throw new JspTagException("ConvertTag: "+ex);
        }
        return SKIP_BODY;
    }
}
```

The `ExpressionEvaluatorManager.evaluate()` method takes five parameters:

- The name of the attribute
- The object representing the value of the attribute
- The `Class` of the attribute
- The current tag (the `this` variable)
- The `PageContext` for the JSP (the `pageContext` variable)

The `evaluate()` method returns the new value of the attribute with any expressions evaluated and converted into a string representation.

Using this new custom tag supporting the expression language (tag name `<convertEl>`), the currency converter can be written as shown in Listing 11.4.

LISTING 11.4 `convert-el.jsp` **with Full Expression Support**

```
<%@ taglib uri="/converter" prefix="conv" %>
<%@ taglib uri="/jstl-c" prefix="c" %>
<c:set var="dollar" value="${param.dollar}"/>
<HTML>
  <HEAD><TITLE>Currency Converter Using Tags</TITLE></HEAD>
  <BODY>
    <H1>Currency Converter</H1>
    <c:if test='${dollar != null and dollar != ""}'>
      <BIG>
        USD <c:out value="${dollar}"/> =
        GBP <conv:convertEl dollarValue='${dollar}'/>
      </BIG>
    </c:if>
    <FORM>
      <P>Enter dollar value: <INPUT TYPE='text' NAME='dollar'></P>
      <INPUT TYPE='submit' VALUE='Convert'>
    </FORM>
  </BODY>
</HTML>
```

Flow Control Tags

JSTL provides flow control tags for adding programming capabilities to a JSP. The following tags are available:

Tag	Description
`if`	Simple `if` statement with no `else` clause
`choose/when/otherwise`	Combine to form a case statement
`forEach`	Iterates over a range or a collection of values
`forTokens`	Iterates over a tokenized string using a `java.util.Tokenizer` object
`catch`	Catches thrown exceptions within the body of the tag

Each of the tags is discussed briefly in the rest of this section.

The <if> Tag

Use of the <if> tag is fairly intuitive and has already been shown in the previous sections as a replacement for the Java `if` statement. The body of the <if> tag is only evaluated if the test attribute of the tag has the value `true`.

The <choose>, <when>, and <otherwise> Tags

The <choose>, <when>, and <otherwise> tags are used in conjunction with each other to provide a programming case construct as follows:

```
<choose>
  <when test=expression>
    ...
  </when>
  ...
  <otherwise>
    ...
  </otherwise>
</choose>
```

The <choose> tag can only contain <when> and <otherwise> tags and whitespace—no other text is allowed. All <when> tags must be defined before the optional <otherwise> tag. A <when> tag must have a single `test` attribute that evaluates to a Boolean value. There are no attributes to <choose> and <otherwise>.

The first <when> clause that has a `test` value of `true` is the one chosen for processing (all others are ignored). If no <when> clause evaluates to `true`, the <otherwise> clause (if present) is processed.

Listing 11.5 shows a simple use of the <choose> tag in the currency converter example.

LISTING 11.5 Using the <choose> Tag in `currency-case.jsp`

```
<%@ taglib uri="/converter" prefix="conv" %>
<%@ taglib uri="/jstl-c" prefix="c" %>
<c:set var="dollar" value="${param.dollar}"/>
<HTML>
  <HEAD><TITLE>Currency Converter (Case)</TITLE></HEAD>
  <BODY>
    <H1>Currency Converter</H1>
```

LISTING 11.5 Continued

```
    <c:choose>
      <c:when test='${dollar== null}'>
        <P>
          Enter a USD amount in the field below and press Convert to obtain
          the equivalent GBP amount.
        </P>
      </c:when>
      <c:when test='${dollar ==""}'>
        <P>
          You didn't enter a USD amount in the field below
          - try again this time specifying an amount.
        </P>
      </c:when>
      <c:otherwise>
        <BIG>
          USD <c:out value="${dollar}"/> =
          GBP <conv:convertEl dollarValue='${dollar}'/>
        </BIG>
      </c:otherwise>
    </c:choose>
    <FORM>
      <P>Enter dollar value: <INPUT TYPE='text' NAME='dollar'></P>
      <INPUT TYPE='submit' VALUE='Convert'>
    </FORM>
  </BODY>
</HTML>
```

In Listing 11.5, the `<choose>` tag is used to customize the appearance of the form. Note that there are better ways of handling errors than shown in this example (see Chapter 12, "Error Handling").

The `<forEach>` Tag

The `<forEach>` tag is the most comprehensive of the flow control tags. Think of all the ways you might want to iterate over data, and the `<forEach>` tag will probably do it. The `<forEach>` tag will iterate

- From a defined start to end value like a Java `for` loop
- For all or part of a Java array, `java.util.Collection`, `java.util.Iterator`, or `java.util.Enumeration`

- For all keys in a `java.util.Map`
- Over a comma-separated list of values in a `String`

The only obvious omission of a standard Java collection is `java.sql.ResultSet`, and that is not needed because of the way the Database (`sql.tld`) package `<query>` tag obtains the results from an SQL select statement. The database package is discussed briefly in the later section called "Database and XML Tags."

The `<forEach>` tag has several attributes:

- `var` defines a loop variable.
- `items` defines the collection to iterate.
- `begin`, `end`, and `step` attributes are used to restrict how much of the collection will be included in the iteration. If no collection is specified, the `begin`, `end`, and `step` attributes are used to specify a range of values for the iteration.
- `varStatus` defines a `javax.servlet.jsp.jstl.core.LoopTagStatus` variable that includes supplementary information about the loop.

Listing 11.6 revisits the currency table example from Chapter 10 to use the `<forEach>` tag to generate the row and column indexes for the table.

LISTING 11.6 Using `for` Loops in `currency-table.jsp`

```
<%@ taglib uri="/converter" prefix="conv" %>
<%@ taglib uri="/jstl-c" prefix="c" %>
<HTML>
  <HEAD><TITLE>Currency Conversion Table</TITLE></HEAD>
  <BODY>
    <H1>Currency Table</H1>
    <TABLE BORDER="1">
      <TR>
        <TH> </TH>
        <c:forEach var='i' begin='0' end='9'>
          <TH><c:out value='${i}'/></TH>
        </c:forEach>
      <TR>
      <c:forEach var='i' begin='0' end='90' step='10'>
        <TR>
          <TD ALIGN="right"><B><c:out value='${i}'/></B></TD>
          <c:forEach var='j' begin='0' end='9'>
            <TD ALIGN="right"><conv:convertEl dollarValue='${i+j}'/></TD>
```

LISTING 11.6 Continued

```
          </c:forEach>
        </TR>
      </c:forEach>
    </TABLE>
  </BODY>
</HTML>
```

Iterating over a collection is simply a matter of specifying the collection in the `items` attribute. The following example lists the cookies in the HTTP request:

```
<c:forEach var='i' items='${pageContext.request.cookies}'>
  <c:out value='${i.name}'/>=<c:out value='${i.value}'/><BR>
</c:forEach>
```

Iterating over a map is a little more complex because an entry in the map has two components: the key and the value associated with the key. Items in a `Map` are actually `java.util.Map.Entry` objects with `key` and `value` properties.

The following code gets the `Map` of all request parameters and displays the parameter name together with the parameter's values:

```
<c:forEach var='p' items='${pageContext.request.parameterMap}'>
  <P>
     <c:out value='${p.key}'/>:<BR>
     <c:forEach var='v' items='${p.value}'>
       <c:out value='--> ${v}'/><BR>
     </c:forEach>
  </P>
</c:forEach>
```

Using the `varStatus` attribute of the `<forEach>` tag to define a `LoopTagStatus` variable is shown in the following example:

```
<c:forEach var='p' items='${pageContext.request.parameterMap}'>
  <P>
    <c:out value='${p.key}'/>:<BR>
    <c:forEach var='v' items='${p.value}' varStatus='status'>
      value [<c:out value='${status.count}'/>] = <c:out value='${v}'/><BR>
    </c:forEach>
  </P>
</c:forEach>
```

In this example, the <forEach> loop labels each request parameter value with an index number obtained from the count property of the LoopTagStatus variable.

The <forTokens> Tag

The <forTokens> tag encapsulates the java.text.StringTokenizer functionality for a JSP and uses the following attributes:

- items specifies the string to be tokenized.
- delim defines the token delimiters (if delim is omitted the string is treated as a single token).
- var holds the token for each iteration.

The following example shows how the currency converter shown in Listing 11.3 could be modified to allow the user to enter a list of numbers in the dollar field of the form:

```
<H1>Currency Converter</H1>
<c:forTokens var='d' items='${param.dollar}' delims='     ,;'>
  <P><BIG>
    USD <c:out value="${d}"/> =
      GBP <conv:convertEl dollarValue='${d}'/>
  </BIG></P>
</c:forTokens>
```

In this example, the HTTP dollar request parameter is tokenized using the space, tab, comma, and semicolon as separators for the amounts entered by the user.

The <catch> Tag

The <catch> tag is used to prevent uncaught exceptions from being propagated to the JSP error page mechanism (see Chapter 12). Any uncaught exceptions in the body of the tag are caught and assigned to an expression variable defined in the var attribute of the tag. The variable is set to null if no exception is thrown.

The following fragment shows how a <catch> tag can be used to catch the exception thrown by the ConvertElTag when a non-numeric value is given as the dollarValue:

```
<c:otherwise>
  <c:catch var='ex'>
    <BIG>
```

```
      USD <c:out value="${dollar}"/> =
      GBP <conv:convertEl dollarValue='${dollar}'/>
    </BIG>
  </c:catch>
  <c:if test='${ex != null}'>
    <P>
      Error: <c:out value='${ex.message}'/><BR>
      <c:out value="${dollar}"/> is not a vaid amount.
      You must enter a numeric value in the field below.
    </P>
  </c:if>
</c:otherwise>
```

This example uses an `<if>` tag to test whether the exception was thrown and outputs the exception `message` property together with a simple error message. If the `<convertEl>` tag throws an exception, any text written to the JSP before the exception occurs is retained.

CAUTION

The `<catch>` tag has limited use and functionality and is a poor alternative to a well-designed error-handling mechanism as discussed in Chapter 12.

URL Tags

The JSTL core package includes useful tags for writing URLs to a Web page. The URL tags all support URL rewriting to support session tracking for clients that do not support cookies (see Chapter 8, "Session Tracking").

The following tags can be used when writing URLs to a Web page:

Tag	Use
`<url>`	Writes a URL to the JSP or to an expression variable
`<redirect>`	Sends an HTTP redirect response to the client
`<import>`	Allows the output of another URL to be imported onto this page
`<param>`	Allows HTTP request parameters to be added to an enclosing tag

The `<url>` tag specifies the URL in the `value` attribute and normally writes the rewritten URL to the JSP, but if a `var` attribute is defined, the URL is saved as a `java.net.URL` variable and nothing is written to the page.

The following example uses a <url> tag to add an ACTION attribute to a simple currency converter form:

```
<FORM ACTION="<c:url value='currency-converter.jsp'/>">
  <P>Enter dollar value(s): <INPUT TYPE='text' NAME='dollar'></P>
  <INPUT TYPE='submit' VALUE='Convert'>
</FORM>
```

TIP

Always use the <url> tag to add an ACTION to a <FORM>, even if the default action is appropriate. This way your Web pages will use URL rewriting to work with clients that do not support cookies.

The following example shows how the exchangeRate request parameter can be added to the currency-converter.jsp URL and saved as a variable called month:

```
<c:url var='month' value='currency-converter.jsp'>
  <c:param name='exchangeRate' value='0.690'/>
</c:url>
```

This URL variable can then be used to define a hypertext link as follows:

```
<P><A HREF="<c:out value='${month}'/>">
    Conversion using previous week's average rate</A></P>
```

The <redirect> tag is similar to the <url> tag but uses the url attribute to define the redirect URL. The following example redirects the browser to the Tomcat home page:

```
<c:redirect url='http://localhost:8080/index.html'/>
```

The <import> tag serves a similar purpose to the <jsp:include> tag, because it includes the content of another URL on the current page. The <import> tag can include pages from outside the current application (something <jsp:include> cannot do) and can be more efficient than <jsp:include> in some situations.

Formatting Tags

In Chapter 4, "Basic Principles of Servlets," you were shown how important it is to consider the potential international use of your application and think about local formatting conventions. The examples have made use of Locale and NumberFormat classes to ensure pages format currency values correctly but have stopped short of using resource bundles so as to keep the examples (relatively) simple.

The good news is that the JSTL includes an Internationalization package for supporting

- Number formatting
- Time and date formatting
- Message formatting using resource bundles

The required TLD file is `jakarta-taglibs/tld/fmt.tld`. A JSP using the formatting package should include the directive `<%@ taglib uri="/jstl-fmt" prefix="fmt" %>`.

The JSTL formatting package uses the client's locale for formatting unless you override it in the Web application.

Locales

Before looking into number formatting, you should review how you plan to support localization in your application. Basically you have three choices:

- Ignore locales so that your Web pages look the same regardless of server and client location
- Use the locale of the server
- Use the locale of the client

The example currency converters have been written to meet the first criterion so that when you run the examples in your location, the screen display will be the same as the ones shown in the figures in the book.

The JSTL formatting package uses the client locale for formatting date and accessing resource bundles. The `HttpRequest.getLocales()` method is used to obtain the `Accept-Language` HTTP header fields for determining the client's preferred locale.

You can override the default locale behavior, on a per-page basis, by adding a `<setLocale>` tag to your JSP, specifying the required language and country code (defined by ISO-639 and ISO-3166) in the `value` attribute. The following example forces a page to format according to U.S. English conventions:

```
<fmt:setLocale value='en_US'/>
```

The `<setLocale>` tag cannot have a body and is used to set a scoped variable defining the locale (`page` scope is the default). It is possible to change locales on the same page simply by inserting a new `<setLocale>` tag where the new locale is required.

CAUTION

Do not use `<setLocale>` to specify the locale in `application` scope; doing so will set the default locale for all pages in your application for all clients. If this functionality is required, you should use the `javax.servlet.jsp.jstl.fmt.locale` Web application context parameter as discussed next.

The Web application locale information can be specified in the `javax.servlet.jsp.jstl.fmt.locale` Web application context parameter. The following example sets an application to use U.S. English:

```
<context-param>
  <param-name>javax.servlet.jsp.jstl.fmt.locale</param-name>
  <param-value>en-US</param-value>
</context-param>
```

Use this approach if you want your application pages to always use the same locale regardless of the client's settings.

Number Formatting

The `<formatNumber>` tag is used to format numeric values, currencies, and percentages. The `type` attribute defines the type of number and defaults to `number`: other values are `currency` and `percentage`.

Simple number formatting uses a `pattern` attribute to define the appearance of the formatted number using the patterns defined in the `java.text.DecimalFormat` API. The following example formats a variable called `rate` to use comma-separated thousand groups and must have at least two digits before and after the decimal point:

```
<fmt:formatNumber value='${rate}' pattern='#,#00.00'/>
```

The `<formatNumber>` tag writes the value to a JSP unless a `var` attribute is used to save the formatted value as a `String` expression variable.

Currency formatting uses the `currencyCode` attribute to define the currency to be formatted. The following example formats the variable `amount` as a U.S. dollar value:

```
<fmt:formatNumber type='currency' currencyCode='USD' value='${amount}'/>
```

The `<parseNumber>` tag is used to read formatted numbers and save them in a `java.lang.Number` expression variable. Listing 11.7 shows all this put together into a JSTL-based currency converter.

LISTING 11.7 JSTL Currency Converter convert-fmt.jsp

```
<%@ taglib uri="/converter" prefix="conv" %>
<%@ taglib uri="/jstl-c" prefix="c" %>
<%@ taglib uri="/jstl-fmt" prefix="fmt" %>
<fmt:parseNumber var="dollar" value="${param.dollar}"/>
<c:set var="rate"><conv:rate/></c:set>
<HTML>
  <HEAD><TITLE>Currency Converter Using JSTL</TITLE></HEAD>
  <BODY>
    <H1>Currency Converter</H1>
    <P>
       Current conversion rate:
       <fmt:formatNumber value='${rate}' pattern='0.0000'/>
    </P>
    <c:if test='${dollar != null and dollar != ""}'>
      <BIG>
        <fmt:formatNumber type='currency' currencyCode='USD'
                          value="${dollar}"/> =
        <fmt:formatNumber type='currency' currencyCode='GBP'
                           value="${dollar*rate}"/>
     </BIG>
    </c:if>
    <FORM>
      <P>Enter dollar value: <INPUT TYPE='text' NAME='dollar'></P>
      <INPUT TYPE='submit' VALUE='Convert'>
    </FORM>
    <A HREF='homepage'>Home page</A>
  </BODY>
</HTML>
```

The example in Listing 11.7 uses `<parseNumber>` to read a formatted number into the `dollar` variable. The `<rate>` tag (shown in Chapter 10) simply returns the current exchange rate and this is stored in the `rate` variable. The dollar and converted pound amounts are written to the page using the `<formatNumber>` tag with the value written to four-digit decimal precision. All of this occurs using the client's number formatting conventions.

Unlike the previous currency converter examples, this one will display number formats according to your location rather than always look the same regardless of client and server location. The following code could be used to format the numbers for a fixed location as used in examples in other chapters:

```
<fmt:setLocale value="en_US"/>
<fmt:formatNumber type='currency' currencyCode='USD' value="${dollar}"/>
<fmt:setLocale value="en_GB"/>
<fmt:formatNumber type='currency' currencyCode='GBP' value="${dollar*rate}"/>
```

Other Formatting

The JSTL formatting package contains several other tags for formatting numbers and messages. These are as follows:

Tag	Purpose
`bundle`	Defines a resource bundle for messages
`message`	Writes a message using a resource bundle
`param`	Defines a value for parametric replacement in a message
`requestEncoding`	Defines the request character encoding for correct decoding of request parameters (used when clients do not specify the `Content-Type` header field)
`timeZone`	Defines a time zone for date and time manipulation
`formatDate`	Formats dates
`parseDate`	Parses dates

As you can see, the JSTL authors have put a lot of effort into supporting internationalization and localization. Using these tags will improve the usability of your Web pages and reduce development time.

Database and XML Tags

The JSTL includes a database package and an XML package for supporting applications that store and retrieve data using databases or XML.

The database package tags support `javax.sql.DataSource` connections as well as direct JDBC connections. The database package uses a `<query>` tag to support select statements and an `<update>` tag to support insert, update, and delete statements. Both tags use the tag body to define the SQL statement, and the `<param>` tag can be used to define the values for `?` parameter markers in the SQL in the same manner as SQL-prepared statements in JDBC.

Listing 11.8 gives a flavor of how to use the SQL query tag for accessing the exchange rates from the `jdbc/conversion` data source discussed in Chapter 9, “Databases and Tomcat.”

LISTING 11.8 JSTL Database Tags in `exchange.jsp`

```
<%@ taglib uri="/jstl-c" prefix="c" %>
<%@ taglib uri="/jstl-sql" prefix="sql" %>
<HTML>
  <HEAD><TITLE>Exchange Rates</TITLE></HEAD>
  <BODY>
    <H1>Currency Exchange Rates</H1>
    <sql:query var='rates' dataSource='${"jdbc/conversion"}'>
      SELECT src,dst,rate FROM Exchange
      ORDER BY src
    </sql:query>
    <TABLE border='1'>
      <TR><TH>From</TH><TH>To</TH><TH>Rate</TH></TR>
      <c:forEach var='row' items='${rates.rows}'>
        <TR>
          <TD><c:out value='${row.src}'/></TD>
          <TD><c:out value='${row.dst}'/></TD>
          <TD><c:out value='${row.rate}'/></TD>
        </TR>
      </c:forEach>
    </TABLE>
    <P><A HREF='homepage'>Home page</A></P>
  </BODY>
</HTML>
```

The XML package provides tags that support parsing existing XML documents and writing new XML documents. This is unfortunately too large a subject to do justice to here. Readers interested in using XML and JSTL should read the JSTL specification and study the examples provided with the JSTL download from the Jakarta Web site.

Summary

Custom tag libraries support the object-oriented objective of code reuse. Many standard tag libraries will support the functionality you need for your pages, and using them will save you design, development, and testing time.

The JSP Standard Tag Library (JSTL) was specified and developed during 2001 and 2002 and is due to be incorporated into the JSP 2.0 specification. The JSTL uses an expression language (EL) to simplify the evaluation of variables and expressions used within custom tags. The simple expression syntax for accessing JSP implicit objects,

JavaBean properties, and Java collections will widen the appeal of JSP and JSTL Web page development to programmers not literate in Java. JSTL provides packages for programming like constructs, number and text formatting, SQL database access, and XML document manipulation.

12

Error Handling

IN THIS CHAPTER

- User Input Errors
- Pages Accessed Out of Order
- Handling HTTP Response Errors
- Servlet Exception Handling
- JSP Error Handling
- Error Handling in Custom Tags

In Chapter 6, "Troubleshooting Servlets and JSPs," you saw how to track and debug common JSP and servlet errors while developing your application. That chapter dealt mainly with compile-time errors. The emphasis in this chapter is on how to write your Web application to handle those runtime errors that cannot be avoided.

In this chapter, you will be looking at the techniques you can use to ensure that your Web application gracefully handles all those error conditions that you hope will never happen but that inevitably do. These errors include

- Runtime exceptions
- Incorrect user input
- Pages accessed out of order
- Failure of supporting systems such as databases
- Security or permission failures
- Lack of server resources

Errors generally fall into one of two categories:

- Those caused by users doing the unexpected, such as incorrectly filling in a form or mistyping a URL
- System failures, which include bugs in your code, communication failures, and running out of resources

These types of errors should be handled in slightly different ways, but in both cases, it is important that they are handled elegantly:

- When necessary, present the end user with an appropriate message.
- If possible, set up your application so that it will take steps to recover from the error.
- Log the error if it is a system failure.
- Notify the Web server administrator if it is a critical error.

TIP

As a general policy, you should never present a user with a Web page showing a Java stack trace. Use the techniques demonstrated in this chapter to hide errors that present stack traces behind more user-friendly Web pages.

User Input Errors

All but the simplest Web applications are likely to require some user input. Data entered into HTML forms can be (and should be) subjected to client-side validation with JavaScript, as this saves a request-response cycle if there are preventable errors. But JavaScript provides only the simplest data integrity checking, and data validated with JavaScript is not completely reliable. Your servlet must therefore always validate user input, because no matter how carefully you design your form and no matter how many instructions your users are given, there will always be the possibility of errors.

The way your servlet handles user input errors is important to the end user. There is nothing more annoying than an application that either fails to handle user errors properly or simply crashes, either with no output or with an error message such as a Java stack trace that is meaningless to the user. To provide the end user with the best browsing experience, you should always

- Validate all the errors on a form in one go
- Return the completed form with the invalid items identified
- Provide a message to indicate the error and what data should be entered to make the entry valid

Good object-oriented design dictates that you should encapsulate the error handling into separate classes. The best way of doing this is to use custom tags.

TIP

To support internationalization, you should use resource bundles so you can customize the error messages according to local languages and conventions.

Listings 12.1 and 12.2 show a revised currency converter servlet and form that incorporate a simple error reporting mechanism. They use a request attribute to highlight user input errors.

LISTING 12.1 `CurrencyConverter.java doGet()` Method with Error Handling

```
public void doGet(HttpServletRequest req, HttpServletResponse res)
             throws ServletException, IOException {

    Currency dollars = Currency.getInstance(Locale.US);
    Currency pounds = Currency.getInstance(Locale.UK);
    try {
        double oldValue = Double.parseDouble(req.getParameter("amount"));
        if (oldValue <= 0) {
            req.setAttribute("error", "Value must be greater than zero");
        }
        else {
            double newValue = oldValue * EXCHANGE_RATE ;
            String result = dollars.getSymbol(Locale.US) +
                format(dollars, oldValue) + " = " +
➥ pounds.getSymbol(Locale.UK) +
                format(pounds, newValue);
            req.setAttribute("result", result);
        }
        req.getRequestDispatcher ("/currency-form.jsp").forward(req, res);
    }
    catch (NumberFormatException e) {
        req.setAttribute("error", "Non numeric value cannot be converted");
        req.getRequestDispatcher ("/currency-form.jsp").forward(req, res);
    }
}
```

Listing 12.1 shows the currency converter servlet that validates the user input. When an error is detected, the servlet adds a request attribute, called `error`, whose value is the error message. Runtime errors (such as `NumberFormatException`) also create the request `error` attribute. If the currency value is converted successfully, a `result` attribute is added to the request.

Whether the currency value is converted successfully or not, the servlet forwards the request to the JSP page shown in Listing 12.2.

LISTING 12.2 currency-form.jsp with Added Error Reporting

```
<% String error = (String) request.getAttribute("error"); %>
<% String result = (String) request.getAttribute("result"); %>
<% String amount = request.getParameter("amount"); %>

<HTML>
    <HEAD><TITLE>Currency Form</TITLE></HEAD>
    <BODY>
        <FORM METHOD=GET ACTION="CurrencyConverter">
            <H1>Currency Converter</H1>
            <P>Use this form to convert US Dollars to UK Pounds Sterling</P>
            Type in the amount to be converted in the box
            <INPUT TYPE=TEXT name="amount"
➥ value="<%= amount==null?"1":amount %>"/>
            <INPUT TYPE=SUBMIT value="CONVERT" />
            <P><FONT color="RED" > <%= error==null?"":error %> </FONT></P>
            <P><FONT size="7"><%= result==null?"":result %></FONT></P>
        </FORM>
    </BODY>
</HTML>
```

The JSP form in Listing 12.2 displays a form in which the user can enter a value to convert. At the end of the form, the JSP uses the `result` and `error` request attributes to display the successful conversion or an error message.

Figures 12.1 and 12.2 show the output generated by this JSP in response to a user entering valid and invalid amounts.

For the sake of simplicity, the JSP uses a request attribute rather than a custom tag, but the principle is the same. In a more sophisticated application, you would simply replace the first line of Listing 12.2 with an appropriate custom tag that delivers the error message. You would also allow the addition of multiple error messages to the request and display all detected failures rather than a single error message. (Imagine how annoying it would be if the Java compiler only displayed one error message at a time.)

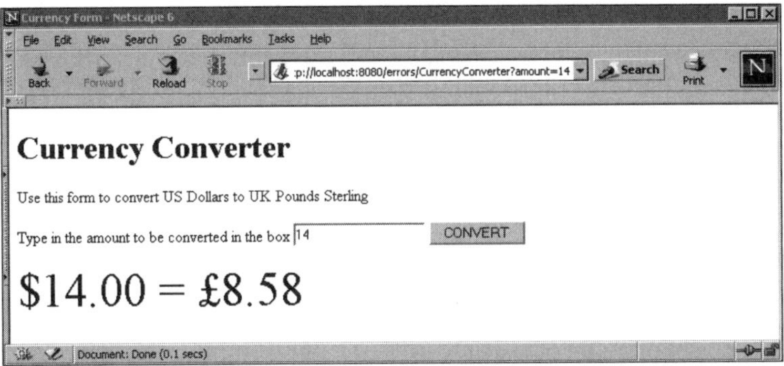

FIGURE 12.1 The currency converter form with valid data entered.

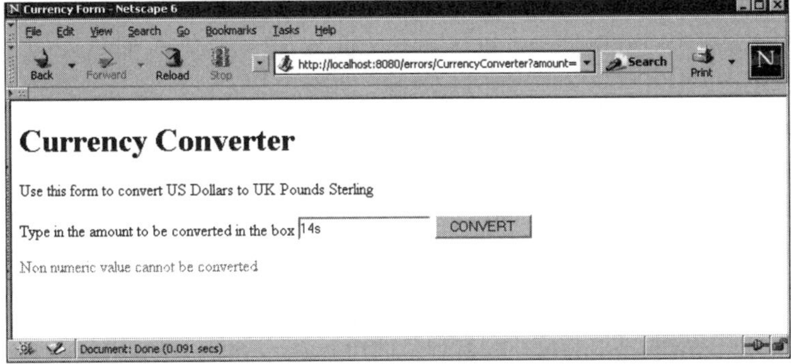

FIGURE 12.2 The currency converter form with invalid data entered.

Pages Accessed Out of Order

No matter how carefully you design your Web application with a logical flow from page to page, users (and particularly hackers) will mess things up by accessing pages in the wrong order. If your servlet has preconditions that should be set up by previous servlets, you must ensure that it validates those preconditions before servicing the request.

A failure to validate preconditions will leave your application in complete disorder and potentially insecure.

In addition to accessing pages out of order, users will

- Access bookmarked pages with invalid or out-of-date request parameters
- Manually type in URLs and omit parameters or mistype parameter names
- Try to bypass any login or registration screens

When validating preconditions, you should use the same error reporting techniques that you used for invalid user input. However, you should redirect users to a suitable starting Web page so you can guide them through the logical progression of your Web pages.

TIP

Consider using HTML page refresh elements to show an error page for a few seconds before redirecting the user to a new Web page.

To reduce the chances of pages being accessed out of order, you should provide users with as little information as possible about your application structure. Wherever possible, hide URLs and parameters by using URL mappings and welcome pages to direct users to the pages you want them to use. Don't allow access to directory listings (Tomcat's default behavior for a directory without a welcome file) and ensure that every servlet checks parameters and security information. This will protect your application not only from malicious users, but also from curious, lazy, or inept users.

Handling HTTP Response Errors

HTTP errors can be generated either by Tomcat (when it detects a problem) or by a servlet using the `HttpServletResponse.sendError()` method. In either case, Tomcat will return an error page to the client. You can improve on the standard Tomcat error handling mechanism by replacing the default error page with one of your own. You can use error pages to handle both HTTP client errors (response codes 400–499) and internal server errors (response codes 500–599).

Configure error pages in the Web application deployment descriptor using one or more `<error-page>` elements. The following example shows how to configure the application to catch the ubiquitous HTTP 404 error and return your own application-specific error page:

```
<error-page>
    <error-code>404</error-code>
    <location>http404.html</location>
</error-page>
```

Your error page should include some or all of the following:

- A simple error message
- A link to your Web application home page
- Any other links you feel are useful

- Automatic refreshing or forwarding to a valid page
- A link for sending email to the Webmaster

If the location of the error page is a servlet or JSP, Tomcat sets the request attributes listed in Table 12.1. These attributes can be used by the error page to modify the response to the client.

TABLE 12.1 Request Attributes Set for an Error Page

Attribute	Description
`javax.servlet.error.status_code`	The HTTP error status code
`javax.servlet.error.message`	The exception error message
`javax.servlet.error.request_uri`	The URI of the servlet that caused the error
`javax.servlet.error.servlet_name`	The logical name of the servlet in which the error occurred

The following code shows how a general-purpose error page (one that is being used to handle many HTTP error conditions) can determine the actual HTTP error code and which Web page generated the error:

```
Integer httpError =
➥ (Integer)req.getAttribute("javax.servlet.error.status_code");
String requestURI =
➥ (String)req.getAttribute("javax.servlet.error.request_uri");
if (httpError.intValue() == HttpServletResponse.SC_NOT_FOUND) {
    System.out.println ("Bad URL " + requestURI);
    // ...
}
```

Server errors should almost certainly be handled differently than client errors. Your application can often recover from client errors by simply redirecting the user to another Web page. It usually can't recover from server errors, however, as they are often caused by fatal internal errors (such as unavailable databases or logic errors in the Java code). With servlet errors, it might be fitting to present users with a problem report form or the Webmaster's email address so they can give an account of the error. At the very least, you should log the error and handle it in a graceful manner. You'll learn how to log errors in Chapter 13, "Logging Using Tomcat."

CAUTION

You will not be able to catch an HTTP 500 error generated by Tomcat when your servlet fails because of an uncaught exception. Uncaught exceptions must be caught using the `<exception-type>` element, as shown in the next section, "Servlet Exception Handling."

Servlet Exception Handling

There is a well-known saying that goes like this:

> There are two certainties in life—death and taxes.

As a Java programmer, you might be inclined to alter this adage slightly:

> There are three certainties in life—death, taxes, and runtime exceptions.

When a runtime exception occurs, you should never present a user with a Web page showing a stack trace. In general, you should catch all exceptions in the Web application and take appropriate action to inform the client what has happened.

When a fatal exception occurs, there is often nothing to do but catch the exception, clean up the data, and tell the client that a serious error has occurred. In this case, you can use the `HttpServletResponse.sendRedirect()` method to redirect the client to another Web page that will display a suitable error message. Alternatively, you can use `HttpServletResponse.sendError()` with an appropriate HTTP error code and use the deployment descriptor error page mechanism discussed in the previous section, "Handling HTTP Response Errors."

You can define an error page for uncaught exceptions in the deployment descriptor for your Web application by adding one or more `<error-page>` elements for each uncaught exception class you wish to catch. You can use the following example to catch applications that throw an `SQLException` due to database errors:

```
<error-page>
    <exception-type>java.sql.SQLException</exception-type>
    <location>/database-error.jsp</location>
</error-page>
```

When handling uncaught exceptions, Tomcat will set all the request attributes shown in Table 12.1 and the following exception-specific attributes:

Attribute	Description
`javax.servlet.error.exception_type`	Holds a `java.lang.Class` object representing the type of exception
`javax.servlet.error.exception`	The exception object

Tomcat also sets `javax.servlet.error.status_code` to 500 for all uncaught exceptions.

Whatever method you use to handle an exception, you should save as much information as possible. You should log all exceptions and save a stack trace for investigation. The use of the J2SE 1.4 logging API and the Apache Software Foundation Log4J framework is covered in Chapter 13.

CAUTION

Any uncaught exceptions that do not have matching `<error-page>` elements will be caught by the Catalina container and reported as HTTP 500 errors. Consider adding an `<error-page>` element to catch `java.lang.Exception` so that all exceptions not explicitly listed in another `<error-page>` element are handled cleanly.

JSP Error Handling

With a JSP page directive, you can redirect the client to a specified URL when an uncaught exception occurs. For example, you can use the following JSP page directive to redirect the request to the `error.jsp` page:

```
<%@ page errorPage="error.jsp" %>
```

The `error.jsp` page itself must include the page directive `isErrorPage`:

```
<%@ page isErrorPage="true" %>
```

This directive indicates that this page is the target for an `errorPage` directive and also defines an extra implicit object called `exception` (class `java.lang.Exception`) that supports access to the exception that caused the error.

Here's a very simple error page that prints out a message and saves the exception stack trace to Tomcat's log file:

```
<%@ page isErrorPage="true" %>
<HTML>
    <HEAD><TITLE>Application Error</TITLE></HEAD>
    <BODY>
        <P>Application failure - contact the Webmaster</P>
        <P><%= exception.getMessage() %></P>
        <% application.log(exception.getMessage(), exception); %>
    </BODY>
</HTML>
```

If you have defined an error page for a JSP with the `errorPage` directive and an `<error-page>` element in the deployment descriptor, the JSP `errorPage` directive will take precedence.

Error Handling in Custom Tags

The JSP specification provides the `TryCatchFinally` interface, which you can use to clean up after an exception is thrown in a JSP custom tag. The `TryCatchFinally` mechanism was covered in detail in Chapter 10, "Custom Tags and TagLibs" (see the section titled "Exception Handling"). A brief review is included here.

The interface defines two methods that are called by Tomcat when an exception occurs:

Method	Description
`doCatch()`	Called if an exception occurs in `doStart()`, `doEndTag()`, `doAfterBody()`, `doInitBody()`, or while executing the body of the tag
`doFinally()`	Always called after `doEndTag()` if an exception has occurred

If you need to clean up or reset any data when an exception occurs, you should put the code in either the `doCatch()` or the `doFinally()` method as dictated by the logic of your tag.

You should only use the custom tag `TryCatchFinally` mechanism to catch any exceptions for which your tag can provide some form of error recovery, so that the tag writes sensible information to the Web page.

If you decide to allow your custom tag to throw an exception, you should clearly indicate this in the documentation for your tag. As a simple example, you might decide that a custom tag that encapsulates access to a database can throw an `SQLException` to indicate database failure. This will allow the JSP developer to decide on the best error recovery strategy for database errors.

Summary

In this chapter, you have studied various techniques for handling user input errors, internal errors, and uncaught exceptions within your Java code. In particular, you have seen how to

- Write your application so that it handles invalid user input in a user-friendly way
- Configure error handling for HTTP errors and servlet exceptions using the deployment descriptor
- Use and write JSP error pages
- Use the `TryCatchFinally` interface in custom tags

Errors do not occur only during development or testing. When a Web application goes live, you may not be around to witness any failures. In the following chapter, you will see how you can use logging to save debugging and auditing information to Tomcat log files.

13 Logging Using Tomcat

IN THIS CHAPTER

- Tomcat Logger Elements
- J2SE 1.4 Logging API
- Jakarta Log4j

Logging is an important but often neglected part of any enterprise application. Although the term *logging* is frequently used synonymously with debugging, there are many uses for logging; these include

- Providing an audit trail for security purposes
- Performance tuning
- Tracking usage patterns
- Tracing for debugging and error handling

In this chapter, you will look at two aspects of logging with Tomcat. First, you will see how to configure the Tomcat logger element to output debugging and tracing information to the system console and Tomcat log files. Second, we will show you how to add logging to your Web application using both the standard J2SE 1.4 logging API and the Jakarta log4j API. These two logging facilities have been chosen for two reasons:

- Log4j is well established and is used in a large number of projects.
- Although only introduced in J2SE 1.4, the `java.util.logging` package can be regarded as the standard logging mechanism and you should consider it carefully before using an alternative.

Too often, and for too long, developers have been using `System.out.println()` for logging and debugging statements. Although simple to implement, this method of tracing application execution has a number of disadvantages:

- There is no way of switching logging on or off at runtime.
- There is no mechanism for specifying logging priority or message severity except by the content of the message.
- Additional functionality (such as e-mailing an administrator) has to be explicitly coded.
- You have to redirect the console output to a file in order to obtain a permanent copy of the log data.
- It is easy to forget debugging messages, which inevitably pop up to embarrass you when the system goes live.

The J2SE and log4j logging APIs discussed in this chapter address all these issues, but before addressing these topics, we will look at the logging facilities provided by Tomcat.

Tomcat Logger Elements

Tomcat `<Logger>` elements define the destinations for logging, debugging, and error messages generated by Tomcat (including the output from `ServletContext.log()` methods and any generated stack traces). Logger elements are configured in the Tomcat `<CATALINA_HOME>/conf/server.xml` file in any of the following three component elements, where each level corresponds to a Catalina container:

Logger Element Level	Description
`<Engine>`	Handles logging messages for the entire engine, including connectors defined in the surrounding service. This element also handles logging for subsidiary hosts and contexts, unless overridden by a logger element defined at host or context level.
`<Host>`	Handles logging messages for the host and all contexts in the host, unless overridden by a logger element defined at the context level.
`<Context>`	Handles logging messages for the specific context.

Tomcat's default `server.xml` file defines several logger elements including the default logger defined for the engine component in the default Tomcat-Standalone service, as shown in the following example:

```
<Logger className="org.apache.catalina.logger.FileLogger"
        directory="logs"  prefix="localhost_log." suffix=".txt"
        timestamp="true"/>
```

Any log messages written from your Web application using the `ServletContext.log()` method will be written to the logging file defined by the `<Logger>` element shown in the previous example.

The `<Logger>` `className` attribute `className` specifies which type of logger implementation to use. There are three to choose from:

- `org.apache.catalina.logger.FileLogger`—Saves logging information to disk
- `org.apache.catalina.logger.SystemOutLogger`—Saves logging information to Tomcat's standard output stream (the window in which Tomcat was started)
- `org.apache.catalina.logger.SystemErrLogger`—Saves logging information to Tomcat's standard error stream (the window in which Tomcat was started)

In most circumstances you will want to use a `FileLogger` so that you have a permanent record of the logging data stored on disk.

Using a `FileLogger`

If a `FileLogger` is specified, you can use the following attributes to define the destination file:

- `directory`—Name of the directory where the log file will be placed. Specify either the absolute pathname or one that is relative to `<CATALINA_HOME>` (default is `<CATALINA_HOME>/logs`).
- `prefix`—Log filename prefix (default is `catalina`).
- `suffix`—Log filename suffix (default is `.log`).
- `timestamp`—Set to `true` to time and date stamp logged messages (default is `false`).

The generated logging filename adds the current date in `YYYY-MM-DD` format between the filename prefix and suffix components; you cannot change this naming convention.

If, for example, you are running Tomcat on April 1, 2002, the default log file will be called `<CATALINA_HOME>/logs/catalina_log.2002-04-01.txt`.

TIP

Always timestamp log entries. With a multi-threaded application, you cannot rely on the order in which messages are logged to determine their order of execution.

As with all disk-based log files, you should take care to ensure that they do not get too large and become unmanageable. Tomcat automatically rolls the log files over at midnight. Because the logging filename includes the current date in YYYY-MM-DD format, Tomcat log files are kept indefinitely unless you take explicit action to archive them or delete them from the disk.

Using Tomcat's Internal Logging

Two things control the amount of logging that Tomcat undertakes. The first is the amount of debugging defined by the `debug` attribute to the `<Connector>`, `<Engine>`, `<Host>`, and `<Context>` elements in the `server.xml` file. The `debug` attribute can have a value between `0` (no debugging messages) and `9` (lots of debugging messages).

The second item that controls the volume of Tomcat logging is the `verbosity` attribute of the `<Logger>` element itself. There are five verbosity levels:

- 0—Fatal
- 1—Error (the default)
- 2—Warning
- 3—Information
- 4—Debug

Messages with a numerically higher level than the configured verbosity level are silently ignored.

NOTE

Messages without a verbosity level are always logged. Most of Tomcat's log messages do not have a verbosity level, so changing the `<Logger>` verbosity level has a minimal effect on the volume of Tomcat's logging messages.

TIP

To increase the amount of Tomcat's logging for just the application you are testing, you should create a `<Logger>` element at the application `<Context>` level and also increase the debug level on the `<Context>`. Reset the debugging level to `0` when the problem has been found.

Logging Using Tomcat Valves

Tomcat also uses components called *valves* (see Chapter 19, "Tomcat Valves") to create logging messages. A `<Valve>` element represents a component that is inserted into the request-processing pipeline for a Tomcat container (`Engine`, `Host`, or `Context`). Tomcat provides two valves that can be used to log request activities. These are discussed briefly in the rest of this section, and Chapter 19 includes full details on how to configure and use valves with your applications.

An `AccessLogValve` creates a log file to track page hits. Various information fields from the request and response can be logged, including the following:

- Remote hostname
- Local port on which this request was received
- Request method (`GET`, `POST`, and so on)
- Request query string
- Requested URL path
- HTTP status code of the response
- Date and time of the request

Tomcat has the following `AccessLogValve` defined in the `server.xml` file to log all requests directed to the `localhost` virtual host:

```
<Valve className="org.apache.catalina.valves.AccessLogValve"
    directory="logs"  prefix="localhost_access_log." suffix=".txt"
    pattern="common"/>
```

NOTE

Depending on the version of Tomcat you are using, this valve may be commented out.

The generated filename for the `AccessLogValve` includes the current date in the YYYY-MM-DD format between the prefix and suffix components of the filename.

A `RequestDumperValve` can be used to dump the request activity information to the `<Logger>` element configured for the associated container. This has the advantage over the `AccessLogValve` that all the logging is contained in the one file. Be warned, however, this valve can generate a lot of information and degrade performance; see Chapter 19 for more information.

J2SE 1.4 Logging API

Figure 13.1 shows the J2SE 1.4 logging architecture using a UML sequence diagram. All of the logging classes are defined in the `java.util.logging` package; a summary of some of the classes is also provided in Table 13.1.

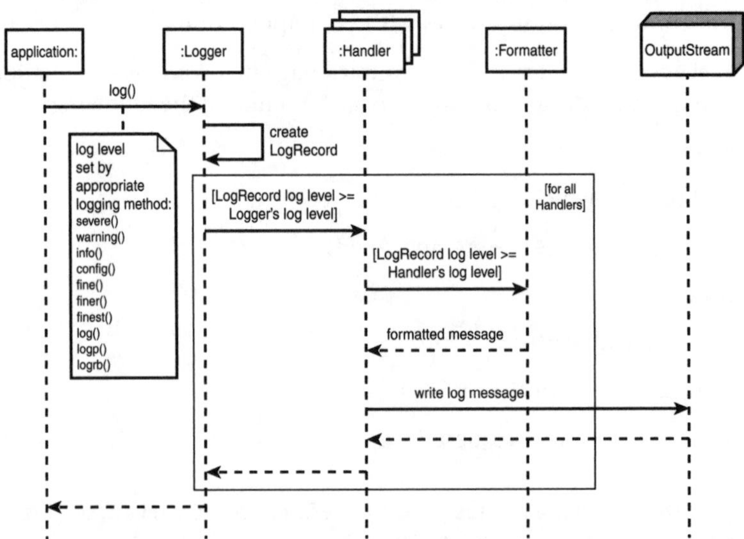

FIGURE 13.1 Logging architecture sequence diagram.

TABLE 13.1 `java.util.logging` Classes

Class	Description
`Logger`	Converts a log message into a `LogRecord` object, which is passed to one or more `Handler` methods for publication
`Handler`	Takes log records from a Logger and publishes them
`ConsoleHandler`	Publishes log records to `System.err`
`FileHandler`	Publishes log records to a file
`MemoryHandler`	Buffers log records in a buffer in memory
`SocketHandler`	Publishes log records to a network stream
`Level`	A set of logging levels that are applied to log messages
`LogRecord`	Encapsulates logging messages with an associated logging level
`Formatter`	Formats `LogRecords`, sub-classes `SimpleFormatter` and `XMLFormatter`
`SimpleFormatter`	Formats a `LogRecord` in a human-readable format
`XMLFormatter`	Formats a `LogRecord` into an XML element

At the simplest level, an application sends messages to a `Logger` object, which converts the input into a `LogRecord` object. The `LogRecord` is passed to one or more `Handler` methods for publication. The `Handler` uses a `Formatter` to localize and format the `LogRecord` before publishing it to an output stream.

The `LogRecord` created by the `Logger` object has an associated log level. The following table shows the seven predefined log levels:

Log Level	Use
SEVERE	When a fatal error occurs that the user will see
WARNING	To warn end users about something
INFO	To provide end users with information
CONFIG	For configuration information (useful for developers)
FINE	For debugging
FINER	For more detailed debugging
FINEST	For really detailed debugging

`SEVERE` is defined to have the highest priority and `FINEST` the lowest. Each `Logger` and `Handler` object also has an associated log level. Only messages with an equal or higher priority than both the `Logger` and `Handler` levels will be processed. All other messages are silently ignored.

You can also create log filter objects that can be used to filter log messages according to any criteria you wish to define (not just the log level). A log filter implements the `java.util.logging.Filter` interface and can be associated with a Logger or a Handler object. A `Logger` or `Handler` can only have one associated filter object.

Logger Objects

Logger objects are used to log messages and normally have names. It is conventional to name logger objects using the same naming convention as Java packages—for example, `com.samspublishing.app`. The logger namespace is hierarchical: Children at a lower level inherit changes made at a higher level. For example, if you set the log level to `INFO` for `com.samspublishing`, the log level for `com.samspublishing.app` logger will by default be set to `INFO`.

NOTE

The API also provides for anonymous (unnamed) loggers primarily intended for use with applets.

A child `Logger` object inherits the attributes of its parent object. In the previous example, the `com.samspublishing.app` logger will inherit from the `com.samspublishing` `Logger` (if it exists), which in turn inherits from a `com` `Logger` (if one exists). This hierarchical structure allows `Handler` objects to be defined for a parent `Logger` and then used by a child logger.

You obtain a logger by passing its name to the `Logger.getLogger()` method as follows:

```
Logger appLogger = Logger.getlogger("com.samspublishing.app");
```

The `Logger.getLogger()` method obtains the `Logger` object associated with the specified name. A default `Logger` (see the later section "Setting Default Logging Configuration") is created if no `Logger` is currently associated with the name.

TIP

There is a useful variant to the `getLogger()` method that takes the name of a resource bundle to support localization of log messages.

To create a log message, you can use one of the many logging methods available in the `Logger` class. Although log methods are provided that give fine control over what is logged, most of the time you will probably use one of the seven convenience methods that corresponds to the log level you require. For example, to write an `INFO`-level message, use

```
appLogger.info("informational message");
```

You can control the level of logging for a given `Logger` object using the `Logger.setLevel()` method. Messages of a lower priority than the level set on the `Logger` object will be silently ignored.

Use the following to set the logging level to `FINE`:

```
appLogger.setLevel(Level.FINE);
```

You can also turn logging on and off with the special logging levels of `ON` and `OFF`. To switch off logging in your servlet use

```
appLogger.setLevel(Level.OFF);
```

TIP

The API for the logging classes states that they are multi-thread safe. However, none of the methods is declared as `synchronized`, so `synchronization` must be at a lower level. In a heavily multi-threaded environment, it is therefore possible for log messages to become intermingled. To ensure log messages do not become confused, you might want to call the logging methods from within a synchronized block, synchronizing on the `Logger` object. However, use of synchronized blocks will normally slow down the performance of your application.

Because logger objects are multi-thread safe, you can store them in an instance variable that is initialized from the `HttpServlet.init()` method.

Handler Objects

Handlers are used by `Logger` objects to publish messages. A `Logger` object can have multiple `Handler` objects to enable log messages to be copied to different output streams. There are five default `Handler` classes, which are probably sufficient for most needs:

- `ConsoleHandler` prints to the application's standard error stream; for servlets, this is the Tomcat startup window.
- `StreamHandler` writes to any `OutputStream`.
- `FileHandler` writes to a specified file or a group of rotating files.
- `SocketHandler` writes to a TCP/IP port.
- `MemoryHandler` writes to a buffer in memory.

You can define your own `Handler` class if the default classes do not meet your requirements.

The default `Logger` object is configured with a single `ConsoleHandler` with a logging level set to `INFO`. This means that log messages of `INFO` or above will appear in the Tomcat startup window. This default behavior is defined in a properties file (`<JAVA_HOME>/jre/lib/logging.properties`). See the section "Setting Default Logging Configuration" later in this chapter.

You must add extra handlers to a named `Logger` object if you want to route your messages to different logging locations. Use the `Logger.addHandler()` method to add a new handler as shown in the following code:

```
Logger appLogger = Logger.getlogger("com.samspublishing.app");
FileHandler logfile = new FileHandler("C:/logs/test.log");
logfile.setLevel(Level.FINEST);
appLogger.addHandler(logfile);
```

CAUTION

Note the `FileHandler` pathname separator is always / regardless of the operating system being used.

The previous example shows how to use the `Handler.setLevel()` method to set the logging level for the handler. The default logging level for all handlers is set to `INFO` in the logging configuration file (see the section "Setting Default Logging Configuration" later in this chapter).

A log message will only be output if the message logging level is equal to or higher than the levels set in the `Logger` and the `Handler` objects. Multiple `Handler` objects can be set to different logging levels to vary the amount of logging sent to each separate location. The `Logger` used in the previous example will log `INFO` and higher messages to the console and all messages to the `test.log` file.

You can use the `Logger.removeHandler()` method to remove an unwanted handler. To remove a handler, you must obtain a list of handlers from the `Logger` using the `getHandlers()` method and remove the one you don't want.

TIP

To remove the default `ConsoleLogger` object, you would not use the `removeHandler()` method because the console logging is associated with the global `Logger` that is the parent of all loggers. Instead, you would use the `Logger.setUseParentHandlers()` method as shown later in Listing 13.3.

Formatter Objects

The final component of the logging mechanism is a `Formatter` object that is used to format the log records. The J2SE Logging API provides two formatters, but you can easily write your own custom formatter.

The `SimpleFormatter` class writes a log record as a two-line summary with the following structure:

```
<Date> <Time> <Java class> <method>
<Log level>: <Message>
```

For example:

```
13-May-2002 16:23:31 CurrencyConverter init()
INFO: servicing requests
```

The `XMLFormatter` provides similar logging information but this time as an XML element, as shown in the following example:

```
<?xml version="1.0" encoding="windows-1252" standalone="no"?>
<!DOCTYPE log SYSTEM "logger.dtd">
<log>
```

```
  <record>
    <date>2002-05-13T19:03:18</date>
    <millis>1021312998157</millis>
    <sequence>0</sequence>
    <logger>myLogger</logger>
    <level>INFO</level>
    <class> CurrencyConverter </class>
    <method>init</method>
    <thread>10</thread>
    <message>servicing requests</message>
  </record>
</log>
```

Each `Handler` has a single `Formatter` object that is used to format the log record. You use the `Handler.getFormatter()` and `Handler.setFormatter()` methods to define the formatter for the handler. The default formatter is set in the logging configuration file and depends on the class of the handler—for example, the `ConsoleHandler` uses a `SimpleFormatter` whereas the `FileHandler` class uses an `XMLFormatter`.

You can define your own formatter class by extending the abstract `Formatter` class and defining a `format()` method that takes a `LogRecord` as a parameter. Listing 13.1 shows a very basic formatter that formats the date, the log level, and the message on a single line.

LISTING 13.1 BasicFormatter.java

```
import java.util.*;
import java.util.logging.*;

public class BasicFormatter extends Formatter {

   public String format(LogRecord record) {
      StringBuffer buffer = new StringBuffer();
      buffer.append(new Date() + " : ");
      buffer.append(record.getLevel().toString() + " : ");
      buffer.append(record.getMessage() + "\n");
      return buffer.toString();
   }
}
```

Setting Default Logging Configuration

The default logging configuration is defined in `<JAVA_HOME>/jre/lib/logging.properties`. You may edit this file or define your own properties file to change the default logging configuration. The `logging.properties` configuration file defines global handlers and properties for all applications. Listing 13.2 shows an example default `logging.properties`.

LISTING 13.2 Example `logging.properties` File

```
############################################################
#       Default Logging Configuration File
#
# You can use a different file by specifying a filename
# with the java.util.logging.config.file system property.
# For example java -Djava.util.logging.config.file=myfile
############################################################
# By default we only configure a ConsoleHandler, which will only
# show messages at the INFO and above levels.
handlers= java.util.logging.ConsoleHandler

# To also add the FileHandler, use the following line instead.
#handlers= java.util.logging.FileHandler, java.util.logging.ConsoleHandler

# Default global logging level.
# This specifies which kinds of events are logged across all loggers.
# Note that the ConsoleHandler also has a separate level
# setting to limit messages printed to the console.
.level= INFO

############################################################
# Handler specific properties.
# Describes specific configuration info for Handlers.
############################################################

# default file output is in user's home directory.
java.util.logging.FileHandler.pattern = %h/java%u.log
java.util.logging.FileHandler.limit = 50000
java.util.logging.FileHandler.count = 1
java.util.logging.FileHandler.formatter = java.util.logging.XMLFormatter

# Limit the message that are printed on the console to INFO and above.
java.util.logging.ConsoleHandler.level = INFO
```

LISTING 13.2 Continued

```
java.util.logging.ConsoleHandler.formatter = java.util.logging.SimpleFormatter
############################################################
# Facility specific properties.
# Provides extra control for each logger.
############################################################
com.xyz.foo.level = SEVERE
```

The `handlers` property specifies a comma-separated list of `Handler` objects. A default `ConsoleHandler` is defined in the configuration file as follows:

```
handlers=java.util.logging.ConsoleHandler
```

A default logging level of `INFO` is specified for all handlers using the `.level` property. Use this property to increase or decrease the default logging level:

```
.level=INFO
```

You can override the default level for a specific handler by prefixing the `.level` property name with the handler class name. The following example restricts the console logging level to `SEVERE`:

```
java.util.logging.ConsoleHandler.level=SEVERE
```

You can also add configuration for an individually named logger by using the logger name as the prefix to the `.level` property as follows:

```
com.sams.appLogger.level=WARNING
```

If you define your own `logging.properties` file, you must specify the file using the JVM command-line property `java.util.logging.config.file`, as shown in the following example:

```
-Djava.util.logging.config.file=F:\Projects\logging.conf
```

The easiest way to specify a `logging.properties` file for Tomcat is to add the property to the environment variable `CATALINA_OPTS`. You can do this as follows for Unix:

```
CATALINA_OPTS=
➥ -Djava.util.logging.config.file=/usr/local/tomcat/logging.properties
```

and as follows for Windows:

```
set CATALINA_OPTS=
➥ -Djava.util.logging.config.file=C:\Tomcat\logging.properties
```

Add this variable definition to the appropriate Tomcat startup file for Unix:

```
<CATALINA_HOME>/bin/catalina.sh
```

and this definition for Windows:

```
<CATALINA_HOME>\bin\catalina.bat
```

Adding Logging to the Currency Converter

Listing 13.3 shows the Currency Converter servlet with some simple logging added.

LISTING 13.3 `CurrencyConverter.java` with Added Logging

```
import java.io.*;
import java.util.*;
import java.util.logging.*;
import java.text.*;
import javax.servlet.*;
import javax.servlet.http.*;

public class CurrencyConverter extends HttpServlet {
    private static final double EXCHANGE_RATE = 0.613;
    private static Logger convLogger = Logger.getLogger("convLogger");

    public void init() {
        convLogger.setLevel(Level.INFO);
        try {
            FileHandler logfile = new FileHandler("F:/Tomcat/logs/conv.log");
            logfile.setLevel(Level.INFO);
            logfile.setFormatter(new BasicFormatter());
            convLogger.addHandler(logfile);
            convLogger.setUseParentHandlers(false);
        }
        catch (IOException e) {
            convLogger.warning("Failed to set up logfile");
        }
    }

    private String format (Currency currency, double value) {
        NumberFormat nf = NumberFormat.getInstance();
        nf.setMaximumFractionDigits(currency.getDefaultFractionDigits());
        nf.setMinimumFractionDigits(currency.getDefaultFractionDigits());
        return nf.format(value);
```

LISTING 13.3 Continued

```
    }

    public void doGet(HttpServletRequest req, HttpServletResponse res)
                 throws ServletException, IOException {

        Currency dollars = Currency.getInstance(Locale.US);
        Currency pounds = Currency.getInstance(Locale.UK);
        try {
            double oldValue = Double.parseDouble(req.getParameter("amount"));
            if (oldValue <= 0) {
                req.setAttribute("error", "Value must be greater than zero");
            }
            else {
                double newValue = oldValue * EXCHANGE_RATE ;
                String result = dollars.getSymbol(Locale.US) +
                  format(dollars, oldValue) + " = "
                  + pounds.getSymbol(Locale.UK) + format(pounds, newValue);
                req.setAttribute("result", result);
                if (convLogger.isLoggable(Level.INFO)) {
                    convLogger.info("Converted " + result + " using rate " +
                       EXCHANGE_RATE);
                }
            }
            req.getRequestDispatcher ("/currency-form.jsp").forward(req, res);
        }
        catch (NumberFormatException e) {
            req.setAttribute("error", "Non numeric value cannot be converted");
            req.getRequestDispatcher ("/currency-form.jsp").forward(req, res);
        }
    }
}
```

This example uses a couple of `Logger` methods not previously discussed. In the `HttpServlet.init()` method, the example sets up a `FileHandler` to log messages to a file. If the file handler is created successfully, the `Logger.setUseParentHandlers(false)` method is called to stop the child `Logger` from using the handlers defined by the parent `Logger`. In this case, the parent is the global handler that has the `ConsoleHandler` defined, so calling this method switches off console logging.

In Listing 13.3, the servlet `doGet()` method calls `convLogger.isLoggable(Level.INFO))` to see whether messages at the `INFO` level will be logged before logging the message. This check avoids the expensive operation of creating the message string if the log message will be discarded.

You have just seen how to set up and use the J2SE Logging API. You will now have a chance to compare this with logging using Jakarta log4j.

Jakarta Log4j

The Jakarta log4j project (see `http://jakarta.apache.org/log4j`) was created a number of years ago and has had a significant influence on the J2SE Logging API.

The two logging packages share the same basic components: `Logger`, `Level`, `Handler`, and `Formatter`. In log4j, these components are called `Logger`, `Priority`, `Appender`, and `Layout` respectively. Both packages use a naming hierarchy to pass logger properties onto child loggers, and they can both write log messages to the console and to files. We will now look at each of the three main components—`Loggers`, `Appenders`, and `Layouts`—in turn.

Log4j Logger Components

While there are implementation differences, for all practical purposes the log4J logger component is equivalent to the J2SE 1.4 Logging API logger object. It has the same hierarchical naming structure and, if not explicitly assigned a logging level, it will inherit one from a logger higher in the hierarchy.

Log4j has only five logging levels, which correspond to the J2SE logging levels as shown here:

Log4j Logging Level	J2SE Logging Level
FATAL	SEVERE
ERROR	SEVERE
WARN	WARNING
INFO	INFO
DEBUG	FINE/FINER/FINEST

There is no log4j level corresponding to the J2SE `CONFIG` level.

The log4j logger object is obtained using the `Logger.getLogger()` static method, and there are a number of convenience methods to log messages at each log level. The following code sample should strike you as being very similar to the J2SE logging:

```
import org.apache.log4j.Logger;
    // application code not included
    Logger log4jLogger = Logger.getLogger("com.samspublishing.app");
    log4jLogger.setLevel(Level.WARN);
    log4jLogger.warn ("some warning message");
```

There is a special root logger that is the ancestor of all other loggers. You retrieve the root logger using the `Logger.getRootLogger()` method. Properties set for the root logger, such as the logging level, will be inherited by all other loggers, which provides a simple way of setting default behavior.

NOTE

`Logger` components were previously known as `Categories`.

Log4j Appender Components

`Appender` components work like J2SE handlers and publish log messages to a destination. It is here that log4j shows some of its greater maturity and its superior functionality over J2SE logging. For example, along with the console and file `Appender`, log4j also supports logging to

- Unix `Syslog` daemons
- Microsoft NT `EventLoggers`
- Remote servers
- JMS message domains
- Email

You can attach multiple `Appenders` to a logger. Messages are published to all the `Appender` destinations attached to a logger and to any additional destinations defined by `Appenders` attached to ancestor loggers in the logger hierarchy. For example, attaching a file `Appender` to the root logger will cause all messages from all loggers to be printed to this file (that is assuming the message is of sufficiently high enough priority to be printed).

Log4j Layout Component

A `Layout` is associated with an `Appender`, and is used to format the log message. Log4j has a standard formatter called `PatternLayout` that is more flexible than the J2SE `SimpleFormatter`. `PatternLayout` lets you specify the output format according to conversion patterns similar to those used in the C language `printf` function. In most cases, this will save you the effort of writing your own formatter. Some of the more commonly used conversion characters are given in the following table:

Conversion Characters	Output
%c	The name of the logger associated with the log message.
%d	The date the log message was generated. This may be followed by a date format specifier—for example, %d{yyyy-mm-dd HH:mm:ss}.
%m	The log message.
%n	Line separator character.
%p	The log message priority level.
%r	The number of milliseconds that have elapsed since the application was started.
%t	The name of the thread that generated the log message.
%%	A % character.

For example:

```
%d{yyyy-mm-dd HH:mm:ss} %p %c %m%n
```

will generate a line with the following content:

```
2002-07-04 09:17:16 WARN com.samspublishing.app some warning message
```

Other text can be added to the pattern string to make the output easier to read. For example:

```
%d{yyyy-mm-dd HH:mm:ss} - %p [%c] %m%n
```

will change the previous output to look like the following:

```
2002-07-04 09:17:16 - WARN [com.samspublishing.app] some warning message
```

Log4j Configuration

As with J2SE logging, you can configure log4j through a properties file. Log4j has the advantage that if you place the `log4j.properties` file under the `WEB-INF/classes` directory of your Web applications, log4j will find the properties file and initialize itself; this is not true of the J2SE Logging API.

Here is a sample configuration file that creates a single `Appender`, which is attached to the root logger:

```
# Set root logger level to WARN.
log4j.rootLogger=WARN, Default

# Default is a ConsoleAppender.
log4j.appender.Default=org.apache.log4j.ConsoleAppender

# Default uses a PatternLayout.
log4j.appender.Default.layout=org.apache.log4j.PatternLayout
log4j.appender.Default.layout.ConversionPattern=%d{yyyy-mm-dd HH:mm:ss} - %p %m%n
```

Obtaining Log4j

Log4j methods are in a package called `org.apache.log4j`, which is available for download from

`http://jakarta.apache.org/log4j/`

Download the log4j JAR file and add this to the `WEB-INF/lib` directory of your Web application. If you standardize on log4j for all your Web applications, you can add the log4j JAR file to `<CATALINA_HOME>/lib`. On a development workstation, you may prefer to add the log4j JAR file as a Java extension so that the log4j classes are accessible by your Java compiler or IDE.

For more information on log4j, read the documentation on the Jakarta log4j Web site.

Summary

Good logging can greatly enhance an application by providing a useful audit trail with built in debugging should things go wrong. In this chapter, you have seen how to configure Tomcat logging for your Web applications and how to specify different log files for each application.

Both the J2SE 1.4 Logging API and Jakarta log4j packages have been presented for comparison. Although there is a great deal of similarity between the packages, log4j has been around for a number of years and has superior functionality. Having said this, the J2SE 1.4 Logging API must be considered the standard logging facility; its functionality will almost certainly improve with future releases of J2SE.

14 Access Control

IN THIS CHAPTER

- Access Control Mechanisms
- Security Realms
- Configuring a `JDBCRealm`
- Configuring a Tomcat `MemoryRealm` or `JNDIRealm`
- Protecting Web Applications with Declarative Security
- Programmatic Security
- Tomcat's Single Sign-on Feature

All real-world Web applications require some form of security to protect resources from damage by malicious users and to safeguard data confidentiality. This chapter is concerned with the following aspects of user security:

- Authentication—The means whereby users identify themselves and are validated by the system
- Authorization—The process by which an authenticated user is granted access to resources
- Confidentiality—The mechanism used to ensure that information is only made available to authorized users

All three security aspects can be addressed by ensuring your Web application provides a satisfactory access control mechanism.

Complete confidentiality and data integrity (ensuring data is not intercepted or changed in transit) requires encryption of the data as it is transported across the network. This aspect of security is covered in Chapter 23, "Securing Web Applications Under Tomcat."

You will also see in this chapter how to configure Tomcat's single sign-on facility. This enables users to be authenticated for all Web applications on a particular host through a single login form, whereas by default, users must authenticate themselves separately for each Web application.

Tomcat provides one further form of access control. You can ask Tomcat to check the IP address or host name for every incoming request against a configured "accept" or "deny" list. How to add this safeguard and configure the accept and deny lists is covered in Chapter 16, "Configuring Tomcat," and Chapter 19, "Tomcat Valves."

NOTE

If you are using Tomcat 4.0, there are no tools to help you configure access control mechanisms in Tomcat; you will have to manually edit the appropriate Tomcat configuration file.

Tomcat 4.1 provides the Tomcat Web Server Administration Tool. The examples in this chapter use the beta 1 version of the Administration Tool; the descriptions of this tool and screen snapshots may differ slightly from the final release.

Access Control Mechanisms

With Web applications, there are two mechanisms for enforcing user access control:

- Declarative—Involves using information stored separately from the application's servlet and JSP code
- Programmatic—Uses programming logic added to the servlets and JSPs

Declarative Security

Declarative security is also known as *container-managed security*; Tomcat, as the alternative name implies, manages this. With declarative security, you add security constraints to the Web application's deployment descriptor. Declarative security applies to entire resources and can be implemented and modified with no changes to the application code. By using declarative security, you can ensure that a consistent security model is applied across all components in the Web application.

With declarative security, Tomcat grants access to resources based not on users, but on security roles. A *security role* is a logical grouping of users. Typical roles might be patrons, administrators, staff, students, or customers. Access to specific Web application resources is granted to all users possessing a particular role. Users can have any number of roles associated with their username. In this way, roles are similar to the groups in Unix and Windows environments.

Programmatic Security

Programmatic security, which is enforced within Web application code, can provide authorization at a much finer level of granularity than declarative security. This finer granularity means you can now protect items within a resource. Programmatic authorization can also be based on a username (also known as a *principal name*) as well as a role. But programmatic security has several drawbacks:

- The security model is hard-coded. This can compromise the reusability of a component.

- If an application is assembled from several components, it can be difficult to ensure that the security model is applied consistently across all components.
- If the security policy changes, every component must be revisited to verify and possibly update the security authorization.

Whichever security mechanism you use, they both authenticate users using user credentials stored in a security realm. We will now look at the components of a security realm in more detail.

Security Realms

A *security realm* provides the information used to authenticate users. A realm is a collection of usernames, roles, and passwords that identify valid users of a Web application.

Tomcat 4.0 does not provide any tools to set up or administer security realms. In Tomcat 4.1, you can either manually configure a security realm by editing the `<CATALINA_HOME>/conf/server.xml` file or use the Tomcat Web Server Administration Tool. This tool is a Web application accessed via the following URL:

```
http://localhost:8080/admin/
```

The Tomcat Web Server Administration Tool can also be used to maintain the `MemoryRealm` definitions in the `tomcat-users.xml` file as discussed in the "Using a `MemoryRealm`" section.

Using the Administration Tool has this great advantage: Tomcat immediately recognizes changes made to the configuration. If you manually edit the `server.xml` file, you will have to stop and restart Tomcat for any changes to take effect.

Whichever method you use, you should use a security realm to implement your site's security policy and security model for the applications.

CAUTION

If you are used to configuring security realms in other servlet containers or a J2EE environment, you may find that the names and attributes of the Tomcat security realms are different from those you are familiar with. This is because the Java Servlet Technology specification does not define how a container should provide the interface to the user authentication information, only what capabilities it should provide.

Tomcat defines a Java interface (`org.apache.catalina.Realm`) that can be used by components to provide access to user credentials. Although you can write your own security realm, the Jakarta Tomcat team has provided three implementations of this interface, which provide ample functionality for most purposes:

- JDBCRealm—Authentication information is stored in a relational database, accessed via a JDBC driver.
- JNDIRealm—Authentication information is stored in a directory server, accessed via a JNDI provider.
- MemoryRealm—Authentication information is stored in an in-memory object collection, which is initialized from an XML document (<CATALINA_HOME>/conf/tomcat-users.xml).

The MemoryRealm uses a plain text configuration file that is only read at startup, so any change to the authentication in the MemoryRealm will require Tomcat to be stopped and restarted. This realm is better suited to a development environment than a live server.

Both the JDBCRealm and the JNDIRealm allow changes to take place dynamically while Tomcat is running. It is also easier to secure access to these realms. For these reasons, they are the preferred realms for a live environment.

Configuring a Security Realm

Security realms are configured in Tomcat's server.xml file. You must place a <Realm> element in the configuration file in the <Engine>, <Host>, or <Context> element. Where a <Realm> element is defined will determine the realm's scope, and therefore, which Web applications will share the authentication information. The scope is illustrated in the following table:

Element Where Realm Is Defined	Scope of Authentication Information
<Engine>	All Web applications on all virtual hosts, unless overridden by a <Realm> element at a lower level
<Host>	All Web applications for this virtual host unless overridden by a <Realm> element at the <Context> level
<Context>	The enclosing Web application only

NOTE

Tomcat does not complain if you configure more than one security realm in any particular context; however, all but the last one will be ignored.

The `<Realm>` element has a number of attributes, many of which are specific to the realm and are discussed later in the sections specific to each type of realm. The following attributes are common to all realms:

- `className`—The fully qualified Java classname of this realm implementation. You must specify one of the following:

  ```
  org.apache.catalina.realm.JDBCRealm
  org.apache.catalina.realm.JNDIRealm
  org.apache.catalina.realm.MemoryRealm
  ```

- `debug` (optional)—The level of debugging logged by this realm; the default is zero (0).

- `digest` (optional)—The digest algorithm used to store passwords in encoded formats. If not specified, passwords are stored in clear text.

Digested Passwords

By default, passwords are stored in clear text, which (if you are concerned about security) is not ideal. Anyone with access to the storage medium used by the security realm will be able to easily obtain user credentials and use them to gain unauthorized access to your Web application. Unless you can guarantee that you have secured the resource holding the password information (which can be problematic), having easily readable passwords can defeat the whole point of adding authentication to your Web application in the first place. To solve this problem, each of Tomcat's security realms also supports the concept of *digesting passwords*.

A digested password is one that is encoded using well-known digest algorithms that Tomcat then uses to authenticate the user. By comparing the digest of the password entered by the user against the stored digest, Tomcat can determine whether the user provided the correct password. Although with some algorithms more than one password can generate the same digest, the algorithms used are complex enough to make this a rare occurrence. The key point about the digest value is that it cannot be used to recover the original password, so anyone gaining access to the digests does not have access to the original passwords.

Tomcat supports the following well-documented digest algorithms:

- MD2
- MD5
- SHA

NOTE

For more information on each of these digest techniques, refer to the following RFC documentation available from the Internet Engineering Task Force Web site `www.ietf.org`:

MD5—RFC 1321

MD2—RFC 1319

SHA—RFC 2841

TIP

You can use methods in the JDK 1.4 `java.security.MessageDigest` class to add support for digest algorithms in your applications.

To instruct Tomcat to use digest passwords, you should set the `digest` attribute in the security realm configuration, as shown in the following example:

```
<Realm className="org.apache.catalina.realm.MemoryRealm" digest="MD5" />
```

You can now store the password in its encoded form, preventing the casual hacker from gaining unauthorized access to your Web application. How to create digested passwords is covered in the section addressing adding users to a `JDBCRealm`.

Configuring a `JDBCRealm`

A `JDBCRealm` offers flexibility and convenience. You may find your application already needs to manage persistent user data, and a `JDBCRealm` allows you to utilize the same storage medium for both authentication and user data.

Configuring a `JDBCRealm` is really quite straightforward. Perform the following steps (each is described in more detail in the following sections):

NOTE

The `mySQL` database has been used to demonstrate configuring a `JDBCRealm`, but you may substitute any JDBC database.

1. Create a database (or utilize an existing one) and create tables in that database to store the end user credentials (usernames, passwords, and roles).
2. In your selected database, configure a database account and password and grant this account access to user credential tables. This is the account Tomcat will use to access the database of end user credentials.

3. Add end user credentials to the database.
4. Add a <Realm> element to Tomcat's server.xml file.

Creating a User Database

Use the following SQL statements to create the authentication tables in your database:

```
create table users (username varchar(20) primary key, password varchar(40));
create table roles (role varchar(20) primary key);
create table userroles (
    username varchar(20) not null references users(username),
    role varchar(20) not null references role(role),
        primary key (username, role));
```

It is not strictly necessary to create all three tables, because Tomcat only uses the users and userroles tables. The third table should be used to ensure referential integrity and prevent annoying errors creeping into your database due to mistyped usernames and roles.

NOTE

The MySQL database does not support referential integrity, but you can still use the previous create table statements because the syntax (if not the functionality) is supported.

You do not need to use the same names for the tables and columns as used here (the actual table and column names used are specified in the Tomcat <Realm> element). You can add any extra columns you want.

CAUTION

The name of the column used to store the username must be the same in the users and userroles tables.

Creating a Tomcat Database User

The database username and password for the Tomcat user are stored in plain text in Tomcat's server.xml file. Anyone with access to this file potentially also has access to the Tomcat database account. For security reasons, it is a good idea for the Tomcat database user to be given minimal security privilege in your selected database. Tomcat never writes to the database, so you should set up the Tomcat user with read-only access.

Adding Users and Roles

How users are added to the security realm will be very dependent on

- The size of the user community
- The dynamic nature of the community
- Whether users can add or change their own details

There are a number of ways to add user credentials to the database. The simplest way is to use your database's SQL interface; if you are adding a number of users, however, this way can be both tedious and error prone (particularly if using digested passwords). Other methods include using batch scripts or a Java program to load, modify, or delete users. If the user community is very dynamic or you want users to change their own passwords, you will probably find it worthwhile to write a Web interface to manage users.

Whatever mechanism you choose, use the following SQL to add a new user and role, replacing *`user`*, *`password`*, and *`role`* with the appropriate values:

```
insert into users values ('user','password');
insert into userroles values ('user','role');
```

If you are using plain text passwords, it is a simple matter to replace the *`user`* and *`password`* parameters with their appropriate values; but if you are using digested passwords, there is more work to be done.

To generate the digest password, you will have to use the required digest algorithm designated in the `<Realm>` element. Tomcat provides two methods for generating digested passwords:

- Using the `RealmBase.Digest()` static method
- From the command line using the `RealmBase` class

From within an application, you can call the static `org.apache.catalina.realm.RealmBase.Digest()` method, passing in the password and the digest algorithm as the two `String` parameters. For example, the following servlet code obtains the username from a request parameter. It then generates an encoded password (from the username) using the MD5 algorithm:

```
String user = req.getParameter("name");
String MD5password = RealmBase.Digest(user, "MD5");
PreparedStatement insert = con.prepareStatement
➥ ("insert into users (username,password) values (?,?)");
insert.setString(1,user);
```

```
insert.setString(2,MD5password);
insert.execute();
```

The RealmBase class also has a main() method, so you can run it as a command line utility. The following example uses MD5 to digest the password garfield:

```
> java org.apache.catalina.realm.RealmBase -a MD5 garfield
garfield:97c2bd1615963162bd4e0caca037ba9e
```

TIP

To use either of these methods for generating digested passwords, you will need to add <CATALINA_HOME>/server/lib/catalina.jar to your CLASSPATH.

Configuring Tomcat to use a JDBCRealm

Now you must add the JDBCRealm definition to Tomcat's server.xml file. The <Realm> element for a JDBCRealm has a number of extra attributes that are described in Table 14.1.

TABLE 14.1 Attributes for JDBCRealm

Attribute	Description
connectionName	The database account used to access the database containing the end user credentials
connectionPassword	The password for the database account
connectionURL	The URL to use for the database connection
driverName	The classname of the JDBC driver
userTable	The name of the table in the database where usernames and passwords are stored
userRoleTable	The name of the table that contains at least one row for each role assigned to a user in the userTable
userNameCol	The name of the column that holds the username in both the userTable and the userRoleTable
userCredCol	The name of the column that holds the user's password in the userTable
roleNameCol	The name of the column that holds the role name in the userRoleTable

As an example, Listing 14.1 shows the <Realm> element that is used by the application built later in this chapter.

LISTING 14.1 `JDBCRealm` Configuration in Tomcat's `server.xml` File

```
<Context path="/access" docBase="access-control" debug="0" reloadable="true">
    <Realm  className="org.apache.catalina.realm.JDBCRealm" debug="0"
        driverName="org.gjt.mm.mysql.Driver"
        connectionURL="jdbc:mysql://localhost/security"
        connectionName="Tomcat" connectionPassword="catalina"
        userTable="users" userNameCol="username" userCredCol="password"
        userRoleTable="userroles" roleNameCol="role"
        digest="MD5" />
</Context>
```

To configure a `JDBCRealm`, you can either manually add an entry such as the previous one to Tomcat's `server.xml` file, or you can use Tomcat's Administration Tool.

In the Administration Tool, select in the left-hand panel the host or context where you want the `JDBCRealm` to be configured, and choose Create New User Realm from the Available Actions list.

NOTE

With the beta version used while writing this chapter, it was not possible to configure a new user realm at the Engine component level.

From the list associated with the `Type:` property, select `JDBCRealm`. This will bring up the form shown in Figure 14.1.

The properties on the form correspond to the attributes of the `<Realm>` element. Fill in the appropriate values (such as those in Listing 14.1) and save the form. This saves the new configuration to memory. You must click on the Commit Changes button in the top frame to write the configuration to the `server.xml` file.

CAUTION

When you commit the changes, the entire server configuration is written replacing the old `server.xml` file. Any comments in the original `server.xml` file are lost.

Having defined the end user database, you can now add declarative security constraints to your Web application. Before you learn how to do that, let's briefly look at the other two Tomcat realms.

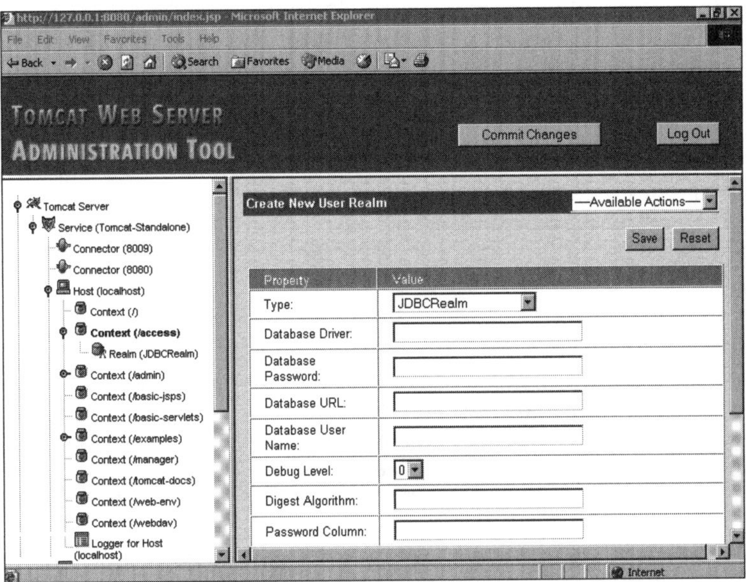

FIGURE 14.1 Configuring a `JDBCRealm` using Tomcat Administration Tool.

Configuring a Tomcat `MemoryRealm` or `JNDIRealm`

Most developers will use the Tomcat `JDBCRealm` to store end user credentials, so our discussion of the other realms will be fairly brief.

Using a `MemoryRealm`

Although the `MemoryRealm` is very easy to set up and use, its implementation has not been designed for production use. If you choose to use a `MemoryRealm`, you should be aware of the following drawbacks:

- The user credentials are stored in an XML document (by default `conf/tomcat-users.xml`), and access to this file should be protected to prevent the circumvention of your access control.
- There is no DTD or schema to validate the contents of the XML document.
- There is no easy way to prevent errors in the data (a mistyped role name will prevent the user from accessing the application).
- The file is only read when Tomcat starts up, so any changes to this file mean Tomcat has to be stopped and restarted before they will be recognized.

You can manually configure users in the tomcat-users.xml file as follows:

```
<tomcat-users>
    <role rolename="administrator"/>
    <role rolename="patron"/>
    <user name="tom" password="rose" roles="administrator" />
    <user name="ben" password="lily" roles="patron" />
    <user name="sam" password="daisy" roles="administrator, patron" />
</tomcat-users>
```

NOTE

The Tomcat 4.0 tomcat-users.xml file does not include <role> elements, because the roles are derived from the <user> elements. In Tomcat 4.1, any roles defined in the <user> elements that do not have <role> element definitions are automatically added to the tomcat-users.xml file when Tomcat starts up.

If you use Tomcat 4.1, you can use the Tomcat Administration Tool to add users and roles. First, create the roles you require by selecting User Definition, Roles in the left panel; then, choose Create New Role from the Available Actions list. Fill in the role name and a description (optional).

Similarly, to create a user, select User Definition, Users and choose Create New User from the Available Actions list. This will bring up the form in Figure 14.2.

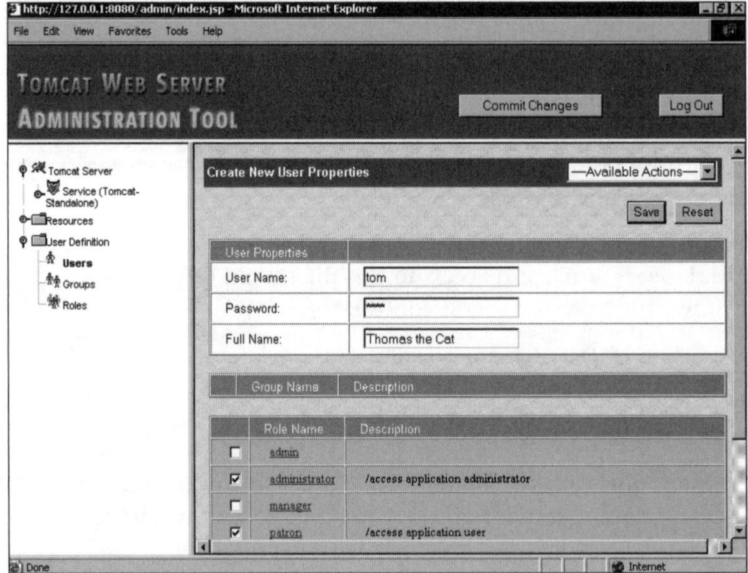

FIGURE 14.2 Creating users using the Tomcat Administration Tool.

Complete the user definition form by providing the User Name, Password, and Full Name values (optional), and select the roles you want to associate with the user. Save this form and click Commit Changes to write out a new tomcat-users.xml file.

NOTE

Users created using the Administration Tool are effective immediately. On the other hand, Tomcat will need to be stopped and restarted in order for it to recognize new users added by editing the tomcat-users.xml file.

You can enter the user passwords in plain text or you can use the command-line utility provided with the org.apache.catalina.realm.RealmBase class to create digested passwords.

NOTE

To enter a digested password, you will have to cut and paste the digested password (from the command-line utility output) into the tomcat-users.xml file or the Password field in the Administration Tool.

The MemoryRealm supports the following optional attribute:

- pathname—Pathname of the configuration file used to initialize the contents of the MemoryRealm (default is <CATALINA_HOME>/conf/tomcat-users.xml).

Use the Tomcat Administration Tool to add a MemoryRealm (use the procedure for JDBCRealm, but this time select MemoryRealm on the Create New User Realm form. Alternatively, you can add the following realm definition to Tomcat's server.xml:

```
<Realm className="org.apache.catalina.realm.MemoryRealm" />
```

TIP

The big advantage of the MemoryRealm is that it is quick to implement and, typing errors aside, is unlikely to go wrong. If you are debugging problems with your access control mechanism, temporarily replacing your JDBCRealm or JNDIRealm with a MemoryRealm can help to determine whether the problem is with the underlying security realm or with your application deployment (or the code, if you are using programmatic security).

Using a JNDIRealm

In a JNDIRealm, user information is stored in a directory server (typically an LDAP server) accessed by a JNDI provider. You will need to be familiar with X.500 naming conventions to follow the example configuration of a JNDIRealm using LDAP.

To set up a JNDIRealm in Tomcat's server.xml file, you will need to supply the information in Table 14.2 as attributes to the <Realm> element.

TABLE 14.2 Attributes to the JNDIRealm Element

Attribute	Description
connectionName	The directory server username used to establish a JNDI connection.
connectionPassword	The directory server password used to establish a JNDI connection.
connectionURL	The directory server URL used to establish a JNDI connection.
roleName	The name of the directory server attribute containing the user's role name.
roleSearch	An LDAP search pattern for selecting roles in this realm. This uses the syntax supported by the java.text.MessageFormat class: Use {0} to substitute in the distinguished name or {1} to substitute in the username of the user you want the roles for.
userPassword	The name of the directory server attribute (in the user element) that contains the user password.
userPattern	An LDAP search pattern for selecting users in this Realm. Use {0} to substitute in the distinguished name of the user you want to select.

The following is an example of a JNDIRealm configuration using an LDAP server:

```
<Realm  className="org.apache.catalina.realm.JNDIRealm" debug="0"
    connectionURL="ldap://localhost:389"
    connectionName="cn=Manager,dc=mycompany,dc=com"
    connectionPassword="catalina"
    userPassword="userPassword"
    userPattern="cn={0},dc=mycompany,dc=com"
    roleName="cn" roleSearch="(uniqueMember={0})" />
```

Using a JNDIRealm has the advantage of enabling your Web application to utilize an existing security schema inside your directory server; this is possible as long as the existing schema conforms to the following requirements:

- Each user is represented by an individual user element in the top level DirContext that is accessed via the connectionURL attribute.
- The user element must have the following characteristics:
    - The distinguished name (dn) attribute of the element contains the username that is presented for authentication.
    - There must be an attribute that contains the user's password, either in clear text or digested form.

- Each group of users that has been assigned a particular role is represented by a *user group* element in the top level `DirContext` that is accessed via the `connectionURL` attribute.
- The *user group* element must have the following characteristics:
  - The element includes an attribute (whose name is configured by the `roleName` attribute of the `<Realm>` element) containing the name of the role represented by this element.
  - The set of all possible groups of interest can be selected by an LDAP search pattern configured by the `roleSearch` attribute of the `<Realm>` element.
- There must be an administrator username and password that Tomcat can use to establish a connection to the directory server, with at least read access to the information.

As with a `JDBCRealm` or a `MemoryRealm`, you can either manually add the `JNDIRealm` to the `server.xml` file or use the Create New User Realm form in the Administration Tool.

Protecting Web Applications with Declarative Security

As already mentioned, declarative security requires no changes to application code. The security configuration is defined in the Web application's deployment descriptor.

For the examples in this chapter, a version of the currency converter application has been added to a new Web application called `access-control`. This application uses the following JSPs and servlets, which have been shown in earlier chapters:

JSP or Servlet	Description
`currency-form.jsp`	Allows users to enter values to be converted
`CurrencyConverter.java`	Servlet that performs the actual conversion
`Rates.jsp`	Provides an administrator interface to change exchange rates

NOTE

This code is available online. If desired, you can download all the code for this application from the Sams Publishing Web site (go to `www.samspublishing.com` and enter this book's ISBN, 0672324393, in the search box and follow the link for Chapter 14).

The following `<Context>` element in the `server.xml` file uses a `JDBCRealm` for this new Web application context:

```
<Context path="/access" docBase="access-control" debug="0"
           reloadable="true">
    <Realm  className="org.apache.catalina.realm.JDBCRealm" debug="0"
        driverName="org.gjt.mm.mysql.Driver"
        connectionURL="jdbc:mysql://localhost/security"
        connectionName="Tomcat" connectionPassword="catalina"
        userTable="users" userNameCol="username" userCredCol="password"
        userRoleTable="userroles" roleNameCol="role" digest="MD5" />
</Context>
```

Authentication in the Deployment Descriptor

Restricting access to resources is configured in the deployment descriptor using two elements: A `<login-config>` element defines the authentication method, and one or more `<security-constraint>` elements define the mapping between roles and resources.

The `<login-config>` has an `<auth-method>` element that defines the authentication method that will be used to obtain the user credentials. A Web application can use one of the following authentication methods:

- HTTP Basic
- HTTP Digest
- HTTPS Client
- Form-Based

These are discussed in the following sections.

HTTP Basic Authentication

HTTP Basic authentication is the simplest mechanism to use. With this method, you rely on the browser to generate an appropriate login form. Figure 14.3 shows the authentication form produced by Netscape 6.

CAUTION

The usernames and passwords are sent in simple base64 encoding. In most cases, you should use a secure transport mechanism (such as SSL) in conjunction with HTTP Basic authentication to prevent unauthorized network sniffing of the username and password.

HTTP Basic authentication is configured in the deployment descriptor as follows:

```
<login-config>
    <auth-method>BASIC</auth-method>
</login-config>
```

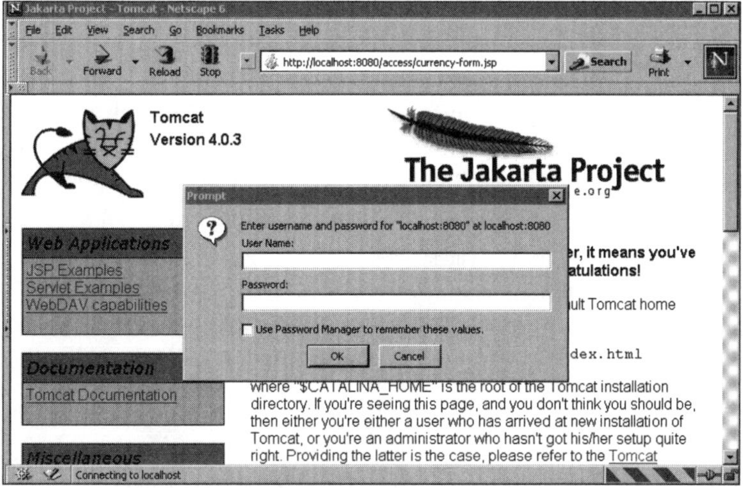

FIGURE 14.3 User authentication in Netscape 6.

HTTP Digest Authentication

HTTP Digest authentication, like HTTP Basic authentication, uses a login form generated by the browser, but in this case the password is transmitted in an encoded form. However, browser support for HTTP Digest authentication is not yet widely available; therefore, this authentication is not commonly used.

More information on HTTP Digest authentication can be found in RFC 2617 from `www.ietf.org`.

HTTPS Client Authentication

HTTPS Client authentication uses HTTP over SSL and is a strong authentication mechanism. For this mechanism to work, the user must possess a digital certificate. SSL and digital certificates are covered in Chapter 23.

Form-Based Authentication

Form-Based authentication uses the same mechanism as HTTP Basic authentication except now your application must provide both the authentication form and an error page to display when authentication fails. This has a number of advantages over HTTP Basic authentication:

- You can design the look and feel of the login form to match your application.
- Extra information can be provided on the form including a link for new users to register.
- The error form can be user friendly, providing links to other parts of your application.

Form-Based authentication is configured in the `web.xml` file with a `<form-login-page>` element that defines the custom authentication form and error page respectively. An example `<login-config>` element is shown here:

```
<login-config>
    <auth-method>FORM</auth-method>
    <form-login-config>
        <form-login-page>/login.html</form-login-page>
        <form-error-page>/login-error.html</form-error-page>
    </form-login-config>
</login-config>
```

The login form itself must be designed to the criteria in the Servlet specification. The form must send a request that

- Uses a `POST` method (so that the username and password are not passed in the query string)
- Has an `action` of `j_security_check`
- Uses a `j_username` parameter to pass the username
- Uses the `j_password` parameter to pass the user's password

Tomcat performs an authentication on the user credentials in the `POST` request.

Listing 14.2 shows the use of these parameters in a very simple authentication form.

LISTING 14.2 Simple Authentication Form

```
<HTML>
  <HEAD>
    <TITLE>Login Error</TITLE>
  </HEAD>
  <BODY>
    <FORM method="POST" action="j_security_check">
      <H1>Login Form</H1>
      <P>Type in your user name and password and click on the login button</P>
```

LISTING 14.2 Continued

```
      <TABLE width="35%" border="0">
        <TR>
          <TD>User:</TD><TD><INPUT type="text" name="j_username"></TD>
        </TR>
        <TR>
          <TD>Password:</TD><TD><INPUT type="password" name="j_password"></TD>
        </TR>
      </TABLE>
      <P><INPUT type=SUBMIT value="Login" name="SUBMIT" /></P>
    </FORM>
  </BODY>
</HTML>
```

This form is shown in Figure 14.4.

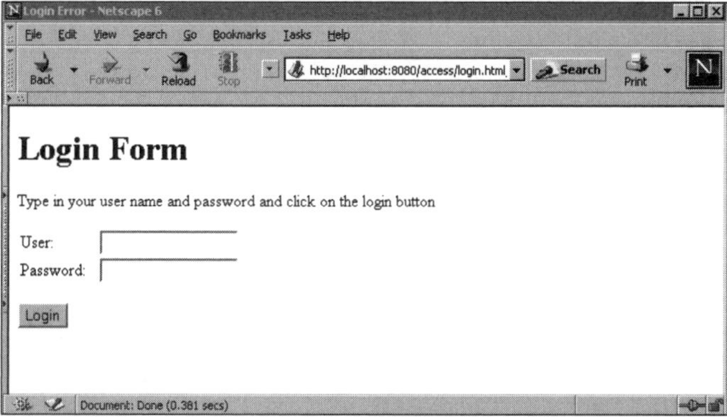

FIGURE 14.4 Simple authentication form—`login.html`.

The page defined by the `<form-error-page>` element is displayed when the login fails (an invalid user is entered or a valid user supplies an invalid password—you don't know which). You should design this page so that it presents users with an appropriate message and gives them the chance to give up or log in again.

Adding Declarative Security Constraints

So far, you have configured a security realm and told Tomcat and the browser what form of authentication method is required. The final step in securing your application is to place security constraints on your Web application resources.

You add authorization to your application with the <security-constraint> element in the deployment descriptor.

NOTE

The <security-constraint> element must appear in the deployment descriptor after any <resource-ref> elements and before the <login-config> element.

You use a <security-constraint> element to associate access control with Web application resources. The <security-constraint> element has a number of sub elements, as described in the following sections.

The <web-resource-collection> Element

In the <web-resource-collection> element, you must supply a name for this collection followed by a list of the URL patterns that this constraint applies to. Use the same URL patterns as defined in your <servlet-mapping> elements, as shown here:

```
<web-resource-collection>
    <web-resource-name>Patrons - ordinary users</web-resource-name>
    <url-pattern>/CurrencyConverter</url-pattern>
    <url-pattern>/currency-form</url-pattern>
</web-resource-collection>
```

CAUTION

You will also need to protect access to the actual resource names (such as currency-form.jsp). Although you could also add the real name to the <web-resource-collection>, this could be error prone (you would have to remember to add every page twice and test the page access twice). A far better solution is to add servlet mappings that will prevent users from accessing the resources by their real names. You do this by adding a servlet mapping that will redirect clients to a specified page if the real name is used. In the following case, an attempt to access a JSP using its full name will simply redirect the user to the Home Page servlet:

```
<servlet-mapping>
    <servlet-name>Home Page</servlet-name>
    <url-pattern>*.jsp</url-pattern>
</servlet-mapping>
```

The <auth-constraint> Element

The <auth-constraint> subelement is used to specify which roles (defined in the realm) can access the Web resources. The following example authorizes both the user and the administrator roles access to the resources in the `<web-resource-collection>`:

```
<auth-constraint>
    <role-name>patron</role-name>
    <role-name>administrator</role-name>
</auth-constraint>
```

The <user-data-constraint> Element

The `<user-data-constraint>` element has a `<transport-guarantee>` subelement that defines how the data should be sent between client and server. The `<transport-guarantee>` can have one of three values:

- `INTEGRAL`—The transport mechanism should guarantee data integrity; that is, the data cannot be changed in transit.
- `CONFIDENTIAL`—The data should be transported in such a manner that it cannot be observed in transit (it is encrypted).
- `NONE`—There are no guarantees about the integrity or confidentiality of the data.

The `INTEGRAL` and `CONFIDENTIAL` values require the use of SSL (see Chapter 23); if you define either of these transport guarantees without SSL, you will not be able to access protected resources.

The following element sets no transport guarantees:

```
<user-data-constraint>
    <transport-guarantee>NONE</transport-guarantee>
</user-data-constraint>
```

Complete Currency Converter Deployment Descriptor

Listing 14.3 is the full `web.xml` file for the currency converter application. You will see that there are two security constraints. Administrators and patrons can access the `currency-form` JSP and the `CurrencyConverter` servlet, but only administrators can access the `rates` JSP used to set the exchange rates.

LISTING 14.3 Deployment Descriptor

```
<!DOCTYPE web-app
    PUBLIC "-//Sun Microsystems, Inc.//DTD Web Application 2.3//EN"
    "http://java.sun.com/dtd/web-app_2_3.dtd">
```

LISTING 14.3 Continued

```
<web-app>

    <display-name>Currency Converter</display-name>
    <description>Simple currency converter application</description>

    <servlet>
        <servlet-name>Currency Converter</servlet-name>
        <servlet-class>CurrencyConverter</servlet-class>
    </servlet>

    <servlet>
        <servlet-name>Currency Form</servlet-name>
        <jsp-file>/currency-form.jsp</jsp-file>
    </servlet>

    <servlet>
        <servlet-name>Rates</servlet-name>
        <jsp-file>/rates.jsp</jsp-file>
    </servlet>

    <servlet>
        <servlet-name>Home Page</servlet-name>
        <jsp-file>/currency-homepage.jsp</jsp-file>
    </servlet>

    <servlet-mapping>
        <servlet-name>Currency Converter</servlet-name>
        <url-pattern>/CurrencyConverter</url-pattern>
    </servlet-mapping>

    <servlet-mapping>
        <servlet-name>Currency Form</servlet-name>
        <url-pattern>/currency-form</url-pattern>
    </servlet-mapping>

    <servlet-mapping>
        <servlet-name>Rates</servlet-name>
        <url-pattern>/rates</url-pattern>
    </servlet-mapping>

    <servlet-mapping>
        <servlet-name>Home Page</servlet-name>
```

LISTING 14.3 Continued

```
        <url-pattern>*.jsp</url-pattern>
    </servlet-mapping>

    <servlet-mapping>
        <servlet-name>Home Page</servlet-name>
        <url-pattern>/servlet/*</url-pattern>
    </servlet-mapping>

    <welcome-file-list>
        <welcome-file>/currency-homepage.jsp</welcome-file>
    </welcome-file-list>

    <error-page>
        <error-code>403</error-code>
        <location>/http403.html</location>
    </error-page>

    <resource-ref>
        <res-ref-name>jdbc/security</res-ref-name>
        <res-type>javax.sql.DataSource</res-type>
        <res-auth>Container</res-auth>
    </resource-ref>

    <resource-ref>
        <res-ref-name>jdbc/conversion</res-ref-name>
        <res-type>javax.sql.DataSource</res-type>
        <res-auth>Container</res-auth>
    </resource-ref>

    <security-constraint>
        <display-name>Web App Access Control - Administrators</display-name>
        <web-resource-collection>
            <web-resource-name>Administration</web-resource-name>
            <url-pattern>/rates</url-pattern>
        </web-resource-collection>
        <auth-constraint>
            <role-name>administrator</role-name>
        </auth-constraint>
        <user-data-constraint>
            <transport-guarantee>NONE</transport-guarantee>
        </user-data-constraint>
    </security-constraint>
```

LISTING 14.3 Continued

```
    <security-constraint>
        <display-name>Web App Access Control - patrons</display-name>
        <web-resource-collection>
            <web-resource-name>Patrons - ordinary users</web-resource-name>
            <url-pattern>/CurrencyConverter</url-pattern>
            <url-pattern>/currency-form</url-pattern>
        </web-resource-collection>
        <auth-constraint>
            <role-name>patron</role-name>
            <role-name>administrator</role-name>
        </auth-constraint>
        <user-data-constraint>
            <transport-guarantee>NONE</transport-guarantee>
        </user-data-constraint>
    </security-constraint>

    <login-config>
        <auth-method>FORM</auth-method>
        <form-login-config>
            <form-login-page>/login.html</form-login-page>
            <form-error-page>/login-error.html</form-error-page>
        </form-login-config>
    </login-config>

</web-app>
```

You will notice that there are a couple of extra resources defined in this deployment descriptor that you have not seen before. There is a home page (used also as a welcome page), which has no security constraints on it. This is not essential to demonstrate the use of access control, but in a real application, it is usually a good idea to provide at least one page that anyone can access, either to find out about your application or to contact you.

The other extra resource is the `http403.html` page. The previously mentioned `<form-error-page>` is displayed if a user fails to login, whereas this page will be displayed if a valid user (one that is defined in your security realm) tries to access an unauthorized page.

And that is all there is to declarative security. If your application requires authorization that cannot be specified in the deployment descriptor, you will need to use programmatic security as described in the next section.

Programmatic Security

You should use programmatic security when declarative security alone is insufficient to express your application's security model. This will usually be when you need to change functionality according to an individual user's identity. An example of this is allowing all users to display some information (such as a telephone list) but only allowing users to update their own data.

The `HttpServletRequest` interface provides the following methods to support programmatic security:

- `getRemoteUser`—Obtains the username used for authentication
- `isUserInRole`—Determines whether the user is in a specified security role
- `getUserPrincipal`—Returns a `java.security.Principal` object containing information about the authenticated user

NOTE

The `java.security.Principal` interface represents an abstract notion of an end user or any entity (individual, corporation, login ID) known as a *principal*. At present, it provides limited information about the principal, but in the future it may be extended.

The `isUserInRole()` method takes as its parameter a `String` representing the user role name. Although this can be the actual role name defined in the security realm, it is far better to use the name associated with a `<security-role-ref>` element. The `<security-role-ref>` element is declared in the deployment descriptor and provides a way of hiding the actual role names. This has the obvious advantage that the security realm administrator can change the role names without affecting your programmatic security.

The syntax for the `<security-role-ref>` element is straightforward. For example, use the following to map the real security role `administrator` onto the role reference `admin` used in the code:

```
<security-role-ref>
    <role-name>admin</role-name>
    <role-link>administrator</manager>
</security-role-ref>
```

`<security-role-ref>` elements are defined inside the appropriate `<servlet>` element in the `web.xml` file; therefore, the reference only applies to that servlet.

The servlet in Listing 14.4 shows an example use of programmatic security for accessing the security information in the example `JDBCRealm`. If the authenticated user is an administrator (role reference `admin`), the whole user table is printed; otherwise, just the row corresponding to the user's login name is displayed.

You could extend this example to display the `userroles` table (and `roles` table if you have one). You could also use this servlet as the basis of a simple security administration tool and enable administrators to add, modify, or delete user entries and users to change their passwords.

LISTING 14.4 `ListTables` Servlet

```
import javax.servlet.http.*;
import java.io.*;
import java.sql.*;
import javax.naming.*;
import javax.sql.*;

public class ListTables extends HttpServlet {

    private void printRows (PrintWriter out, ResultSet rows)
        throws SQLException{
     out.println ("<TABLE width='35%' border='0'>");
     while (rows.next()) {
        out.println ("<TR>");
        out.println(" <TD>" + rows.getString(1)+ "</TD><TD>" +
rows.getString(2) + "</TD>");
        out.println ("</TR>");
    }
    out.println ("</TABLE>");
    }

    public void doGet(HttpServletRequest req, HttpServletResponse res)
                throws ServletException, IOException {
    res.setContentType("text/html");
    PrintWriter out = res.getWriter();
    try {
        Context init = new InitialContext();
        Context ctx = (Context) init.lookup("java:comp/env");
        DataSource ds = (DataSource) ctx.lookup("jdbc/security");
        Connection con = ds.getConnection();
        PreparedStatement select = con.prepareStatement(
            "SELECT * FROM userroles WHERE username like ?");
```

LISTING 14.4 Continued

```
        out.println("<H1>User Table</H1>");
        if (req.isUserInRole("admin"))
            select.setString(1,"%");
        else
            select.setString(1,req.getUserPrincipal().getName());
        ResultSet rows = select.executeQuery();
        if (rows != null)
            printRows(out, rows);
    }

    catch (SQLException ex) {
        System.out.println("SQL Exception thrown: "+ex);
        ex.printStackTrace();
    }
    catch (NamingException ex) {
        System.out.println("Naming Exception thrown: "+ex);
        ex.printStackTrace();
        }
    }
}
```

The example in Listing 14.4 uses a `PreparedStatement` to precompile the SQL select statement as follows:

```
PreparedStatement select = con.prepareStatement(
    "SELECT * FROM userroles WHERE username like ?");
```

The value of the parameter in this statement is then set according to the user's role as follows:

```
if (req.isUserInRole("admin"))
    select.setString(1,"%");
else
    select.setString(1,req.getUserPrincipal().getName());
```

If the user is an administrator, the parameter is set to the special SQL `%` token that represents any character string. Otherwise, it is set to the username obtained from the `Principal` object.

Tomcat's Single Sign-on Feature

As already described, a security realm can be configured within the <Engine> or <Host> elements in Tomcat's server.xml file. While this can be used to ensure that all the Web applications for the container or a particular host share the same security information, users still have to authenticate themselves for each separate Web application.

If you want your users to be able to log in once for all of your Web applications, you can add the following Tomcat valve to the <Host> element in the server.xml file (how Tomcat valves work is covered in Chapter 19, "Tomcat Valves"):

```
<Host name="localhost" ...>
  ...
  <Valve className="org.apache.catalina.authenticator.SingleSignOn"/>
  ...
</Host>
```

The single sign-on facility only works at the host level, so Web applications running in different hosts will each still require users to authenticate themselves separately.

When the single sign-on facility is configured, the first time a user accesses a protected resource, she logs in using the mechanism defined for the Web application containing the resource. Thereafter, the user will not need to log in again to access protected resources in different applications.

If you are going to use the single sign-on facility, you should be aware of the following features:

- All Web applications configured for the host must share the same security realm. If you have a <Realm> element defined at the <Context> level, that application cannot take part in the single sign-on.
- If a user logs out of one application (either explicitly by closing the browser or because a session has been invalidated or timed out), the user will be invalidated for all applications and will be required to log in again the next time he accesses a protected resource.
- Cookies are used to transmit a token that associates each request with the saved user identity. So, the single sign-on facility can only be utilized in client environments that support cookies.

Because you have to share the identical authentication information across all applications, the single sign-on facility may have limited applicability. But if the feature is appropriate for your site, it costs nothing to configure—and your users will definitely appreciate it.

Summary

This chapter has covered access control. You have seen the two approaches: declarative and programmatic security. Declarative security has the advantage that it can be added to a Web application at deployment time and requires no changes to the application code. It is also relatively easy to change the security model. Programmatic security, on the other hand, has to be designed in from the start, but it does give you more fine-grained control. It allows the same JSPs or servlets to alter their functionality based on the user's role or principal name.

Access control is just one aspect of security. Later in the book, in Chapter 23, we will look at using SSL to ensure data integrity and confidentiality and also discuss using the Java Security Manager to prevent rogue servlets from damaging your system.

15

Administering Tomcat in a Live Environment

IN THIS CHAPTER

- Essential Information for Tomcat Administrators
- Starting and Stopping Tomcat
- Using the Tomcat Manager Application
- Administering Web Applications Manually
- General Tomcat Housekeeping

In this and the following chapter (Chapter 16, "Configuring Tomcat"), we address the main elements of Tomcat administration. Tomcat administrators come in many flavors. You may be a developer administering Tomcat on your own system; a system administrator running Tomcat in a development environment, a live environment, or both; or a mixture of these. Whatever your role, your responsibilities as administrator are fundamentally the same:

- Making Tomcat available to your user community and to end-user clients
- Installing, reloading, and removing Web applications
- Implementing a security policy appropriate for your site
- Performance tuning
- Installing or upgrading Tomcat when required
- Making regular backups
- Undertaking general housekeeping

Chapter 2, "Installing Jakarta Tomcat," covered in detail the installation of Tomcat, the directory structure, and how to configure Tomcat to run multiple instances on a single server. This chapter covers the basics of day-to-day administration.

Chapter 16 covers aspects of administration that are done less often and includes the details of the Tomcat configuration files; this is also where performance is addressed.

Managing security and configuring SSL support are covered in Chapter 14, "Access Control," and Chapter 23, "Securing Web Applications Under Tomcat."

Essential Information for Tomcat Administrators

This section includes the basic background information you will need to administer Tomcat on a daily basis. If you are already familiar with Tomcat and its environment, you can probably skip this section.

CATALINA_HOME

In order to run Tomcat, you need to set an environment variable called `CATALINA_HOME` to the path of the directory into which you have installed Tomcat. This variable is used by the startup and shutdown scripts to locate the various Tomcat configuration files and directories.

CATALINA_BASE

In most circumstances, all Web applications will be stored under `CATALINA_HOME` and a single copy of Tomcat will be running on the system. In multi-user development environments, there are distinct advantages to each developer running her own instance of Tomcat on a shared server. With separate instances of Tomcat, developers can set up special environments (for, say, debugging purposes) without affecting the remainder of the Tomcat user community. In this case, the `CATALINA_BASE` variable is set to point to a Tomcat directory specific to each developer. Setting up Tomcat for multiple instances is discussed in detail in Chapter 2.

Tomcat Directories

The complete list of Tomcat files and directories was described in Chapter 2, Table 2.1. The abbreviated list in Table 15.1 shows directories that are of primary interest to you as a system administrator administering Tomcat on a daily basis.

TABLE 15.1 Principal Tomcat Files and Directories

File or Directory	Contents
`bin/`	All the binary executables and scripts (both Windows/NT `.bat` and Unix `.sh`) to run Tomcat and various utilities
`conf/`	Tomcat configuration files
`logs/`	Tomcat log files
`webapps/`	Web applications and WAR files
`webapps/tomcat-docs/`	HTML documentation for Tomcat
`work/`	Tomcat temporary files and directories for each Web application

The configuration files in `<CATALINA_HOME>/conf` are essential for the correct running of Tomcat (more on these files in Chapter 16). You should make regular backups of these files and save a copy before editing them.

Tomcat creates various log files under `<CATALINA_HOME>/logs` on a daily basis. The log files are a useful source of information for when you need to diagnose a problem with Tomcat or one of the Web applications. Tomcat cycles log files each day, and you should archive or remove old files to free up disk space.

The Web applications stored in `<CATALINA_HOME>/webapps` should be backed up on a regular basis and always when upgrading a Web application.

The `<CATALINA_HOME>/work` directory contains temporary files created by Tomcat for each Web application. It may also contain unpacked Web Application Resource (WAR) files. There is no need to back up the files in this directory because if accidentally removed, they will be re-created when Tomcat is restarted.

What Is a Web Application?

Although Tomcat can and does serve static pages, its real purpose is to run dynamic Web components called servlets and Java Server Pages (JSPs). The term *Web application* was coined to describe a collection of these different Web components that together form a single application that can be accessed from a Web client.

The dynamic nature of Web applications means there is more to them than just writing the component servlets and JSPs; the developer also has to tell Tomcat how the Web application should be deployed (made available to the end user). This is done in the deployment descriptor file, which is also known as the `web.xml` file.

A Web application therefore consists of

- Servlets
- JSPs
- Static HTML pages
- Helper classes, usually packaged in JAR files
- A deployment descriptor

Each Web application has its own context path or root (it is also the name usually used to refer to the Web application). The context path is usually the name of the directory where the Web application is stored (in Tomcat's `webapps` directory) but can be set to a different name in Tomcat's `server.xml` configuration file (see Chapter 16).

The context path is used in the URL to access the Web application. For example, the index page of a Web application with a context path of `examples` might be accessed using the following URL (presuming Tomcat is configured to listen on port 8080 on `localhost`):

```
http://localhost:8080/examples/index.html
```

A Web application also has a predetermined directory structure. If the directory structure is not correct, Tomcat may fail to start a Web application; it will certainly fail to serve the components correctly.

Web Application Resource Files

If a Web application is to be installed or upgraded, it will normally be handed over to you in the form of a Web Application Resource (WAR) file. A WAR file is simply an archive file that contains all the components for the Web application in their correct directory structure. Developers use WAR files to simplify distribution of their Web applications.

There is no need to unpack the WAR file; simply place it in Tomcat's `webapps` directory. On startup, Tomcat checks for any WAR files in the `webapps` directory and extracts any it finds, except when the following conditions are true:

- A subdirectory of the same name as the WAR file already exists in the `webapps` directory.
- You configure Tomcat not to unpack WAR files in the `server.xml` file (see Chapter 16).

TIP

Always remember to remove the old application directory from the `webapps` directory when using a WAR file to replace an existing Web application.

If Tomcat is configured not to unpack WAR files, the application will be installed and run directly from the WAR file. This can simplify administration, but there will be an initial delay while Tomcat unpacks the WAR file into its working directory.

Tomcat will only recognize new or upgraded Web applications at startup or when using the Manager Application described in the "Using the Tomcat Manager Application" section. To reduce the number of times you take Tomcat out of service, you should use the Manager Application to manage the upgrade and maintenance of

Web applications.

Java Libraries and Tomcat

Many Web applications require helper class files, images, and other resources that are stored in libraries or Java Archive (JAR) files. JAR files typically contain third-party tools that are used by developers in their Web applications, such as JDBC database drivers. If the JAR file is not specific to a particular application, you should install it separately from the Web application so it can be shared by other Web applications.

Within the Tomcat directory structure, you can place these JAR files in a number of places. Where a resource is placed will determine its visibility to the Web applications:

- Web application specific—To restrict visibility of a resource to a particular Web application, place library JAR files in the application's `/WEB-INF/lib` directory.
- All Web applications—For library classes and resources that are to be shared across all Web applications, place JAR files in `<CATALINA_HOME>/share/lib`.
- Web applications and Tomcat—Libraries to be shared by Tomcat and all Web applications should be placed in `<CATALINA_HOME>/common/lib`.

NOTE

JDBC drivers must be installed in `<CATALINA_HOME>/common/lib` if they are used as datasources (see Chapter 9, "Databases and Tomcat").

At startup, Tomcat employs various class loaders to make these resources available, so there is no need to add these directories to the Java `CLASSPATH` variable. From the perspective of a Web application, libraries are loaded in the following order:

- `/WEB-INF/lib/*.jar`
- `<CATALINA_HOME>/common/lib/*.jar`
- `<CATALINA_HOME>/share/lib/*.jar`

If, after first installing a new Web application, you find that it does not work due to a missing class file or JDBC driver, you may not have installed the necessary JAR files in the locations required by Tomcat. Check with the Web application developer which JAR files are required and install any missing ones.

Starting and Stopping Tomcat

How to start and stop Tomcat is covered in detail in Chapter 2. A summary of the Tomcat startup and shutdown procedures is also presented here for completeness.

How to Start Tomcat

Tomcat is started using a command file in the `<CATALINA_HOME>/bin` directory. On Unix, this file is `startup.sh`; on Windows, it is `startup.bat`. On a Windows 2000/NT/XP platform, Tomcat can also be run as an NT service. In this case, you start up and shut down Tomcat as you would any other NT service using the Administrative Tools, Services menu.

If Tomcat is started interactively rather than as a Unix daemon process or a Windows server, the window in which Tomcat is started is designated as Tomcat's console window. Here, Tomcat displays some diagnostic messages in addition to writing them to the log files.

CAUTION

Closing down or pressing Ctrl+C in this console window will shut down Tomcat. Shutting down Tomcat in this manner is not recommended—particularly in a live environment.

By shutting down Tomcat this way, you will prevent any applications that rely on a graceful shutdown to save state (such as session information) from working correctly.

Automatic Startup of Web Applications

When Tomcat starts up, it puts into service all the Web applications (either as unpacked Web application directories or as WAR files) found in the `webapps` directory.

When Tomcat starts up a Web application, it checks that (among other things)

- The Web application base directory exists and is readable
- The application's `web.xml` file is well-formed (there are no syntax errors)

If either of these checks fails, the Web application will not be started. Tomcat reports any errors in its log file. The default location of this log file is `<CATALINA_HOME>/logs`; the log file is named after the current host and date, such as `localhost_log.2002-06-27.txt`. Some (but not all) messages are also written to the Tomcat console window.

Tomcat Shutdown

A script is provided in the `<CATALINA_HOME>/bin` directory to shut down Tomcat cleanly. For Unix systems, this script is called `shutdown.sh`; for Windows, it's `shutdown.bat`. If Tomcat is run as an NT service, you should stop it using the Administrative Tools, Services menu.

TIP

Remember to add the Tomcat shutdown to your standard system shutdown scripts or procedures. Note that NT services are automatically stopped when a Windows system is shut down or rebooted.

When Tomcat is shut down with the shutdown script, each Web application is gracefully taken out of service. This gives Web applications a chance to save persistent data or do any other cleanup operations.

Obviously, on a live system you should restrict the amount of time Tomcat is out of service to an absolute minimum, to minimize the disruption to users. In the next section, you will see how using the Tomcat Manager Application helps you minimize Tomcat's downtime.

Using the Tomcat Manager Application

This section discusses the Tomcat Manager Application, which you can use to administer Web applications. In particular, the Tomcat Manager Application allows you to

- List all Web applications
- Start or stop individual applications
- Install or deploy applications
- Remove or undeploy applications
- Display session information for an application

The Tomcat Manager Application is itself a Web application and is provided with the Tomcat server.

Securing Access to the Manager Application

The Tomcat Manager Application is protected by a security constraint, which means you have to log in to use it. Before you can run the Manager Application, you must first set up a user in the <CATALINA_HOME>/conf/tomcat-users.xml file that has a role of manager, as shown here:

```
<user name="tomcat" password="tomcat" roles="manager" />
```

This user entry must be added between the <tomcat-user> and </tomcat-user> tags.

NOTE

If you have installed Tomcat 4.1, you were given the opportunity to configure the Manager Application user at installation. You can always manually add or modify the user at a later date if required.

TIP

With Tomcat 4.1, there is an admin role for running the Tomcat Web Server Administration Tool. Unless you have a good reason for separating the roles of manager and admin, you should create a single user and allocate it both roles as shown in the following example tomcat-users.xml file:

```
<tomcat-users>
    <role rolename="admin" />
    <role rolename="manager" />
    <user username="tomcat" password="tomcat" roles="admin,manager" />
</tomcat-users>
```

The tomcat-users.xml file is read into memory at startup, so you will need to stop and restart Tomcat in order for any changes to this file to be recognized.

TIP

For added security, you may prefer to configure the Manager application to use a JDBCRealm or JNDIRealm (see Chapter 14). You should in any case restrict access to the tomcat-users.xml file because it contains the unencrypted password for the administration user.

Using the Manager Application

The Tomcat Manager Application has two Web interfaces:

- A minimal interface designed to be accessed from scripts (the default)
- A more user-friendly HTML interface

The default interface is fine for infrequent use or for incorporating the Manager Application into your own administration scripts. For most purposes, the HTML interface provides a much more convenient way to administer applications.

To change from the default command line manager application to use the HTML interface, you must edit the Manager Application's `web.xml` file.

NOTE

For Tomcat 4.0, this file is `<CATALINA_HOME>/manager/WEB-INF/web.xml`. For Tomcat 4.1, it is `<CATALINA_HOME>/server/webapps/manager/WEB-INF/web.xml`.

Edit the Manager Application's `web.xml` file and change the servlet class for the Manger servlet from `org.apache.catalina.servlets.ManagerServlet` to `org.apache.catalina.servlets.HTMLManagerServlet`, as shown in bold in the following example:

```
<servlet>
    <servlet-name>Manager</servlet-name>
    <servlet-class>org.apache.catalina.servlets.HTMLManagerServlet</servlet-class>
    <init-param>
        <param-name>debug</param-name>
        <param-value>2</param-value>
    </init-param>
</servlet>
```

When using the HTML interface, all administration is done through the one screen, as shown in Figure 15.1.

This interface is intuitive and provides an easy way to monitor and manage Web applications.

Regardless of whether you use the simple or graphic administration interface, the same commands are available, as listed in Table 15.2. You always use the following URL, followed by the name of the command, to access the application:

```
http://localhost:8080/manager/
```

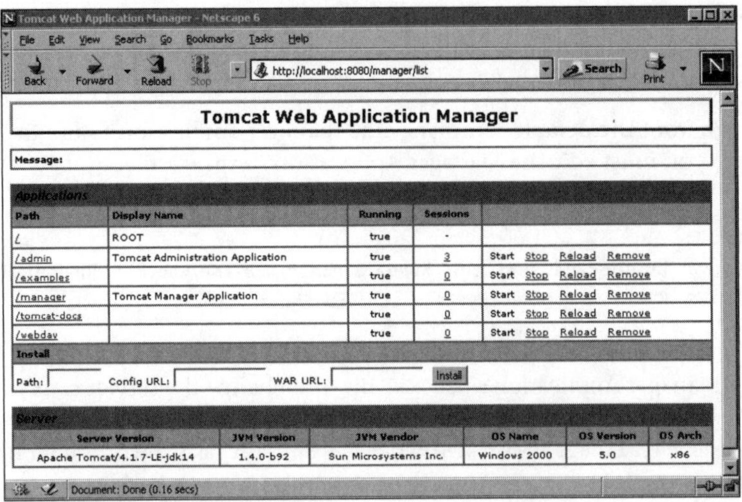

FIGURE 15.1 Tomcat Manager Application HTML interface.

TABLE 15.2 Tomcat Manager Application Commands

Command	Description
`install`	Installs a Web application from a WAR file or unpacked directory.
`list`	Lists the currently installed Web applications, along with their status (running/stopped) and the number of active sessions.
`reload`	Reloads a particular Web application.
`remove`	Gracefully shuts down and uninstalls the Web application. Depending on the version of Tomcat 4 being used, this command may not physically remove application files and directories—if Tomcat does not remove the directory, you should remove it yourself, or the application will reappear the next time Tomcat is restarted.
`session`	Lists session information about a Web application.
`start`	Starts a Web application.
`stop`	Stops a Web application.

The commands are designated as extra path information added to the Manager Application URL. For example, you use the following to run the list command:

```
http://localhost8080:/manager/list
```

For the HTML interface, this command displays the output already seen in Figure 15.1. For the default interface, it simply lists the Web applications and their current status, as shown in Figure 15.2.

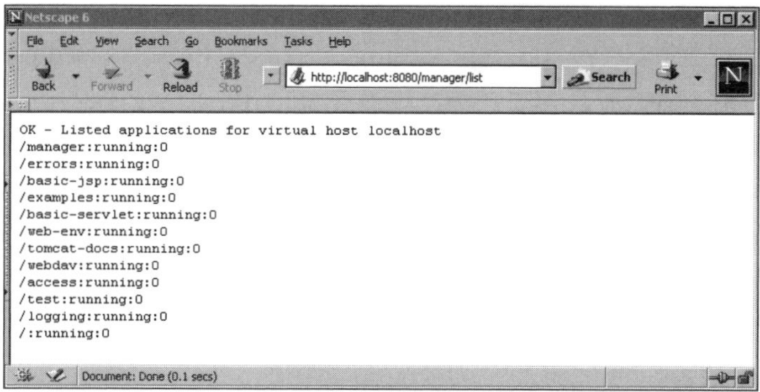

FIGURE 15.2 Use of Tomcat Manager Application list command.

If you use the HTML interface to start, stop, reload, remove, or display session information for an application, you simply select the appropriate link on the page displayed by the `list` command (shown in Figure 15.1).

If you use the default interface, you will need to add the required Web application name to the Manager Application URL. All the commands, apart from `list`, require the name of the Web application to be supplied in the form of an HTTP request parameter called `path`. For example, you would use the following to reload the `logging` application:

```
http://localhost:8080/manager/reload?path=/logging
```

Installing a Web Application

To install a new application, you must supply the Manger Application's `install` command with either the URL of a WAR file or the pathname of the directory that contains the Web application. This WAR file URL is supplied as the `war` parameter, and has to be in one of the following formats:

- `file:/` followed by the absolute path of a directory that contains the unpacked version of the Web application (for example, `file:/D:/Tomcat4/webapps/logging`).
- `jar:file:/` followed by the absolute path of WAR file, terminated by `!/` (for example, `jar:file:/D:/Tomcat4/webapps/logging.war!/`).
- `jar:http://` followed by the location of a remote WAR file, terminated by `!/` (for example, `jar:http://www.samspublishing.com/4393/logging.jar!/`).

If you use the HTML interface, you install a Web application using the form fields on the `http://localhost:8080/manager/install` page. In the `Path:` field, enter the context path for the Web application preceded by a `/`. In the `War URL:` field, enter the location of the Web application using one of the formats listed previously.

If you use the default interface, you must supply the path and location values as parameters to the `install` URL. For example, you would use the following to install a new application called `cats` from an already unpacked WAR file:

```
http://localhost:8080/manager/install?path=/cats&war=file:/D:/Tomcat4/webapps/cats
```

Using the default interface to replace the logging application from a WAR file, you would use the following two commands:

```
http://localhost:8080/manager/remove?path=/logging
http://localhost:8080/manager/install?path=/logging&war=
➥ jar:file:/D:/Tomcat4/webapps/logging.war!/
```

CAUTION

If you are running Tomcat 4.0, the `remove` command does not delete the physical files from the disk. You should remove the files manually after issuing the `remove` command and before issuing the `install` command.

Administering Web Applications Manually

If you choose not to use the Tomcat Manager Application, you can still install and remove applications manually. The major disadvantage of doing things manually is that you have to stop and restart Tomcat each time in order for it to recognize the changes you have made to the `webapps` directory.

To install an application, you must stop Tomcat, copy the application directory or WAR file to Tomcat's `webapps` directory, and restart Tomcat. To remove an application, first stop Tomcat, remove the Web application directory or WAR file, and then restart Tomcat. To upgrade an application, you must remove the old application first and then install the new application.

It is not possible to temporarily stop and restart a Web application except through the Manager Application. All applications are started when Tomcat is started; there is no way to tell Tomcat not to start an installed Web application.

General Tomcat Housekeeping

On a day-to-day basis, Tomcat does not require much in the way of housekeeping. Here are a couple of tasks you might like to add to your administration procedures:

- Tomcat creates new log files every day and never deletes them. You should monitor the `logs` directory and archive or remove old log files.
- Back up the Tomcat directories, especially the Web applications and Tomcat configuration files.

Summary

This chapter covered the basic administration tasks required to start Tomcat and manage the Web applications. You have been introduced to the Tomcat Application Manager, which provides a simple and effective way of monitoring and administering applications. The HTML interface to the Manager Application, in particular, provides a useful monitoring tool to keep a watch on what is happening in the Tomcat server.

In Chapter 16, we will delve more deeply into Tomcat's configuration and also look at changes that can be made to improve performance.

16

Configuring Tomcat

IN THIS CHAPTER

- An Overview of Configuring the Tomcat Server
- Tomcat 4.1 Web Server Administration Tool
- Configuring Hosts
- Changing Tomcat Port Numbers
- Tomcat Server Configuration
- Performance Issues
- Configuring Access to Users' Home Directories
- Controlling Client Access to Tomcat
- Tomcat Default Deployment Descriptor
- Managing Tomcat Users
- Running Tomcat as a Service Under Windows

Chapter 15, "Administering Tomcat in a Live Environment," covered the basics of Tomcat administration—that is, those actions you are likely to undertake on a regular basis. In this chapter, you will look at the Tomcat configuration in more detail.

An Overview of Configuring the Tomcat Server

Much of Tomcat's configuration is accomplished through editing the four configuration files:

- `server.xml`—Server configuration file.
- `web.xml`—Defines default values for all Web applications loaded by Tomcat.
- `tomcat-users.xml`—Defines users and roles that are used for access control.
- `catalina.policy`—Contains a set of security policies enforced by the Tomcat JVM. The configuration and use of this file is covered in Chapter 23, "Securing Web Applications Under Tomcat."

Tomcat 4.1 introduced the Tomcat Web Server Administration Tool, which simplifies much of the administration and allows changes to be made and recognized while Tomcat is running. If you are using Tomcat 4.0, you will have to manually edit the configuration files and restart Tomcat to make the changes effective. All the four configuration files listed previously can be found in the `<CATALINA_HOME>/conf` directory.

CAUTION

The Tomcat configuration files are XML documents. You should therefore be comfortable with the syntax and structure of a well-formed XML document before making changes to these files.

When making changes in a live environment, it is advisable to use the Tomcat Web Server Administration Tool (where possible) because the tool will ensure that the required attributes to the directives are supplied and that the syntax is correct.

Tomcat 4.1 Web Server Administration Tool

The Tomcat Web Server Administration Tool is a Web-based utility introduced with Tomcat 4.1. This administration utility can be used to configure Tomcat server components, users, and other resources. The tool is accessed through a browser using the following URL:

```
http://localhost:8080/admin/
```

TIP

On a Windows platform the tool can be accessed via a shortcut provided in the Programs menu.

Creating an Administration User

The Administration Tool is password protected; you will need to create a user configured with the `admin` role in the `tomcat-users.xml` file.

NOTE

A suitable user was created as part of the Tomcat 4.1 installation.

The following is an example `tomcat-users.xml` file that defines a user called `admin`, with password `tomcat`, and the roles of `admin` and `manager`:

```
<?xml version='1.0'?>
<tomcat-users>
  <role rolename="admin"/>
  <role rolename="manager"/>
  <user username="admin" password="tomcat" roles="admin,manager"/>
</tomcat-users>
```

The `admin` role allows that user to run the Tomcat Web Server Administration Tool, and the `manager` role allows the user to run the Tomcat Web Application Manager Tool.

Using the Administration Tool

The Tomcat Web Server Administration Tool screen is divided into three areas as shown in Figure 16.1.

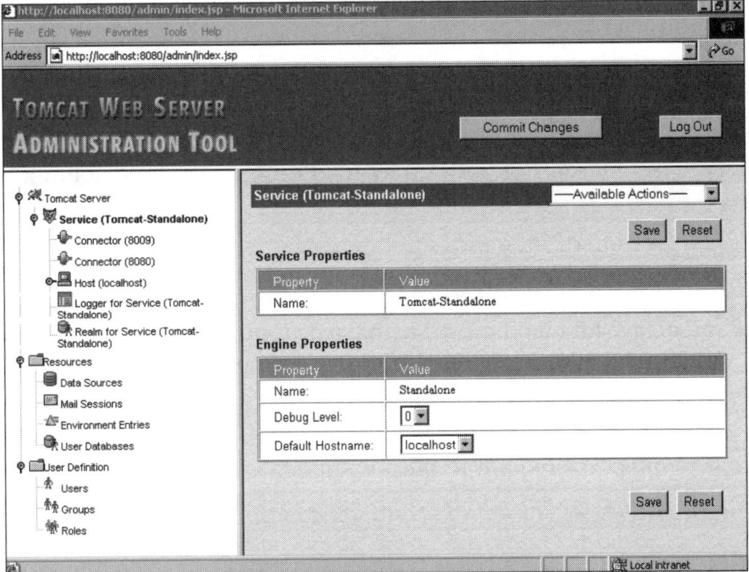

FIGURE 16.1 Tomcat Web Server Administration Tool.

The panels provide the following functionality:

- The top panel contains a button to commit any changes made. Only after clicking on this button are any changes to Tomcat's configuration written out to disk.
- The left panel shows the current configuration in a hierarchical representation; click the twister icons to hide or reveal more of the configuration.
- The right panel either shows details about the configuration or contains a form to add new elements. At the top of this panel is a pull-down list showing the Available Actions for the item selected in the left panel. Typically, these actions allow you to create or delete Tomcat components.

This chapter focuses on the structure of the `server.xml` file and the attributes and elements required to configure Tomcat. Using the Administration Tool to perform the configuration is not shown in each case. Using the Administration Tool is straightforward, as long as you are aware of the meaning and use of the underlying configuration elements.

NOTE

The Administration Tool used in this chapter is from a beta release of Tomcat 4.1. The final version may have different functionality and appearance than the one shown here.

Configuring Hosts

Tomcat uses the concepts of hosts and virtual hosts to service incoming HTTP requests.

- A *host* is either the IP address of the server running Tomcat or a registered DNS entry on the system that refers to the server.
- A *virtual host* (under Tomcat) is a named component that services requests and must match either a registered DNS name or an entry in the local `hosts` file.

The hostname is provided by the client as part of the URL, and Tomcat uses this hostname to direct the request to the appropriate virtual host.

The Tomcat `server.xml` file comes configured with a single virtual host (`localhost`).

NOTE

By convention, most systems have `localhost` configured in the system hosts file to map onto the special loopback IP address `127.0.0.1`.

There are many reasons why you might want to add virtual hosts, some of which are listed here:

- To simplify migration of applications from one system to another (you need only change the DNS entry; users can continue to use the same URL)
- To provide a different application base directory to load balance page hits across different physical disks for performance
- To provide a development setup that reflects the real environment

- To reflect the virtual host configuration of another Web server when integrating Tomcat into that Web server (see Chapter 22, "Integrating Tomcat with a Web Server")
- To provide a logical grouping of Web applications that share things in common (for example, the same security policy, user base, or ownership)

To operate Tomcat as a standalone Web server, you must configure at least one host. If you have more than one host defined, you will need to designate one of them as the default host (see the `defaultHost` attribute in the section "Configuring the Engine Component"). The default host will handle all requests that are directed to a nonexistent virtual host (that is, a request directed to a registered DNS name that has no virtual host in the `server.xml` file).

Host Aliases

Where you have more than one DNS network name that represents the same system, host aliases allow you to map the many names to the same Tomcat virtual host.

The process of configuring virtual hosts and host aliases is covered in the section "Tomcat Server Configuration."

Changing Tomcat Port Numbers

Requests are routed to hosts via components called connectors. Connectors are associated with TCP/IP ports. Each connector configured in Tomcat has its own unique port number (which is not only unique in Tomcat but cannot be used by any other Web server or application running on the same system).

By default, Tomcat listens on port 8080 for HTTP connections from client browsers. Reasons why you might want to change this default port number include the following:

- If Tomcat is the only Web server running on the system, you might want to change to port 80 (the default HTTP port). If you use port 80, users no longer have to specify the port number as part of the URL.
- To avoid a clash with another Web server or application on the same system.
- When you are setting up Tomcat for multiple instances on the same system, each instance will require its own unique set of port numbers (see Chapter 2, "Installing Jakarta Tomcat").

Similarly, if you use other connectors (to provide secure access or to connect to another Web server), you may need to change other port numbers to avoid clashes.

TIP

The system command `netstat -a` will show which ports are currently in use.

Connectors are defined in the `server.xml` file. To change the port number, simply edit the port attribute to the appropriate connector (or use the Administration Tool). The following table is a list of ports defined in the default `server.xml` file:

Tomcat Port	Used For
8080	Non-secure HTTP/1.1 requests
8443	Secure SSL requests
8008	Requests from another Web server using WARP
8009	Requests from another Web server using AJP
8082	Proxy requests from another Web server
8084	Non-secure HTTP/1.0 requests
8005	Shutdown port

Not all the connectors connected with these ports are enabled by default and you should comment out or remove any that are not required. How to configure connectors is covered in the following section.

Tomcat Server Configuration

The `server.xml` file contains configuration directives that affect Tomcat's behavior. The file has a hierarchical structure and defines a number of containers that are able to process client requests and generate responses.

Listing 16.1 shows the default `server.xml` file shipped with the Tomcat 4.1 distribution; it has been edited for clarity (and to save space).

LISTING 16.1 Tomcat's `server.xml` File

```
<Server port="8005" shutdown="SHUTDOWN" debug="0">
  <Listener className="org.apache.catalina.mbeans.ServerLifecycleListener"
            debug="0"/>
  <Service name="Tomcat-Standalone">

    <!-- Define a non-SSL Coyote HTTP/1.1 Connector on port 8080 -->
    <Connector className="org.apache.coyote.tomcat4.CoyoteConnector"
               port="8080"
               minProcessors="5" maxProcessors="75"
```

LISTING 16.1 Continued

```
             enableLookups="true" redirectPort="8443"
             acceptCount="10" debug="0" connectionTimeout="20000"
             useURIValidationHack="false" />

    <!-- Define a Coyote/JK2 AJP Connector on port 8009 -->
    <Connector className="org.apache.coyote.tomcat4.CoyoteConnector"
             port="8009" minProcessors="5" maxProcessors="75"
             enableLookups="true" redirectPort="8443"
             acceptCount="10" debug="0" connectionTimeout="20000"
             useURIValidationHack="false"
             protocolHandlerClassName="org.apache.jk.server.JkCoyoteHandler"
    />
    <!-- Define a Proxied HTTP/1.1 Connector on port 8082 -->
    <Connector className="org.apache.coyote.tomcat4.CoyoteConnector"
             port="8082" minProcessors="5" maxProcessors="75"
             enableLookups="true"
             acceptCount="10" debug="0" connectionTimeout="20000"
             proxyPort="80" useURIValidationHack="false" />

    <!-- Define the top level container in our container hierarchy -->
    <Engine name="Standalone" defaultHost="localhost" debug="0">

      <!-- Global logger unless overridden at lower levels -->
      <Logger className="org.apache.catalina.logger.FileLogger"
              prefix="catalina_log." suffix=".txt"
              timestamp="true"/>

      <!-- Because this Realm is here, an instance will be shared globally -->
      <Realm className="org.apache.catalina.realm.MemoryRealm" />

      <!-- Define the default virtual host -->
      <Host name="localhost" debug="0" appBase="webapps"
            unpackWARs="true" autoDeploy="true">

        <!-- Logger shared by all Contexts related to this virtual host -->
        <Logger className="org.apache.catalina.logger.FileLogger"
                directory="logs"  prefix="localhost_log." suffix=".txt"
              timestamp="true"/>

        <!-- Tomcat Examples Context -->
        <Context path="/examples" docBase="examples" debug="0"
                 reloadable="true" crossContext="true">
```

LISTING 16.1 Continued

```
        <Logger className="org.apache.catalina.logger.FileLogger"
                prefix="localhost_examples_log." suffix=".txt"
          timestamp="true"/>
        <Ejb name="ejb/EmplRecord" type="Entity"
             home="com.wombat.empl.EmployeeRecordHome"
             remote="com.wombat.empl.EmployeeRecord"/>

        <Environment name="maxExemptions" type="java.lang.Integer"
                     value="15"/>
        <Parameter name="context.param.name" value="context.param.value"
                   override="false"/>
        <Resource name="jdbc/EmployeeAppDb" auth="SERVLET"
                  type="javax.sql.DataSource"/>
        <ResourceParams name="jdbc/EmployeeAppDb">
          <parameter><name>user</name><value>sa</value></parameter>
          <parameter><name>password</name><value></value></parameter>
          <parameter><name>driverClassName</name>
            <value>org.hsql.jdbcDriver</value></parameter>
          <parameter><name>driverName</name>
            <value>jdbc:HypersonicSQL:database</value></parameter>
        </ResourceParams>
        <Resource name="mail/Session" auth="Container"
                  type="javax.mail.Session"/>
        <ResourceParams name="mail/Session">
          <parameter>
            <name>mail.smtp.host</name>
            <value>localhost</value>
          </parameter>
        </ResourceParams>
        <ResourceLink name="linkToGlobalResource"
                      global="simpleValue"
                      type="java.lang.Integer"/>
      </Context>
    </Host>
  </Engine>
</Service>

<!-- Define an Apache-Connector Service -->
<Service name="Tomcat-Apache">

  <Connector className="org.apache.catalina.connector.warp.WarpConnector"
```

LISTING 16.1 Continued

```
               port="8008" minProcessors="5" maxProcessors="75"
               enableLookups="true" appBase="webapps"
               acceptCount="10" debug="0"/>

    <Engine className="org.apache.catalina.connector.warp.WarpEngine"
            name="Apache" debug="0">

      <Logger className="org.apache.catalina.logger.FileLogger"
              prefix="apache_log." suffix=".txt"
              timestamp="true"/>

      <Realm className="org.apache.catalina.realm.MemoryRealm" />
    </Engine>
  </Service>
</Server>
```

CAUTION

There is no DTD or XML schema for the `server.xml` file, so if you manually edit this file you cannot validate any changes you make prior to starting up Tomcat. You may still check the syntax, and confirm that the XML is well formed, using an XML parser or XML-aware browser.

You will now look at the elements in the `server.xml` file in more detail. All the elements discussed are common to both Tomcat 4.0 and 4.1; any differences in how they are configured are highlighted in the appropriate sections.

Configuring the Server Element

The server element is denoted by the XML `<Server>` tag. The server element is at the outermost level of the `server.xml` file and represents the entire Tomcat Java Virtual Machine (JVM). A Tomcat server is not itself a container, which means it does not process requests, so you can't define elements that apply only to requests, such as logger and valve elements, at this level.

The `<Server>` element has the following attributes:

`<Server>` **Attribute**	**Description**
`port`	The TCP/IP port on which the server listens for the shutdown command (default 8005)
`className`	(optional) The Java classname of the server implementation (default `org.apache.catalina.core.StandardServer`)

<Server> **Attribute**	**Description**
`shutdown`	The string that must be received via the above TCP/IP port to shut the server down (default `SHUTDOWN`)

A server can contain one or more service elements.

Configuring the Service Element

A Tomcat service is denoted by the XML `<Service>` tag and handles all requests received on specified TCP/IP ports. In Listing 16.1 there are two services defined:

```
<Service name="Tomcat-Standalone">
  ...
</Service>
<Service name="Tomcat-Apache">
   ...
</Service>
```

The `Tomcat-Standalone` service handles all requests received directly from browsers and the `Tomcat-Apache` service handles requests forwarded to Tomcat from an Apache server.

The `<Service>` element has the following attributes:

<Service> **Attribute**	**Description**
`className`	(optional) The Java classname of the service implementation (default `org.apache.catalina.core.StandardService`)
`name`	The display name for this service (used in log messages)

Nested in a `<Service>` element are one or more connectors and elements and a single engine component. Connectors define how to handle incoming requests and the engine component undertakes the request processing.

Configuring Connectors

Tomcat connectors are denoted by the XML `<Connector>` tag and are used to define how to handle incoming requests. Listing 16.1 includes two types of connectors:

- Coyote (supports HTTP and AJP)
- Webapp (supports WARP)

The Coyote connector supports the HTTP/1.1 protocol and handles all requests directed at the service from clients. This connector allows Tomcat to operate as a standalone server (by serving static pages as well as executing JSPs and servlets). This connector can also be used with the Apache Jserv Protocol (AJP) to integrate Tomcat with another Web server (see Chapter 22).

The Webapp connector is used to integrate Tomcat with Apache using the WARP protocol. This is discussed further in Chapter 22.

There are a large number of attributes for a `<Connector>` element as shown in the following table:

`<Connector>` **Attribute**	**Description**
`className`	The Java classname of the connector implementation. The `className` depends on the type of connector and the version of Tomcat (see note below).
`port`	The TCP port number on which this connector will listen for incoming requests.
`acceptCount`	(optional) The maximum number of requests that will be queued when all request processing threads are in use (default `10`).
`debug`	(optional) The debugging level for the connector. Determines the amount of log messages created (default `0`).
`enableLookups`	(optional) Set this to `false` if you want calls to `request.getRemoteHost()` to return the IP address in String form rather than perform DNS lookup to return the actual host name (default `true`).
`maxProcessors`	(optional) Maximum number of threads for this connector. Sets the maximum number of simultaneous requests that can be handled (default `20`).
`minProcessors`	(optional) The number of threads created when connector is first started (default `5`).
`redirectPort`	(optional) The TCP/IP port that the request will be directed to if it requires SSL transport.
`scheme`	(optional) The name returned by calls to `request.getScheme()` (default `http`).

`<Connector>` **Attribute**	**Description**
`secure`	(optional) Set to `true` to have calls to `request.isSecure()` return `true` (default `false`).
`protocolHandlerClassName`	(required for AJP) Must be set to `org.apache.jk.server.JkCoyoteHandler` to use the JK2 handler to support AJP.

NOTE

The connector `className` is set according to the protocol supported by the connector and the version of Tomcat.

- For Tomcat 4.1 and HTTP/1.1 or AJP, use `org.apache.coyote.tomcat4.CoyoteConnectort`.
- For Tomcat 4.0 and HTTP/1.1, use `org.apache.catalina.connector.http.HttpConnectort`.
- For Tomcat 4.0 and AJP, use `org.apache.ajp.tomcat4.Ajp13Connectort`.

  For both versions of Tomcat, the Webapp connector uses the `org.apache.catalina.connector.warp.WarpConnector.class`.

The following attributes are optional and specific to the HTTP connector:

HTTP `<Connector>` **Attribute**	**Description**
`bufferSize`	The size (in bytes) of the buffer to be provided for input streams (default `2048`)
`connectionTimeout`	The number of milliseconds the HTTP connector will wait after connection is established for the request URI line (default `60000`)
`proxyName`	The name returned by `request.getServerName()` if the HTTP connector is being used in a proxy configuration
`proxyPort`	The port number returned by `request.getServerPort()` if the HTTP connector is being used in a proxy configuration
`tcpNoDelay`	Sets the `TCP_NO_DELAY` option on the server socket; this usually improves performance (default `true`)

If the connector is to be used for secure traffic, you enable SSL by adding a `<Factory>` element inside the connector as follows:

```
<Connector className="org.apache.coyote.tomcat4.CoyoteConnector"
           port="8443" minProcessors="5" maxProcessors="75"
           enableLookups="true"
           acceptCount="10" debug="0" scheme="https" secure="true"
           useURIValidationHack="false">
  <Factory className="org.apache.catalina.net.SSLServerSocketFactory"
           clientAuth="false" protocol="TLS"
           keystoreFile=".keystore" />
</Connector>
```

Configuring SSL is covered in detail in Chapter 23.

Configuring the Engine Component

The engine component is denoted by the XML `<Engine>` tag and performs the request processing for a service. It processes all the requests received via connectors and returns the response to the same connector. There must only be one `<Engine>` element defined in a `<Service>` and it is placed after the connectors.

The `<Engine>` element has the following attributes.

`<Engine>` **Attribute**	**Description**
`name`	Display name of this engine (used in log messages)
`defaultHost`	(optional) The name of the default `<Host>`, which will process requests directed to host names that are not defined elsewhere in the `server.xml` file
`className`	(optional) Java classname of the engine implementation to use (default `org.apache.catalina.core.StandardEngine`)

Within the `<Engine>` element, you can have the following nested elements:

- `<Host>`—Virtual host definitions, the name of one must match the `defaultHost` attribute (for more on hosts see the next section).
- `<Logger>`—Optional logger to process all messages for the engine (including nested hosts unless overridden at lower level) and the connectors associated with the engine in the surrounding service (see Chapter 13, "Logging Using Tomcat").

- `<Realm>`—Optional security realm to be used by all hosts (see Chapter 14, "Access Control").
- `<Valve>`—You can add Tomcat valves to an `<Engine>` element to log client access and provide client access control, (see Chapter 19, "Tomcat Valves").
- `<Listener>`—Listener elements enable you to associate a Java class with engine lifecycle events (see Chapter 7, "The Web Application Environment").

NOTE

A Tomcat engine component cannot be selected in the Administration Tool. The previous components are configured in the service that encloses the engine.

Configuring the Host Components

Each `<Host>` element defined in the `server.xml` file represents a different virtual host. The default `server.xml` file is distributed with one virtual host (called `localhost`); you may change this or add more as required.

The `<Host>` element has the following attributes:

`<Host>` **Attribute**	**Description**
`appBase`	The directory where all the applications are stored (path can be absolute or relative to `<CATALINA_HOME>`).
`autoDeploy*`	(optional) Indicates whether Web applications should be automatically deployed. See the "Application Deployment" section.
`name`	Network name for this virtual host.
`className`	(optional) Java classname of the host implementation to use (default `org.apache.catalina.core.StandardHost`).
`debug`	(optional) Level of logging for this host (default `0`).
`deployXML*`	(optional) Set to `false` to disable deploying applications using an XML context file (default `true`). See the section "Application Deployment."
`liveDeploy*`	(optional) Set to `false` to stop Web applications copied to the `Tomcat webapps` directory while Tomcat is running from being automatically deployed (default `true`). See the section "Application Deployment."

<Host> Attribute	Description
unpackWARs	(optional) If true, deployed WAR files are unpacked into a directory structure under appBase; if false, the application is run directly from the WAR file (default true). See the section titled "Application Deployment."
workDir	(optional) Pathname to a scratch directory to be used by applications for this host (default <CATALINA_HOME>/work/<*host*>).

* *only available in Tomcat 4.1*

Application Deployment

In Tomcat 4.0, applications were deployed as WAR files or Web application directories in the Tomcat webapps directory. If new applications are added to this webapps directory, Tomcat has to be restarted for the new Web application to become available (unless it was deployed using the Tomcat Web Application Manager). With Tomcat 4.1, this restriction has been removed. Setting the attribute liveDeploy to true (which is the default) will ensure that Web applications added to the webapps directory (while Tomcat is running) are automatically deployed.

With Tomcat 4.1, you can replace the WAR file or the unpacked application directory in the webapps directory with an XML file. This XML file contains a single <Context> element (see the section "Configuring Application Contexts") that, among other things, defines where the Web application files are located. To enable this feature, set the deployXML attribute to true.

CAUTION

Applications deployed using deployXML="true" run without a security manager (even if one is configured as described in Chapter 23). You should therefore consider setting deployXML to false if developers are able to add their own applications to the webapps directory.

If autoDeploy is set to true, Web applications in Tomcat's webapps directory that are not explicitly mentioned in a <context> element in the server.xml file will receive an automatically generated context. Properties set for the DefaultContext element will be applied to this application (see the "Configuring Application Contexts" and "Configuring the DefaultContext Element" sections).

Host Aliases

Host aliases allow you to have more than one DNS network name that is resolved to the same Tomcat virtual host. An <Alias> element specifies the alternative name and is nested inside a <Host> element as the following example shows:

```
<Host name="www.samspublishing.com" ...>
  ...
  <Alias>samspublishing.com</Alias>
  ...
</Host>
```

NOTE

All hostnames and aliases used in the `server.xml` file must be valid DNS names for the host running Tomcat.

Configuring Application Contexts

Application contexts are used to represent Web applications. Application contexts are denoted by `<Context>` elements and are only found nested in `<Host>` elements. You use `<Context>` elements to define Web application specific properties and resources. Not every Web application will require a `<Context>` element; you can use a `<DefaultContext>` element to set properties for all Web applications, including those that are not represented by an explicit `<Context>` element.

If `autoDeploy` is set to `true` for the enclosing `<Host>` element, Web applications will receive an automatic context even if there is no `<Context>` or `<DefaultContext>` element.

Context elements can be configured in the `server.xml` file or in Tomcat 4.1 in separate XML files stored in the `webapps` directory.

Each context has two required attributes:

- `docBase`—The *document base* (also known as the *context root* or *document root*) describes the pathname of the application WAR file or the unpacked application directory.
- `path`—The context path used in the URL to designate the application.

The `index.html` page for the following example context (from the `server.xml` file in Listing 16.1)

```
<Context path="/examples" docBase="examples" debug="0"
         reloadable="true" crossContext="true">
```

would be referenced using

```
http://localhost:8080/examples/index.html
```

The names chosen for all the context paths for an application must be unique within the virtual host.

A list of commonly used context attributes are given in the following table (apart from `docBase` and `path`, they are all optional):

`<context>` **Attribute**	**Description**
`cookies`	Set to `false` to disable the use of cookies for session identification. If session identification is then required, the application should use URL rewriting (default `true`).
`docBase`	The directory for this Web application, or the pathname to the Web application WAR file. The pathname may be absolute or relative to the `webapps` directory.
`override`	Must be set to `true` for settings in this context element to override any corresponding settings in the `DefaultContext` element (default `false`).
`path`	The context path for the Web application, which is provided in the URL to select the Web application.
`reloadable`	If set to `true`, Tomcat will monitor the `/WEB-INF/classes/` and `/WEB-INF/lib` for updated files and automatically reload the Web application if a class file is replaced (default `false`).
`debug`	The level of debugging that is logged by the associated Logger (default is `0`—no logging).
`workDir`	Pathname to a scratch directory (default `<CATALINA_HOME>/work`).

Tomcat recognizes the special context path `""` (an empty string) as denoting the default Web application for this host. The following example defines a default application that resides in the `<CATALINA_HOME>/webapps/welcome` directory:

```
<Context path="" docBase="welcome" debug="0"/>
```

The default application will process all requests not assigned to other explicit contexts and is where clients will be directed if they simply enter your site's hostname in the URL. If you only have one Web application, you could make this the default Web application, but it is more likely that you will want the default Web application to be a portal to your site.

NOTE

The default Web application should not be confused with the `DefaultContext`. The former defines an application that will handle requests directed to unknown contexts. The `DefaultContext` defines properties for applications that do not have an explicit context element of their own.

Configuring the `DefaultContext` Element

The `<DefaultContext>` element can be nested in a `<Host>` or `<Engine>` component to provide default configuration properties for all Web applications, including those with automatically created contexts. The `<DefaultContext>` element has only a subset of the `<Context>` attributes and is normally used to set the `cookies` or the `reloadable` attributes. For example, if you want to enable automatic reloading of all Web applications (see the "Performance Issues" section), you should add the following:

```
<DefaultContext reloadable="true" />
```

Other Components in the `server.xml` File

Other components can be nested in an `<Engine>`, `<Host>`, or `<Context>` element; most of them have been covered in detail in other chapters of this book. These components include

Component	Description
Loaders	Defines the class loader used for Web applications.
Valves	A valve is used to pre-process requests; a number of valves are provided with Tomcat (see Chapter 19).
Loggers	Loggers define the destination for general debugging and error messages (see Chapter 13).
Realms	A realm provides access to a collection of usernames, passwords, and roles that can be used to implement access control (see Chapter 14).

The `<Loader>` element defines the class loader used to load Web applications. Unless you have specific requirements for how Java classes are loaded, it is unlikely that you will want to change from the standard loader (`org.apache.catalina.loader.WebappLoader`); however, you might want to change its attributes.

The `<Loader>` element has a `checkInterval` attribute, which, if the Web application has been configured to be `reloadable`, can be used to set the number of seconds between checks for modified classes and resources (the default is 15 seconds). The following example sets the check interval to 2 minutes:

```
<Context ...>
  <Loader checkInterval="120">
</Context>
```

You can only nest a `<Loader>` element within a `<Context>`, so the new `checkInterval` will only apply to a single Web application.

Performance Issues

If you are using Tomcat in a pure development environment, performance is probably not a topic of great concern. For a live server, on the other hand, you need to think carefully about the Tomcat configuration and whether to enable features that may adversely affect performance. The following sections look at three areas that require consideration in a live environment:

- Information gathering
- Integrating Tomcat with another Web server
- Automatic Web application deployment

Information Gathering

Tomcat valves can be used to monitor client requests by saving information to log files. Setting high debug levels to certain Tomcat components can also provide lots of information about client requests and what Tomcat is doing. In a development environment, this information can be used for debugging and simple auditing, but you should be aware that the gathering process will degrade server performance. On a heavily used server this could be significant.

In a live environment, only two scenarios should require information gathering:

- Auditing information required to satisfy the requirements of the site security policy
- Debugging information switched on for a period while a problem investigation is in progress

In all other situations, monitoring and debugging should be switched off.

Integrating Tomcat with Another Web Server

Tomcat is a Web server designed to serve dynamic content in the form of servlets and JSPs. Other Web servers have been optimized to serve static content. If your site's Web applications have significant static content, you can increase performance and general system scalability by integrating Tomcat with another Web server such as Apache or IIS. Apache or IIS are then used to serve the static pages leaving Tomcat to serve only the dynamic content. Integrating Tomcat with Apache or IIS is covered in detail in Chapter 22.

Automatic Web Application Reloading

In a development environment, it is often useful to set automatic reloading of Web applications in the `server.xml` file. In most live environments this feature should be disabled and the Tomcat Web Application Manager used to reload applications when required. Doing so has the following advantages:

- You retain control of if and when applications are updated.
- Tomcat server processing is not wasted constantly checking the webapps directory for changes.

In a live environment, set the reloadable attribute to false in the <DefaultContext> element. You can then use the Tomcat Web Application Manager to reload applications as required.

Configuring Access to Users' Home Directories

On a multiuser system, it can be useful to provide users with an area where they can store resources (that you, as the site administrator, do not have to maintain). Tomcat supports this capability by being able to map a subdirectory of the user's home directory onto a URL. The user's subdirectory for Web resources is usually called public_html.

For Unix systems, the user's home directory is determined from the users' entry in the /etc/passwd file.

For Windows systems, you will need to designate a folder to contain the user's home directories. This folder is known as the homeBase. Under the homeBase folder, each user will require his or her own home directory named after the user.

CAUTION

The Tomcat server must have read access to the public_html directory of individual users' home directories.

To configure access to the user's home directory, you need to create a <Listener> element inside a <Host> element in Tomcat's server.xml file. The syntax is different depending on whether you are configuring a Unix or a Windows system.

Under Unix you would add the following:

```
<Host...>
...
  <Listener className="org.apache.catalina.startup.UserConfig"
            directoryName="public_html"
            userClass="org.apache.catalina.startup.PasswdUserDatabase"/>
  ...
</Host>
```

On a Windows system you would use the following, replacing `C:\Home` with wherever you choose to place the `homeBase` folder:

```
<Host name="localhost" ...>
    ...
    <Listener className="org.apache.catalina.startup.UserConfig"
              directoryName="public_html"
              homeBase="C:\Home"
              userClass="org.apache.catalina.startup.HomesUserDatabase"/>
    ...
</Host>
```

NOTE

On a Windows system, if you have more than one location for the `homeBase` folders, you can define multiple `<Listener>` elements for each `homeBase`.

After you have configured the mapping onto the user's home directories, the home directory is referred to using the context name *~username*. The following example shows how to access a page in the `public_html` directory of a user called `peggy`:

```
http://localhost:8080/~peggy/index.html
```

For the example Windows configuration shown previously, this URL will access the file `C:\Home\peggy\public_html\index.html`. For the Unix configuration, this will access the file `public_html/index.html` in the `peggy` user's home directory.

Controlling Client Access to Tomcat

There are a number of ways of controlling client access to Tomcat Web applications. Developers can implement security constraints that require individual users to authenticate themselves (login) to an application (see Chapter 14). At the server level, you can configure allow and deny lists that constrain which hosts (identified by their IP address or hostname) are given access to Tomcat.

Before looking at the configuration in detail, the following example shows how you might restrict access to your development Tomcat servers to only your own workstation:

```
<Valve classname="org.apache.catalina.valves.RemoteAddrValve"
    allow="127.0.0.1" />
```

The `allow` and `deny` lists are provided as attributes to one of the two Tomcat valves: the Remote Host Filter or the Remote Address Filter. Tomcat valves are discussed in detail in Chapter 19. These two valve components can be configured at the following levels in the `server.xml` file:

- `Engine`—The valve applies all requests directed to the associated Tomcat service.
- `Host`—The valve applies only to the virtual host in which it is defined.
- `Context`—The valve only applies to the individual Web application configured in this context.

The Remote Address Filter compares IP addresses, whereas the Remote Host Filter compares DNS hostnames. Both valves use the same rules for determining access:

- Both the `allow` and `deny` lists are optional.
- If the `allow` attribute is present, a hostname or IP address *must* match one of the `allow` patterns to gain access to the server.
- If the `deny` attribute is present, a hostname or IP address *must not* match a pattern in the `deny` attribute if the request is to proceed.
- If both the `allow` and `deny` attributes are present, the hostname or IP address *must* match one of the `allow` patterns and *must not* match a `deny` pattern.

CAUTION

Be careful that the patterns you place in the deny list do not match IP addresses or hostnames that you want to be allowed.

The `allow` and `deny` lists consist of comma-separated Java regular expression patterns (see the `java.util.regexp.Pattern` documentation). If you are administering Tomcat in a Unix environment, you are probably familiar with regular expressions, but be aware that Java regular expressions use an extended form of Unix regular expressions. If you are not familiar with regular expressions, the following section gives a brief introduction.

Java Regular Expressions

A regular expression consists of a character string where some or all of the characters are used to represent other characters. The whole string is then used for pattern matching. The following is a small extract of the regular expression special characters and their meaning:

`.`	Matches any single character
`[abc]`	Matches any character in the set *a, b,* or *c*
`[^abc]`	Matches any character not in the set *a, b,* or *c*
`[a-z]`	Matches any character in the range *a* to *z*, inclusive
`a|b`	Matches *a* or *b*
`(a)`	Defines a subexpression
`?`	Matches zero or one repetition of the preceding expression
`*`	Matches zero or any number of repetitions of the preceding expression
`+`	Matches one or more repetitions of the preceding expression
`\`	Escapes the meaning of a special character

Because `.` matches any one character and `*` matches zero or more repetitions of the previous expression, the regular expression `.*` can be used to match any character string of any length including a zero length or null string.

The Remote Host Filter

You use the Remote Host Filter valve to allow or deny access to particular hosts using the DNS hostname.

The Remote Host Filter has the following attributes:

Attribute	Description
`className`	Java classname for this valve—`org.apache.catalina.valves.RemoteHostValve`
`allow`	(optional) A comma-separated list of patterns that are compared to the remote client's hostname to allow the request
`deny`	(optional) A comma-separated list of patterns that are compared to the remote client's hostname to block the request

For example, the following valve element will deny Tomcat access to requests from hosts that includes `hacker` in the URL:

```
<Valve classname="org.apache.catalina.valves.RemoteHostValve"
    deny=".*hacker.*" />
```

The following example only allows access to domains ending in `uk` or `com`:

```
<Valve classname="org.apache.catalina.valves.RemoteHostValve"
    allow=".*\.uk,.*\.com" />
```

The Remote Address Filter

The Remote Address Filter compares IP addresses to determine whether a client should gain access to Tomcat. It has the following attributes:

Attribute	Description
className	Java classname for this valve—org.apache.catalina.valves.RemoteAddrValve
allow	(optional) A comma-separated list of patterns that are compared to the remote client's hostname to allow the request
deny	(optional) A comma-separated list of patterns that are compared to the remote client's hostname to block the request

For example, you could use the following to allow only clients running on a particular subnet:

```
<Valve classname="org.apache.catalina.valves.RemoteAddrValve"
    allow="123\.104\.93\..*" />
```

Tomcat will block any requests received from other sources and return an HTTP 403 "Forbidden" error.

Tomcat Default Deployment Descriptor

Most Web applications require a deployment descriptor which is found in the /WEB-INF/web.xml file in the application directory. This file is processed by Tomcat when a Web application is loaded and is used to define properties and resources for the Web application.

Before looking at the application specific deployment descriptor, Tomcat first processes a default web.xml file, which sets default values for all Web applications. This file is found in <CATALINA_HOME>/conf/web.xml.

NOTE

As with all web.xml files, the Tomcat web.xml file has to comply with the servlet specification and is validated with a DTD available from Sun Microsystems, Inc. (for the Servlet 2.3 specification this is http://java.sun.com/dtd/web-app_2_3.dtd). A prototype web.xml file is included in Appendix B.

Tomcat's default web.xml file is used to configure a number of interesting features.

Built-in Servlets

The Tomcat web.xml file has a number of definitions for Tomcat built-in servlets. These servlets are used by Tomcat to manage resources of various kinds.

Invoker Servlet

The Invoker servlet is used to execute anonymous servlet classes. These servlets do not have a <Servlet> element in the application web.xml file.

Anonymous servlets are mapped to the URL pattern /servlet/* using the following servlet mapping:

```
<servlet-mapping>
    <servlet-name>invoker</servlet-name>
    <url-pattern>/servlet/*</url-pattern>
</servlet-mapping>
```

You can add additional anonymous servlet mappings if required. For example, the following would enable anonymous servlets to be addressed using /anon/*:

```
<servlet-mapping>
    <servlet-name>invoker</servlet-name>
    <url-pattern>/anon/*</url-pattern>
</servlet-mapping>
```

Alternatively, you could remove the anonymous servlet mapping which would force developers to create a web.xml entry for every servlet and stop them being accessed using /servlet/*. Doing so would aid Web application security and access control by ensuring Web resources are only accessed using URL patterns defined by the developer.

JSP Servlet

When Tomcat serves a JSP page for the first time, it translates and compiles the JSP into a conventional servlet. The built-in JSP servlet performs this task.

The JSP servlet has a number of initialization parameters that you might want to modify when using Tomcat in a live environment:

Initialization Parameter	Use
keepgenerated	The default is to keep the generated Java source code when a page is compiled. To save space in a live-environment, set this parameter to false.
logVerbosityLevel	The level (and therefore amount) of messages produced by the JSP servlet. The levels are FATAL, ERROR, WARNING, INFORMATION, and DEBUG. Messages are written to the Tomcat log file.

Initialization Parameter	Use
`reloading`	In a live environment, all JSPs should be precompiled when the Web application is deployed (see Chapter 5, "Basic Principles of JSPs"). If this has been done, you can set reloading to `false`, which stops Jasper (the Tomcat JSP container) from checking for JSPs that have been modified (and therefore require to be translated and recompiled). This will speed up access to JSPs.

An example entry for the JSP servlet that modifies these parameters is

```
<servlet>
    <servlet-name>jsp</servlet-name>
    <servlet-class>org.apache.jasper.servlet.JspServlet</servlet-class>
    <init-param>
        <param-name>logVerbosityLevel</param-name>
        <param-value>WARNING</param-value>
    </init-param>
    <init-param>
        <param-name>keepgenerated</param-name>
        <param-value>false</param-value>
    </init-param>
    <init-param>
        <param-name>reloading</param-name>
        <param-value>false</param-value>
    </init-param>
</servlet>
```

The servlet mapping for this servlet maps all URLs ending in `.jsp`:

```
<servlet-mapping>
    <servlet-name>jsp</servlet-name>
    <url-pattern>*.jsp</url-pattern>
</servlet-mapping>
```

Add additional servlet mappings if you need to map other files' extensions onto the JSP servlet. Or remove this mapping if you want to only use explicit JSP mappings in each Web application.

Default Servlet

The default servlet serves static resources that are not mapped onto other servlets with servlet mappings. The default servlet has a number of initialization parameters that affect its behavior, including `listings` and `readonly`.

In a security conscious live-environment, you should set the `listings` parameter to `false` (default is `true`) to prevent clients from browsing directories in the Web application. In addition, `readonly` should be `true` (the default) to prevent clients issuing HTTP `PUT` and `DELETE` requests. If `readonly` is `false`, the integrity of a Web application could be compromised by external sources adding or deleting Web application resources.

The following servlet definition should be used to turn off directory listings:

```
<servlet>
    <servlet-name>default</servlet-name>
    <servlet-class>
        org.apache.catalina.servlets.DefaultServlet
    </servlet-class>
    <init-param>
        <param-name>debug</param-name>
        <param-value>0</param-value>
    </init-param>
    <init-param>
        <param-name>listings</param-name>
        <param-value>false</param-value>
    </init-param>
    <load-on-startup>1</load-on-startup>
</servlet>
```

The CGI and SSI Servlets

Tomcat also provides servlets to serve Common Gateway Interface (CGI) scripts and to handle Server-Side Include (SSI) directives in HTML pages. Both these servlet elements are commented out in the distributed `web.xml` file. Uncomment both the servlet element and the corresponding servlet mapping enable support for CGI or SSI. You will also need to rename the appropriate jar files in the `<CATALINA_HOME>/server/lib/` directory. For CGI support, rename `servlets-cgi.renametojar` to `servlets-cgi.jar`; for SSI, rename `servlets-ssi.renametojar` file to `servlets-ssi.jar`.

NOTE

If the Web applications have a large number of CGI scripts and SSIs, you should consider allowing another Web server (such as Apache) to handle these resources.

Session Timeout

Another default you can set in Tomcat's `web.xml` file for all Web applications is the session timeout. The following entry in Tomcat's `web.xml` file sets the session timeout to 30 minutes, which is fine for most situations:

```
<session-config>
    <session-timeout>30</session-timeout>
</session-config>
```

On a busy site with a large number of concurrent clients, the memory allocated to supporting session data could become significant. Reducing this default timeout may help reduce memory usage. Developers have the option of increasing the session timeout for individual applications by setting the session timeout in the application's `web.xml` file.

MIME Mapping

MIME mappings defined in the default `web.xml` file are used by Tomcat to generate the `Content-Type` HTTP header in the response sent back to the client. The MIME type is determined from the filename extension, as shown in this example for an Adobe PDF file:

```
<mime-mapping>
    <extension>pdf</extension>
    <mime-type>application/pdf</mime-type>
</mime-mapping>
```

A large number of MIME mappings are provided in Tomcat's `web.xml` file and you may add additional ones as needed.

NOTE

MIME types are registered with the Internet Assigned Number Authority (IANA: `www.iana.org`). The use of non-registered MIME types may cause unexpected results and is not recommended.

Welcome Files

If a request URL specifies the name of a directory rather than a specific resource, Tomcat looks for a designated welcome file and returns this to the client. The welcome file is simply a resource with a special name as configured in the welcome-file list. Typically, a developer will use a welcome file as the introductory page to the application. You should add any additional files that should be considered as welcome files. The following adds the HTML files with a prefix of `default` to the welcome file list:

```
<welcome-file-list>
    <welcome-file>index.html</welcome-file>
    <welcome-file>index.htm</welcome-file>
    <welcome-file>index.jsp</welcome-file>
    <welcome-file>default.html</welcome-file>
    <welcome-file>default.htm</welcome-file>
</welcome-file-list>
```

NOTE

Tomcat parses this list in order, but this functionality should not be depended on. Avoid having multiple welcome files in the same directory.

New welcome files should be added with caution, so as not to cause unexpected effects with existing applications; a welcome file required for a specific application should be added to that application's `web.xml` file and not to Tomcat's default `web.xml` file.

Managing Tomcat Users

Tomcat provides the simple `tomcat-users.xml` file for configuring users, passwords, and roles. You can either edit this file directly or use the Administration Tool to maintain user information.

When Tomcat 4.1 is installed (see Chapter 2), you are asked to provide a password for the `Admin` user. Tomcat then creates the `tomcat-users.xml` file as shown here:

```
<?xml version="1.0" ?>
<tomcat-users>
<role rolename="admin" />
<role rolename="manager" />
<role rolename="role1" />
<role rolename="tomcat" />
<user username="admin" password="tomcat" roles="admin,manager" />
<user username="role1" password="tomcat" roles="role1" />
<user username="tomcat" password="tomcat" roles="tomcat" />
<user username="both" password="tomcat" roles="tomcat,role1" />
</tomcat-users>
```

NOTE

The Tomcat 4.0 tomcat-users.xml file does not include <role> elements because the roles are derived from the <user> elements. In Tomcat 4.1, any roles defined in the <user> elements that do not have <role> element definitions are automatically added to the tomcat-users.xml file when Tomcat starts up.

Of these, only the admin user and the admin and manager roles are required; the other users and roles are provided as examples only and can be safely deleted.

NOTE

The admin role provides access to the Administration Tool. The manager role is used to access the Application Manager.

CAUTION

As you can see, passwords are stored in plain text. Therefore, access to this file should be protected in multi-user systems to reduce the risk of malicious attack on your Web server. Chapter 14 describes how digested passwords can be created and added to this file.

You add users to this file by adding a new <user> element. For example, the following will add peggy as a user who can use the manager application:

```
<user username="peggy" password="sue" roles="manager" />
```

You can use the Administration Tool to do the same thing, as shown in Figure 16.2.

NOTE

Tomcat 4.1 also allows you to create a *group,* which is a collection of roles. You can then assign the group to individual users. Use groups to simplify administration if you have a large number of roles.

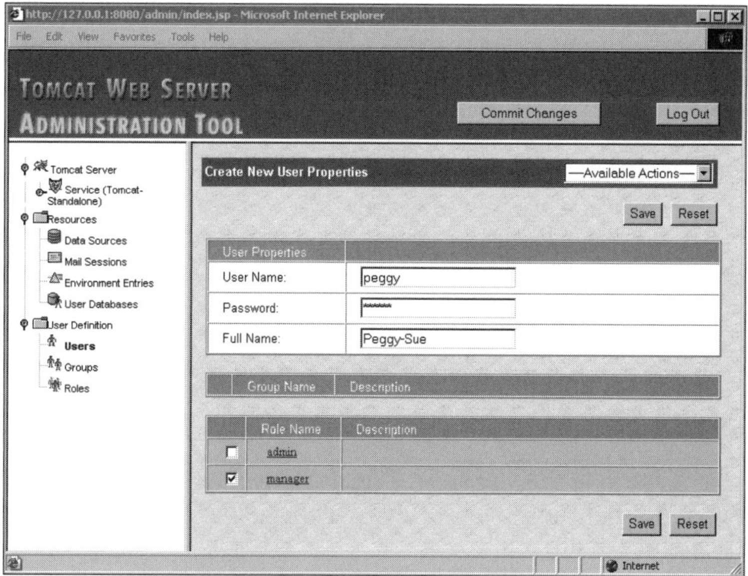

FIGURE 16.2 Adding a user using the Tomcat Web Server Administration Tool.

Running Tomcat as a Service Under Windows

To install Tomcat 4.1 as an NT service under Windows, you need to select the NT Service check box at install time (see Chapter 2). Tomcat will be installed as a service with the name Apache Tomcat 4.1 and set to start up automatically when Windows is rebooted.

NOTE

It is not possible to install the Tomcat NT Service feature later without reinstalling Tomcat, which will overwrite your current configuration.

If you are using Tomcat 4.0, the Tomcat service is not automatically installed, and you will need to perform the following steps to run Tomcat as an NT service.

First, create a batch file containing the following:

```
set SERVICENAME=Apache Tomcat 4.0
set JAVACLASSPATH=%CLASSPATH%
set JAVACLASSPATH=%JAVACLASSPATH%;"%CATALINA_HOME%\bin\bootstrap.jar"
set JAVACLASSPATH=%JAVACLASSPATH%;"%CATALINA_HOME%\common\lib\servlet.jar"
set JAVACLASSPATH=%JAVACLASSPATH%;"%JAVA_HOME%\lib\tools.jar"
```

```
%CATALINA_HOME%\bin\tomcat.exe
➥ -install "%SERVICENAME%" "%JAVA_HOME%\jre\bin\server\jvm.dll"
➥ -Djava.class.path=%JAVACLASSPATH%
➥ -Dcatalina.home="%CATALINA_HOME%"
➥ -Xrs
➥ -start org.apache.catalina.startup.Bootstrap -params start
➥ -stop org.apache.catalina.startup.Bootstrap -params stop
➥ -out "%CATALINA_HOME%\logs\stdout.log"
➥ -err "%CATALINA_HOME%\logs\stderr.log"
```

NOTE

All the options for the `tomcat.exe` command must be on a single line.

Run this batch file to install Tomcat as a service. The service will be installed but will not be started. To start the service, either issue the following command in a command prompt window

```
> net start "Apache Tomcat 4.0"
```

or use the NT Services Manager (found on the Windows NT control panel or the Windows 2000/XP Start menu under Administrative Tools, Services).

To uninstall the Tomcat NT service, first stop the service and then issue the following command:

```
%CATALINA_HOME%\bin\tomcat.exe -uninstall "Apache Tomcat 4.0"
```

This `uninstall` command works for both Tomcat 4.0 and 4.1 (for Tomcat 4.1 you will have to supply the 4.1 service name `Apache Tomcat 4.1`).

Summary

This chapter has provided an overview of the main administrative tasks you will need to undertake to configure Tomcat. It has covered in some detail the structure and use of three main configuration files: `server.xml`, `web.xml`, and `tomcat-users.xml`.

You have also seen how to set Web application defaults, how to improve Tomcat performance, how to provide access to users' home directory, how to control client access to Tomcat, and finally, how to run Tomcat as an NT service under Windows.

Tomcat configuration is also covered in other chapters in this book: Chapters 2, 15, and 23. For even more information on any of these topics, you should study the Tomcat online documentation.

PART III
Advanced Topics

IN THIS PART

17 Architectures

IN THIS CHAPTER

- Architecture and Design
- Component Architecture
- Frameworks
- Model-1 Architecture
- Model-2 Architecture
- MVC Architecture
- A Model-2/MVC Currency Converter

Most of the chapters in this book are standalone: They discuss a single topic with minimal reference to the topics in the other chapters. This chapter is where many of the different features of Tomcat development are integrated under the single concept of architecture.

A Web application *architecture* dictates how the different components are put together to form a complete package. Well-constructed applications that conform to a defined architecture are easy to understand, develop, maintain, and enhance; badly constructed applications are not.

This chapter discusses the structure and role of simple component and framework architectures as well as the model-1, model-2, and Model-View Controller (MVC) architectures found in Web applications.

As the Java Web application technology matures, the development community gains a better understanding of how to design its solutions. A good point of reference for the latest thinking on Web architecture and J2EE design patterns is `http://developer.java.sun.com/developer/technicalArticles/J2EE/patterns/`.

Architecture and Design

Giving thought to application architecture is important because a well-constructed architecture enables you to combine the component Web technologies in the most effective manner. A good understanding of technology is essential, but simply using the technology without proper regard for the overall system architecture leads to problems. Good architecture will help by

- Reducing development time
- Improving code reuse
- Simplifying system maintenance
- Facilitating future feature enhancements

As you will see, an understanding of the different Web application architectures will help you design your applications in the most efficient and suitable manner.

Component Architecture

A component architecture builds a system from reusable components. Object-oriented languages facilitate the use of components, as the class and object nature of the languages map easily onto components. But non-OO languages (such as HTML/JSP Web pages) can still be used to develop reusable components.

Component systems use large numbers of simple reusable components. The straightforward nature of the components supports good design and rapid development. If a component's requirements change radically, an existing one can be thrown away and a new component designed to replace it.

Components are

- Small well-encapsulated objects (each object does one job, and does that job well)
- Minimally dependent on other components (leads to low coupling between components)
- Eminently reusable (reducing development time as less new code needs to be written and tested)

You are probably already using components in development, as the following Java technologies are all examples of components:

- JavaBeans (Chapter 5, "Basic Principles of JSPs")
- TagLibs (Chapter 10, "Custom Tags and TagLibs")
- JSTL (Chapter 11, "JSP Expression Language and JSTL")
- Servlets (Chapter 4, "Basic Principles of Servlets")
- JSPs (Chapter 5)
- Data Access Objects (DAOs) (Chapter 9, "Databases and Tomcat")

- Filters (Chapter 18, "Servlet Filters")
- Valves (Chapter 19, "Tomcat Valves")

Components are often used in conjunction with a framework architecture.

Frameworks

A *framework* is a collection of objects or classes that provide the structure to support the components you develop. Think of a framework as the plumbing that joins your classes together and you won't be far wrong. Frameworks solve a set of problems or make it easier for you to solve your problems.

A framework is not usually a complete working program but something that requires you to provide functionality that is added into a basic skeleton. A framework may be a simple non-functional program that you extend to implement your system, or it may be a collection of Java classes that you incorporate into your system.

Examples of frameworks discussed in this book include

- The `Servlet` and `HTTPServlet` classes that provide the basic functionality for all servlets and JSPs (see Chapter 4)
- The `TagSupport` and `TagBodySupport` classes provided for developing custom tags (see Chapter 11)
- The Jakarta Struts package used to develop MVC Web applications (see Chapter 20, "Frameworks and Jakarta Struts")
- The Jakarta Cactus package used for testing Web resources (see Chapter 21, "Testing with Jakarta Cactus")

Frameworks are common features of modern programming.

Model-1 Architecture

A model-1 architecture is a Web application containing standalone servlets and JSPs with minimal communication between each component. Typically, there is little separation of functionality and no clear differentiation between business rules (policy), implementing functionality (computation), and presentation of the results. A good model-1 system will use JavaBeans, DAOs, and other components to achieve some separation of functionality. Model-1 architectures are mainly suitable for small applications. Figure 17.1 shows a typical model-1 architecture.

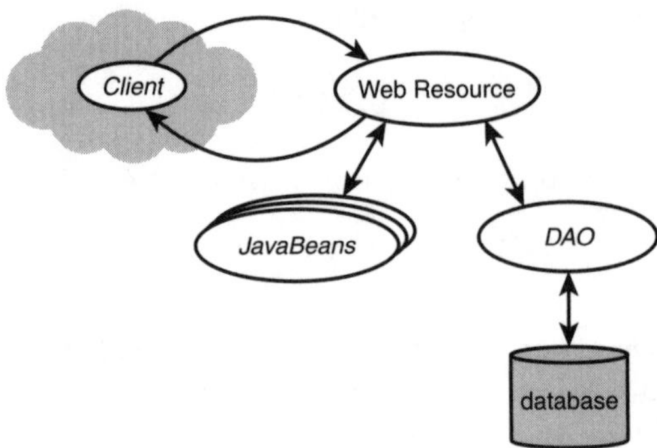

FIGURE 17.1 Model-1 architecture.

In a model-1 architecture, a client request for a Web resource is routed to a single servlet or JSP that validates the request, undertakes any data manipulation required, and formats the response for returning to the client. Most of the examples presented in the other chapters of this book are model-1 architectures.

As a Web application grows and adds more functionality, the following problems manifest themselves with the model-1 architecture:

- Increasingly complex pages
- Excessive duplication of code
- Inconsistencies between components in the application

The natural step forward to solve many of the problems with the model-1 architecture is to refactor the Web application to use a model-2 or MVC architecture.

Model-2 Architecture

A model-2 architecture separates the data presentation functionality from the business logic and flow control. Essentially, all requests are routed to a controller servlet, which performs common operations such as fetching and validating request parameters, maintaining session data, and interfacing to the supporting Java beans and other classes. A typical model-2 architecture is shown in Figure 17.2.

In a model-2 architecture, a client request for a Web resource is routed to the controller servlet or JSP, which validates the request and undertakes any data manipulation required. The request is then forwarded to a view JSP that may do further data manipulation before formatting the response for returning to the client. Large applications may use several controller servlets to represent the different functional areas of their application.

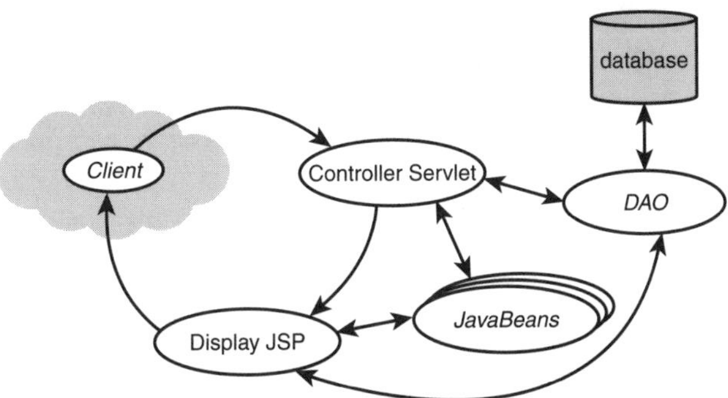

FIGURE 17.2 Model-2 architecture.

The advantage of a model-2 architecture is that the controller servlet undertakes common operations prior to handing the request on to a JSP. The JSP is primarily focused on the presentation of the data. The model-2 structure ensures that the servlet does little or no HTML formatting, and the JSP requires little or no Java programming—targeting the strengths of both technologies.

The logical extension to the model-2 architecture is the MVC architecture that separates managing the data model from the flow-control logic from the view JSP. Model-2 architectures that use well-encapsulated data objects such as JavaBeans and DAOs are usually MVC architectures.

MVC Architecture

An MVC architecture is similar to the model-2 architecture, but there is a clear separation between the following component areas of the application:

- Model—Responsible for maintaining the persistent data and session information
- View—Responsible for formatting and presenting the data for the client and should not undertake data manipulation or validation
- Controller—Responsible for controlling the actions of the model and passing control to the required view component

Figure 17.3 shows a typical MVC architecture.

In an MVC architecture, a client request for a Web resource is routed to the controller, which validates the request and invokes any required operations on the components in the model. Typically, data validation is performed partly by the controller and partly by the model. After the data model has been updated, control is passed to the view component. Any data that the view needs for display is passed with the request (typically as references to JavaBeans containing the required data). In some cases it is expedient to allow the view JSP read-only access to the data model; it is important, however, that the view does no data manipulation but simply retrieves and formats the data correctly for the client.

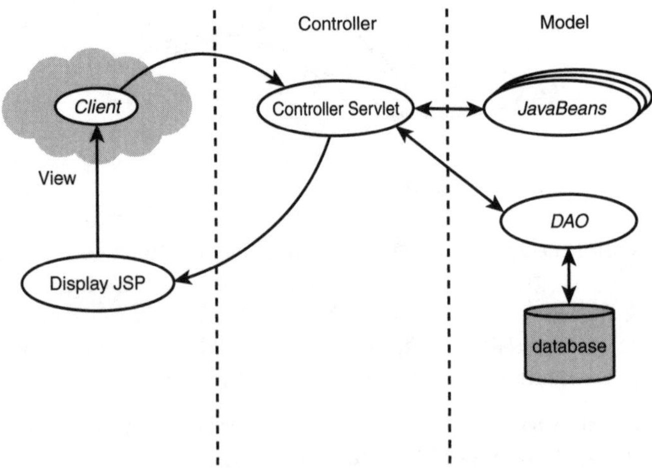

FIGURE 17.3 Model-View-Controller (MVC) architecture.

MVC components are highly replaceable. A well-designed MVC architecture may well support several views for the same controller and model. An obvious example for Web applications is the support of PC clients and mobile phone clients. A single controller can handle both HTTP and WAP requests and update the same data model. The request can be forwarded to an HTML view or a WML view component as appropriate.

Multiple controllers can interface to the same model and possibly use the same view components. An application could use a separate controller to support a Java Swing–based GUI that manipulates the same data model as the Web interface. This GUI application would also implement the view component of the architecture.

A good example of an MVC architecture is in Jakarta Struts, which is discussed in Chapter 20.

A Model-2/MVC Currency Converter

The example in this section shows a simple model-2/MVC implementation of the currency converter. The home page for this example is shown in Listing 17.1.

LISTING 17.1 Home Page JSP: `homepage.jsp`

```
<HTML>
  <HEAD>
    <TITLE>Chapter 17, Architectures</TITLE>
  </HEAD>
  <BODY>
    <H1>Chapter 17, Architectures</H1>
    What would you like to do?
    <UL>
        <LI><A HREF=><%=response.encodeURL("rate.do")%>'>
            Examine the exchange rate</A></LI>
        <LI><A HREF=><%=response.encodeURL("convert.do")%>'>
            Convert a currency amount</A></LI>
    </UL>
  </BODY>
</HTML>
```

The two URL links on the JSP in Listing 17.1 refer to `rate.do` and `convert.do` for examining the exchange rate and accessing a currency conversion form respectively. These links are routed to the single controller servlet shown in Listing 17.2.

LISTING 17.2 Controller Servlet: `Action.java`

```
import java.io.*;
import java.sql.*;
import java.text.*;
import javax.naming.*;
import javax.servlet.*;
import javax.servlet.http.*;
import converters.*;


public class Action extends HttpServlet
{
    public void doGet(HttpServletRequest request, HttpServletResponse response)
        throws ServletException, IOException {

        // find real web resource
        String forward = request.getServletPath();
        if (forward.endsWith(".do"))
            forward = forward.substring(1,forward.length()-3)+".jsp";
        else
```

LISTING 17.2 Continued

```
            throw new ServletException(
                "Action servlet called with illegal path: "+forward);

        // build and validate view page attributes
        HttpSession session = request.getSession();
        String amount = request.getParameter("amount");
        try {
            ConverterBean convert =
                (ConverterBean)session.getAttribute("convert");
            if (convert == null)
                session.setAttribute("convert",convert=new ConverterBean());
            String from = request.getParameter("countryFrom");
            String to = request.getParameter("countryTo");
            if (from!=null && from.length()>0 && to!=null && to.length()>0)
                convert.setCountries(from,to);
            if (amount!=null && amount.length()>0)
                convert.setAmount(amount);
        }
        catch (NamingException ex) {
            request.setAttribute("exception",ex);
            forward = "databaseError.jsp";
        }
        catch (SQLException ex) {
            request.setAttribute("exception",ex);
            forward = "databaseError.jsp";
        }
        catch (ParseException ex) {
            request.setAttribute("message",
              "<FONT color='red'>Invalid value for amount: "+amount+"</FONT>");
        }
        catch (IllegalArgumentException ex) {
            request.setAttribute("message",
              "<FONT COLOR='red'>"+ex.getMessage()+"</FONT>");
        }

        // forward request
        request.getRequestDispatcher(forward).forward(request,response);
    }

    public void doPost(HttpServletRequest request, HttpServletResponse response)
        throws ServletException, IOException {
```

LISTING 17.2 Continued

```
        doGet(request,response);
    }
}
```

The servlet in Listing 17.2 responds to Web requests for pages with names ending in `.do`. The pages routed through the controller servlet must be clearly identified as distinct from ordinary Web pages. Using a simple naming scheme simplifies the `web.xml` file, and the same `.do` convention is used by Struts (see Chapter 20). The controller servlet must be able to differentiate each different request it receives; otherwise, it will not be able to invoke the correct functionality or pass the request on to the appropriate JSP.

The first step for the controller servlet is to either convert the page name into a similar JSP name (replacing `.do` with `.jsp`) or reject the request if the page name is wrong. Next, the servlet retrieves a currency converter bean from the session or creates a new one if the converter does not already exist.

This application is a little more functional than the usual currency converter examples, as it allows the client to specify the conversion currencies (the bean gets the exchange rates from the database developed in Chapter 9). If the user has defined the conversion currencies (the `countryFrom` and `countryTo` parameters), the servlet updates the bean to use the new currencies. The `Action` servlet sets the conversion amount for the bean to the value of the `amount` parameter if one is supplied. At this point, the currency conversion bean has collated all the information necessary to construct the client response.

If any data validation errors occur while creating the currency conversion bean, the servlet adds a `message` attribute, representing the error, to the request. If a fatal error occurs (such as database failure), the request is routed to a generic error page with the `Exception` passed as a request attribute.

Finally, the servlet forwards the request to the JSP for displaying the results.

The currency conversion JSP shown in Listing 17.3 is the ultimate target of the `convert.do` link on the home page in Listing 17.1. The exchange rate page (`rate.jsp`) is similar to the one in Listing 17.3 but displays the exchange rate in place of the currency conversion form. It is not shown here because it does not introduce any new concepts.

LISTING 17.3 Currency Conversion Form: `convert.jsp`

```
<%@ page import="converters.*" %>
<% ConverterBean convert = (ConverterBean)session.getAttribute("convert"); %>
<% String amount = request.getParameter("amount"); %>
```

LISTING 17.3 Continued

```
<% if (amount==null) amount = ""; %>
<% String message = (String)request.getAttribute("message"); %>
<HTML>
  <HEAD>
    <TITLE>Currency Converter</TITLE>
  </HEAD>
  <BODY>
    <H1>Currency Converter</H1>
    <FORM ACTION='<%=response.encodeURL("convert.do")%>'>
      <P>Amount to convert:
          <INPUT TYPE='text' NAME='amount' VALUE='<%=amount%>'></P>
      <%@ include file="country.jsf" %>
      <P><INPUT TYPE='submit' VALUE='Submit'></P>
    </FORM>
    <% if (message != null) { %>
        <%= message %>
    <% } else if (amount.length()>0) { %>
      <H2>
        <%= convert.getAmount() %> =
        <%= convert.getConvertedAmount() %>
      </H2>
    <% } %>
    <P><A HREF=><%=response.encodeURL("homepage")%>'>Return to home page</A></P>
  </BODY>
</HTML>
```

The example in Listing 17.3 deliberately uses embedded Java actions on the JSP to keep life simple. In reality, supporting custom tags (especially those in JSTL) would be used to access the Java objects defined at the start of the page. This currency converter JSP displays the currency conversion form together with the ability to select the source and destination countries for the currency conversion.

The page in Listing 17.3 uses the JSP `<%@ include>` mechanism to include the `country.jsf` page within this form. Creating this part of the form as a separate component enables the same form fields to be used on other pages. Listing 17.4 shows the country selection form.

LISTING 17.4 Country Selection Form `country.jsf`

```
<TABLE>
  <TR><TH COLSPAN='2'>Change Currency Conversion Countries</TD></TR>
  <TR>
```

LISTING 17.4 Continued

```
    <TD>Convert from:</TD>
    <TD>
      <SELECT NAME='countryFrom'>
        <OPTION></OPTION>
        <OPTION>Canada</OPTION>
        <OPTION>Germany</OPTION>
        <OPTION>United Kingdom</OPTION>
        <OPTION>United States</OPTION>
      </SELECT>
    </TD>
  <TR>
  <TR>
    <TD>To:</TD>
    <TD>
      <SELECT NAME='countryTo'>
        <OPTION></OPTION>
        <OPTION>Canada</OPTION>
        <OPTION>Germany</OPTION>
        <OPTION>United Kingdom</OPTION>
        <OPTION>United States</OPTION>
      </SELECT>
    </TD>
  <TR>
</TABLE>
```

The final file needed for this example is `web.xml`; its main purpose is to map `*.do` requests onto the `Action` servlet. The `web.xml` file is shown in Listing 17.5.

LISTING 17.5 `web.xml` Deployment Descriptor for the Model-2/MVC Example

```
<?xml version="1.0" encoding="ISO-8859-1"?>
<!DOCTYPE web-app
  PUBLIC "-//Sun Microsystems, Inc.//DTD Web Application 2.2//EN"
  "http://java.sun.com/j2ee/dtds/web-app_2_2.dtd">
<web-app>
  <servlet>
    <servlet-name>Action</servlet-name>
    <servlet-class>Action</servlet-class>
  </servlet>
  <servlet>
    <servlet-name>Home</servlet-name>
```

LISTING 17.5 Continued

```
    <jsp-file>homepage.jsp</jsp-file>
  </servlet>
  <servlet-mapping>
    <servlet-name>Action</servlet-name>
    <url-pattern>*.do</url-pattern>
  </servlet-mapping>
  <servlet-mapping>
    <servlet-name>Home</servlet-name>
    <url-pattern>/homepage</url-pattern>
  </servlet-mapping>

  <welcome-file-list>
    <welcome-file>homepage.jsp</welcome-file>
  </welcome-file-list>

  <resource-ref>
    <res-ref-name>jdbc/conversion</res-ref-name>
    <res-type>javax.sql.DataSource</res-type>
    <res-auth>Container</res-auth>
  </resource-ref>
</web-app>
```

NOTE

This example uses the same JDBC data source as the currency converter application shown in Chapter 9. The currency conversion bean `ConverterBean` is not shown here but the bean source code and other files used in this example can be downloaded from the supporting Web site on `http://www.samspublishing.com` (search for the book's ISBN, 0672324393).

This example shows the benefits of the model-2/MVC architectures in allowing common functionality to be easily factored out and made available to multiple Web resources. The clear separation of controller and data model functionality simplifies the writing of the JSPs and ensures servlets and other components are not aware of the HTML language used to present the data back to the client. Changing this example to use XML for presenting data to the client will only affect the JSP component.

Summary

Good design requires an understanding of the use of components, frameworks, and the three main Web application architectures:

- Model-1—Uses one Web resource to validate the request, retrieve and update the data, and format the client response
- Model-2—Separates the process of data validation and manipulation from the formatting of the response into a controller servlet and a view JSP
- MVC—Is a variant of the model-2 architecture where the control flow of the request is further separated out from the data model, creating the three distinct application areas of model, view, and controller

Small, simple Web applications can use the model-1 architecture, but larger applications should use the model-2 or MVC approach because it facilitates better separation of functionality and greater component reuse.

18

Servlet Filters

IN THIS CHAPTER

In this chapter, you will look at the use of servlet filters in your Web applications and how they can simplify the design and be reused to speed up coding. In Chapter 19, "Tomcat Valves," you will find out about an alternative type of filter called a valve. Valves are propriety to Tomcat and there are other differences in the way they operate, which are covered in Chapter 19.

What Is a Servlet Filter?

A *servlet filter* is a special Web application component (introduced in the Servlet 2.3 specification) that dynamically intercepts requests and responses. A servlet filter can be used to transform, use, or add to the information contained in the request or response objects. You can think of filters as preprocessing the request before a servlet receives it or post-processing the response after a servlet has sent it back to the client. A real advantage of filters is that it is possible to add a filter to an existing Web application without having to recompile or change any existing servlet or JSP code.

NOTE

It is not always the case that, when you add a filter, the existing code does not change. For example, you can use filters to encapsulate common code that you can then remove from individual Web resources.

Filters provide a mechanism for encapsulating reusable functionality that can then easily be applied to some or all servlets in an application.

As Figure 18.1 shows, filters can also be chained together to form a pipeline.

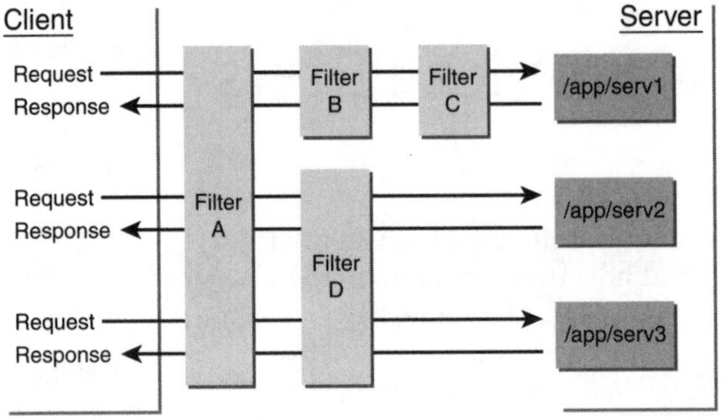

FIGURE 18.1 Using filters with Web resources.

In Figure 18.1, filter A is applied to all three servlets (which could also be JSPs); filters B and C are applied only to `serv1`; and filter D is applied to both `serv2` and `serv3`. Filter A might be doing security checking that needs to be applied to all servlets, whereas filter D may be setting up a Java bean that is used by both `serv2` and `serv3`. Filters B and C could be doing form validation that is only used once in this small application, but could be reused if the application is extended or used in another application.

Implementing a Filter

A filter implements the `javax.servlet.Filter` interface. This interface defines three methods:

Filter Interface Method	Called
`init()`	When the filter instance is created
`destroy()`	When a filter instance is taken out of service
`doFilter()`	Each time a request is transmitted through the filter chain

The `init()` method is called once when the filter is instantiated.

NOTE

When Tomcat starts up, it creates a single filter instance. It does not create a new instance for each request or each servlet.

The init() method has access to a FilterConfig object passed as a parameter. You can use the FilterConfig object in the init() method to obtain any filter initialization parameters configured in the web.xml file. You can also use the FilterConfig object to obtain a reference to the ServletContext object, which gives access to the servlet initialization parameters and attributes.

CAUTION

Because there is only one filter instance, you should not save the ServletContext object in a filter instance variable. Instead use FilterConfig.getServletContext() to obtain a reference to the ServletContext in which the init() method is executing.

As usual, you should use the destroy() method to remove any resources created in the filter.

The doFilter() method is where the filter processing takes place. The parameters to the doFilter() method include a reference to the ServletRequest, ServletResponse, and FilterChain objects.

The FilterChain object provides a mechanism for invoking a series or pipeline of filters. Tomcat calls the doFilter() method each time a request is received for the servlet at the end of the filter chain. Each doFilter() method in the chain can add to or amend information in the request object before it passes control on to the next filter in the chain by calling the FilterChain.doFilter() method. If this is the last filter in the chain, Tomcat will use the call to the FilterChain.doFilter() method to pass control to the servlet at the end of the chain. When the servlet has constructed the response and terminates execution, control is passed back to the last filter in the chain, which continues execution immediately after the call to FilterChain.doFilter(). At this point the doFilter() method can do further processing on the response object. It is therefore possible to have the same doFilter() method both preprocess the request and postprocess the response.

CAUTION

Using a single filter to perform both preprocessing of the request and postprocessing should be avoided where possible because it is likely to reduce the reusability of your filter code.

If the doFilter() method returns without calling FilterChain.doFilter(), access to the servlet is blocked and an empty response is returned to the client; because this can lead to unpredictable results, you should avoid simply returning from doFilter() without constructing a response. If an error occurs within the filter that makes continuing with the request processing meaningless, you have two choices—either create an appropriate response in the filter, or throw an exception and allow your Web application error handling mechanism to deal with it.

A simple example filter will help you understand how to use filters.

Simple Filter Example

The filter in Listing 18.1 provides a page hit counter that can be used to gather statistics on the number of requests generated by the client. For each request, it stores the URL and the page hit count as an entry in a HashMap that is stored in the application context.

LISTING 18.1 PageHitCountFilter That Records Page Hits

```
package sams.filters;

import java.io.*;
import java.util.*;
import javax.servlet.*;
import javax.servlet.http.*;

public class PageHitCountFilter implements Filter {

    private FilterConfig filterConfig = null;

    public void init(FilterConfig filterConfig) throws ServletException {
        this.filterConfig = filterConfig;
    }

    public void destroy() {
        this.filterConfig = null;
    }

    public void doFilter(ServletRequest request, ServletResponse response,
            FilterChain chain) throws IOException, ServletException {

        if (filterConfig == null)
            throw new ServletException();

        ServletContext context = filterConfig.getServletContext();
        if (request instanceof HttpServletRequest) {
            HttpServletRequest httpReq = ((HttpServletRequest) request);

            HashMap hitCountMap = (HashMap) context.getAttribute("hitCounts");
            if (hitCountMap == null) {
```

LISTING 18.1 Continued

```
                context.setAttribute("hitCounts", hitCountMap = new HashMap());
            }
            String servletName = httpReq.getServletPath();
            Integer hits = (Integer) hitCountMap.get(servletName);
            if (hits == null)
                hits = new Integer(1);
            else
                hits = new Integer (hits.intValue() + 1);
            hitCountMap.put(servletName, hits);
            context.setAttribute("hitCounts", hitCountMap);
        }
        chain.doFilter(request, response);
    }
}
```

CAUTION

The implementation of `HashMap` is not synchronized, and therefore it is feasible that page hits will be lost. For this example, this is probably not important; but when it is, you should synchronize on an object that encapsulates the map, use a `HashTable`, or use a `synchronizedMap()` as shown here:

```
Map m = Collections.synchronizedMap(new HashMap());
```

You can now use a JSP (such as the one shown in Listing 18.2) to display the page hits saved in the `HashMap` object. The `HashMap` is saved in the application context so the page hit count applies to all users accessing the application.

LISTING 18.2 `hits.jsp` Displays Page Hit Counts on the Client

```
<%@ page import="java.util.*" %>
<% HashMap map = (HashMap)application.getAttribute("hitCounts"); %>

<HTML>
    <HEAD><TITLE>Application Page Hits</TITLE></HEAD>
    <BODY>
        <H1><A href='homepage'>
            <img src="images/tomcat.gif" border="0"></A>
            Application Page Hits
        </H1>
        <BR>
        <TABLE width="50%" border="1" cellspacing="0">
```

LISTING 18.2 Continued

```
        <TR>
            <TH>Page</TH><TH>Hits</TH>
        </TR>
        <%
            if (map != null) {
                Iterator i = map.entrySet().iterator();
                while (i.hasNext()) {
                    Map.Entry e = (Map.Entry) i.next();
                    %>
                        <TR>
                            <TD><%= e.getKey() %></TD>
                            <TD><%= e.getValue() %></DT>
                        </TR>
                    <%
                }
            }
        %>
        </TABLE>
    </BODY>
</HTML>
```

You can, of course, simplify this JSP by using custom tags to encapsulate access to the page counter statistics, but for demonstration purposes, this does the job. The next section shows you how to deploy this filter.

Deploying a Filter Under Tomcat

Filters are configured, like other components, in the deployment descriptor. You use `<filter>` elements to define a filter. Filters must appear after any context parameters and before any listener or servlet definitions.

A `<filter>` element must have the following subelements:

- `<filter-name>`—Unique name for this filter
- `<filter-class>`—The fully qualified name for the class implementing this filter

You can also provide filter initialization parameters using the `<init-params>` subelement.

The following element can be used to define the example page hit count filter:

```
<filter>
    <filter-name>Page Hit Count Filter</filter-name>
    <filter-class>sams.filters.PageHitCountFilter</filter-class>
</filter>
```

Filters are attached to servlets and JSPs using the `<filter-mapping>` element. A filter can be attached to a specific servlet by specifying a `<servlet-name>` element:

```
<filter-mapping>
    <filter-name>Page Hit Counter Filter</filter-name>
    <servlet-name>Currency Form</servlet-name>
</filter-mapping>
```

To map a filter onto more than one Web resource, use the `<url-pattern>` element to specify a URL mapping. The following example shows the example page hits filter applied to all servlets:

```
<filter-mapping>
    <filter-name>Page Hit Counter Filter</filter-name>
    <url-pattern>/*</url-pattern>
</filter-mapping>
```

Figure 18.2 shows the statistics displayed by the `hits.jsp` page after a few accesses to pages in the application.

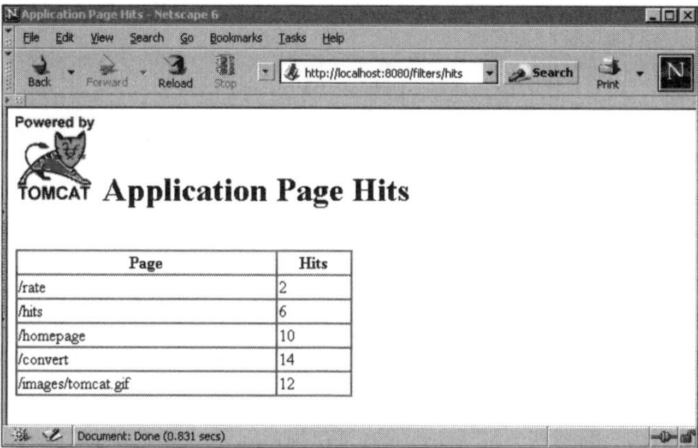

FIGURE 18.2 Displaying application page hits.

Other Uses for Filters

So far, you have seen one use for a filter: a reusable component that can be applied to one or more servlets without affecting the existing application. However, servlet filters can also be used for the following purposes:

- To provide authorization and blocking of requests
- To provide logging and auditing
- To modify or add data to the request
- To modify or format the data sent back to the client
- To implement a model-2 architecture

Relying on filters to provide security features such as authorization, logging, and auditing has the advantage that these functions can be added to existing Web applications without the need to change the application code. Using filters for this task also helps to ensure that the security functions are applied consistently across the entire application and greatly simplifies incorporating any required changes to the security model.

Using Wrapper Methods to Modify Request and Response Objects

A filter can be used to modify both the request object and modify or transform the response. A filter could modify the request to

- Set or override HTTP headers
- Add, remove, or modify attributes and parameters

There are many reasons why you might want to modify the response. These are just a few:

- Transforming the response for non-HTML clients
- Compressing data or scaling images to reduce Web download times
- Applying XSLT transformations to XML documents to support different types of clients

To override request methods, you must wrap the request in an object that extends `ServletRequestWrapper` or `HttpServletRequestWrapper`. To modify the response, you must similarly wrap the response in an object that extends `ServletResponseWrapper` or `HttpServletResponseWrapper`.

The "wrapped" object is then passed down the chain. Wrapper methods default to delegating the call to the wrapped request or response object, so you only need override those methods required to provide the required functionality.

Wrapping the Request

Listings 18.3 and 18.4 show how to use a filter to wrap the request and override a request method. Listing 18.3 simply wraps the request in a `HttpServletRequestWrapper` and passes it on down the filter chain. Listing 18.4 shows an example of the use of a class that extends `HttpServletRequestWrapper` to override the `ServletRequest.getLocale()` method.

> **NOTE**
>
> The `ServletRequest.getLocale()` method uses the HTTP `Accept-Language` header to determine the locale of the client.

With the filter in place, when the servlet at the end of the filter chain calls the `HttpServletRequest.getLocale()` method, the wrapped method `RequestWrapper.getLocale()` shown in Listing 18.4 is called instead. For this example, the `getLocale()` method simply returns `Locale.US`, overriding any client supplied value, but it could easily be modified to obtain a `Locale` stored as user preference data in a database.

LISTING 18.3 `RequestWrapperFilter.java`

```
package sams.filters;

import java.io.*;
import javax.servlet.*;
import javax.servlet.http.*;

public class RequestWrapperFilter implements Filter {

    public void init(FilterConfig filterConfig) throws ServletException {}
    public void destroy() {}

     public void doFilter(ServletRequest request, ServletResponse response,
            FilterChain chain) throws IOException, ServletException {

        HttpServletRequestWrapper wrapper =
            new RequestWrapper((HttpServletRequest) request);
```

LISTING 18.3 Continued

```
        chain.doFilter(wrapper, response);
    }
}
```

LISTING 18.4 RequestWrapper.java

```
package sams.filters;

import java.util.*;
import javax.servlet.http.*;

public class RequestWrapper extends HttpServletRequestWrapper {

    public RequestWrapper(HttpServletRequest request){
      super(request);
    }

    public Locale getLocale() {
        return Locale.US;
    }
}
```

You can use the same mechanism to override any `HttpServletRequest` method.

Modifying the Response

To modify the response, the filter has to capture the response before it is returned to the client, thereby preventing the servlet from closing the response output stream. This is achieved by overriding the `getWriter()` method to use a buffer into which the servlet at the end of the filter chain writes its response.

Listings 18.5 and 18.6 shows a filter that adds a simple text message at the end of the HTML response body. Listing 18.5 is the filter, and Listing 18.6 shows the methods overridden in the wrapper. After saving the original output stream, it wraps the response in a `HttpServletResponseWrapper` and passes it on down the filter chain. When the `doFilter()` method returns, the filter searches the body of the response for the HTML `</body>` end tag. It then writes the response to that point to the original output stream, adds some new text, and finally completes the HTML page with `</BODY></HTML>`.

LISTING 18.5 ResponseWrapperFilter.java

```
package sams.filters;

import java.io.*;
import javax.servlet.*;
import javax.servlet.http.*;

public class ResponseWrapperFilter implements Filter {

    public void init(FilterConfig filterConfig) throws ServletException {}
    public void destroy() {}

     public void doFilter(ServletRequest request, ServletResponse response,
            FilterChain chain) throws IOException, ServletException {

        PrintWriter out = response.getWriter();
        HttpServletResponseWrapper wrapper =
            new ResponseWrapper((HttpServletResponse) response);
        chain.doFilter(request, wrapper);

        String body = wrapper.toString();

        int endpos = body.toLowerCase().indexOf("</body>");
        if (endpos > 0) {
            out.write(body.substring(0, endpos));
            out.write("<P>Extra text added by ResponseWrapperFilter</P>");
            out.write("</BODY></HTML>");
        }
        else
            out.write(body);
        out.close();
    }
}
```

The `ResponseWrapper` class extends `HttpServletResponseWrapper` and simply uses a `CharArrayWriter` character buffer object to replace the normal `PrintWriter` output stream. When the target servlet calls `ServletRequest.getWriter()`, it uses the `CharArrayWriter` buffer from this `ResponseWrapper` class to write the response.

LISTING 18.6 `ResponseWrapper.java`

```
package sams.filters;

import java.io.*;
import java.util.*;
import javax.servlet.http.*;

public class ResponseWrapper extends HttpServletResponseWrapper {

    private CharArrayWriter out;

    public ResponseWrapper(HttpServletResponse response) {
        super(response);
        this.out = new CharArrayWriter();
    }

    public PrintWriter getWriter() {
        return new PrintWriter(out);
    }

    public String toString() {
        return out.toString();
    }
}
```

In Listing 18.5 a simple text string was added to the end of the response, but of course you could add any data you wanted. In a similar fashion, you could use a filter like to this to add page hit counter data to dynamically generated pages.

Using a Filter as a Model-2 Architecture

Finally, you will see how you can use a filter in an application that implements a model-2 architecture. In this scenario, the filter can be used to replace the controller servlet described in Chapter 17, "Architectures." The advantage of implementing a model-2 architecture using filters is that it is possible to retrofit the model-2 architecture into an existing application with relatively few changes to the existing code.

In the example filter in Listing 18.7, you might recognize the code in the `doFilter()` method. Apart from the obvious changes required to make this an implementation of a `Filter`, this code is almost identical to the `doGet()` method from the controller servlet `Action.java` shown in Chapter 17 (Listing 17.1).

LISTING 18.7 A Filter Acting as Controller in a Model-2 Architecture

```
package sams.filters;

import java.io.*;
import java.sql.*;
import java.text.*;
import javax.naming.*;
import javax.servlet.*;
import javax.servlet.http.*;
import converters.*;

public class ActionFilter implements Filter {

    public void init(FilterConfig filterConfig) throws ServletException {}
    public void destroy() {}

    public void doFilter(ServletRequest request, ServletResponse response,
             FilterChain chain) throws IOException, ServletException {

        if (request instanceof HttpServletRequest) {
            HttpServletRequest httpReq = ((HttpServletRequest) request);

            HttpSession session = httpReq.getSession();
            String amount = httpReq.getParameter("amount");
            try {
                ConverterBean convert =
                    (ConverterBean)session.getAttribute("convert");
                if (convert == null)
                    session.setAttribute("convert",convert=new ConverterBean());
                String from = httpReq.getParameter("countryFrom");
                String to = httpReq.getParameter("countryTo");
                if (from!=null && from.length()>0 && to!=null && to.length()>0)
                        convert.setCountries(from,to);
                if (amount!=null && amount.length()>0)
                        convert.setAmount(amount);
            }
            catch (NamingException ex) {
                httpReq.setAttribute("exception",ex);
                httpReq.getRequestDispatcher("databaseError.jsp").
                    forward(request,response);
            }
            catch (SQLException ex) {
```

LISTING 18.7 Continued

```
                httpReq.setAttribute("exception",ex);
                httpReq.getRequestDispatcher("databaseError.jsp").
                    forward(request,response);
            }
            catch (ParseException ex) {
                httpReq.setAttribute("message",
                    "<FONT color='red'>Invalid value for amount: " +
                        amount + "</FONT>");
            }
            catch (IllegalArgumentException ex) {
                httpReq.setAttribute("message",
                  "<FONT COLOR='red'>"+ex.getMessage()+"</FONT>");
            }
            chain.doFilter(httpReq, response);
        }
        else
            chain.doFilter(request, response);
    }
}
```

You can use this filter along with the JSPs provided in Chapter 17 (you will need to change any URL references ending in `.do` to the actual URL mapping for the JSP) to provide another version of a model-2 currency converter application.

The additions to the `web.xml` file required to deploy this application and attach the filter to the Currency Form and Rates JSPs are shown in Listing 18.8.

LISTING 18.8 `web.xml` Elements Required to Implement a Model-2 Architecture Filter

```
<filter>
    <filter-name>M2 Action Filter</filter-name>
    <filter-class>sams.filters.ActionFilter</filter-class>
</filter>

<filter-mapping>
    <filter-name>M2 Action Filter</filter-name>
    <servlet-name>M2 Currency Form</servlet-name>
</filter-mapping>
```

LISTING 18.8 Continued

```
<filter-mapping>
    <filter-name>M2 Action Filter</filter-name>
    <servlet-name>M2 Rates</servlet-name>
</filter-mapping>

<servlet>
    <servlet-name>M2 Currency Form</servlet-name>
    <jsp-file>/convert.jsp</jsp-file>
</servlet>

<servlet>
    <servlet-name>M2 Rates</servlet-name>
    <jsp-file>/rate.jsp</jsp-file>
</servlet>

<servlet-mapping>
    <servlet-name>M2 Rates</servlet-name>
    <url-pattern>/rate</url-pattern>
</servlet-mapping>

<servlet-mapping>
    <servlet-name>M2 Currency Form</servlet-name>
    <url-pattern>/convert</url-pattern>
</servlet-mapping>
```

You have now seen two ways of implementing a model-2 architecture in a Web application. You might be wondering whether you should implement the model-2 architecture using a servlet (as in Chapter 17) or in a filter as shown here. If you use servlets, you will have to map URL patterns onto the model-2 controller servlet, whereas a model-2 filter simply intercepts requests for the target Web resource. The filter approach is somewhat more secure because users cannot bypass the filter, whereas with a servlet-based approach it is possible to enter the URL of the target Web resource (which has to be prevented in other ways). Malicious users will always try to identify and enter the target Web resource in an attempt to break the security of your Web application.

On balance, the security aspects give a slight advantage to using filters to implement model-2 controllers rather than servlets.

Summary

As you have seen in this chapter, the filter mechanism provides a way to encapsulate functionality in a component that can be reused in different contexts. Filters can add to, modify, or redirect requests and also modify the contents of any response.

As well as being portable and reusable, filters are easy to add to existing applications. These features make filters a useful additional component in the Web application writer's toolbox.

19 Tomcat Valves

IN THIS CHAPTER

Tomcat valves are similar to servlet filters in that they can be used to preprocess request objects. However, unlike filters, which are server-independent, valves are proprietary to Tomcat. Also, valves are only inserted in the request-processing pipeline and therefore cannot be used to modify response objects. For these reasons, it is unlikely that you would want to write a valve yourself. With that in mind, this chapter will only describe the purpose and use of the valves that are provided with Tomcat 4.

Introduction to Tomcat Valves

If you have read Chapter 18, "Servlet Filters," you know that servlet filters are reusable components that can be attached to resources in a Web application and are configured in the `web.xml` file. Valves are also reusable components, but they are attached to a Tomcat container (`Engine`, `Host`, or `Context`) and are configured using a `<Valve>` element in the `server.xml` file.

A valve attached to an `Engine` container will preprocess all requests received by the connectors that are associated with that `Engine` (that is, requests received by the service in which the `Engine` is nested). Similarly, a valve attached to a `Host` preprocesses all requests targeted at a particular virtual host. The lowest granularity for a valve is an individual `Context`, where it will preprocess all requests referencing that `Context`—it is not possible to attach a valve to an individual servlet or group of servlets.

Bundled with Tomcat 4 are the following valves:

- Access Log Valve
- Remote Address Filter
- Remote Host Filter

- Request Dumper Valve
- Single Sign On Valve

You can configure a Tomcat valve by editing the `server.xml` file and adding the `<Valve>` element within the appropriate container. Alternatively, you can use the Create New Valve action in the Tomcat Web Server Administration Tool. You can also use the Tomcat Web Server Administration Tool to remove Tomcat valves.

TIP

If you use the Administration Tool, it will verify that the syntax is correct and all the required attributes have been specified.

Let's look at each of the Tomcat valves in turn.

Access Log Valve

The Access Log Valve is used to log information about client requests. It is a useful tool for debugging and simple auditing, but you should be aware that using it degrades server performance. On a heavily used server, this could be significant.

CAUTION

Information is logged for every client request, including not only page requests but also individual graphics and any other objects that generate a client request. If client redirection is used (as it is with welcome files and temporary redirects), there can be more than one log entry for every page.

Table 19.1 shows the attributes for the `<Valve>` element definition for the Access Log Valve.

TABLE 19.1 Access Log Valve Attributes

Attribute	Description
`className`	The Java classname for this valve—`org.apache.catalina.valves.AccessLogValve`.
`directory`	(optional) The directory where the log file is placed. This may be an absolute pathname or relative to `<CATALINA_HOME>` (default is `logs`).
`pattern`	(optional) Used to define the information that is logged. A formatting pattern is made up of a combination of text and pattern identifiers (default is `common`; see Table 19.2 for more information).
`prefix`	(optional) Defines the prefix added to the name of each log file (default is `access_log`).

TABLE 19.1 Continued

Attribute	Description
`resolveHosts`	(optional) If `resolveHosts` is set to `true`, the client DNS hostname is logged rather than the numeric IP address (default is `false`). Setting this attribute to `true` could affect performance because it necessitates looking up the client hostname for each client request.
`suffix`	(optional) Defines the suffix added to the name of each log file (default is no suffix).

The `pattern` attribute is made up of pattern identifiers that are replaced by the appropriate value from the client request. Table 19.2 lists the pattern identifiers.

TABLE 19.2 Access Log Valve Pattern Identifiers

Identifier	Description
`%a`	Remote IP address
`%A`	Local IP address
`%b`	Bytes sent, excluding HTTP headers, or `-` if zero
`%B`	Bytes sent, excluding HTTP headers
`%h`	Remote hostname (or IP address if `resolveHosts` is false)
`%H`	Request protocol
`%l`	Remote logical username from `identd` (always returns `-`)
`%m`	Request method (`GET`, `POST`, and so on)
`%p`	Local port on which this request was received
`%q`	Query string (prepended with `?`)
`%r`	First line of the request (method and request URI)
`%s`	HTTP status code of the response
`%S`	User session ID
`%t`	Date and time of the request
`%u`	Remote user that was authenticated (if any); otherwise, `-`
`%U`	Requested URL path
`%v`	Local server name
`common`	Combination of `%h`, `%l`, `%u`, `%t`, `%r`, `%s`, and `%b`
`combined`	Same as `common` with the values of the `Referer` and `User-Agent` HTTP headers added: `%h`, `%l`, `%u`, `%t`, `%r`, `%s`, `%b`, `%{Referer}i`, and `%{User-Agent}i`

The `server.xml` file supplied with Tomcat 4 comes with an Access Log Valve defined in the `Tomcat-Standalone localhost` container:

```
<Valve className="org.apache.catalina.valves.AccessLogValve"
       directory="logs" prefix="localhost_access_log."
       suffix=".txt" pattern="common" resolveHosts="false"/>
```

NOTE

This valve is commented out in the default `server.xml` file for Tomcat 4.1 but is uncommented in Tomcat 4.0.

This `<Valve>` element dictates that the log file has prefix `localhost_access_log` and suffix `.txt` and will be found in the `<CATALINA_HOME>/logs` directory.

With the default `common` pattern, the Access Log Valve generates entries in the log file similar to the following:

```
127.0.0.1 - - [17/Jun/2002:10:59:57 00] "GET / HTTP/1.1" 302 -
127.0.0.1 - - [17/Jun/2002:10:59:57 00] "GET /index.jsp HTTP/1.1" 200 -
127.0.0.1 - - [17/Jun/2002:11:00:13 00] "GET /admin/index.jsp HTTP/1.1" 302 -
127.0.0.1 - - [17/Jun/2002:11:00:13 00] "GET /admin/login.jsp HTTP/1.1" 200 -
127.0.0.1 - - [17/Jun/2002:11:00:13 00] "GET /admin/admin.css HTTP/1.1" 304 -
```

You can also configure or remove an Access Log Valve using the Tomcat Web Server Administration Tool. Figure 19.1 shows how to set up an Access Log Valve for all requests directed to the standalone `Engine`.

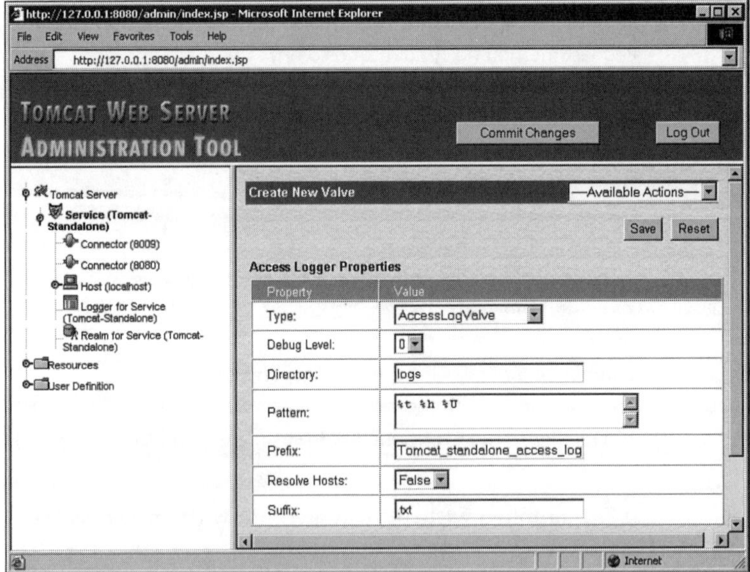

FIGURE 19.1 Configuring an Access Log Valve using the Tomcat Web Server Administration Tool.

NOTE

You cannot select the Engine container in the Tomcat Web Server Administration Tool. Accessing the Service (Tomcat-Standalone) entry in the left-hand panel provides access to the Engine element.

Remote Address Filter

This valve was covered in detail in Chapter 16, "Configuring Tomcat," in the section titled "Controlling Client Access to Tomcat." The Remote Address Filter checks the IP address of the client that submitted a request against a list of IP addresses defined in the `allow` and `deny` attributes of the `<Valve>`.

TIP

If you prefer to use DNS hostnames, you should configure a Remote Host Filter as described in the following section.

Based on the results of this comparison, the request is then either blocked or allowed. You can apply a Remote Address Filter with any Tomcat container (`Engine`, `Host`, or `Context`).

The Remote Address Filter has the attributes listed in Table 19.3.

TABLE 19.3 Remote Address Filter Attributes

Attribute	Description
`className`	The Java classname for this valve—`org.apache.catalina.valves.RemoteAddrValve`
`allow`	(optional) A comma-separated list of patterns that are compared to the remote client's IP address to allow the request
`deny`	(optional) A comma-separated list of patterns that are compared to the remote client's IP address to block the request

Although both the `allow` and `deny` attributes are optional, you need at least one for this filter to have any effect. The patterns used in the `allow` and `deny` attributes use a pattern-matching syntax where `.*` matches any character.

NOTE

This is actually a simplification. See Chapter 16 for more information about the pattern-matching syntax.

For example, you could use the following to only allow hosts on a local subnetwork (replace the IP address with one appropriate for your site):

```
<Valve classname="org.apache.catalina.valves.RemoteAddrValve"
    allow="123\.123\.123\.. *" />
```

If the `allow` attribute is present, an IP address *must* match one of the `allow` patterns for the request to proceed. If an IP address matches a pattern in the `allow` attribute (or if the `allow` attribute is not present), it is then compared to the patterns in the `deny` attribute. Only if the IP address *does not* match a pattern in the `deny` attribute is the request allowed to proceed.

To protect access to Tomcat from any other computer on the network, you could configure a Remote Address Filter as follows:

```
<Valve classname="org.apache.catalina.valves.RemoteAddrValve"
    allow="127\.0\.0\.1" />
```

With this filter in place, Tomcat will block any requests received from other sources and return an HTTP 403 "Forbidden" error.

Remote Host Filter

The Remote Host Filter works the same way as the Remote Address Filter, except that it compares the hostname of the client (rather than the IP address) to the regular expressions in the `allow` and `deny` attributes.

The Remote Address Filter has the same attributes as the Remote Host Filter (see Table 19.3).

As with the Remote Address Filter, if the `allow` attribute is present, a hostname *must* match one of the `allow` patterns, and it *must not* match a pattern in the `deny` attribute if the request is to proceed.

For example, the following `<Valve>` element will deny access to all hosts whose hostname includes the word *devil*:

```
<Valve classname="org.apache.catalina.valves.RemoteHostValve"
    deny=".*devil.*" />
```

Request Dumper Valve

The Request Dumper Valve logs details of HTTP requests. As with the previous valves, you can configure the Request Dumper Valve at the `Engine`, `Host`, or `Context` level. This valve does not create its own log file but sends its output to whatever `Logger` element is defined for the `Engine`, `Host`, or `Context` element.

This valve has only a single attribute, which is the Java `className` for the valve. Use the following element to configure a Request Dumper Valve in the `server.xml` file:

```
<Valve className="org.apache.catalina.valves.RequestDumperValve"/>
```

Listing 19.1 shows the information logged for a single request. From this you can see that the Request Dumper Valve is a useful tool for debugging.

LISTING 19.1 Output Generated by the Request Dumper Valve

```
===============================================================
REQUEST URI       =/access/CurrencyConverter
          authType=null
 characterEncoding=null
     contentLength=-1
       contentType=null
       contextPath=/access
            cookie=JSESSIONID=89F7CCC2D9998D93D5687733EFBB27EE
            header=host=localhost:8080
            header=user-agent=Mozilla/5.0 (Windows; U; Windows NT 5.0; en-GB;
➥ rv:0.9.4) Gecko/20011128 Netscape6/6.2.1
            header=accept=text/xml, application/xml, application/xhtml+xml,
➥ text/html;q=0.9, image/png, image/jpeg, image/gif;q=0.2, text/plain;q=0.8,
➥ text/css, */*;q=0.1
            header=accept-language=en-gb
            header=accept-encoding=gzip, deflate, compress;q=0.9
            header=keep-alive=300
            header=connection=keep-alive
            header=cookie=JSESSIONID=89F7CCC2D9998D93D5687733EFBB27EE
            header=referer=http://localhost:8080/access/currency-form
            locale=en_GB
            method=GET
         parameter=amount=1
          pathInfo=null
          protocol=HTTP/1.1
       queryString=amount=1
        remoteAddr=127.0.0.1
        remoteHost=127.0.0.1
        remoteUser=null
        requestedSessionId=89F7CCC2D9998D93D5687733EFBB27EE
            scheme=http
```

LISTING 19.1 Continued

```
      serverName=localhost
      serverPort=8080
     servletPath=null
        isSecure=false
---------------------------------------------------------------
```

NOTE

In the actual log file, each line is prefixed with a time stamp, the string `RequestDumperValve`, and the name of the context, as shown in the following:

`2002-06-17 17:05:42 RequestDumperValve[/access]:`

This information has been removed from each line of Listing 19.1 for the sake of clarity.

CAUTION

The use of the Request Dumper Valve is not recommended for a production system. Not only does it generate vast amounts of output, which for a busy system will rapidly devour disk space, but it also adversely affects performance.

Single Sign On Valve

You can only configure the Single Sign On Valve at the `Host` level. It allows users who have authenticated themselves to one application to have their identity recognized by all other Web applications on the same virtual host. The use of the Single Sign On Valve was covered in detail in Chapter 14, "Access Control."

Table 19.4 shows the attributes for the Single Sign On Valve.

TABLE 19.4 Single Sign On Valve Attributes

Attribute	Description
`className`	The Java classname for this valve—`org.apache.catalina.authenticator.SingleSignOn`
`debug`	(optional) Level of debugging generated by this valve (default is `0`)

Summary

Valves are components proprietary to Tomcat that can be used to preprocess requests. The five valves provided with Tomcat can be used to aid debugging, to implement part of a security policy, or to improve the user interface with the Web server.

20 Frameworks and Jakarta Struts

IN THIS CHAPTER

- Installing Jakarta Struts
- Struts Architecture
- A Simple Struts JSP
- Defining the Struts Controller in `web.xml`
- Simple Struts Action Mappings
- Form Validation
- Custom Action Controllers
- Defining the View JSP
- Other Struts Features

A framework is designed to provide a basic structure that you can use as a starting point for building a finished product. In a Web application, this means providing a set of supporting classes, servlets, JSPs, and tags that can be incorporated into different applications without change.

Good frameworks require significant development effort, but the payback comes when you use the framework to develop new applications. Development time will be reduced because the framework provides basic functionality that can be reused across many applications. Furthermore, a framework will impose a standard design pattern and structure for all Web applications, thereby imposing consistency and helping less-experienced developers to produce better quality solutions.

This chapter does not provide you with the skills to write your own framework, because that would require a book in itself. But then, why write your own framework when there are several already available? In this chapter, you will look at using one of these, Jakarta Struts, to build a simple application. This chapter summarizes the basic Struts architecture and shows you how to use the Struts TagLib and form validation capabilities.

Because Struts is a large subject, this chapter will only provide the information needed to get you started. Another book in this series from Sams Publishing, *Struts Kick Start* (ISBN 0-672-32472-5), is devoted entirely to developing Struts applications. Apart from *Struts Kick Start*, you should read the Struts documentation and example applications in the Struts archive to build on the knowledge you gain from this chapter.

You should be comfortable with using custom tags, TagLibs, and Tag Library Descriptor (TLD) files in order to follow the Struts-based converter shown in this chapter. Refer to Chapter 10, "Custom Tags and TagLibs," for information about TagLibs.

Installing Jakarta Struts

Jakarta Struts is available from http://jakarta.apache.org/struts and can be downloaded as a binary distribution containing Struts, associated documentation, and sample applications. You should download the binary archive from the latest production release (the examples use Struts 1.0.2) and unpack the archive to a temporary location. Unpacking the downloaded file will create a jakarta-struts-1.0.2 directory containing lib and webapps subdirectories. The lib directory contains the following files:

File	Description
*.dtd	DTD files for validating the XML configuration files
jdbc2_0-stdext.jar	Classes required for the Struts JDBC data sources (this JAR file is already included in the Tomcat installation)
struts.jar	Classes required for Struts
*.tld	TLD files for the Struts TagLibs

To deploy a Struts-based Web application, you must include the struts.jar file in the WEB-INF/lib directory of your application. To compile your servlets, you will need to add the struts.jar file to your CLASSPATH or install the JAR file as a standard Java extension.

NOTE

If you are using Tomcat 4.1, the Admin tool (see Chapter 16, "Configuring Tomcat") is based on Struts and the Struts JAR, XML, and TLD files. They can be found in the <CATALINA_HOME>/webapps/admin/WEB-INF directory tree. You can use these files instead of downloading the Struts archive if this is more convenient.

You do not have to make any configuration changes to Tomcat. Struts is just a collection of Java class files to include with your application.

TIP

For your application to run, you must have a copy of struts.jar in the WEB-INF/lib directory of every application that uses Struts. The Tomcat class loader will not load the Struts classes from any other location; adding `struts.jar` to `<CATALINA_HOME>/lib` or as a Java standard extension does not work.

You will also need to add the required TLD files to your application's `WEB-INF` directory and include the appropriate `<taglib>` element in the `web.xml` file (as discussed in Chapter 10).

The `webapps` directory of the Struts binary distribution contains the following WAR files:

WAR File	Description
`struts-blank.war`	A simple Web application
`struts-documentation.war`	A copy of the documentation available on the Struts Web site
`struts-example.war`	Examples of using Struts
`struts-exercise-taglib.war`	Test pages for developers who are enhancing the Struts TagLibs, useful for examples of how to use the custom tags
`struts-template.war`	Example application showing the use of Struts templates
`struts-upload.war`	Example of how to upload files using Struts

To access the Struts examples and documentation, you should copy the WAR files to `<CATALINA_HOME>/webapps` and stop and restart Tomcat to install the different Struts contexts.

Struts Architecture

Struts uses a Model-View Controller (MVC) architecture (see Chapter 17, "Architectures") that separates out the business logic (model) from the presentation logic (view) and the data flow (control) between various components. Figure 20.1 shows the key components of a Struts application.

In Figure 20.1, the client request is routed to the Struts `ActionServlet` object that is the main controller for the framework. There is only one `ActionServlet` for all Web resources in the application, and it is provided with Struts. The `ActionServlet` uses the information in the client request to pass control to an action controller. There is normally one action controller for each Web resource, and you have to write these controllers yourself.

The `ActionServlet` can populate an optional `ActionForm` object with the HTTP request parameters. An `ActionForm` is used to encapsulate form parameters and can also be used to validate the request parameters.

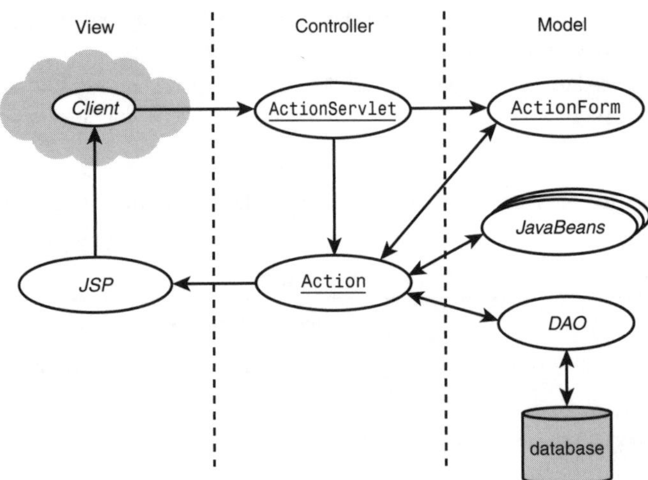

FIGURE 20.1 Key components of a Struts application.

An individual action controller uses the `ActionForm` and other supporting Java objects such as beans and Data Access Objects (DAO) to generate the result data for the request. This data is forwarded to a JSP, which builds the response for the client.

The Struts configuration file (`WEB-INF/struts-config.xml`) determines the mapping between HTTP requests, action controller objects, and `ActionForm` objects.

Struts is primarily for Web form processing and handles the common Web server headache of the client not completing a form correctly. Struts simplifies form validation and the resubmission of an incorrectly completed form. The form is returned to the client with the previous field values already filled in and an appropriate error message added. Struts is most useful for projects with many forms. Although using the Struts framework increases the overall complexity of an application, its features (internationalization and a consistent form processing approach) will give you a good return on your investment very quickly.

Struts is a good match for enterprise sized solutions (it is used by Tomcat, WebSphere, and at least one of Sun Microsystems' blueprint examples). It may take you some time to become comfortable working with Struts because it utilizes servlets, JSPs, TagLibs, and XML configuration files—all the things you are studying in the other chapters of this book.

A Simple Struts JSP

This chapter uses Struts to develop a currency converter application along the lines of those used in previous chapters. This Struts converter has a single home page with links to a page displaying the current exchange rate and a second page that provides a form for submitting values to convert.

To create a Struts application, you will have to perform the following steps, which are explained in detail in the rest of this chapter:

1. Define links to the Web resources in your application using a URL of the form `*.do`.
2. In the `web.xml` file, map the URL pattern `*.do` onto the `ActionServlet` page.
3. For each Web resource, add an `<action>` mapping entry to the `struts-config.xml` file.
4. For each form in your application, write an `ActionForm` validation subclass and add a `<form-bean>` entry to the `struts-config.xml` file.
5. For each Web resource in your application, write an `Action` subclass controller object to implement the request (this is the target of the `<action>` mapping in `struts-config.xml`).
6. For each Web resource, write a JSP that displays the results of the action controller.

The Struts converter includes error handling, but keeps the currency conversion and data presentation as simple as possible.

The starting point for the converter is the home page shown in Listing 20.1, with links to two Web resources: examining exchange rates and performing a currency conversion.

LISTING 20.1 Home Page `index.jsp`

```
<%@ taglib uri="/WEB-INF/struts-html.tld" prefix="html" %>
<html:html locale="true">
  <HEAD>
    <TITLE>Chapter 20, Frameworks and Jakarta Struts</TITLE>
  </HEAD>
  <BODY>
    <H1> Chapter 20, Frameworks and Jakarta Struts</H1>
    What would you like to do?
    <UL>
        <LI><html:link page="/rate.do">
            Examine the exchange rate</html:link></LI>
        <LI><html:link page="/convert.do">
            Convert a currency amount</html:link></LI>
```

LISTING 20.1 Continued

```
    </UL>
  </BODY>
</html:html>
```

Struts provides an `html` TagLib, with support for several HTML tags, which is used in Listing 20.1. The `html` tag library acts as a bridge between the actual HTML tag and the supporting Struts framework. The following tags are used in Listing 20.1:

Tag	Use
`<html:html locale="true">`	Writes the `<HTML>` tag to the page and creates a `Locale` object from the HTTP request `Accept-Language` header field
`<html:link>`	Adds an HTML `<A>` tag with URL rewriting on the `<A>` tag's `HREF` value

There are about 20 HTML tags in the library, which are mostly used for supporting HTML forms. You should study the Struts HTML tags and use them on your Web pages to gain the most benefit from using Struts.

In Listing 20.1, the `<html:link>` is used to add two hypertext links to the Web page. The two links used refer to the resources `/rate.do` and `/convert.do`. These are not real Web pages but action-mapping names that are used by the `ActionServlet` controller for routing the request to the appropriate action controller. The `<html:link>` tag adds the Web application name to the front of the action name and subjects the resultant pathname to URL rewriting. As outlined, the request routing is defined in the following configuration files:

- `web.xml`—Used to map the URLs onto the controller servlet
- `struts-config.xml`—Used to map the requests onto action forms, action controllers, and view JSPs

The `struts-config.xml` file helps support the division of labor between Java code and Web designers. By modifying the `struts-config.xml` file, Web designers can reorganize the site structure without having to know (or recompile) any Java code. Likewise, the Java developers can develop component functionality with minimal need to dirty their hands with HTML or learn the overall site structure.

Configuring Struts using these files is discussed in the following sections.

Defining the Struts Controller in `web.xml`

Conventionally, all Web resource names used in a Struts application end in `.do`. All requests are routed to the single `ActionController` servlet that uses the URL pathname to determine the actions required to support the request.

The `web.xml` file will be similar for most applications because all requests are handled by the single `ActionServlet` object, which is configured by the separate `struts-config.xml` file. Listing 20.2 shows the `web.xml` file used for the Struts converter.

LISTING 20.2 The `web.xml` for a Struts Application

```
<?xml version="1.0" encoding="ISO-8859-1"?>
<!DOCTYPE web-app
  PUBLIC "-//Sun Microsystems, Inc.//DTD Web Application 2.2//EN"
  "http://java.sun.com/j2ee/dtds/web-app_2_2.dtd">
<web-app>
  <servlet>
    <servlet-name>action</servlet-name>
    <servlet-class>org.apache.struts.action.ActionServlet</servlet-class>
    <init-param>
      <param-name>application</param-name>
      <param-value>converter</param-value>
    </init-param>
  </servlet>
  <servlet-mapping>
    <servlet-name>action</servlet-name>
    <url-pattern>*.do</url-pattern>
  </servlet-mapping>
  <welcome-file-list>
    <welcome-file>index.jsp</welcome-file>
  </welcome-file-list>

  <taglib>
    <taglib-uri>/WEB-INF/struts-bean.tld</taglib-uri>
    <taglib-location>/WEB-INF/struts-bean.tld</taglib-location>
  </taglib>
  <taglib>
    <taglib-uri>/WEB-INF/struts-html.tld</taglib-uri>
    <taglib-location>/WEB-INF/struts-html.tld</taglib-location>
  </taglib>
  <taglib>
    <taglib-uri>/WEB-INF/struts-logic.tld</taglib-uri>
    <taglib-location>/WEB-INF/struts-logic.tld</taglib-location>
  </taglib>
```

LISTING 20.2 Continued

```
  <resource-ref>
    <res-ref-name>jdbc/conversion</res-ref-name>
    <res-type>javax.sql.DataSource</res-type>
    <res-auth>Container</res-auth>
  </resource-ref>
</web-app>
```

The `web.xml` file in Listing 20.2 defines a single servlet (class `org.apache.struts.action.ActionServlet`) and maps the URL pattern `*.do` onto this servlet. By default, the `ActionServlet` uses the `WEB-INF/struts-config.xml` configuration file to route the request to an appropriate controller; a different configuration file pathname could be specified as an initialization parameter to the servlet.

The Struts philosophy is to develop applications that use resource bundles (see the `java.util.ResourceBundle` API documentation) to support multinational clients. You have already seen part of this support in the `locale=true` attribute of the `<html:html>` tag. A resource bundle base name for the application is defined in the `application` initialization parameter to the servlet. The `converter` resource bundle name maps onto the `WEB-INF/classes/converter.properties` file which is discussed later in the "Form Validation" section.

NOTE

The example JSPs deliberately use simple English text on the page to keep the listings as easy to understand as possible. A real application would use the Struts `<bean:message>` tag to support internationalized messages.

The remainder of the example `web.xml` file defines the Struts tag library files and a data source resource reference for accessing the conversion rates.

Simple Struts Action Mappings

When the `ActionServlet` services a request, it uses the `struts-config.xml` file to determine the action it should take. For example, consider the following simple link to the exchange rates page used in Listing 20.1:

```
<html:link page="/rate.do">Examine the exchange rate</html:link>
```

The following <action> tag in `struts-config.xml` tells the servlet to forward the rate request to `/rate.jsp` page:

```
<action path="/rate" forward="/rate.jsp"/>
```

The `ActionServlet` uses the request name without the `.do` suffix to match the request to the `path` attribute of the <action> definition.

The exchange rates page is a simple Web resource that does not validate any request parameters and does not require a custom controller to be written. For this page the `ActionServlet` simply forwards the request without providing any additional functionality. However, the `ActionServlet` really comes into its own when dealing with requests from HTML forms.

Form Validation

The Struts `ActionServlet` controller can be configured to support form-based requests by storing the form parameters in a supporting `ActionForm` bean. The second link in Listing 20.1 points to the `/convert.do` action, and the associated entry in `struts-config.xml` for this link is

```
<action     path="/convert"
            type="converters.ActionConvert"
            name="convertForm"
            scope="request"
            input="/convert.jsp"
            validate="true">
  <forward name="modelError" path="/modelError.jsp"/>
</action>
```

This <action> entry defines the following attributes:

Attribute	Description
`path`	The request path for this action mapping
`type`	A custom action object (class `converters.ActionConvert` shown in Listing 20.5)
`name`	A form validation bean name
`scope`	The scope for the form bean (`request` or `session`)
`input`	The form to be returned to the client if the form validation fails (usually the form that submitted the request)
`validate`	Set to `true` to call the `validate()` method on the form bean to validate the request parameters

The <action> element also contains a <forward> element that is used to map an alias name onto an actual Web resource. The example maps the modelError name onto the /modelError.jsp page and is used to handle errors in the custom action controller discussed in the section "Custom Action Controllers."

Defining an Action Form Bean

The action form bean must be defined in the struts-config.xml file using a <form-bean> element as shown in the following example:

```
<form-bean name="convertForm" type="converters.ConvertForm"/>
```

An action form bean is a Java bean with properties for each field on the HTML form that it supports. The converter form bean has a single property called amount and represents the following HTML form (the complete JSP is shown in Listing 20.7):

```
<html:form action="/convert.do">
  <P>Amount to convert: <html:text property="amount" /></P>
  <P><html:submit>Convert</html:submit></P>
</html:form>
```

The action form bean itself is shown in Listing 20.3.

LISTING 20.3 Action Form Bean ConvertForm.java

```
package converters;

import javax.servlet.http.*;
import org.apache.struts.action.*;

public class ConvertForm extends ActionForm {

    private String amount;

    public void setAmount (String amount) { this.amount = amount; }
    public String getAmount () { return amount; }

    public void reset(ActionMapping mapping, HttpServletRequest request) {
        amount = null;
    }

    public ActionErrors validate(ActionMapping mapping,
                                 HttpServletRequest request) {
        ActionErrors errors = new ActionErrors();
```

LISTING 20.3 Continued

```
        if (amount == null)
            errors.add("amount", new ActionError("convert.enter.amount"));
        else if (amount.length() == 0)
            errors.add("amount", new ActionError("convert.no.value"));
        else {
            try {
                double doubleAmount = Double.parseDouble(amount);
            }
            catch (NumberFormatException ex) {
                errors.add("amount",
                           new ActionError("convert.bad.amount",amount));
            }
        }
        return errors;
    }
}
```

An action form bean must extend the `org.apache.struts.action.ActionForm` class and provide JavaBean properties for all the parameters in the HTML request. It may optionally override the `validate()` method to support property validation.

When the `ActionServlet` object processes a request for this action, the form's properties are set to the equivalent request parameters. If the `<action>` tag sets the validate attribute to `true`, the `validate()` method of form action bean class is called to validate the properties.

Validating Form Parameters

The `validate()` method on an action form bean must return an `org.apache.struts.action.ActionErrors` collection if it detects a problem with the form parameters. Returning null or an empty collection from `validate()` indicates that the form is valid. If the `ActionServlet` receives a non-empty `ActionErrors` collection from `validate()`, it will forward the request to the Web resource in the `input` attribute of the `web.xml` `<action>` element instead of forwarding it to the action controller. The input form can use the `<html:errors/>` tag to display the messages in the `ActionErrors` collection.

The example code uses the `ActionErrors` mechanism to display messages as well as errors. Each message added to the collection is an `org.apache.struts.action.ActionError` object constructed from a message key that categorizes the message and an error message. The error message must be a key into the application resource bundle (see the `java.util.ResourceBundle` API) specified as the `application` initialization parameter in the ActionServlet's <servlet> entry in the web.xml file as shown in Listing 20.2.

The resource bundle mechanism uses the message key to obtain the actual message from the resource properties file. Listing 20.4 shows the resource bundle file used by the Struts converter.

LISTING 20.4 Resource Bundle File converter.properties

```
errors.header=
errors.footer=

convert.enter.amount=<B>Enter an amount to convert</B>
convert.no.value=<I>You did not specify a value to convert</I>
convert.bad.amount=<FONT COLOR="red">ERROR: {0} is not a valid number</FONT>

convert.naming.error=Failed to lookup datasource JNDI name
convert.database.error=SQL error when accessing the database
```

The ActionErrors mechanism uses the message keys errors.header and errors.footer to write text before and after the error messages when they are written to the Web page. These have been defined as empty strings in the example properties file.

This convert.bad.amount message uses a second form of ActionError constructor, which uses a parameter to include in the message (the underlying mechanism is java.text.MessageFormat).

TIP

This example uses a resource bundle with the base name converter. The converter.properties file defines the keys and default messages that are used to write text to the Web pages. You can provide additional resource bundles for different languages by adding the ISO language two-letter extension to the base name. For example, if you provided a resource bundle called convert_fr.properties, any client that prefers text in French (fr) (as defined by the HTTP request Accept-Language header field) will get the messages from this file rather than the default file. If you need to differentiate between countries ostensibly speaking the same language, you can add the ISO country code after the language. Using files convert_en_US.properties and convert_en_GB.properties will let you customize your messages for American and British English.

On the Web page, you use the <bean:message key='*key*'> tag to write internationalized messages to your Web page.

Only if your action form class successfully validates the request parameters does the ActionServlet forward the request to the custom action controller specified in the type attribute of the <Action> element.

Custom Action Controllers

A custom action controller implements the business logic of your Web resource and is invoked after successful validation of any request parameters. The action controller should retrieve and update any data required to service the request before passing the request onto a JSP that will display the results of the request.

An action controller must extend the org.apache.struts.action.Action class and override the perform() method. Listing 20.5 shows the custom controller for the Struts converter form.

LISTING 20.5 Custom Action Controller ActionConvert.java

```
package converters;

import java.io.*;
import java.sql.*;
import java.text.*;
import javax.naming.*;
import javax.servlet.*;
import javax.servlet.http.*;
import org.apache.struts.action.*;

public class ActionConvert extends Action
{
    public ActionForward perform(ActionMapping mapping, ActionForm actionForm,
            HttpServletRequest request, HttpServletResponse response)
            throws IOException, ServletException {
        ActionErrors errors = null;
        try {
            ConverterBean convert = new ConverterBean();
            ConvertForm form = (ConvertForm)actionForm;
            convert.setAmount(form.getAmount());
            request.setAttribute("amount",convert.getAmount());
            request.setAttribute(
                "convertedAmount",
                convert.getConvertedAmount()
            );
            return mapping.findForward("convert");
```

LISTING 20.5 Continued

```
        }
        catch (ParseException ex) {
            errors = new ActionErrors();
            errors.add("database", new ActionError("convert.bad.amount"));
        }
        catch (NamingException ex) {
            errors = new ActionErrors();
            errors.add("database", new ActionError("convert.naming.error"));
        }
        catch (SQLException ex) {
            errors = new ActionErrors();
            errors.add("database", new ActionError("convert.database.error"));
        }
        saveErrors(request,errors);
        return mapping.findForward("modelError");
    }
}
```

The parameters to the `Action.perform()` method are

- `ActionMapping`—Used to forward the request
- `ActionForm`—A reference to the action form bean (for the request parameters)
- `HttpServletRequest`—The servlet request object
- `HttpServletResponse`—The servlet response object

NOTE

Overloaded versions of `perform()` are provided that use the generic `ServletRequest` and `ServletResponse` objects or the `ActionServlet` object, but most applications will not override these versions.

In Listing 20.5 the Struts converter custom action controller (`ActionConvert`) uses a simple `ConverterBean` to do the required currency conversion. The servlet obtains the value of the amount from the action form object and calls the bean's `getConvertedAmount()` method to obtain the converted value as a correctly formatted `String` for the currency. Similarly, the bean's `getAmount()` method returns the original value as a correctly formatted string. The servlet adds the original and converted amounts to the request object as the `amount` and `convertedAmount` attributes. These attributes can be retrieved by the view JSP that builds the response to send back to the client (shown in Listing 20.7).

After successfully adding the attributes to the request object, the action controller forwards the request to the view component of the framework. The `ActionMapping.findForward()` method accepts the name of a page and forwards the request to this page. The page name must be defined in a `<forward>` mapping element in `struts-config.xml`, either in the `<action>` element for the controller, or in a `<global-forwards>` element as shown in Listing 20.6.

LISTING 20.6 Struts Configuration File `struts-config.xml`

```
<?xml version="1.0" encoding="ISO-8859-1" ?>
<!DOCTYPE struts-config PUBLIC
          "-//Apache Software Foundation//DTD Struts Configuration 1.0//EN"
          "http://jakarta.apache.org/struts/dtds/struts-config_1_0.dtd">
<struts-config>
  <form-beans>
    <form-bean name="convertForm"
               type="converters.ConvertForm"/>
  </form-beans>

  <global-forwards>
     <forward  name="home"      path="/index.jsp"/>
     <forward  name="convert"   path="/convert.jsp"/>
     <forward  name="rate"      path="/rate.jsp"/>
  </global-forwards>

  <action-mappings>
    <action    path="/convert"
               type="converters.ActionConvert"
               name="convertForm"
               scope="request"
               input="/convert.jsp"
               validate="true">
      <forward name="modelError" path="/modelError.jsp"/>
    </action>
    <action    path="/rate"
               forward="/rate.jsp" />
    <action    path="/home"
               forward="/index.jsp" />

  </action-mappings>
</struts-config>
```

CAUTION

Because the Action Servlet reads the `struts-config.xml` file once at startup, any changes to this file while Tomcat is running will not be detected. Use the Tomcat Manager Application (See Chapter 15, "Administering Tomcat in a Live Environment") to reload the application, or stop and restart Tomcat.

Listing 20.6 shows the complete `struts-config.xml` file for the Struts converter. The configuration includes a set of `<global-forwards>` that define `<forward>` mapping elements that apply to all `<action>` mappings. A `<forward>` element inside an `<action>` element (such as the `modelError` example) is specific to that one action. In this example, if the action controller detects an error from the supporting `ConverterBean` object, the request is forwarded to the `modelError` page instead of the data input form.

Once your action controller has updated the model data, it must forward the request to the view JSP.

Defining the View JSP

The final stage of the Struts converter is to create the view JSP that will display the results of the request. A view JSP should only display the results of the request; all request processing should be performed by the action form bean and action controller objects.

In the Struts converter, the view JSP is the same form as the one used to submit the data, but in many applications, a separate JSP is used to display the results of the request. A more complex action controller may support several different view pages and forward the request to a different page depending upon the nature of the request. For example, a request that queries a database may forward the results to one page if data rows were returned, and to another page of no data rows were returned.

The currency view form is shown in Listing 20.7.

LISTING 20.7 Currency Form `convert.jsp`

```
<%@ taglib uri="/WEB-INF/struts-bean.tld" prefix="bean" %>
<%@ taglib uri="/WEB-INF/struts-html.tld" prefix="html" %>
<%@ taglib uri="/WEB-INF/struts-logic.tld" prefix="logic" %>
<html:html locale="true">
  <HEAD>
    <TITLE>Currency Converter</TITLE>
  </HEAD>
```

LISTING 20.7 Continued

```
  <BODY>
    <H1>Currency Converter</H1>
    <html:form action="/convert.do">
      <P>Amount to convert: <html:text property="amount" /></P>
      <P><html:submit>Convert</html:submit></P>
    </html:form>
    <html:errors/>
    <logic:present name="convertedAmount">
      <H2>
        <bean:write name="amount"/> =
        <bean:write name="convertedAmount"/>
      </H2>
    </logic:present>
    <P><html:link page="/home.do">Return to home page</html:link></P>
  </BODY>
</html:html>
```

As you can see, the view form has been simplified by the removal of all the control and model functionality into the other components of the Struts framework.

Struts includes support for all of the HTML form tags in the `html` library. You should use these tags for all your forms as they provide the framework for supporting form field validation. The simple currency form (extracted from Listing 20.7) is shown here:

```
<html:form action="/convert.do">
  <P>Amount to convert: <html:text property="amount" /></P>
  <P><html:submit>Convert</html:submit></P>
</html:form>
```

The following points highlight the benefits of using the Struts HTML tags:

- The `action` attribute of the `<html:form>` tag is subject to URL rewriting to cater to clients that do not support cookies.
- The `<html:text>` field inserts an `<INPUT TYPE='TEXT'>` tag on the page setting the `<INPUT> NAME` attribute to the value of the `property` attribute. Furthermore, the `<INPUT> VALUE` attribute is set to the value of the named property obtained from an action form object if one is present. This mechanism allows faulty form data to be returned to the client for correction without the client having to reenter all the data.

- The `<html:submit>` tag represents an `<INPUT TYPE='SUBMIT'>` tag with the tag value (the text on the button) set to the body of the `<html:submit>` tag.

Other Struts tags support similar functionality for form-related tags in HTML as described in the Struts documentation.

On the Web page in Listing 20.7, the `<html:errors/>` tag retrieves the `ActionErrors` collection associated with the request and displays any messages in the collection. The resource bundle messages `errors.header` and `errors.footer` are added before and after any messages that are written to the page. If the `ActionErrors` collection is empty or does not exist, no information is written to the Web page. The `<html:errors>` tag can define the `property` attribute to restrict the display to those messages stored against a specific key (the first parameter to the `ActionError` constructor used to create the message).

The `<logic:present>` tag in Listing 20.7 is used to test whether an attribute has been defined in the page, request, session, or application scope of the JSP. The required attribute is specified by the `name` attribute of the tag, and the scope can optionally be defined in the `scope` attribute; by default all scopes are examined. The following snippet from Listing 20.7 determines whether the `convertedAmount` attribute is present in any of the JSP scopes:

```
<logic:present name="convertedAmount">
  <BIG>
    USD <bean:write name="amount"/> =
    GBP <bean:write name="convertedAmount"/>
  </BIG>
</logic:present>
```

The action controller adds the `convertedAmount` attribute to the request when a currency amount is successfully converted, and this `<logic:present>` tag is used to conditionally include the currency conversion results.

The Struts `<bean:write>` tag is used to write the string value of an attribute to the JSP. In the previous snippet, the two `<bean:write>` tags write the unconverted and converted currency amounts to the page.

Finally, Figure 20.2 shows the Struts-based currency conversion form displaying the results of a successful conversion operation (note that the value in the amount field on the form is populated from the previous invocation of this form).

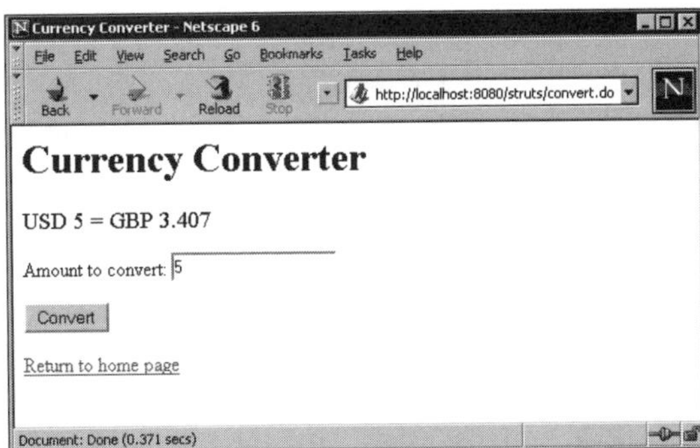

FIGURE 20.2 Struts-based currency converter form.

As you can see, Struts provides a good framework for developing your applications. The `html` TagLib and action form beans support your forms in a logical manner and allow rapid implementation of form-based applications. The separation of business logic into the custom action controller and presentation logic into the view JSP will improve the design and implementation of your application.

Other Struts Features

In addition to the basic MVC framework, Struts provides several tag libraries for supporting JSP development, as shown in Table 20.1.

TABLE 20.1 Struts TagLibs

TagLib	Notes
`bean`	Tags for creating and using scripting variables (beans) and page, request, session, and application-scoped attributes
`logic`	Tags for conditional inclusion, iterative loops, and request forwarding or redirection
`html`	Tags for supporting HTML elements such as form fields
`template`	Tags for defining pro-forma templates for Web pages to support using a consistent look and feel across multiple pages

Some of the Struts custom tags (principally those in the logic library) provide functionality that is now available in the JSP Standard Tag Library (JSTL) and the proposed Java Server Faces (JSF) specification. The Struts developers are committed to enhancing Struts to be compatible with JSTL and JSF, so expect to see changes to the TagLibs as the JSTL and JSF standards mature.

Summary

Frameworks provide a basis on which to build new Web applications. By providing some of the infrastructure for a Web application, using a good framework

- Reduces development time
- Promotes good design and development practices

One of the more popular frameworks is the Jakarta Struts project (`http://jakarta.apache.org/struts`), which implements an MVC architecture. Struts provides a main controller servlet; all you have to do is implement

- A controller object for each of your Web resources
- A form validation object for each form you define
- Supporting beans and Java classes to implement the data model
- View JSPs to display the results for each request

Struts includes a comprehensive suite of TagLibs that interoperate with the MVC framework to simplify the development of many common Web applications with features such as form validation and URL rewriting.

21 Testing with Jakarta Cactus

IN THIS CHAPTER

- Cactus Overview
- Cactus Architecture
- Cactus Test Life Cycle Methods
- Testing a Currency Converter Servlet
- Cactus Test Environment
- Running the Example Cactus Test

Testing is an important area of software development that is sadly often neglected. For Web applications, developers have had the added difficulty of not being able to easily unit test application components in isolation. With the development of the Jakarta Cactus testing framework, developers now have a mechanism for unit-testing their Web components. The Jakarta Cactus framework sets up the necessary environment with a Web server (such as Tomcat) for unit-testing servlets, JSPs, tag libraries, and filters.

The purpose of this chapter is to show you how to configure Cactus to run tests in a Tomcat server; it is not a commentary on the principles of testing. With this in mind, this chapter covers writing, configuring, and running Cactus tests.

Cactus Overview

Cactus is a framework for running Unit tests on server-side Web application components. It provides support for testing

- Servlets
- JSPs
- Tag libraries
- Filters

Cactus uses and extends the popular JUnit open source regression testing framework and uses the Jakarta log4j logging package. Further information on JUnit is available from `http://JUnit.org`; log4j is discussed in Chapter 13, "Logging Using Tomcat."

Cactus also provides custom Jakarta Ant tasks for automating the test process using Ant build scripts (more information on Ant is available from `http://jakarta.apache.org/ant`).

This chapter will concentrate on writing and running a simple test for a Currency Converter servlet. Full details of the other features of Cactus are available in the documentation provided with the Cactus download, or online at `http://jakarta.apache.org/cactus`.

Downloading Cactus

You can download the latest version of Cactus from `http://jakarta.apache.org/cactus`. Unpack the Cactus archive to create a direc-tory named after the version of Cactus you have downloaded (the examples use `jakarta-cactus-13-1.3`). Inside the `cactus` directory you will find the following subdirectories:

Directory	Description
`web`	Web resources (not class files) needed to use Cactus
`sample-servlet`	An example test suite for a servlet
`lib`	JAR files required for using Cactus
`doc`	Cactus documentation

To run tests, you will need to add the Cactus JAR files from the `lib` subdirectory to your `CLASSPATH`. You will also need to add these JAR files to the Web application you are testing as described in the "Cactus Test Environment" section.

Cactus Architecture

A Cactus test suite is a single Java class that defines a number of methods that comprise the tests to run. The tests are initiated from a client `TestRunner` program that manages the client side of the test. The `TestRunner` program issues an HTTP request to a Cactus redirector object on the server that undertakes the server-side testing. The results of the server-side tests are returned to the client, where they can be logged to a file or displayed in a GUI display client. Figure 21.1 shows a simple diagram of the Cactus Architecture.

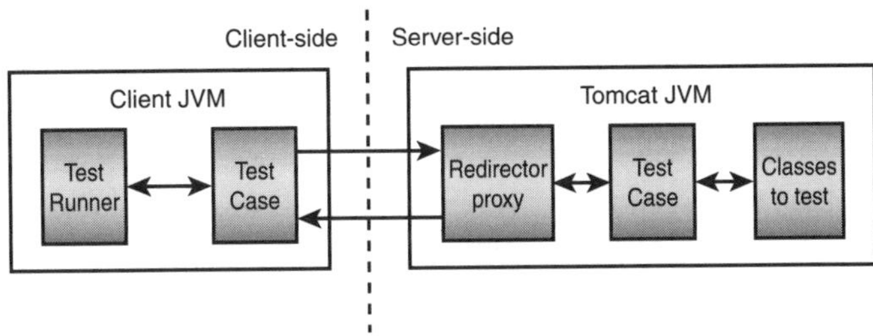

FIGURE 21.1 Cactus architecture.

In Figure 21.1, the server-side redirector acts as a proxy for your test case class. All HTTP requests generated by the test program are sent to the redirector servlet. This servlet then redirects the request to an instance of the Web component being tested. There is a redirector for each of the Web component types:

- Servlet Redirector—For testing servlets
- JSP Redirector—For testing JSPs and custom tag libraries
- Filter Redirector—For testing servlet filters

Each redirector proxy performs the following functions:

- Creates an instance of the test case class using Java Reflection.
- Sets specific implicit objects to create the environment for the test case (which objects are set up depends on the redirector being used).
- Creates instances of wrapper classes for server objects (such as `HttpServletRequest`, `ServletConfig`, and `ServletContext`). You can use these wrapper classes to override standard methods to set up appropriate values and conditions for the test case.
- Creates an HTTP session (unless this is explicitly switched off).

To write a Cactus test suite, you must define in the Java test class methods for each test to be performed. These methods follow a simple naming convention as described in the following section.

Cactus Test Life Cycle Methods

A Cactus test uses a single class to define both the client-side and server-side test methods; herein lies much of confusion (and initial difficulties) with Cactus. Two separate instances of the test class are created: one on the client and the other on the server. You must be clear in your own mind which methods run on the client and which run on the server, because these two distinct sets of methods cannot share instance variables defined in the class.

For each individual test in a Cactus test class, you must define a public method with a name starting with `test`—for example, `testXXX()`. This method undertakes the test on the server. The `testXXX()` method indicates a test failure by throwing an exception.

In addition to the `testXXX()` method, you can define the following client-side methods named after your test method:

- `beginXXX()`—Run on the client side before the test is performed and typically used to define HTTP request parameters.
- `endXXX()`—Run on the client side after the test has completed and normally used to test values in the HTTP response, such as cookies and header fields. The `endXXX()` method is not called if a test fails.

On the server side, the following two optional methods can be defined for configuring the server context for the test:

- `setUp()`—Initializes any server-side values required for the test and is often used to define initialization parameters or data source objects needed by the Web resource
- `tearDown()`—Releases any resources allocated in `setUp()`

If multiple `test*()` methods are defined in a single test class, the server-side `setUp()` and `tearDown()` methods are common to all tests. The client-side `begin*()` and `end*()` methods, on the other hand, are specific to each test.

Figure 21.2 shows a simplified UML sequence diagram of the sequence of method calls for running a single `testXXX()` case.

The same life cycle methods are used for testing servlets, JSPs, filters, and custom tags. To illustrate how to write a Cactus test suite, the following section shows a simple test for a currency converter servlet.

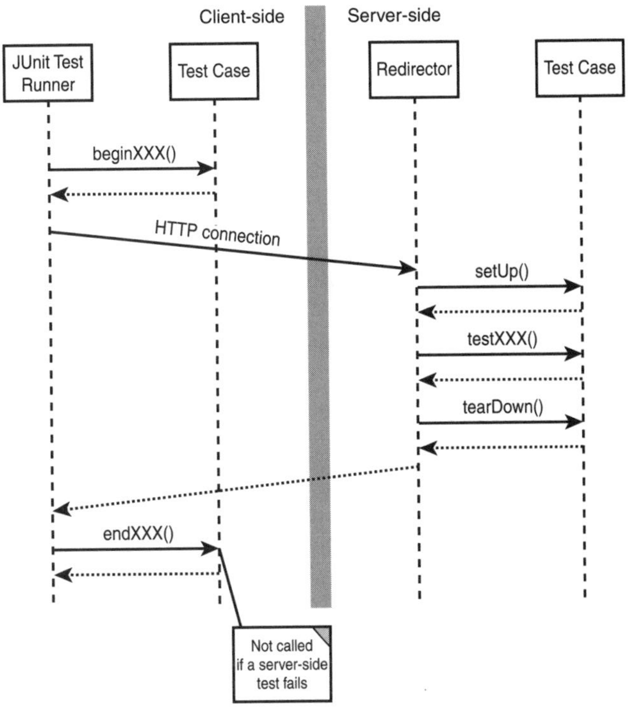

FIGURE 21.2 Simplified UML sequence diagram for the Cactus execution cycle.

Testing a Currency Converter Servlet

This section will test the Currency Converter servlet shown in Listing 21.1. This is a simple model-2 (see Chapter 17, "Architectures") servlet that performs the currency conversion before forwarding the request to a JSP for display.

LISTING 21.1 The Currency Converter Servlet `CurrencyConverter.java`

```
import java.io.*;
import java.util.*;
import java.text.*;
import javax.servlet.*;
import javax.servlet.http.*;

public class CurrencyConverter extends HttpServlet {

   private String format (Currency currency, double value) {
```

LISTING 21.1 Continued

```
        NumberFormat nf = NumberFormat.getInstance();
        nf.setMaximumFractionDigits(currency.getDefaultFractionDigits());
        nf.setMinimumFractionDigits(currency.getDefaultFractionDigits());
        return nf.format(value);
    }


    public void doGet(HttpServletRequest request, HttpServletResponse response)
                 throws ServletException, IOException {
    HttpSession session = request.getSession();
    if (session.getAttribute("rate")==null)
        session.setAttribute("rate","0.615");
    Currency dollars = Currency.getInstance(Locale.US);
    Currency pounds = Currency.getInstance(Locale.UK);
    try {
        double oldValue = Double.parseDouble(request.getParameter("amount"));
        if (oldValue <= 0) {
            request.setAttribute("error", "Value must be greater than zero");
        }
        else {
            double exchangeRate =
                Double.parseDouble((String)session.getAttribute("rate"));
            double newValue = oldValue * exchangeRate ;
            String result = dollars.getSymbol(Locale.US) +
            format(dollars, oldValue) + " = " +
            pounds.getSymbol(Locale.UK) + format(pounds, newValue);
            request.setAttribute("result", result);
        }
    }
    catch (NumberFormatException e) {
        request.setAttribute("error", "Invalid number format");
    }
        request.getRequestDispatcher("/currency-form.jsp")
            .forward(request, response);
    }
}
```

The servlet in Listing 21.1 retrieves the exchange rate from an HTTP session attribute called `rate` and uses it to convert the value of the `amount` request parameter. If the conversion is successful, the converted value is added as the `result` request attribute;

but if an error occurs, a request attribute called `error` is created. The request is forwarded to `currency-form.jsp` for displaying the results. The `result` and `error` request attributes are mutually exclusive.

The following simple tests will be defined for this servlet:

- `testValidAmount`—Checks the `result` request attribute for a valid conversion
- `testInvalidAmount`—Checks the `error` request attribute when a non-numeric amount is specified
- `testNegativeAmount`—Also checks the `error` request attribute when a negative amount is specified

The conversion rate used by the servlet will be defined in the `setUp()` method of the test, and each test will define the amount request parameter in the appropriate `begin*()` method.

Listing 21.2 shows the Cactus test class for this servlet.

LISTING 21.2 Currency Converter Cactus Test Class: `TestCurrencyServlet.java`

```
import org.apache.cactus.*;
import javax.servlet.http.*;

public class TestCurrencyServlet extends ServletTestCase {

    public TestCurrencyServlet (String theName) {
        super(theName);
    }

    public static void main(String[] theArgs) {
        junit.swingui.TestRunner.main(
            new String[] {TestCurrencyServlet.class.getName()}
        );
    }

    public static junit.framework.Test suite() {
        return new junit.framework.TestSuite(TestCurrencyServlet.class);
    }

    public void setUp() {
        HttpSession session = request.getSession();
        session.setAttribute("rate", "0.615");
    }
```

LISTING 21.2 Continued

```
    // *** Valid Amount ***

    public void beginValidAmount(WebRequest request) {
        request.addParameter("amount", "103.72");
    }

    public void testValidAmount() throws Exception {
        CurrencyConverter servlet = new CurrencyConverter();
        servlet.doGet(request, response);
        String result = (String) request.getAttribute("result");
        assertNotNull (result);
        String error = (String) request.getAttribute("error");
        assertNull (error);
    }

    // *** Invalid Amount ***

    public void beginInvalidAmount(WebRequest request) {
        request.addParameter("amount", "55c");
    }

    public void testInvalidAmount() throws Exception {
        CurrencyConverter servlet = new CurrencyConverter();
        servlet.doGet(request, response);
        String result = (String) request.getAttribute("result");
        assertNull (result);
        String error = (String) request.getAttribute("error");
        assertNotNull (error);
        assertEquals (error, "Invalid number format");
    }

    // *** Negative Amount ***

    public void beginNegativeAmount(WebRequest request) {
        request.addParameter("amount", "-3");
    }

    public void testNegativeAmount() throws Exception {
        CurrencyConverter servlet = new CurrencyConverter();
        servlet.doGet(request, response);
```

LISTING 21.2 Continued

```
        String result = (String) request.getAttribute("result");
        assertNull (result);
        String error = (String) request.getAttribute("error");
        assertNotNull (error);
        assertEquals (error, "Value must be greater than zero");
    }
}
```

A Cactus servlet test class must extend `org.apache.cactus.ServletTestCase` (as shown in Listing 21.2). A test case for a JSP would extend `org.apache.cactus.JspTestCase`, and a test case for a filter would extend `org.apache.cactus.FilterTestCase`.

The test case must also define the following methods to conform to the Cactus conventions for a test class:

- A constructor with a single `String` parameter that invokes the superclass constructor. The parameter is the test name.
- A `main()` method that starts a JUnit `TestRunner` program.
- A `suite()` method to return a `junit.framework.Test` list of tests to be executed in the test class. This list is obtained from all the `test*` method names in the test class passed as a parameter to a `junit.framework.TestSuite` constructor.

Defining these methods is a simple matter of copying the following boilerplate code:

```
public TestCurrencyServlet (String theName) {
    super(theName);
}

public static void main(String[] theArgs) {
    junit.swingui.TestRunner.main(
    new String[] {TestCurrencyServlet.class.getName()}
    );
}

public static junit.framework.Test suite() {
    return new junit.framework.TestSuite(TestCurrencyServlet.class);
}
```

The boilerplate main() method invokes the JUnit TestRunner class to create the client-side GUI interface. You use the TestRunner class to initiate the test suite.

On the client side, each begin*() method for a test accepts an org.apache.cactus.WebRequest object that represents the HTTP request that will be passed to the server. Similarly, an end*() method takes an org.apache.cactus.WebResponse parameter representing the HTTP response from the server.

CAUTION

Remember that the begin*() method runs on the client. You cannot therefore use begin*() to initialize an instance variable to be used in the actual test that runs on the server.

After calling the begin*() method for a test, the client TestRunner program will send the HTTP request to the Cactus redirector running under Tomcat. This redirector will use a separate instance of the test class to perform the server-side testing.

On the server, the HTTP redirector calls the setUp(), test*(), and tearDown() methods to perform each test. Instance variables in the ServletTestCase superclass provide access to the servlet container's HTTPServletRequest and HTTPServletResponse objects.

In Listing 21.2 the client-side begin*() methods are used to define the amount request parameter used for each test. No end*() methods are used in this example.

The server-side setUp() method in Listing 21.2 creates the session attribute rate containing an example exchange rate. The setUp() method is common to all the test*() methods. Each test*() method creates an instance of the CurrencyConverter servlet and calls the doGet() method passing in the request and response objects defined in the ServletTestCase superclass.

NOTE

If the test servlet defined additional servlet methods such as init(), destroy(), or doPost(), they should be called if required by the test class.

After the doGet() method returns, each test*() method checks whether the servlet has performed correctly by testing for the presence or absence of the result and error attributes in the request object.

Cactus test classes perform the actual testing using assert methods defined in the ServletTestCase superclass, which itself is a subclass of JUnit.framework.Assert. Table 21.1 lists the assert methods available to use in your test case (each method may have several signatures in addition to the basic form shown in the table).

TABLE 21.1 JUnit Assert Package Methods

Method	Description
`assertEquals(`*`expected`*`, `*`actual`*`)`	Uses == for primitives and `equals()` for objects to determine whether the expected value is the same as the actual value
`assertTrue(`*`condition`*`)`	Checks whether the condition is true
`assertFalse(`*`condition`*`)`	Checks whether the condition is false
`assertNull(`*`object`*`)`	Checks whether the object is null
`assertNotNull(`*`object`*`)`	Checks whether the object is not null
`assertSame(`*`expected`*`, `*`actual`*`)`	Checks whether the expected and the actual objects are the same physical object
`assertNotSame(`*`expected`*`, `*`actual`*`)`	Checks whether the expected and the actual objects are not the same physical object
`fail()`	Used to fail a test; can be used to mark code that should not be reached (for example, after something that should have thrown an exception)

If an assert method fails, it throws a `junit.framework.AssertionFailedError`, which is passed back to the client. If a test fails, the `end*()` method for that test is not called by the client-side framework.

The client-side `TestRunner` program runs the entire test suite and reports test passes or failures in its output window. If a test fails, you will be provided with a stack trace identifying the failure and the line of test code containing the assert method name that generated the failure.

It is possible to automate the testing process using Ant scripts. Cactus provides a custom Ant task that will deploy and run your test cases. A tutorial on the Cactus Web site (`http://jakarta.apache.org/cactus/`) describes how to configure and run this task.

To run a Cactus test manually, you will have to create the necessary environment for the client-side `TestRunner` program and the server-side HTTP redirector program as shown in the next section.

Cactus Test Environment

Because every Cactus test has a client-side and a server-side component, you have to configure environments for both the Cactus client program and the server redirector objects.

Before looking at these environments in detail, you will need to decide how to configure your overall test strategy. You have two choices:

- Include the Cactus tests within the existing Web application.
- Create one or more separate Web applications purely for testing.

The advantage of the first approach is that you can add the Cactus configuration to your Web application with very little extra work. The disadvantage is that the testing programs will be included in the final Web application. Including the test programs in the final application is not advisable for the following reasons:

- Test programs can provide security loopholes that can be exploited by hackers.
- Test programs may corrupt live data if they are inadvertently invoked.
- It will not be apparent which components are an essential part of the Web application and which are there for test purposes only.
- Test programs use up valuable server resources (such as memory for class files).

Unless you have a strong reason for not doing so, you should always use separate Web applications for the test environment. You can use automation tools such as Jakarta Ant (or even simple batch or shell scripts) to build the different test and live environments from a common set of source files.

The example test environment will create a new Web application. This application will include its own deployment descriptor, the Web resources being tested, and the Cactus JAR files.

Client-Side Environment

In order to compile and run the client-side Cactus test program, you will need to include the following JAR files from the *<CACTUS_HOME>*`/lib` directory on your `CLASSPATH`:

- `cactus.jar`
- `log4j-1.2rc1.jar`
- `commons-httpclient-20020421.jar`
- `httpunit.jar`
- `junit.jar`
- `aspectjrt.jar`

CAUTION

The client-side JUnit TestRunner program uses a custom class loader that will not load the Cactus JAR files if they are installed as Java extensions (in *<JAVA_HOME>*/jre/lib/ext). You must include the JAR files in the CLASSPATH.

Cactus requires the following configuration files on the client:

- cactus.properties—(mandatory) Used to define the Web server and application URL and the Cactus redirectors, and to enable client-side logging
- log_client.properties—(optional) Used to configure log4j logging in the client (see Chapter 13), but must be included if the cactus.enableLogging=true property is defined in cactus.properties

A sample cactus.properties file is provided with the Cactus distribution. Listing 21.4 shows this file set up for Tomcat running on port 8080 on the localhost with the server-side test deployed under the cactus context. If you are running on a different server or choose a different context for your Web application, you will need to amend this file accordingly.

LISTING 21.4 Client cactus.properties File

```
# Web app Context under which our application to test runs
cactus.contextURL = http://localhost:8080/cactus

# Default Servlet Redirector Name. Used by ServletTestCase test cases.
cactus.servletRedirectorName = ServletRedirector

# Default JSP Redirector Name. Used by JspTestCase test cases.
cactus.jspRedirectorName = JspRedirector

# Default Filter Redirector Name. Used by FilterTestCase test cases.
cactus.filterRedirectorName = FilterRedirector

# Enable Cactus internal logging
cactus.enableLogging = true
```

In Listing 21.4, the values of the redirector properties in the file must correspond to the <servlet-mapping> redirector names in the testing Web application web.xml file (shown in Listing 21.5).

As usual with Java properties files, the cactus.properties file must be in a directory on your client-side CLASSPATH.

TIP

If you decide to put different test cases in separate Web applications, you will require different versions of this file for different test cases. The easiest way of ensuring that Cactus picks up the correct `cactus.properties` file is to include the current directory in your `CLASSPATH` and have a copy of `cactus.properties` where you run the test client.

Finally, you must make sure the compiled Cactus test class can be run from your command-line JVM (in other words, make sure it's on the command-line `CLASSPATH`).

Server-Side Environment

To run the server-side Cactus test suite, Tomcat will require access to the Cactus JAR files listed at the start of the previous section, "Client-Side Environment." The Cactus JAR files can be included in the test Web application `WEB-INF/lib` directory or in `<CATALINA_HOME>/lib`.

If you are testing any JSP pages, you must also include the Cactus JSP Redirector in the Web application. The JSP redirector can be copied from the unpacked Cactus archive file `<CACTUS_HOME>/web/jspRedirector.jsp`. The servlet and filter redirector classes are included in the `cactus.jar` file.

Your test Web application requires a `web.xml` file that includes the Cactus redirector servlet definitions and mappings as shown in Listing 21.5.

LISTING 21.5 Template Cactus Deployment Descriptor: `web.xml`

```
<?xml version="1.0" encoding="ISO-8859-1"?>

<!DOCTYPE web-app
    PUBLIC "-//Sun Microsystems, Inc.//DTD Web Application 2.3//EN"
    "http://java.sun.com/j2ee/dtds/web-app_2_3.dtd">

<web-app>

    <filter>
        <filter-name>FilterRedirector</filter-name>
        <filter-class>
            org.apache.cactus.server.FilterTestRedirector
        </filter-class>
    </filter>

    <filter-mapping>
        <filter-name>FilterRedirector</filter-name>
```

LISTING 21.5 Continued

```
        <url-pattern>/filterRedirector.jsp</url-pattern>
    </filter-mapping>

    <servlet>
        <servlet-name>ServletRedirector</servlet-name>
        <servlet-class>
            org.apache.cactus.server.ServletTestRedirector
        </servlet-class>
    </servlet>

    <servlet>
        <servlet-name>JspRedirector</servlet-name>
        <jsp-file>/jspRedirector.jsp</jsp-file>
    </servlet>

    <servlet-mapping>
        <servlet-name>ServletRedirector</servlet-name>
        <url-pattern>/ServletRedirector</url-pattern>
    </servlet-mapping>

   <servlet-mapping>
        <servlet-name>JspRedirector</servlet-name>
        <url-pattern>/JspRedirector</url-pattern>
    </servlet-mapping>

</web-app>
```

You must add any additional deployment descriptor elements required by the application being tested to the basic Cactus `web.xml` file.

Cactus also uses the following optional server-side configuration files:

- `cactus.properties`—Used to enable server-side logging by defining the `cactus.enableLogging=true` property.
- `log_server.properties`—Used to configure log4j logging on the server (see Chapter 13).

If server-side logging is not required, the `cactus.properties` and `log_server.properties` files can be omitted.

NOTE

If you include the `log_server.properties` on the server side and use log4j logging in your application, messages will be logged to the Cactus log file instead of the application log file.

The server-side property files must be included in the Web application class path; it is common practice to add them to the `WEB-INF/classes` directory.

Running the Example Cactus Test

An instance of the `TestCurrencyServlet` class of Listing 21.2 is run both on the server and on the client. Therefore, to deploy and run this application (without any logging), the following files are needed on the client side:

- Cactus JAR files in the `CLASSPATH`
- `TestCurrencyServlet.class`
- `cactus.properties`

These files are needed on the server side:

- Cactus JAR files in `WEB-INF/lib`
- `web.xml`
- `TestCurrencyServlet.class`
- `CurrencyConverter.class`
- `currency-form.jsp` (the servlet being tested forwards the request to this JSP)

NOTE

The `currency-form.jsp` file is not listed because it simply displays the results of the request and is not relevant to the Cactus tests shown here. The JSP can be downloaded from the accompany Web site at `http://www.samspublishing.com` (search for the book's ISBN: 0672324393).

Running your tests is a simple matter of calling your test case class from a command line window. The following command line will invoke the `TestCurrencyServlet` test client:

```
java TestCurrencyServlet
```

The client-side test program will start, create the GUI display window, and then run the tests defined in the test class. Figure 21.3 shows the output for a successful run of the tests in Listing 21.2.

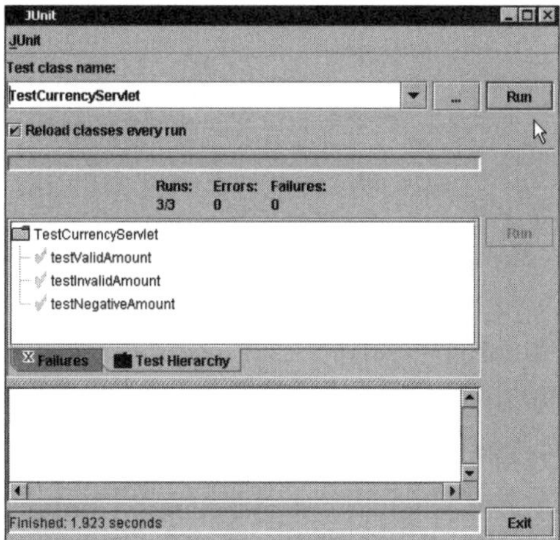

FIGURE 21.3 Cactus client test window.

You have now written and run a simple test for a servlet. Testing JSPs, filters, and tag libraries using Cactus follows a similar approach and is described in the Cactus documentation provided with the download archive under `<CACTUS_HOME>/doc/index.html`.

Summary

This chapter has skimmed the surface of testing servlets with Cactus. You have seen how to write a Cactus test for a servlet and how to set up the client- and server-side environment for running the test. If you want to take Cactus-testing farther, read the Cactus documentation for the following subjects:

- Testing filters, JSPs, and tag libraries
- Automating test scripts using the Cactus custom tasks for use with Jakarta Ant

Using Cactus will reduce the effort and lower the cost of writing tests for your server-side code.

22

Integrating Tomcat with a Web Server

IN THIS CHAPTER

- Obtaining the Web Server/Tomcat Plugin Software
- Integrating Tomcat with Apache
- Integrating with IIS
- Web Access Control and User Credentials
- Functional Separation Using Explicit URLs

Tomcat is a fully functional Web server; in many environments, running Tomcat to serve both static and dynamic Web applications will be perfectly acceptable. There are, however, good reasons for integrating Tomcat with a second Web server. You should consider using Tomcat alongside another Web server under the following circumstances:

- You are adding Tomcat to an existing Web server environment to serve dynamic content.
- You need to take advantage of specific features of another Web server—such as support for Active Server Pages, PHP, Perl scripts, VB scripts, or Server Side Includes (SSI).
- You want to simplify administration and security control by only exposing a single port (for example, just the default port 80) on the Web.
- You are looking to increase performance and scalability by having Tomcat serve the dynamic content and a second Web server serve static pages.

Tomcat was designed specifically to serve dynamic content in the form of servlets and JSPs; and in a live environment with a large amount of static Web pages and heavy usage, this is exactly what you should let it do. Embedding Tomcat into a second Web server, one that is efficient at serving static pages, will take the load off of Tomcat at the cost of some increased complexity with administration.

This chapter covers integrating Tomcat with two different Web servers: the popular Apache HTTP Web server from Apache Software Foundation and Microsoft's Internet

Information Services (IIS) Web server. Apache is a free-to-use commercial grade Web server that has undergone a long period of development and is very stable; because of this, it is used by many organizations. IIS comes with Windows NT, 2000, and XP and is therefore a common Web server in a predominantly Windows environment. Both Web servers can be upgraded to forward HTTP requests to Tomcat by installing a software plugin.

If you are not using either of these Web servers, you should check with either the documentation for your Web server or the Tomcat documentation to see whether your Web server can be integrated with Tomcat.

This chapter presumes you have Apache or IIS installed and running on your system, and you are comfortable with basic administration of your Web server.

Obtaining the Web Server/Tomcat Plugin Software

The following two sections show how to integrate Tomcat with Apache and IIS. Although the principles are the same for both Web servers, the details are necessarily different. In both cases you add a plugin to the Web server to redirect specific URLs to Tomcat, and you add a connector to Tomcat that listens on a specific port for the redirected requests.

Tomcat supports two connectors for integration with a Web server:

- The Webapp connector (previously known as the Warp connector)
- The Coyote JK2 connector (previously known as the AJP connector)

The Webapp connector has the advantage that it runs in its own service under Tomcat and can therefore be configured with its own loggers, realms, and virtual hosts. Running in its own service also means that if you only use Tomcat through another Web server you could, if you wanted, remove the Tomcat standalone service altogether (you might want to do this for security reasons).

NOTE

At the time of writing, there was no Webapp plugin for IIS, and the Webapp connector was found to be unreliable on Windows platforms when used with Apache. Until this is remedied you should use the Coyote JK2 connector when integrating Tomcat with a Web server on a Windows platform.

To enable redirection of requests from Apache or IIS, you will need to download a plugin component from the Tomcat Web site. The connector plugins are provided in binary form for the common platforms. If a binary does not exist for your platform, they are also available in source form for you to build the connector plugin for your particular platform.

Integrating Tomcat with Apache

In order for Tomcat to connect with Apache, you need to add a plugin to Apache that redirects requests through to Tomcat. This redirector or connector comes in the shape of a DLL for Windows platforms or a shared object module for Unix platforms. Tomcat supports both the Webapp connector and the Coyote JK2 connector for integration with Apache.

The following sections provide a systematic guide to configuring Apache to work with Tomcat, first using the Webapp connector followed by the Coyote JK2 connector.

Tomcat Apache Integration Using the Webapp Connector

To integrate Tomcat with Apache using the Webapp connector, you will need to perform the following steps, which are described in detail in the rest of this section:

1. Configure the Webapp connector as a service in Tomcat.
2. Download and install the Webapp connector plugin for Apache.
3. Add a Webapp connector configuration entry to the Apache `httpd.conf` file.
4. Configure Apache to forward requests to Tomcat.

Configure the Webapp Connector in Tomcat

In Tomcat, the Webapp connector is configured in its own service separate from the Tomcat standalone service. This has the advantage that you can create Tomcat virtual hosts (see Chapter 16, "Configuring Tomcat") to correspond to the Apache virtual hosts defined in Apache's `httpd.conf` file.

To add the Webapp connector to Tomcat, you will need to add an entry to Tomcat's `server.xml` file similar to one in Listing 22.1.

LISTING 22.1 Tomcat `server.xml` Configuration for Webapp Connector

```
<Service name="Tomcat-Apache">

    <Connector className="org.apache.catalina.connector.warp.WarpConnector"
     port="8008" minProcessors="5" maxProcessors="75"
     enableLookups="true" appBase="webapps"
     acceptCount="10" />
```

LISTING 22.1 Continued

```
    <Engine className="org.apache.catalina.connector.warp.WarpEngine"
            name="Apache" >

        <Logger className="org.apache.catalina.logger.FileLogger"
                prefix="apache_log." suffix=".txt"
                timestamp="true"/>

        <!--Because this Realm is here, an instance will be shared globally-->
        <Realm className="org.apache.catalina.realm.MemoryRealm" />
    </Engine>
</Service>
```

Listing 22.1 configures the connector (`org.apache.catalina.connector.warp.WarpConnector`) to listen on port 8008 (this must be the same as the port defined in the `WebAppConnection` directive in Apache's `httpd.conf` file).

Depending on the version of Tomcat you use, you may also be able to add the Webapp connector using the Tomcat Web Server Administration Tool. You will need to give the connector a name, define its port number, and specify the Engine as `org.apache.catalina.connector.warp.WarpEngine`.

Download and Install the Webapp Connector Plugin for Apache

Download the following files from the Tomcat Web site (`jakarta.apache.org/tomcat`). Choose the binary download appropriate for your platform or build the plugin from the source code:

- `mod_webapp.so`
- `libapr.dll` (required for Windows only)

For Windows platforms, copy `mod_webapp.so` and `libapr.dll` to the `%`*APACHE_HOME*`%\modules` directory. For Unix platforms, copy `mod_webapp.so` to the `$`*APACHE_HOME*`/libexec` directory.

NOTE

APACHE_HOME refers to the directory where Apache is installed.

Configure the Webapp Connector in Apache

Edit the Apache configuration file (<*APACHE_HOME*>`/conf/httpd.conf`). Find the section titled "Dynamic Shared Object (DSO) Support," and at the end of the

`LoadModule` directives, add the `mod_webapp.so` module. Because the plugin is stored in a different directory under Unix and Windows, the directive needs also to be different to reflect this. For Windows, add

```
LoadModule webapp_module modules/mod_webapp.so
```

For Unix, add

```
LoadModule webapp_module libexec/mod_webapp.so
```

For both platforms, find the end of the `AddModule` directives (in the following configuration section of the `httpd.conf` file) and add the following entry:

```
AddModule mod_webapp.c
```

TIP

At this point you should save the `httpd.conf` file and use the Apache Test Configuration utility to check that you have added the directives correctly and that Apache can find the new module.

Configure Apache to Forward Requests to Tomcat

You tell Apache to configure the Webapp connector and forward requests to Tomcat using `WebApp` directives added to the end of Apache's `httpd.conf` file. First, inform Apache to use the Webapp connector with a `WebAppConnection` directive with the following syntax:

```
WebAppConnection [name] [protocol] [host:port]
```

Where

- *`name`* is a name for connection between Tomcat and Apache, the name must be unique for this instance of Apache.
- *`protocol`* is the protocol used to provide the connection and must be set to `WARP` for the Webapp connector.
- *`host:port`* is where to send the requests—the port must match the port configured for the Webapp connector in Tomcat's `server.xml` file (discussed later).

For example, use the following to connect to Tomcat on port 8008 on the `localhost` using the WARP protocol:

```
WebAppConnection TomcatWarpConnector warp localhost:8008
```

You tell Apache which requests to forward to Tomcat using WebAppDeploy directives. The following example entries will forward requests for the examples and tomcat-docs applications:

```
WebAppDeploy examples TomcatWarpConnector /examples
WebAppDeploy tomcat-docs TomcatWarpConnector /tomcat-docs
```

Assuming Apache is running on localhost on the default Web server port (80), you will be able to access these applications using the following URLs (after completing the configuration):

```
http://localhost/examples
http://localhost/tomcat-docs
```

To bring all this together, Listing 22.2 shows all the additions made to Apache's httpd.conf file to configure the Webapp connector on a Windows platform (... indicates existing text that is not affected). You will see that in Listing 22.2 the WebApp directives are inside a <IfModule> element, which ensures they are only executed if the mod_webapp module is loaded.

LISTING 22.2 Additions to the Apache httpd.conf File to Connect to Tomcat Using the Webapp Connector

```
...
# Dynamic Shared Object (DSO) Support
...
LoadModule webapp_module modules/mod_webapp.so
....
AddModule mod_webapp.c
...
<IfModule mod_webapp.c>
WebAppConnection TomcatWarpConnector warp localhost:8008
WebAppInfo   /webapp-info
WebAppDeploy examples TomcatWarpConnector /examples
WebAppDeploy tomcat-docs TomcatWarpConnector /tomcat-docs
</IfModule>
```

TIP

If you insert the WebApp directives inside a <VirtualHost> element, the Tomcat Web application will only be deployed for that virtual host.

A useful feature when using the Webapp connector is a utility that allows you to call up a Web page to display the status of all configured Webapp connections and deployed applications. You enable this utility with the `WebAppInfo` directive in the `httpd.conf` file, as shown in Listing 22.2 and again here:

```
WebAppInfo /webapp-info
```

After restarting Apache, if you type the URL `http://localhost/webapp-info/` into your browser, it will bring up a page similar to the one shown in Figure 22.1.

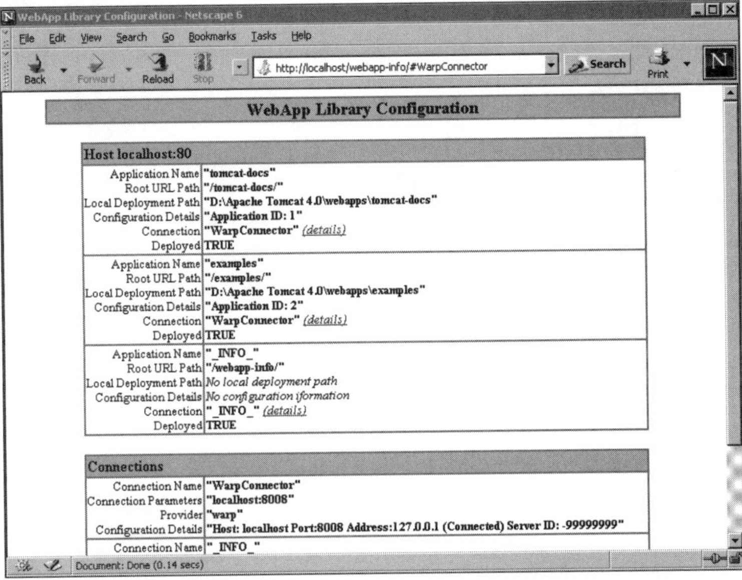

FIGURE 22.1 Output from `webapp-info` showing information about Tomcat applications and the Webapp connector.

To complete the configuration, you will first need to stop and restart Tomcat, and then stop and restart Apache.

CAUTION

You must start up Tomcat before Apache. If you do not, Apache will fail to create the Webapp connection. If you automate the startup of Apache and Tomcat in your system's startup scripts, you must also ensure Tomcat starts before Apache.

To test the connection, you can type the following URL into your browser. This will access the Tomcat documentation through Apache (this presumes you have Apache running on port 80):

```
http://localhost/tomcat-docs/
```

You should now see the `tomcat-docs` index page as shown in Figure 22.2. You can similarly test out the `examples` application.

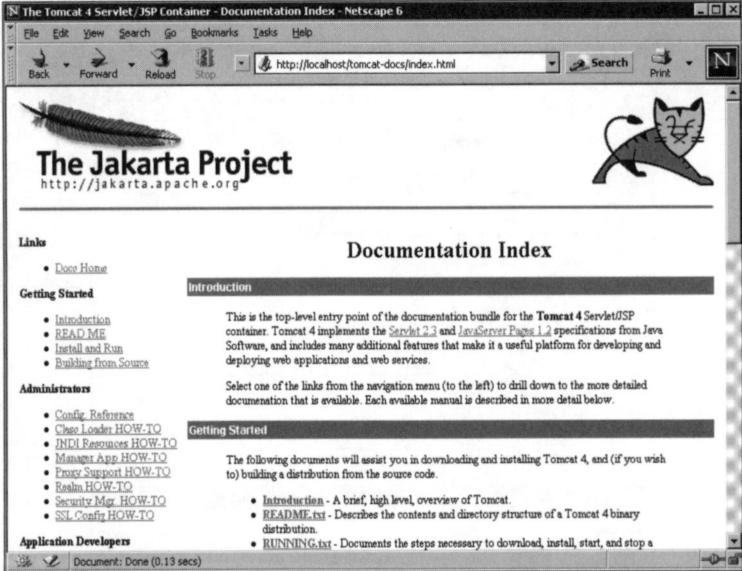

FIGURE 22.2 Tomcat application accessed through Apache.

To add your own Web applications, simply add the relevant `WebAppDeploy` directives to the Apache `httpd.conf` file mapping an Apache URL onto a Tomcat context. You will need to restart Apache after adding new `WebAppDeploy` directives.

Using the Coyote JK2 Connector to Connect Tomcat to Apache

The Coyote JK2 connector uses AJP (Apache JServ Protocol) (also used by the older `jserv` module used to add Java servlet support to Apache). To integrate Tomcat and Apache using the Coyote JK2 connector requires the following steps, described in detail in the rest of this section:

1. Configure the Coyote JK2 connector in Tomcat.
2. Download and install the Coyote JK2 connector plugin for Apache.

3. Add Coyote JK2 connector configuration to the Apache `httpd.conf` file.
4. Configure Apache to forward requests to Tomcat.

Configure the Tomcat Coyote JK2 Connector

To configure the Coyote JK2 connector, you must add a connector to the Tomcat-Standalone service in Tomcat's `server.xml` file. The following entry will configure a Coyote JK2 connector to listen on port 8009 (if this port is already in use you may use any other free port):

```
<Connector className="org.apache.coyote.tomcat4.CoyoteConnector"
           port="8009" minProcessors="5" maxProcessors="75"
           protocolHandlerClassName="org.apache.jk.server.JkCoyoteHandler"
           acceptCount="10" />
```

NOTE

The Coyote JK2 connector is new in Tomcat 4.1: It supports both AJP version 1.3 and AJP version 1.4. For Tomcat 4.0, use the following `Ajp13Connector`, which only supports AJP 1.3.

```
<Connector className="org.apache.ajp.tomcat4.Ajp13Connector"
           port="8009" minProcessors="5" maxProcessors="75"
           acceptCount="10" />
```

Download and Install the Coyote JK2 Connector Plugin for Apache

Download the appropriate `mod_jk` plugin file from the Tomcat Web site. Choose the binary download appropriate for your platform:

- `mod_jk.dll`—for Windows
- `mod_jk.so`—for Unix

For Windows platforms, copy `mod_jk.dll` to the *%APACHE_HOME%*`\modules` directory and, for Unix platforms, copy `mod_jk.so` to the *$APACHE_HOME*`/libexec` directory.

Configure the Coyote JK2 Connector in Apache

Edit the Apache configuration file (*<APACHE_HOME>*`/conf/httpd.conf`) and find the section headed "Dynamic Shared Object (DSO) Support." At the end of the `LoadModule` directives, add an entry for the `mod_jk.so` module. Because the plugin is stored in a different directory under Unix and Windows, the directive on each of these platforms needs also to be different to reflect this.

For Windows, add

```
LoadModule webapp_module modules/mod_jk.dll
```

For Unix, add

```
LoadModule webapp_module libexec/mod_jk.so
```

For both platforms find the end of the `AddModule` directives and add

```
AddModule mod_jk.c
```

> **TIP**
>
> At this point, you should use the Apache Test Configuration utility to check that you have added the directives correctly and that Apache can find the new module.

Configure Apache to Forward Requests to Tomcat

The Coyote JK2 connector uses the notion of a worker process to service requests (a worker is defined as a process instance that is waiting to execute servlet requests on behalf of some other Web server). You define workers in a `workers.properties` file.

An example `workers.properties` file that defines a Tomcat JK2 worker that is listening on port 8009 and uses the AJP version 1.4 protocol is shown in Listing 22.3.

> **NOTE**
>
> For Tomcat 4.0, a `workers.properties` file for AJP 1.3 is shown in Listing 22.4 in the "Integrating with IIS" section.

LISTING 22.3 JK2 Connector `workers.properties` File

```
workers.tomcat_home=" C:\Tomcat4.1"

workers.java_home=D:\j2sdk1.4.0

worker.list=jk2

worker.jk2.port=8009
worker.jk2.host=localhost
worker.jk2.secretkey=secret
worker.jk2.type=ajp14
```

You tell Apache where to find this `workers.properties` file with a `JkWorkersFile` directive in Apache's `httpf.conf` file. You must supply the full pathname of the location of the `worker.properties` file. For example:

```
JkWorkersFile "C:\Tomcat4.1\conf\ApacheJK2\workers.properties"
```

After adding this entry, you can define the Web applications to forward to Tomcat in subsequent `JkMount` directives. The `JkMount` directive has the following syntax:

```
JkMount [web app]/* [worker]
```

To add the Tomcat `examples` and `tomcat-docs` Web applications to Apache, you would use the following:

```
JkMount /examples/* jk2
JkMount /tomcat-docs/* jk2
```

Two further Apache directives, `JkLogFile` and `JkLogLevel`, allow you to define the location of a log file for the JK2 connection and a logging level.

Listing 22.4 shows all the additions made to Apache's `httpd.conf` file to configure the Coyote JK2 connector on a Windows platform (`...` represents existing text in the file that has not been modified). You will see that in Listing 22.4 the `Jk` directives are inside a `<IfModule>` element, which ensures that they are executed only if the `mod_jk` module is loaded.

LISTING 22.4 Additions to the Apache `httpd.conf` File to Connect to Tomcat Using the Coyote JK2 Connector

```
...
# Dynamic Shared Object (DSO) Support
...
LoadModule webapp_module modules/ mod_jk.dll
....
AddModule mod_jk.c
...
<IfModule mod_jk.c>
JkWorkersFile "C:\Tomcat4.1\conf\ApacheJK2\workers.properties"
JkMount /examples/* jk2
JkMount /tomcat-docs/* jk2
JkLogFile " C:\Tomcat4.1\logs\mod_jk.log"
JkLogLevel info
</IfModule>
```

To complete the configuration, you will need to stop and restart Tomcat and Apache.

To test whether the integration has been successful, type the following URL into your browser. This URL accesses the Tomcat documentation through Apache (this presumes you have Apache running on port 80):

```
http://localhost/tomcat-docs/
```

You will now see the `tomcat-docs` index page as shown previously in Figure 22.2.

Integrating with IIS

To integrate Tomcat with Microsoft's IIS, you will configure Tomcat to use the Coyote JK2 connector as described in the following steps (and explained in detail in the rest of this section):

1. Configure the Coyote JK2 connector in Tomcat.
2. Download and install the `isapi_Redirect.dll` plugin for IIS.

Configure the Tomcat Coyote JK2 Connector

To configure the Coyote JK2 connector, you need to add a connector to the Tomcat-Standalone service in Tomcat's `server.xml` file. The following entry will configure a Coyote JK2 connector to listen on port 8009 (if this port is already in use you may use any other free port):

```
<Connector className="org.apache.coyote.tomcat4.CoyoteConnector"
           port="8009" minProcessors="5" maxProcessors="75"
           protocolHandlerClassName="org.apache.jk.server.JkCoyoteHandler"
           acceptCount="10" />
```

NOTE

The Coyote JK2 connector is new in Tomcat 4.1. For Tomcat 4.0 use the following `Ajp13Connector` instead:

```
<Connector className="org.apache.ajp.tomcat4.Ajp13Connector"
           port="8009" minProcessors="5" maxProcessors="75"
           acceptCount="10" />
```

Download the Redirector Plugin for IIS

Tomcat integration with IIS is achieved by adding a filter plugin for IIS that redirects selected IIS requests to Tomcat.

The Tomcat redirector for IIS is made up of the following four files:

- `isapi_redirect.dll`—The IIS server plugin
- `worker.properties`—A configuration file that defines the hosts and ports used by Tomcat
- `uriworkermap.properties`—Maps URL-Path patterns to Tomcat worker processes
- `iis_redirect.reg`—A file that is used to create registry entries in the Windows registry

First, download the `isapi_redirect.dll` from the Tomcat Web site and store it in a local file. You can choose any location for the file, but for security reasons, it is advisable to store the redirector in a directory of its own.

NOTE

For the following example, the `isapi_redirect.dll` has been stored in `%CATALINA_HOME%\bin\IIS` where `%CATALINA_HOME%` is `C:\Tomcat4.1`.

After downloading the redirector DLL, create a `worker.properties` to configure the connector details.

An example `workers.properties` file that defines a `worker` that is listening on port 8009 using the AJP version 1.3 protocol is provided in Listing 22.5.

NOTE

You should use this configuration under Tomcat 4.0 or Tomcat 4.1. Tomcat 4.1 also supports AJP 1.4; a `workers.properties` file for AJP 1.4 is shown in Listing 22.3).

LISTING 22.5 JK2 Connector `workers.properties` File for AJP 1.3

```
workers.tomcat_home="C:\Tomcat4.1"

workers.java_home=D:\j2sdk1.4.0

worker.list=ajp

worker.ajp.port=8009
worker.ajp.host=localhost
worker.ajp.type=ajp13
```

After configuring the `workers.properties` file, you create a `uriworkermap.properties` file to define which URLs should be redirected to Tomcat. The following `uriworkermap.properties` file has redirections for both the `examples` and `tomcat-docs` Web applications:

```
default.worker=ajp13
#
# Sites to be redirected to Tomcat
/examples=$(default.worker)
/examples/*=$(default.worker)
/tomcat-docs=$(default.worker)
/tomcat-docs/*=$(default.worker)
```

NOTE

If you are using AJP 1.4 and the `workers.properties` file from Listing 22.3, you should replace the `default.worker` with the following:

```
default.worker=jk2
```

You will be able to access the Tomcat examples and documentation using the following URLs (assuming IIS is running on the default HTTP port on `localhost`):

```
http://localhost/examples
http://localhost/tomcat-docs
```

Configure IIS to Use the Tomcat Redirector

Now, to configure IIS itself, you first perform the following steps to configure IIS to use the AJP connector:

1. Start the Internet Information Services Manager.

NOTE

The IIS manager can be started by selecting the Internet Services Manager item on the Administrative Tools menu accessed via the Windows start menu; or right-click the My Computer icon on the desktop, select Manage, open Services and Applications in the left panel, and click Internet Information Services.

2. Right-click the Default Web Site and, from the menu, select New and Virtual Directory. This will bring up a Virtual Directory Creation Wizard. Click Next.

3. Give the Virtual Directory an alias name. You may choose any name you want, as you define this name in the Windows registry (`tomcat` has been used here; see Listing 22.5). Click Next.
4. On the following screen, enter the directory where the `isapi_redirect.dll` is located. Click Next.
5. On the next Access Permissions page, set Read and Execute permissions. Click Next.
6. Click Finish.

Second, add the redirector filter to the Default Web Site using the following steps:

1. Right-click the IIS Manager Default Web Site and select Properties.
2. Click the ISAPI Filters tab.
3. Click Add. Give the filter a name (such as `Tomcat Redirector`) and point the Executable to the `isapi_redirect.dll` file. Click OK.

   The filter will appear in the filters box (the status field will be blank at this time). Click OK.

Finally, add Windows registry entries to define the location of the `workers.properties`, `uriworkermap.properties`, log files, and the virtual directory created in IIS. The easy way to add the required Windows registry entries is to copy Listing 22.5 into a file with `.reg` extension, and change the entries as appropriate for your system. Double-clicking the `.reg` file in Windows Explorer will add the definitions to the registry.

LISTING 22.5 Windows Registry Entries for Tomcat

```
REGEDIT4

[HKEY_LOCAL_MACHINE\SOFTWARE\Apache Software Foundation\Jakarta Isapi
➥ Redirector\1.0]
"extension_uri"="/tomcat/isapi_redirect.dll"
"log_file"="C:\\Tomcat4.1\\logs\\iis_redirect.log"
"log_level"="emerg"
"worker_file"="C:\\Tomcat4.1\\conf\\iis
➥ \\workers.properties"
"worker_mount_file"="C:\\Tomcat4.1\\conf\\iis
➥ \\uriworkermap.properties"
```

After the registry entries have been added, you must restart IIS to enable the ISAPI redirector. You can check that the ISAPI redirector filter has been correctly registered by selecting the Default Web Site properties page, where the ISAPI redirector should have a green arrow in the status field.

TIP

If the filter has a red arrow, make sure that the file location is correct.

Ensure that Tomcat is running and test the integration by typing the following URL into your browser to access the Tomcat documentation through IIS:

```
http://localhost/tomcat-docs/
```

You will now see the `tomcat-docs` Web application welcome page as previously shown in Figure 22.2. You can now add additional Web application redirections to the `uri_workermap.properties` file. You will have to restart IIS for changes to this file to be recognized.

Web Access Control and User Credentials

At present, Tomcat cannot share the user authorization credentials of either Apache or IIS. This imposes restrictions on how you control access to your static pages and dynamic Web resources.

If you configure Apache or IIS to require the user to log in to access your Tomcat Web applications, Tomcat will not be aware that the user has logged in. Specifically, the `javax.servlet.http.HttpServlet` methods for accessing user credentials (`getRemoteUser()`, `getUserPrincipal()`, and `isUserInRole()`) will return null or false accordingly. This means you must use Tomcat's authentication mechanism if your application requires access to the end user's principal name or roles.

If you use Tomcat's authentication mechanism, you should ensure that the user does not need to log in to Apache or IIS prior to accessing the Tomcat Web applications; otherwise, the user will have to log in twice.

TIP

If you need to protect access to both static pages and dynamic Web resources, you should put the protected static pages inside a Tomcat application. By doing this you will use the single authentication mechanism provided by Tomcat for all protected resources.

Functional Separation Using Explicit URLs

If Tomcat and your Web server cannot be integrated, not all is lost. A simple solution can be achieved using explicit URL host and port names in your hyperlinks.

One approach to running Tomcat in conjunction with a Web server is to run the static Web server on one host and the Tomcat dynamic Web server on a separate host. For example:

```
<A href='http://www.host.com/static-pages/index.html'>Static Pages</A>
<A href='http://dynamic.host.com/dynamic-webapp/hompage.jsp'>Dynamic Content</A>
```

Alternatively, you can run the two Web servers on the same system provided each server connects to a different port number.

It is possible to direct Web requests to either server simply by specifying the appropriate `hostname:port` in the URL. For example, if the following links were included in a Web page, the first link would route the request to Tomcat on its default 8080 port, whereas the second would send the request to the default Web server on port 80:

```
<A href='http://www.host.com:8080/dynamic-webapp/hompage.jsp'>Dynamic Content</A>
<A href='http://www.host.com/static-pages/index.html'>Static Pages</A>
```

This simple approach has the advantage that no configuration is required to make this work in either Tomcat or the default Web server. It has, however, some major disadvantages:

- It exposes your site architecture to external clients.
- Developers need to hard-code hostnames and port numbers in URLs making it difficult to change the architecture.
- There is no possibility of information sharing between the two Web servers.

For these reasons, using the URL to redirect requests to different Web servers should only be used when Tomcat cannot be integrated with your Web server.

Summary

This chapter has covered the steps required to integrate Tomcat with the two popular Web servers Apache and IIS. In both cases you need to download and install a connector plugin for the Web server and configure the Web server to redirect specific URL patterns to Tomcat.

Tomcat uses two forms of connector to integrate with Apache and IIS—the Webapp and the Coyote JK2 connector. The Coyote JK2 connector supports the AJP protocol, whereas the Webapp connector uses the WARP protocol. There are advantages in using the Webapp connector, but at present, it is not recommended for use on Windows platforms.

You have also seen how to provide functional separation using explicit URLs to direct clients to either Tomcat or another Web server. You should use this method only where integrating Tomcat is impractical.

23

Securing Web Applications Under Tomcat

IN THIS CHAPTER

- SSL Overview
- Configuring SSL with Tomcat
- Enabling Secure Login
- Protecting Secure Web Resources with a Filter
- Using a Security Manager

Chapter 14, "Access Control," introduced the concept of protecting Web resources so that only authorized users can gain access to them. This chapter looks at the closely related security topic of enabling features that ensure data integrity and confidentiality. This chapter also discusses how to protect the Tomcat server from errors within its own Web applications by using a security manager.

Ensuring the confidentiality of data in a Web application entails using a Secure Socket Layer (SSL) for transferring data between the client and the server. Web resources accessed using an SSL connection use HTTPS (URL protocol `https:`) rather than HTTP (protocol `http:`). In this chapter, you will be shown how to use secure user login and SSL to improve the security of your Tomcat Web applications.

SSL Overview

SSL is a TCP/IP socket connection that uses Public Key Encryption (PKE) to secure the exchange of data between two hosts. PKE uses digital certificates to publish a public encryption key that is used to encrypt and decrypt data, allowing the secure transfer of data between two hosts.

SSL is an open standard that was originally developed by Netscape. More details on the SSL specification can be found at `http://wp.netscape.com/security/techbriefs/ssl.html`.

Although you do not need to know the details of PKE and digital certificates to use SSL, the following discussion of these technologies will help you follow the steps required to configure SSL in Tomcat.

Public Key Encryption

PKE is based on complex numerical algorithms that generate two message keys for encrypting and decrypting data. Data encrypted using one key can only be decrypted using the other key. One key is made publicly available (the public key), whereas the other is kept private to the key holder (the private key). The keys used in PKE are normally very large numbers: Modern systems use numbers of 1024 bits (approximately 140 decimal digits). Several public key algorithms are in use, with RSA being the most popular.

With PKE, a message encrypted with a public key can only be decrypted by the holder of the associated private key. Any client can encrypt data for a server using the server's public key with the assurance that only the server will be able to decrypt the data. Using public keys to encrypt messages ensures data confidentiality.

Conversely, a message encrypted with a private key can be decrypted and read by any recipient by using the associated public key. The recipient is assured of the origin of the data because only the private key holder could have encrypted the original message. Using private keys to encrypt a message is the basis of digital contracts where the sender must not be able to repudiate their actions.

The drawback to using PKE is the computational cost of encrypting and decrypting the messages. Simpler symmetric encryption techniques that use a single key to both encrypt and decrypt the data (such as DES) are significantly faster in operation. Consequently, a common use of PKE is to allow two parties to exchange a symmetric encryption key in a secure manner prior to using that symmetric key to encrypt messages.

How SSL Uses PKE

SSL uses PKE to exchange a symmetric encryption key to be used for the duration of the session between Web client and Web server. The exact steps are as follows:

1. A client contacts your server requesting a secure connection.
2. Your server sends its digital certificate to the client.
3. The client generates a unique session key to encrypt all communications between client and server.
4. The client encrypts the session key with your server's public key and sends the key to the server.

5. Your server decodes the session key using its private key.
6. Subsequent data exchanged between the client and server is encrypted using the session key.

Digital Certificates

Public keys are published using digital certificates meeting the X509 international standard. X509 defines a format for representing public keys and other information about an entity (it could be a user, a program, a company, or anything that has a public key). More information on X509 can be found on the International Telecommunications Union (ITU) Web site at `http://www.itu.int/`.

Digital certificates must be signed by a Certification Authority (CA) to prove their validity. The most widely known CAs are

- VeriSign Inc. (`http://www.verisign.com`)
- TrustCenter (`http://www.trustcenter.de`)
- Thawte Consulting (`http://www.thawte.com`)

A signed digital certificate contains a message digest of the certificate encrypted using the CA's private key. Any recipient of the certificate can decrypt the digest using the CA's public key and verify that the rest of the certificate has not been corrupted or modified. Therefore, the client can trust the public key in the certificate as being the public key of the owner of the certificate. However, the client must trust the CA to have authenticated the owner of the certificate in the first place. Ultimately, the security of digital certificates depends on trusting the CA issuing the certificate.

Configuring SSL with Tomcat

Configuring Tomcat to use SSL is usually only necessary when running Tomcat as a standalone Web server. When running Tomcat behind another Web server such as Apache or Microsoft IIS (see Chapter 22, "Integrating Tomcat with a Web Server"), you would normally configure the SSL security in the main Web server. In this case, Tomcat is still aware that communication takes place over a secure connection, but it does not participate in the SSL encryption or decryption.

To configure Tomcat to use SSL, you will have to do the following:

1. Obtain a digital certificate from a CA, or create a self-certified digital certificate for your server.
2. Enable Tomcat's SSL Connector.

Managing digital certificates can be problematic because you have to keep a record of which digital certificate belongs to which third party. To make life easier, you can use simple utilities to keep the digital certificates in a database known as a key store.

Sun Microsystems' Java Runtime Edition (JRE) includes a `keytool` utility that will store digital certificates in a password-protected key store. Each certificate is stored against an alias (or key) that you can use to retrieve the certificate.

NOTE

If you are using JRE 1.3 or earlier, you will have to download and install the Java Security Extensions (JSSE) package from `http://java.sun.com/products/jsse` to obtain the security classes needed to support SSL. If you are using JRE 1.4, the JSSE classes are included in the JRE.

The following subsections discuss how to add certificates to a key store end enable the Tomcat SSL connector.

Creating a Self-Certified Digital Certificate

If you already have a digital certificate for your server, you should follow the instructions in the "Installing a Digital Certificate from a Certification Authority" section.

If you do not have a digital certificate for your server, you can use the JRE `keytool` utility to create one for development and testing purposes. This form of certificate is called a *self-certified certificate*, because it has not been verified by a CA. Most browsers will warn the end user if they receive a certificate that has not been verified by a trusted CA. On a live Tomcat server, you must obtain a verified digital certificate from a CA.

NOTE

If you want a verified digital certificate for a live Tomcat server, you will have to submit a request to a suitable CA (see the list in the section titled "SSL Overview"). The Web site for your chosen CA will describe how to apply for a certificate, what information you need to supply, and what fees will be charged. The CA will require additional information that will allow it to satisfy itself that you are who you say you are, and you are not trying to obtain a false certificate in order to compromise security for another person or company.

Tomcat requires the digital certificate to be stored in a key store database against the `tomcat` alias. The following `keytool` command will generate a self-certified digital certificate based on the RSA algorithm (the public key algorithm used by SSL) and store it against the `tomcat` alias in the `.keystore` database in Tomcat's home directory (if the key store does not exist, a new file will be created):

```
> keytool -genkey -alias tomcat -keyalg RSA -keystore <CATALINA_HOME>/.keystore
```

When you enter this `keytool` command, you will be prompted for a password for the key store database. You must enter a password to protect access to the database. Tomcat uses the default password `changeit`, but you are advised to select another password to protect your key store from other users. If you choose another password, you will have to specify the password in the SSL `<Connector>` entry in Tomcat's `server.xml` file (see the section "Enabling the Tomcat SSL Connector").

After entering the password for the database you will be prompted for the X500 fields for the digital certificate. When prompted with "What is your first and last name?" you should enter the name of the host running Tomcat (`localhost` if you are a developer running Tomcat on your workstation). The other fields on the certificate can contain any information you want to provide.

NOTE

If you don't set the name on the certificate to be the same as the Tomcat server hostname, the Web browser receiving the certificate will issue a warning to the end user indicating there is a mismatch between the server name and the certificate name.

Finally you will be prompted for a password for accessing the digital certificate within the key store. The certificate password must be the same as the one you used to protect the key store (Tomcat uses the same password for accessing the key store and the certificate).

The following example shows the complete interactive dialog for creating a self-certified digital certificate for `localhost` using the password `secret`:

```
> keytool -genkey -alias tomcat -keyalg RSA -keystore <CATALINA_HOME>/.keystore
Enter keystore password:  secret
What is your first and last name?
  [Unknown]:  localhost
What is the name of your organizational unit?
  [Unknown]:  Tomcat - Kick Start
What is the name of your organization?
  [Unknown]:  Sams Publishing
What is the name of your City or Locality?
  [Unknown]:  Indianapolis
What is the name of your State or Province?
  [Unknown]:  Indiana
What is the two-letter country code for this unit?
  [Unknown]:  US
Is CN=localhost, OU=Tomcat Kick Start, O=SAMS Publishing, L=Indianapolis, ST=
Indiana, C=US correct?
  [no]:  yes
```

```
Enter key password for <tomcat>
        (RETURN if same as keystore password):
```

You can now enable Tomcat's SSL connector as described in the section "Enabling the Tomcat SSL Connector."

Installing a Digital Certificate from a Certification Authority

If you have a verified digital certificate for your server obtained from a CA, you must install this in a key store database using the JRE `keytool` command. If you do not have a verified certificate, you must either use a self-certified certificate or obtain a verified certificate as described in the section "Creating a Self-Certified Digital Certificate."

To use a verified digital certificate, you must add the CA's chain certificate to the key store. The CA's chain certificate contains the information needed to contact the CA to verify the certificate issued by the CA. You can obtain the chain certificate for your CA from its Web site. The following table shows the location of the chain certificates for the popular CAs:

CA	Chain Certificate URL
VeriSign Inc.	`http://www.verisign.com/support/install/intermediate.html`
TrustCenter	`http://www.trustcenter.de/certservices/cacerts/en/en.htm#server`
Thawte Consulting	`http://www.thawte.com/html/RETAIL/sgc/index.html`

If you save the CA's chain certificate in a local file called `chain.cert`, the following command will add this certificate to the `.keystore` database in Tomcat's home directory (if the database does not exist, a new file will be created):

```
> keytool -import -alias root -keystore <CATALINA_HOME>/.keystore
➥ -trustcacerts -file chain.cert
```

When you enter this `keytool` command, you will be prompted for a password for the key store database. You must enter a password to protect access to the database. Tomcat uses the default password `changeit`, but you are advised to select another password to protect your key store from other users. If you choose another password, you will have to specify the password in the SSL `<Connector>` entry in Tomcat's `server.xml` file (see the section "Enabling the Tomcat SSL Connector"). The examples in this chapter use the password `secret`.

Once you have added the chain certificate, you can add your server's own certificate. The following `keytool` command will add a digital certificate stored in the file `server.cert` to the key store database:

```
> keytool -import -alias tomcat -keystore <CATALINA_HOME>/.keystore
➥ -trustcacerts -file server.cert
```

You will have to provide a password to protect the certificate and you must use the same password you used for the key store. Tomcat uses the same password to open the database and to access the certificate. You can now enable Tomcat's SSL connector as described in the next section.

Enabling the Tomcat SSL Connector

To enable SSL support in Tomcat, you must add an entry for the SSL connector to the file `<CATALINA_HOME>/conf/server.xml`. If you are using Tomcat 4.1, you can use the Tomcat Web Server Administration Tool to configure the SSL Connector. If you are using Tomcat 4.0, or you want to manually edit the `server.xml` file, you should follow the steps described in the upcoming section titled "Manually Editing `server.xml`."

Using the Tomcat 4.1 Administration Tool

If you use the Tomcat 4.1 Administration Tool (`http://localhost:8080/admin`) to enable the SSL connector, you will have to perform the following steps:

1. Select the Service (Tomcat-Standalone) entry in the left-hand panel.
2. Choose Create New Connector from the Available Actions drop down list in the right panel.
3. On the subsequent form, provide the following field values:

Field	Value
Type	`HTTPS`
Port number	`8443`
Key store filename	`.keystore`
Key store password	`secret`

Use the Save button to save these changes in memory and then use the Commit Changes button to save the values to the `server.xml` file.

Manually Editing `server.xml`

Tomcat 4.1 introduced a new Coyote HTTP/1.1 connector to replace the `HttpConnector` class. Consequently, the `<Connector>` entry in `server.xml` has a slightly different syntax for Tomcat 4.0 and Tomcat 4.1 as shown in the following examples.

If you are using Tomcat 4.1, you must add the following SSL `<Connector>` element to the `server.xml` file to enable the SSL connector:

```
<Connector className="org.apache.coyote.tomcat4.CoyoteConnector"
           port="8443" minProcessors="5" maxProcessors="75"
           enableLookups="true"
           acceptCount="10" debug="0" scheme="https" secure="true"
           useURIValidationHack="false">
  <Factory className="org.apache.coyote.tomcat4.CoyoteServerSocketFactory"
           clientAuth="false" protocol="TLS"
           keystoreFile=".keystore" keystorePass="secret" />
</Connector>
```

If you are using Tomcat 4.0, you must add the following `<Connector>` element to the `server.xml` file to enable the SSL connector:

```
<Connector className="org.apache.catalina.connector.http.HttpConnector"
           port="8443" minProcessors="5" maxProcessors="75"
           enableLookups="true"
           acceptCount="10" debug="0" scheme="https" secure="true">
  <Factory className="org.apache.catalina.net.SSLServerSocketFactory"
           clientAuth="false" protocol="TLS"
           keystoreFile=".keystore" keystorePass="secret" />
</Connector>
```

For both versions of Tomcat, the `<Connector>` element must be defined inside the `<Service>` element for the Tomcat standalone server.

NOTE

You may find that a commented-out entry for this connector is already present in the `server.xml` file. If you use the one already in the file, you must add the `keystore` and `keystorePass` attributes to the supplied `<Factory>` element.

Because the examples used a password other than `changeit` for the key store, the `<Factory>` element's `keystorePass` attribute has been used to specify the alternate password.

CAUTION

You should ensure that Tomcat's `server.xml` file is protected from read access by other users of the system, because it contains the key store password in plain text.

TIP

If you are running Tomcat on a live system, you will probably want to use the default HTTPS port instead of port 8443 as configured in the examples. If you use the 8443 port, all URLs must include the port number (`https://www.host.com:8443/`), whereas the port number can be omitted if the default HTTPS port is used (`https://www.host.com/`).

You should change the value of the `port` attribute of the `<Connector>` element to the value `443` to use the default HTTPS port. If you change the SSL port number, you should update the `redirectPort` attribute of the other `<Connector>` elements in `server.xml` to reflect your chosen SSL port.

You must stop and restart Tomcat for the changes to the `server.xml` file to be recognized.

Testing the HTTPS Connection

Once you have configured the SSL connection, you can access any Tomcat Web resource using the secure HTTPS protocol simply by entering the URL with the `https:` prefix and a port number of 8443. The following URL accesses the homepage of the `access-control` Web application using HTTPS:

```
https://localhost:8443/access-control
```

If you are using a self-certified certificate, the browser will normally issue a warning indicating that the certificate was issued by an unrecognized certification authority. Figure 23.1 shows the unrecognized certification authority warning dialog box displayed by Netscape 6.

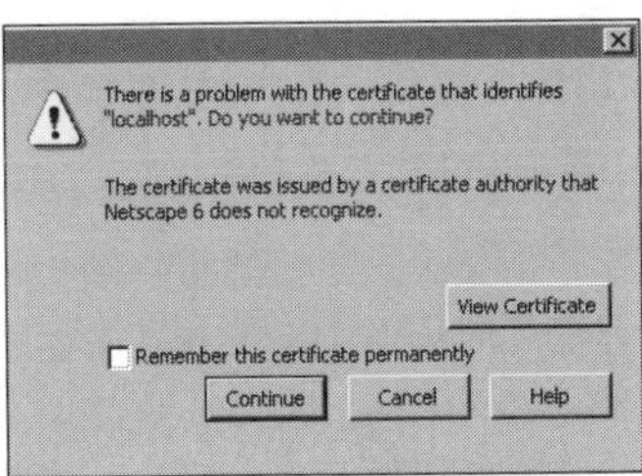

FIGURE 23.1 Netscape warning for self-certified certificate.

After accepting the certificate, your browser will retrieve the Web page using a secure session. Depending on the browser, you may see a broken key icon becoming a whole key or an open padlock closing, indicating that the session is secure. Figure 23.2 shows a Netscape 6 browser with the closed padlock in the bottom right corner of the window showing that the session is secure.

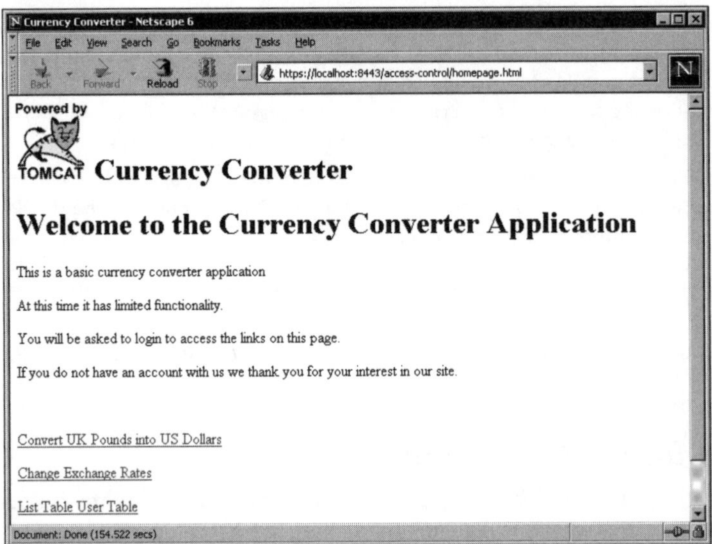

FIGURE 23.2 Netscape 6 with closed padlock icon indicating a secure session.

Now that Tomcat support for HTTPS is enabled, you should use this protocol to access secure Web pages. A simple but unusual approach would be to configure a hypertext link to explicitly use HTTPS as follows:

```
<A HREF='https://localhost:8443/access-control'>Access Control Example</A>
```

It is not uncommon to protect secure pages so that the user must log in before accessing those pages (see Chapter 14). The process of configuring the login negotiation to use SSL is covered in the next section; this is the recommended approach to securing Web pages.

Enabling Secure Login

The simplest way of using SSL when requesting Web resources is to require the client to log in before accessing secured resources. The deployment descriptor's `<security-constraint>` entry for the Web resource should set the `<transport-guarantee>` to `INTEGRAL` or `CONFIDENTIAL` because this necessitates the use of SSL. A value of `INTEGRAL` requires that the data transferred between client and server cannot be changed in transit, whereas `CONFIDENTIAL` means that the data cannot be observed during transmission. It is a common practice to set the `<transport-guarantee>` value to `CONFIDENTIAL` for protecting the data from network sniffers.

If the login process is secured using SSL, all subsequent URLs will use the HTTPS protocol unless explicitly overridden by using a URL defining the `http:` protocol.

The following example shows how to enable SSL in the `web.xml` file for secure access to the Web resources introduced in Chapter 14 (the relevant entries are highlighted in bold):

```
<security-constraint>
    <display-name>Web App Access Control - Administrators</display-name>
    <Web-resource-collection>
        <Web-resource-name>Administration</Web-resource-name>
        <url-pattern>/rates</url-pattern>
    </Web-resource-collection>
    <auth-constraint>
        <role-name>administrator</role-name>
    </auth-constraint>
    <user-data-constraint>
        <transport-guarantee>CONFIDENTIAL</transport-guarantee>
    </user-data-constraint>
</security-constraint>

<security-constraint>
    <display-name>Web App Access Control - ordinary users</display-name>
    <Web-resource-collection>
        <Web-resource-name>Patrons</Web-resource-name>
        <url-pattern>/CurrencyConverter</url-pattern>
        <url-pattern>/currency-form</url-pattern>
        <url-pattern>/ListTables</url-pattern>
    </Web-resource-collection>
    <auth-constraint>
        <role-name>patron</role-name>
        <role-name>administrator</role-name>
    </auth-constraint>
    <user-data-constraint>
         <transport-guarantee>CONFIDENTIAL</transport-guarantee>
    </user-data-constraint>
</security-constraint>
```

Simply by setting the `<transport-guarantee>` element to the value `CONFIDENTIAL`, you have ensured that the login negotiation and subsequent page accesses use SSL. However, you have not prevented a malicious user from bypassing your security and accessing the protected resources directly using the HTTP (insecure) protocol. To do that you must prevent the user from accessing the resources without first logging in.

In Chapter 14, you protected Web resources by mapping URL patterns onto the home page, so that clients could not bypass the login mechanism by using the resource name rather than its protected URL. The URL mappings used to protect all servlets and JSPs are shown in the following example:

```
<servlet-mapping>
    <servlet-name>Home Page</servlet-name>
    <url-pattern>*.jsp</url-pattern>
</servlet-mapping>

<servlet-mapping>
    <servlet-name>Home Page</servlet-name>
    <url-pattern>/servlet/*</url-pattern>
</servlet-mapping>
```

TIP

The default servlet and JSP mappings are defined in `<CATALINA_HOME>/conf/web.xml`. You could delete these mappings from the `web.xml` file to make your site more secure. However, you would need to explicitly add individual mappings for every servlet and JSP used in all of your Web applications if you removed these global mappings.

An alternative means of preventing insecure access to resources is to check that all requests to the resource use a secure protocol. This is discussed in the next section.

Protecting Secure Web Resources with a Filter

If you want to ensure that a Web resource (servlet or JSP) is always accessed using a secure connection, you must add a check to the Web resource to verify that the request is a secure request. The `javax.servlet.ServletRequest.isSecure()` method is used to check that a request uses a secure connection. You can add a call to the `isSecure()` method in a servlet filter and then apply that filter with those resources requiring secure access (filters are described in Chapter 18, "Servlet Filters").

The example in Listing 23.1 shows a simple filter that checks that a request uses a secure connection before forwarding the request.

LISTING 23.1 Secure Access Filter: `HttpsFilter.java`

```
package filters;

import java.io.*;
import javax.servlet.*;
```

LISTING 23.1 Continued

```
public class HttpsFilter implements Filter {

    public void doFilter(ServletRequest request, ServletResponse response,
        FilterChain chain) throws IOException, ServletException {

        if (!request.isSecure())
          request.getRequestDispatcher("/insecure.html")
                .forward(request,response);
        else
            chain.doFilter(request, response);
    }

    public void init(FilterConfig filterConfig) throws ServletException {}
    public void destroy() {}
}
```

In Listing 23.1, the `isSecure()` method on the `javax.servlet.ServletRequest` object is used to test whether the request was made using a secure protocol such as SSL. If this is not the case, the request is forwarded to the `/insecure.html` error page; otherwise the request is passed down the filter chain.

The following `web.xml` entries will apply the filter in Listing 23.1 to the protected Web resources used in the examples from Chapter 14:

```
<filter>
    <filter-name>HTTPS Filter</filter-name>
    <filter-class>filters.HttpsFilter</filter-class>
</filter>

<filter-mapping>
    <filter-name>HTTPS Filter</filter-name>
    <servlet-name>Currency Converter</servlet-name>
</filter-mapping>

<filter-mapping>
    <filter-name>HTTPS Filter</filter-name>
    <servlet-name>List Tables</servlet-name>
</filter-mapping>

<filter-mapping>
    <filter-name>HTTPS Filter</filter-name>
    <servlet-name>Currency Form</servlet-name>
</filter-mapping>
```

Using a filter this way is a fallback security mechanism, because the URL mappings described in the previous section ("Enabling Secure Login") should prevent direct access to the protected Web resources.

Using a Security Manager

Using a security manager allows Tomcat to run Web applications in a sandbox, restricting what the Web application can do and thereby preventing an aberrant Web application from bringing down Tomcat or other Web applications.

All Web applications run within the Tomcat process have the same privileges as any Tomcat object. Imagine a naive Web developer adding the following Java statement to a Web resource:

```
System.exit(1);
```

Each time this statement is executed, Tomcat will exit (not just the Web application). Obviously this is an undesirable situation. Uncontrolled Web applications can also do harm or open up security holes in a system by

- Writing or modifying configuration files
- Providing network socket services
- Executing programs

In much the same way as a Web browser must run applets inside a secure environment called a *sandbox*, Tomcat should run its Web applications in a secure environment.

Enabling the Security Manager

Enabling the security manager is the same for both Unix and Windows environments unless you are running Tomcat as a Windows service. This section describes how to enable the security manager for the different platforms.

The following subsections show how to enable the security manager for Unix, Windows, and the Windows NT Service for both Tomcat 4.1 and Tomcat 4.0.

Enabling the Security Manager for Unix

To enable Tomcat to use a security manager, you should add the `-security` flag on the Tomcat startup command line as shown in the following example:

```
$CATALINA_HOME/bin/startup.sh -security
```

Enabling the Security Manager for Windows

To enable Tomcat to use a security manager, you should add the `-security` flag on the Tomcat startup command line as shown in the following example:

```
%CATALINA_HOME%\bin\startup.bat -security
```

You will need to edit the Start menu shortcuts created when you installed Tomcat to include the `-security` option.

Enabling the Security Manager for the Tomcat 4.1 Windows NT Service

If you run Tomcat as an NT service, you will need to uninstall the existing service and install a new service with the security manager enabled. Tomcat's NT service configuration is discussed in Chapter 16, "Configuring Tomcat." To configure the NT service, you will create simple batch files that use the `<CATALINA_HOME>/bin/tomcat.exe` application to update the service. With Tomcat 4.1, you must have selected the NT Service option when you installed Tomcat (see Chapter 2, "Installing Jakarta Tomcat"); otherwise, the required `tomcat.exe` application is not installed.

For Tomcat 4.1, you can remove the service by creating a batch file with the following commands:

```
set SERVICENAME=Apache Tomcat 4.1
net stop "%SERVICE_NAME%"
%CATALINA_HOME%\bin\tomcat.exe -uninstall "%SERVICE_NAME%"
```

For Tomcat 4.1, you can install the service with a security manager by creating a batch file with the following commands:

```
set SERVICENAME=Apache Tomcat 4.1
set JAVACLASSPATH=%CLASSPATH%;"%CATALINA_HOME%\bin\bootstrap.jar"

%CATALINA_HOME%\bin\tomcat.exe
➥ -install "%SERVICENAME%" "%JAVA_HOME%\jre\bin\server\jvm.dll"
➥ -Djava.class.path=%JAVACLASSPATH%
➥ -Dcatalina.home="%CATALINA_HOME%"
➥ -Djava.endorsed.dirs="%CATALINA_HOME%\common\endorsed"
➥ -Djava.security.manager
➥ -Djava.security.policy=="%CATALINA_HOME%\conf\catalina.policy"
➥ -start org.apache.catalina.startup.BootstrapService -params start
➥ -stop org.apache.catalina.startup.BootstrapService -params stop
➥ -out "%CATALINA_HOME%\logs\stdout.log"
➥ -err "%CATALINA_HOME%\logs\stderr.log"
```

Run the commands to uninstall the existing service before running the commands to install the new (secure) service.

Enabling the Security Manager for the Tomcat 4.0 Windows NT Service

If you run Tomcat as an NT service, you will need to uninstall the existing service and install a new service with the security manager enabled. Tomcat's NT service installation and configuration are discussed in Chapter 16. To configure the NT service, you will create simple batch files that use the `<CATALINA_HOME>/bin/tomcat.exe` application to update the service.

For Tomcat 4.0, you can remove the service by creating a batch file with the following commands:

```
set SERVICENAME=Apache Tomcat 4.0
net stop "%SERVICE_NAME%"
%CATALINA_HOME%\bin\tomcat.exe -uninstall "%SERVICE_NAME%"
```

For Tomcat 4.0, you can install the service with a security manager by creating a batch file with the following commands:

```
set SERVICENAME=Apache Tomcat 4.0
set JAVACLASSPATH=%CLASSPATH%
set JAVACLASSPATH=%JAVACLASSPATH%;"%CATALINA_HOME%\bin\bootstrap.jar"
set JAVACLASSPATH=%JAVACLASSPATH%;"%CATALINA_HOME%\common\lib\servlet.jar"
set JAVACLASSPATH=%JAVACLASSPATH%;"%JAVA_HOME%\lib\tools.jar"

%CATALINA_HOME%\bin\tomcat.exe
➥ -install "%SERVICENAME%" "%JAVA_HOME%\jre\bin\server\jvm.dll"
➥ -Djava.class.path=%JAVACLASSPATH%
➥ -Dcatalina.home="%CATALINA_HOME%"
➥ -Djava.security.manager
➥ -Djava.security.policy=="%CATALINA_HOME%\conf\catalina.policy"
➥ -Xrs
➥ -start org.apache.catalina.startup.Bootstrap -params start
➥ -stop org.apache.catalina.startup.Bootstrap -params stop
➥ -out "%CATALINA_HOME%\logs\stdout.log"
➥ -err "%CATALINA_HOME%\logs\stderr.log"
```

Run the commands to uninstall the existing service before running the commands to install the new (secure) service.

Configuring Web Application Security

With the Tomcat security manager enabled, Web applications are controlled by the security policy defined in the Tomcat security policy file `<CATALINA_HOME>/conf/`

catalina.policy. You might find the default permissions are suitable for your Web site, but you should review and edit this file to add or change the permissions to meet your requirements. If you are new to Java security permissions, you can find more information in the API documentation for java.lang.SecurityManager and the online Java Tutorial available from http://java.sun.com.

The Web applications permissions provided by the default catalina.policy file include the following:

- JNDI name lookup as required for data sources
- Read access to system and JVM properties
- Access to BeanInfo and JAXP facilities

NOTE

When the default catalina.policy file is used with the security manager, Web applications do not have permission to read or write local files or connect to network sockets.

If you encounter problems that prevent your Web applications from working correctly when running with the security manager, you should check whether your application is being denied access to files or network services.

A common problem occurs when using JDBC connections and JNDI data sources. By default, the security manager prevents your Web applications from opening data-source and JDBC connections to a database when the security manager is enabled (database connections are discussed in Chapter 9, "Databases and Tomcat").

NOTE

The Tomcat documentation implies that JNDI data sources will work because the JDBC device drivers are installed in the *<CATALINA_HOME>*/common/lib directory. In practice, you will have to explicitly add permissions to the policy file to enable network connections to the database from your Web application classes.

To enable a Tomcat data source, you will have to add an entry to the catalina.policy file similar to the following example for connecting to the MySQL database on network socket 3306 from within the database Web application:

```
grant codeBase "file:${catalina.home}/webapps/database/WEB-INF/classes/-" {
    permission java.net.SocketPermission "localhost:3306", "connect";
};
```

If you are using a JDBC driver rather than data sources to connect to the database, you will also need to add an entry for the JAR file containing your JDBC driver. The following example enables classes in the MySQL JAR file stored in the `database` Web application to access the database on network socket 3306:

```
grant codeBase "jar:file:${catalina.home}/webapps/database/WEB-INF/lib/
➥mm.mysql-2.0.13-bin.jar!/-" {
    permission java.net.SocketPermission "localhost:3306", "connect";
};
```

If you cannot determine the cause of a problem that occurs when the security manager is enabled, you can switch on security debugging by setting the following environment variable `CATALINA_OPTS=-Djava.security.debug=all` or by adding the `-Djava.security.debug=all` command-line option to the Tomcat startup command. But make sure you have lots of free disk space, because security debugging will generate copious amounts of logging information.

The Tomcat documentation states that the security manager features have not been fully tested, nor have they been submitted for a full security audit. In other words, be careful when using the security manager.

You can run Tomcat without the security manager, but for peace of mind on a live server, you should seriously consider using the security manager. If you use a security manager on a live server, you should, of course, use a security manager for your development and testing activities to ensure your development and live environments are as similar as possible.

Summary

Securing Web resources requires the use of the HTTPS protocol, which uses SSL to encrypt data between Tomcat and the client. To use SSL, you must first have a digital certificate for your server. You store your server's digital certificate in a key store using the JRE `keytool` utility and then configure the Tomcat SSL connector to use the certificate in this key store.

Ensuring the client uses HTTPS to access your protected resources is normally achieved by requiring the client to log in to access the resources and by configuring the login negotiation to use SSL.

To protect Tomcat and other Web applications from a badly written or rogue Web application, you should enable the Tomcat security manager. The security manager runs each Web application in a secure environment, preventing it from causing accidental or malicious damage to other areas of the Web server.

24

Tomcat and J2EE

IN THIS CHAPTER

- J2EE and Tomcat
- Using JNDI
- Sending Email Messages Using JavaMail

This chapter looks at Tomcat in the wider context of the Java 2 Enterprise Edition (J2EE) technologies. Tomcat provides the subset of the J2EE technologies required to implement the servlet and JSP specifications. However, Web applications under Tomcat can utilize other J2EE and Java technologies.

In this chapter, you will look in detail at using JNDI services within your Web application and using JavaMail to send email messages.

J2EE and Tomcat

J2EE is a collection of Java APIs and technologies designed to support enterprise-wide functionality. The following table details key components of J2EE:

Component	Purpose
Java Naming and Directory Interface (JNDI)	An interface to naming and directory services such as Novell Directory Services (NDS) and Lightweight Directory Access Protocol (LDAP)
Enterprise JavaBeans (EJB)	Reusable components that are designed for a scalable transaction, secure, possibly distributed environment
JavaMail	An interface to SMTP, POP3, IMAP, and other mail services
Java Message Service (JMS)	An interface to messaging services
JavaServer Faces (JSF)	A framework for building user interfaces in Web applications

Component	Purpose
JavaServer Pages (JSP)	Web components predominantly written using HTML and HTML-like extensions
Java Servlets	Web components written in Java
J2EE Connector Architecture	An API used to simplify connections to legacy systems

NOTE

At the time of this book's writing (mid 2002), the JavaServer Faces specification was in the early stages of development and provide similar functionality to the Jakarta Struts project discussed in Chapter 20, "Frameworks and Jakarta Struts."

Of the J2EE technologies just listed, Tomcat was designed to support the JSP and servlet Web application technologies, which require Tomcat to also provide a simple JNDI implementation. Tomcat does not implement the EJB or JMS technologies, but your Web applications can easily integrate with an external J2EE server providing these technologies.

All J2EE components are accessed using a JNDI naming service. To use external EJB and JMS components, your Web application must use the JNDI service used by the J2EE components as well as the internal Tomcat JNDI service.

Although using an external JNDI service is discussed in the "Using an External JNDI service" section in this chapter, using EJB and JMS components is too large a subject to cover in this book. If you are interested in using other J2EE technologies, *Sams Teach Yourself J2EE in 21 Days* is a good introduction to the subject.

One aspect of Web applications that does not require a full J2EE implementation is the sending of email. The "Sending Email Messages using JavaMail" section describes how to send email from within your Tomcat Web applications.

Using JNDI

Java Naming and Directory Interface (JNDI) is a Java API that defines an interface to a naming and directory service and not actually an implementation of a naming and directory service. To use JNDI, you must have a naming service implementation and the necessary Service Provider Interface (SPI) classes to use that naming service. SPI classes for the following popular naming services are included with J2SE 1.4:

- Novell Directory Services (NDS)
- Lightweight Directory Access Protocol (LDAP) Internet servers with several different implementations available

- Active Directory from Microsoft (see note)
- CORBA Naming Service

NOTE

JNDI support for Microsoft's Active Directory service is achieved using an LDAP interface.

JNDI is a standard component of J2SDK 1.4 and JDK 1.3 and is also available as a standard Java extension for earlier JDKs.

Naming and directory services provide a repository for storing and retrieving information. Typically a Tomcat Web application will use a JNDI service to

- Define and look up a JDBC data source
- Define and look up a JavaMail session
- Define and look up reusable JavaBean components

Tomcat includes a simple JNDI service that provides the functionality needed to support Web applications, but is not intended as a general-purpose naming and directory service. You will need to use an external naming service if you want to use EJB or JMS components from a J2EE-compliant server.

Using Tomcat's JNDI Service

Using Tomcat's JNDI service for defining and accessing Web application resources requires three stages:

1. Define the resource in Tomcat's `server.xml` file.
2. Define a reference to the resource in the Web applications `web.xml` file.
3. Create and use a JNDI context to look up the resource.

The exact syntax of the `server.xml` and `web.xml` elements used to define specific JNDI resources is described in Chapter 9, "Databases and Tomcat," and in the "Sending Email Messages Using JavaMail" section in this chapter. However, using JNDI to retrieve an object uses the following standard idiom:

1. Create a `javax.naming.InitialContext` object that is used to access the JNDI service.
2. Use the `InitialContext` object to look up the Web application's private `Context` object (always called `java:comp/env`).

3. Use the Web application's `Context` object to retrieve the named object from the server.

The following code taken from Chapter 9 shows how to look up a JDBC data source called `jdbc/conversion` using the Tomcat JNDI service:

```
Context init = new InitialContext();
Context ctx = (Context) init.lookup("java:comp/env");
DataSource ds = (DataSource) ctx.lookup("jdbc/conversion");
```

After you have retrieved the object from the naming service, it can be used like a normally constructed Java object.

Using an External JNDI Service

If you plan to use J2EE components, such as EJB or JMS objects, that are provided by another supplier, you will have to interface to the naming service used by the J2EE supplier. Using an external name service requires your program to define the properties of the service when creating the JNDI `Context` object. At minimum you will need to provide the following information:

- The service provider classes for the naming service
- The location (hostname and port number) of the directory server on your network

An individual JNDI service provider may require additional information.

You will need to make sure that the class files for your JNDI service provider are accessible by your Web application. J2SDK 1.4 includes SPI classes for the LDAP, NDS, and CORBA naming services, but if you use a different naming service, you will need to include the service provider's JAR file in your application's `WEB-INF/lib` directory.

To access an external JNDI service from within a Tomcat Web application, you must provide the server properties in a `Hashtable` that is provided as a parameter to the `javax.naming.InitialContext` constructor.

The following example shows how to access an LDAP server running on port 389 on host address 192.168.0.250:

```
Hashtable env = new Hashtable();
env.put(Context.INITIAL_CONTEXT_FACTORY, "com.sun.jndi.ldap.LdapCtxFactory");
env.put(Context.PROVIDER_URL, "ldap://192.168.0.250:389");
Context init = new InitialContext(env);
```

The `Context.INITIAL_CONTEXT_FACTORY` property defines the SPI class for the name service, and the `Context.PROVIDER_URL` property defines the host running the server.

TIP

To aid program portability, you would normally define the values for the `INITIAL_CONTEXT_FACTORY` and `PROVIDER_URL` properties as Web application context parameters or as servlet initialization parameters.

CAUTION

If you are familiar with JNDI and have previously used the `jndi.properties` file for defining the JNDI context properties, be aware that you cannot use this technique with Tomcat Web applications. The JNDI properties can only be provided in the `Hashtable` parameter passed to the `InitialContext` constructor.

After you have created the JNDI `InitialContext` object that refers to the external naming service, object lookup is the same as for the Tomcat's own JNDI service.

Sending Email Messages Using JavaMail

A common requirement for Web applications is to be able to send email to the user, perhaps confirming some action. Tomcat provides support for sending email using the JavaMail API.

JavaMail is not a component of the J2SE 1.4 but is available as a Java extension and can be downloaded from `http://java.sun.com/products/javamail`. After downloading the JavaMail archive, you should extract the archive contents, which will create a directory named after the JavaMail version (for example, `javamail-1.3`). Copy the `mail.jar` file from the JavaMail directory to the Java extension directory of your JRE or J2SDK directory, or add the `mail.jar` file to your `CLASSPATH` environment variable.

NOTE

Java extensions are installed in the `lib/ext` subdirectory of the JRE or the `jre/lib/ext` subdirectory of the J2SDK.

The JavaMail archive also includes full API documentation, several example applications, and the JavaMail design specification.

Once you have the JavaMail API installed, you can add email support to your Web applications using the following steps (explained in detail in the rest of this section):

1. Define the JavaMail session in Tomcat's `server.xml` file.
2. Define a resource reference to the JavaMail session in the Web application's `web.xml` file.
3. Create a JNDI context and obtain a JavaMail session.
4. Use the JavaMail session to send an email.

Defining the JavaMail Resource

Add a `<ResourceParams>` entry for the JavaMail session to the *`<CATALINA_HOME>`*`/conf/server.xml` file. The `<ResourceParams>` can be defined inside the `<Context>` element for a specific application, or it can be defined inside the `<DefaultContext>` element to make JavaMail available to all Web applications.

An example `<ResourceParams>` element for a JavaMail resource called `mail/session` for the `j2ee` application is shown in the following listing:

```
<Context path="/j2ee" docBase="j2ee" debug="0">
  <ResourceParams name="mail/session">
    <parameter>
      <name>mail.smtp.host</name>
      <value>localhost</value>
    </parameter>
  </ResourceParams>
</Context>
```

In the `<ResourceParams>` element example, the `name` attribute defines the resource name and the `<parameter>` element defines the parameter `mail.smtp.host` to specify the host running the SMTP mail server. The example assumes an SMTP server is running on `localhost` on the default SMTP port (22).

Defining a JavaMail Resource Reference

Within your application's deployment descriptor, you will need to define a resource reference for the JavaMail resource. The following example shows the resource reference entry for the `mail/session` resource defined in the previous section:

```
<resource-ref>
    <res-ref-name>mail/session</res-ref-name>
    <res-type>javax.mail.Session</res-type>
    <res-auth>Container</res-auth>
</resource-ref>
```

The `<res-ref-name>` element must use the same name as the resource definition in the `<ResourceParams>` entry in the `servler.xml` file. The `<res-type>` entry defines the reference as a JavaMail session, and the `<res-auth>` entry specifies that resource authentication is applied by the `Container`. The `<resource-ref>` element must be added after any `<servlet-mapping>` elements in the deployment descriptor (see Appendix B, "Template `web.xml` File").

Creating the JavaMail Connection

When you use resource references in your application, you must use JNDI to look up and access the resource. You have to import the `javax.naming` package to use JNDI. Note that the JNDI methods shown here can throw a `javax.naming.NamingException` error.

The name you defined in the `<res-ref-name>` element is the JNDI name you must use in your code. To resolve the resource associated with this name, you must obtain the JNDI context for your Web application. Use the `javax.naming.Context.lookup()` method to look up the `javax.mail.Session` object as shown in the following code, which uses the example `mail/session` resource:

```
Context init = new InitialContext();
Context ctx = (Context) init.lookup("java:comp/env");
Session mailer = (Session) ctx.lookup("mail/session");
```

Creating and Sending Emails

After you have obtained the JavaMail `Session` object using JNDI, you can use the `Session` to create and send email. The packages containing the required JavaMail classes are `javax.mail` and `javax.mail.internet`. To create an email, you must create a `javax.mail.Message` object using the JavaMail `Session` object. The following example creates an Internet MIME message:

```
Message message = new MimeMessage(mailer);
```

Next, define the sender's email address (which must be a `javax.mail.internet.InternetAddress` object). The following example uses the fictitious address `currency@converter`:

```
message.setFrom(new InternetAddress("currency@converter"));
```

Similarly, you define an array of recipient `InternetAddress` addresses; you can define separate primary (to), copy (cc), and blind copy (bcc) recipients. The following creates a single "to" recipient whose name is defined by the `email` parameter of the HTTP request:

```
InternetAddress to[] = new InternetAddress[1];
to[0] = new InternetAddress(request.getParameter("email"));
message.setRecipients(Message.RecipientType.TO, to);
```

The `InternetAddress` constructor will throw a `javax.mail.internet.AddressException` if the address does not conform to RFC822.

You can define the message subject using the `setSubject()` method as follows:

```
message.setSubject("Currency conversion: "+convert.getAmount());
```

To define the actual message content, you use one of the `Message.setContent()` methods. The following example uses the convenience method that sets the message content using a Java object (in this case a `String` variable called `result`) and the message MIME type (in this case a `text/plain` message):

```
message.setContent(result,"text/plain");
```

Multipart mail messages (messages with attachments) can be defined using another form of the `setContent()` method, which takes a `javax.mail.Multipart` object as its only parameter (see the JDK API documentation).

Finally, you can send the message using the `javax.mail.Transport.send()` method specifying the `Message` object as the method parameter:

```
Transport.send(message);
```

The `send()` method can throw a `javax.mail.MessagingException` should the message fail to send correctly.

Listing 24.1 brings all these steps together to show a simple currency converter servlet that sends the conversion result to an email address specified in the `email` HTTP request parameter.

LISTING 24.1 Sending Email from `ConvertMail.java`

```
import java.io.*;
import java.sql.*;
import java.text.*;
import java.util.*;
import javax.mail.*;
import javax.mail.internet.*;
import javax.naming.*;
import javax.servlet.*;
import javax.servlet.http.*;
import converters.*;
```

LISTING 24.1 Continued

```
public class ConvertMail extends HttpServlet
{
    public void doGet(HttpServletRequest request, HttpServletResponse response)
        throws ServletException, IOException {

        String forward = "converted.jsp";
        HttpSession session = request.getSession();
        String amount = request.getParameter("amount");
        String email = request.getParameter("email");
        try {
            ConverterBean convert =
                (ConverterBean)session.getAttribute("convert");
            if (convert == null)
                session.setAttribute("convert",convert=new ConverterBean());
            if (amount!=null && amount.length()>0) {
                if (email==null || email.length()==0)
                    throw new IllegalArgumentException(
                                    "Email address not defined");
                convert.setAmount(amount);
                String result = convert.getAmount() + " = " +
                    convert.getConvertedAmount();

                Context init = new InitialContext();
                Context ctx = (Context) init.lookup("java:comp/env");
                Session mailer = (Session) ctx.lookup("mail/session");

                Message message = new MimeMessage(mailer);
                message.setFrom(new InternetAddress("currency@converter"));
                InternetAddress to[] = new InternetAddress[1];
                to[0] = new InternetAddress(email);
                message.setRecipients(Message.RecipientType.TO, to);
                message.setSubject("Currency conversion: "+convert.getAmount());
                message.setContent(result,"text/plain");
                Transport.send(message);
                request.setAttribute("message",
                  "<H2>Converted value emailed to "+email+"</H2>");
            }
        }
        catch (NamingException ex) {
            request.setAttribute("exception",ex);
            forward = "databaseError.jsp";
        }
```

LISTING 24.1 Continued

```
        catch (SQLException ex) {
            request.setAttribute("exception",ex);
            forward = "databaseError.jsp";
        }
        catch (AddressException ex) {
            request.setAttribute("exception",ex);
            forward = "databaseError.jsp";
        }
        catch (MessagingException ex) {
            request.setAttribute("exception",ex);
            forward = "databaseError.jsp";
        }
        catch (java.text.ParseException ex) {
            request.setAttribute("message",
              "<FONT color='red'>Invalid value for amount: "+amount+"</FONT>");
        }
        catch (IllegalArgumentException ex) {
            request.setAttribute("message",
              "<FONT COLOR='red'>"+ex.getMessage()+"</FONT>");
        }

        request.getRequestDispatcher(forward).forward(request,response);
    }

    public void doPost(HttpServletRequest request, HttpServletResponse response)
        throws ServletException, IOException {
        doGet(request,response);
    }
}
```

The servlet in Listing 24.1 is a simple variation of the Model 2/MVC servlet shown in Chapter 17, "Architectures." The rest of the Web application files are similar to those shown in Chapter 17 and can be viewed on the book's accompanying Web site (go to `http://www.samspublishing.com` and search for the book ISBN, 0672324393).

As you can see, adding support for sending email from within your Web application is relatively simple. All of the construction of the mail message and negotiation of SMTP is encapsulated within the JavaMail classes.

Summary

This chapter looked at the role of Tomcat in the context of the J2EE specification. Tomcat provides a simple JNDI service, a servlet container, and a JSP container for supporting Web applications.

Web applications for Tomcat can use external J2EE components, such as EJB and JMS objects, but must use an external JNDI service to look up and access these objects.

Tomcat Web applications can be simply extended to use the JavaMail API for sending email messages. Tomcat supports the definition and use of JavaMail resources using JNDI.

25 Web Services and Axis

IN THIS CHAPTER

- Distributed Application Services Overview
- Apache Axis
- A Simple Java Web Service
- A Currency Converter Service

A Web service is what its name implies: a service provided via the Web, such as a currency converter, stock quotation, credit card validation, shopping cart support, and so on. A Web service differs from Web resources such as HTML pages, servlets, and JSPs by using the HTTP protocol as a data exchange medium for supporting client/server applications.

A Web service advertises itself as a service via a URL. A client uses a Web service by sending a request to the URL and receiving the server response. A number of standards such as Simple Object Access Protocol (SOAP); Universal Description, Discovery, and Integration (UDDI); and Web Services Description Language (WSDL) define the manner by which Web services are described, configured, and accessed.

This chapter shows how a simple currency converter can be implemented as a Web service using Jakarta Axis and Tomcat. The examples shown here assume you are familiar with writing and deploying Web applications under Tomcat and simply show how to create Web services under Axis.

Distributed Application Services Overview

The traditional means of providing a distributed application service is to use raw TCP/IP sockets with a proprietary data exchange protocol. Many common Internet services such as Telnet, FTP, SMTP, and POP3 fall into this category. The coded algorithms in both the client and server programs are aware of the socket connectivity and the format of the data packets. This has the drawback of tightly coupling the client/server business logic with the low-level data exchange mechanism.

As the technologies have matured, the raw socket programming approach has generally been replaced by higher-level distributed frameworks such as

- Remote Procedure Calls (RPC)
- Java Remote Method Invocation (RMI)
- Common Object Request Broker Architecture (CORBA)
- Microsoft's DCOM

These distributed programming technologies hide the underlying network communication mechanism behind a functional programming interface. Figure 25.1 shows the basic architecture of all these technologies.

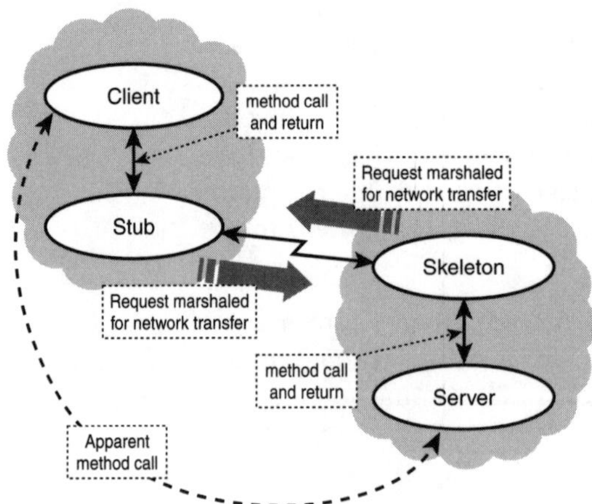

FIGURE 25.1 Generic distributed framework architecture.

Fundamentally, a distributed client program makes what appears to be a simple method (or function) call to a method implemented on the server. The underlying framework takes care of transforming the method call into a network connection and consequent exchange of data.

In reality, the client calls a method on a *stub* object or library. The stub encodes the request parameters into an octet stream for transfer over a TCP/IP socket to the server. At the server end, a *skeleton* object or library reconstructs the parameters from the octet stream and invokes the target method. The process of packing the request for transfer over a network is called *data marshaling*; unpacking the request by the recipient is called *data unmarshaling*. The results from the method call on the server are marshaled up by the skeleton and returned to the client stub. The stub unmarshals the response and returns the results to the client program.

The advantage of a distributed method call architecture is that the client and the server are developed using standard classes and interfaces. The only concession to the network component is the necessity to identify the service the client is using and to handle errors that may arise from the network communication. There is no requirement to handle raw socket connections or explicitly encode data for transfer over the network.

The main disadvantage to the distributed method call mechanism is the need to use TCP/IP services that are normally disabled in the network. In most environments, network routers and firewalls have to be configured to support RMI, CORBA, and DCOM, because these services are normally blocked. In many security-conscious environments, it may not be possible, or desirable, to open up the network to support these protocols. This limits the applicability of these established distributed architectures and certainly rules out using them over the Internet.

Another disadvantage is the limited interoperability between the different frameworks. Although Java RMI is compatible with a subset of the CORBA functionality (by using `javax.rmi.*` rather than `java.rmi.*` classes), it is not compatible with RPC or DCOM. CORBA and DCOM are incompatible, but there is a bridge that will enable DCOM and CORBA to interoperate—with a performance overhead.

Web services address both of the problems identified for distributed computing frameworks. A Web service uses HTTP (this protocol is supported by the Internet and most, if not all, enterprise networks) as the low-level data transfer mechanism. A number of standards listed in Table 25.1 are defined to ensure interoperability between different Web service technologies (such as Java, C++, Perl, .NET, C#, J#, and VB).

TABLE 25.1 Web Service Technologies and Protocols

Standard	Description
SOAP	Simple Object Access Protocol—Combines XML and Multipurpose Internet Mail Extensions (MIME) to provide a standard for transporting data messages over different transport mechanisms. More information about SOAP is available from `http://www.w3.org/2002/ws`.
UDDI	Universal Description, Discovery, and Integration—Defines the standard for organizing, registering, and accessing information about Web services. More information on UDDI is available from `http://www.uddi.org/`.
WSDL	Web Services Description Language—Uses XML to describe operations, data types, and bindings for Web services. For more information on WSDL, access `http://www.w3.org/TR/wsdl`.

The Apache Axis project is an open source implementation of a Web service framework that conforms to the standards in Table 25.1.

CAUTION

Web services are a new and fast-changing technology. The examples in this chapter were correct at the time of writing (mid 2002), but future changes in the standards may require changes to these examples. Similarly, new releases of Tomcat and Axis may require changes to the steps and instructions presented in this chapter.

Apache Axis

Apache Axis is a Java Web application that provides the framework for providing and accessing a Web service. Axis includes

- An `axis` Web application that provides a server container for hosting your Web services
- Tools to support WSDL documents in a Java context
- The `tcpmon` utility for monitoring SOAP messages when debugging a Web service

Axis is available for download via `http://xml.apache.org/axis`.

NOTE

Apache Axis is the third incarnation of the Apache SOAP project. The examples in this chapter use the beta-3 release of Axis, which conforms to SOAP 1.1 with some SOAP 1.2 support.

Installing Axis

Download the Axis archive from `http://xml.apache.org` and extract it to a new directory. Inside the Axis directory you will find the following subdirectories:

Directory	Usage
`docs`	Axis documentation
`lib`	Axis JAR files
`samples`	Some example Web services and clients
`webapps`	The Axis Web application

In the webapps subdirectory of the Axis directory, you will find a further subdirectory called axis. This axis directory is the Axis Web application that must be deployed to Tomcat as indicated in the following steps:

1. Stop Tomcat.
2. Copy the *<AXIS_HOME>*/webapps/axis directory to *<CATALINA_HOME>*/webapps.
3. Now move (not copy) all the JAR files in *<CATALINA_HOME>*/webapps/axis/WEB-INF/lib to *<CATALINA_HOME>*/shared/lib (or *<CATALINA_HOME>*/lib if you are using Tomcat 4.0). If you leave the JAR files inside the Axis Web application, Tomcat will fail to load the Axis class files.
4. Axis uses the Java Activation Framework (JAF) mechanism, and you must download this standard Java extension from http://java.sun.com/products/jaf. You install JAF by copying the activation.jar file from the JAF directory to the Java extensions directory (*<JAVA_HOME>*/jre/lib/ext).
5. Restart Tomcat.
6. Verify that Axis has deployed successfully by browsing to http://localhost:8080/axis and following the link on the home page labeled Visit the Axis Servlet.

NOTE

If you are using Axis beta-3, you can browse http://localhost:8080/axis/happyaxis.jsp, and this page will indicate whether you have configured the Axis Web application correctly.

To develop and deploy an Axis Web service application, you will need to make the Axis JAR files available to your IDE or Java compiler. You can either add the individual JAR files to your CLASSPATH or install them as a standard Java extension by copying <AXIS>/lib/*.jar to *<JAVA_HOME>*/jre/lib/ext. If you do not install Axis as a Java extension, you will need to include the following JAR files in your CLASSPATH:

<CATALINA_HOME>/shared/lib/axis.jar

<CATALINA_HOME>/shared/lib/commons-logging.jar

<CATALINA_HOME>/shared/lib/jaxrpc.jar

<CATALINA_HOME>/shared/lib/saaj.jar

<CATALINA_HOME>/shared/lib/tt-bytecode.jar

<CATALINA_HOME>/shared/lib/wsdl4j.jar

A Simple Java Web Service

The simplest way to develop an Axis Web Service is to create a Java Web Service (JWS) program that provides the service you want to implement. A JWS program is just the source code for a Java class that is stored in a file with a `.jws` extension. When a JWS file is deployed, Axis takes care of registering the service, mapping incoming requests onto the service, and compiling the Java class to create the Web service.

Developing a Web Service

For this example, the simple currency converter shown in Listing 25.1 will be deployed as a Web service. This example is called `CurrencyConverterSimple` because a more functional example is developed later in this chapter. The example in Listing 25.1 delegates the actual currency conversion to a supporting `converters.ConverterBean` class.

LISTING 25.1 Simple Currency Converter Web Service: `CurrencyConverterSimple.jws`

```
import converters.ConverterBean;

public class CurrencyConverterSimple {

    public String convert (String amount)
    throws java.text.ParseException, java.rmi.RemoteException {
        try {
            ConverterBean bean = new ConverterBean();
            return bean.convertAmount(amount);
        }
        catch (java.sql.SQLException ex) {
            throw new java.rmi.RemoteException ("Converter bean failure", ex);
        }
        catch (javax.naming.NamingException ex) {
            throw new java.rmi.RemoteException ("Converter bean failure", ex);
        }
    }
}
```

A JWS file is a Java class that implements one or more public methods that together make up the Web service. The name of the service is the Java class name. A Web service class must have a no-argument constructor. In Listing 25.1, the `CurrencyConverterSimple` service provides a single `convert()` method that returns the converted value of the amount passed as a parameter.

TIP

Many Java IDE compilers do not recognize files with a `.jws` extension. It is best to develop your Web service as a normal `.java` file and rename the `.java` file to `.jws` when it is copied to Axis.

This example, like many other examples in this book, uses a supporting `converters.ConverterBean` class to do the actual currency conversion. The source code for this bean is similar to the other JavaBean converter examples included in this book and is not shown here. The source code and class file for the bean can be downloaded from the Web site accompanying this book: Browse to `http://www.samspublishing.com` and search for this book's ISBN, 0672324393.

To deploy the currency converter Web service you will need to

1. Copy `CurrencyConverterSimple.jws` to *<CATALINA_HOME>*`/webapps/axis`.
2. Copy the following converter JavaBean helper classes to *<CATALINA_HOME>*`/webapps/axis/WEB-INF/classes`:

   ```
   converters.ConverterBean.class
   converters.ConverterBean$CurrencyFormat.class
   ```

3. Add a data source definition for `jdbc/conversion` to *<CATALINA_HOME>*`/conf/server.xml` as described in the following paragraphs.

To ensure that the example models a real-world Web service, the `converters.ConverterBean` class uses a Tomcat data source called `jdbc/conversion` to retrieve the conversion rates from a database. To run the example, you will have to configure a Conversion table in a database and add a suitable data source definition to *<CATALINA_HOME>*`/conf/server.xml`. A suitable database table schema and data source are described in Chapter 9, "Databases and Tomcat." If you have already worked through Chapter 7, "The Web Application Environment," and created the database tables, you can add the following data source definition to the `server.xml` file:

```
<Resource name="jdbc/conversion"
          auth="Container"
          type="javax.sql.DataSource"/>
<ResourceParams name="jdbc/conversion">
    <parameter>
        <name>username</name><value>root</value>
    </parameter>
    <parameter>
        <name>password</name><value>secret</value>
    </parameter>
```

```
    <parameter>
        <name>driverClassName</name><value>org.gjt.mm.mysql.Driver</value>
    </parameter>
    <parameter>
        <name>url</name><value>jdbc:mysql://localhost/test</value>
    </parameter>
</ResourceParams>
```

Add the <Resource> and <ResourceParams> elements either to the <Context> element for axis or to the <DefaultContext> element. By defining the data source <Resource> element in the server.xml file, you will not need to add a <resource-ref> specifying the resource reference entry to the WEB-INF/web.xml file of the axis Web application.

Once you have deployed the JWS file and the converter.ConverterBean class file and added the jdbc/conversion data source, you can access the service using http://localhost:8080/axis/CurrencyConverterSimple.jws. At present, this will not do anything useful, because you have to write a client to access the service. Writing the client requires a little more work.

Developing a Web Service Client

To use a Web service, you must write a client that communicates with the service using UDDI to identify and locate the service and SOAP to exchange messages. You can use the supporting tools provided with Axis to simplify the writing of a Web service client encapsulating most of the UDDI and SOAP coding into generated client-side supporting classes.

The starting point for using a Web service is the Web Service Descriptor Language (WSDL) specification obtained from the Web service provider. A WSDL specification is an XML document that describes the service including its name, URL, method names, method parameters, and method results. In the case of Axis, you can obtain the WSDL for a service by browsing the URL of the service you require and appending a ?wsdl request parameter.

Figure 25.2 shows the WSDL for the CurrencyConverterSimple.jws service obtained by browsing http://localhost:8080/axis/CurrencyConverterSimple.jws?wsdl using Internet Explorer.

TIP

You must use a browser that supports XML in order to see the WSDL file. In non-XML-aware browsers, you will need to view the HTML page source to see the WSDL document.

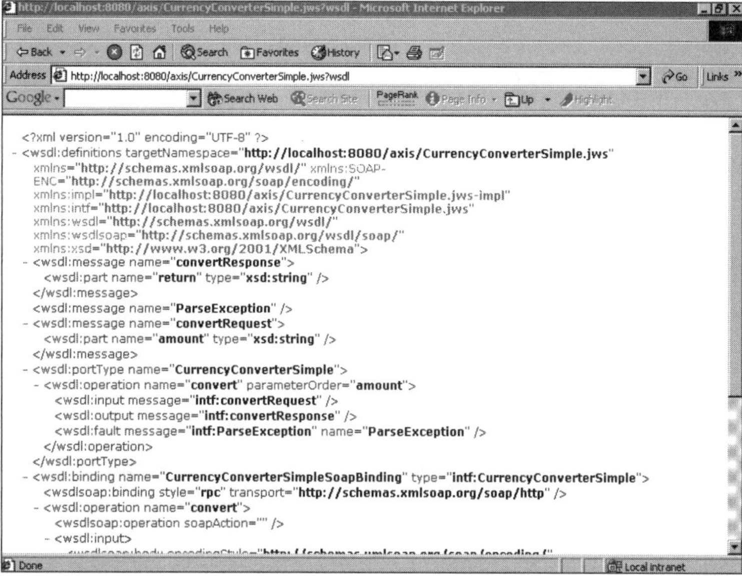

FIGURE 25.2 Simple currency converter WSDL document.

Once you have a WSDL document for a Web service, you will perform the following steps to write a client program:

1. Generate the client-side Java stub and helper classes.
2. Write the client program using the stub and helper classes to access the Web service.
3. Compile and deploy the client-side application.

For the examples in this chapter, you do not need to understand the contents of the WSDL document because Axis provides tools for converting between WSDL and Java code. For more information on WSDL you can look at `http://www.w3.org/TR/wsdl`.

The Axis `WSDL2Java` tool will generate the client-side Java stub and helper classes from the WSDL document.

To generate the client-side files, you will need to have the Axis JAR files in your `CLASSPATH` or installed as a Java extension as previously discussed in the section "Installing Axis." Run the `WSDL2Java` tool from the command line to generate the Java client files for the Simple Currency Converter Service as follows:

```
java org.apache.axis.wsdl.WSDL2Java -p simple
➥ http://localhost:8080/axis/CurrencyConverterSimple.jws?wsdl
```

NOTE

You can use a local filename in place of the Web service URL on the `WSDL2Java` command line if you have been supplied with a WSDL file from another source.

Running `WSDL2Java` will create a subdirectory named after the package name supplied with the `-p` option to the command. The following source files in the `simple` package are created when running the example `WSDL2Java` command:

File	Description
`CurrencyConverterSimple.java`	An interface definition for the Web service for use by the client
`CurrencyConverterSimpleService.java`	A helper class that encapsulates the Web service
`CurrencyConverterSimpleServiceLocator.java`	A helper class that locates the Web service
`CurrencyConverterSimpleSoapBindingStub.java`	The client-side stub class used to marshal and unmarshal the SOAP request
`ParseException.java`	A wrapper class that wraps the `java.text.ParseException` (thrown by the server) inside an `org.apache.axis.AxisFault` exception

As you can see, the generated files are named after the Web service defined in the WSDL document. All you now have to do is write a client that locates the service and then calls the required methods on the service. Listing 25.2 shows a JSP that uses the `CurrencyConverterSimple` service.

LISTING 25.2 The Simple Currency Converter Client: `convert-simple.jsp`

```
<%@ page import="simple.*" %>
<% String amount = request.getParameter("amount"); %>
<HTML>
  <HEAD>
    <TITLE>Currency Converter Simple Client</TITLE>
  </HEAD>
  <BODY>
    <H1>Currency Converter Simple Client</H1>
    <FORM>
      <P>Amount to convert:
```

LISTING 25.2 Continued

```
        <INPUT TYPE='text' NAME='amount'></P>
      <P><INPUT TYPE='submit' VALUE='Submit'></P>
    </FORM>
    <%    if (amount!=null && amount.length()>0) { %>
      <H2>
        <%
          try {
            CurrencyConverterSimpleService service =
                new CurrencyConverterSimpleServiceLocator();
            CurrencyConverterSimple converter =
                service.getCurrencyConverterSimple();
            String gbp = converter.convert(amount);
            out.print("USD ");
            out.print(amount);
            out.print(" = GBP ");
            out.print(gbp);
          }
          catch (org.apache.axis.AxisFault ex) {
            out.print("<FONT COLOR='red'>"+ex.getMessage()+"</FONT>");
          }
        %>
      </H2>
    <% } %>
    <P><A HREF='<%=response.encodeURL("homepage")%>'>Return to home page</A></P>
  </BODY>
</HTML>
```

Listing 25.2 imports the client-side package and then uses the `WSDL2Java` generated helper files to locate and invoke the Web service, as shown in the following lines:

```
CurrencyConverterSimpleService service =
➥ new CurrencyConverterSimpleServiceLocator();
CurrencyConverterSimple converter = service.getCurrencyConverterSimple();
```

Note that the `CurrencyConverterSimple` object obtained from the helper classes is the stub object (class `CurrencyConverterSimpleSoapBindingStub`) that implements the client-side `CurrencyConverterSimple` interface. Calling the `convert()` method on the stub will use SOAP to route the request to the actual server at the URL specified in the WSDL document.

To deploy this client in a Web application called `web-services`, you will need to

1. Copy convert-simple.jsp to *<CATALINA_HOME>*/web-services.
2. Copy the following compiled helper class files to *<CATALINA_HOME>*/web-services/WEB-INF/classes:

```
simple/CurrencyConverterSimple.class
simple/CurrencyConverterSimpleService.class
simple/CurrencyConverterSimpleServiceLocator.class
simple/CurrencyConverterSimpleSoapBindingStub.class
simple/ParseException.class
```

3. Ensure your client Web application has access to the Axis JAR files. If you are deploying the Web application to the same server as the Web service, the Axis JAR files are already accessible as they are stored in *<CATALINA_HOME>*/shared/lib. If you are running the client on a different Web server to Axis, you will need to either include the Axis JAR files in the application's WEB-INF/lib directory or add them to *<CATALINA_HOME>*/shared/lib.

You can now run the Web service client by accessing http://localhost:8080/web-services/convert-simple.jsp.

A Currency Converter Service

The previous simple currency converter example is a good starting point for a Web service but suffers from the drawback that a new server-side object is created to service each incoming request. This is potentially inefficient, and if the currency exchange rate fluctuates, the client may see inconsistent results within a single session.

The following example uses a Web service that is included in the client-side session context. This will ensure that after one currency conversion has been made, all further currency conversions during the session will use the same exchange rate. Axis Web Services defined by JWS files cannot, at present, participate in client-side HTTP sessions, so you will have to explicitly generate the Web service and WSDL documents to include client session support.

To include client session support in the Web service, you will need to perform the following steps instead of creating the JWS file:

1. Define a class prototype for the Web service.
2. Generate a WSDL document from the Java class.
3. Generate the server-side skeleton and service implementation classes.

4. Complete the service implementation class.
5. Compile and deploy the server-side class files.

These steps are explained in the rest of this section.

Defining the Web Service Prototype

Defining a Web service means creating the WSDL document either manually or by using tools supplied by Axis. You can write the WSDL document by hand, but it is much easier to write a Java definition of the service you want and use this to generate the WSDL document.

The simplest way to create the WSDL document from a Java class is to write a simple prototype Java class for your Web service. The prototype service class is a non-functional implementation of the service and is used to generate the WSDL file that is used to create the server-side skeleton files for the service implementation. A class definition for the prototype Currency Converter Service is shown in Listing 25.3.

LISTING 25.3 The Prototype Currency Converter Service `CurrencyConverter.java`

```
package webservices;

public class CurrencyConverter {
    public Conversion convert (String amount)
        throws java.text.ParseException, java.rmi.RemoteException {
        return null;
    }
}
```

CAUTION

The prototype service class is used to generate the WSDL document and server-side files for the Web service. In line with good object-oriented (OO) practice, you might prefer to write your Web service prototype as a Java interface. Do not do this. If you use a Java interface for the prototype, the WSDSL and Java code generation process will generate incorrect Java class definitions (it actually generates an abstract class that cannot be instantiated).

The example currency converter in Listing 25.3 uses a JavaBean helper class to store the results of the convert operation. This `Conversion` helper class is shown in Listing 25.4 and simply holds the original amount and the converted amount as correctly formatted currency strings for display on a JSP.

LISTING 25.4 JavaBean Helper Class: `Conversion.java`

```
package webservices;

public class Conversion {

    private String amount;
    private String convertedAmount;

    public Conversion () {}

    public Conversion (String amount, String convertedAmount) {
        this.amount = amount;
        this.convertedAmount = convertedAmount;
    }

    public String getAmount() { return amount;}
    public void setAmount(String amount)  {this.amount = amount;}

    public String getConvertedAmount() { return convertedAmount;}
    public void setConvertedAmount(String convertedAmount)
        {this.convertedAmount = convertedAmount;}
}
```

The `Conversion` class shown in Listing 25.4 is an example of a user-defined data type that must be characterized in the WSDL file. When an Axis request uses a user defined data type, you must specify how to marshal the data for transfer over the network. The simplest way of handling user-defined data types with Axis is to ensure the class representing the data is a JavaBean (as in the example in Listing 25.4).

Axis provides a generic JavaBean serializer and associated deserializer class that will ensure your JavaBean helper classes can exchange data using SOAP messages. Like the prototype Web service class definition, the `Conversion` helper class is used to generate the WSDL file and is not used in the Web service implementation.

Compile the prototype `CurrencyConverter` and `Conversion` data type classes and ensure they are included in your `CLASSPATH` so they can be accessed by the Axis `Java2WSDL` tool.

Developing the Server-Side Components

After you have a prototype Web service class, you can use the `Java2WSDL` tool to generate the WSDL document. The following command generates the Currency Converter WSDL:

```
java org.apache.axis.wsdl.Java2WSDL
➥   -l "http://localhost:8080/axis/services/CurrencyConverter"
➥   -n "urn:converters"
➥   -p"webservices" "urn:converters"
➥   webservices.CurrencyConverter
```

CAUTION

The Axis JAR files (see the "Installing Axis" section) and your prototype `webservices.CurrencyConverter` class must be included in your `CLASSPATH`; otherwise the `Java2WSDL` application will not run correctly.

This command defines the following parameters:

- `-l "http://localhost:8080/axis/services/CurrencyConverter"`—The URL that will be used to access the Web service
- `-n "urn:converters"`—An XML namespace used within the WSDL document
- `-p"webservices" "urn:converters"`—A mapping of the Web service Java package name onto the XML namespace
- `webservices.CurrencyConverter`—The prototype class file that defines the Web service

The `Java2WSDL` command will generate a WSDL file named after the Web service with a `.wdsl` suffix (`CurrencyConverter.wsdl`). The generated WSDL file is shown in Listing 25.5 for you to examine (and be glad you don't have to write it by hand).

LISTING 25.5 Generated `CurrencyConverter.wsdl`

```
<?xml version="1.0" encoding="UTF-8"?>
<wsdl:definitions
    targetNamespace="urn:converters"
    xmlns:soapenc="http://schemas.xmlsoap.org/soap/encoding/"
    xmlns:wsdlsoap="http://schemas.xmlsoap.org/wsdl/soap/"
    xmlns:apachesoap="http://xml.apache.org/xml-soap"
    xmlns:xsd="http://www.w3.org/2001/XMLSchema"
    xmlns:intf="urn:converters"
    xmlns:wsdl="http://schemas.xmlsoap.org/wsdl/"
    xmlns:impl="urn:converters-impl"
    xmlns="http://schemas.xmlsoap.org/wsdl/">
 <wsdl:types>
  <schema xmlns="http://www.w3.org/2001/XMLSchema"
```

LISTING 25.5 Continued

```
        targetNamespace="urn:converters">
  <import namespace="http://schemas.xmlsoap.org/soap/encoding/"/>
  <complexType name="Conversion">
   <sequence>
    <element name="amount" nillable="true" type="soapenc:string"/>
    <element name="convertedAmount" nillable="true" type="soapenc:string"/>
   </sequence>
  </complexType>
  <element name="Conversion" nillable="true" type="intf:Conversion"/>
 </schema>
</wsdl:types>

  <wsdl:message name="convertResponse">
     <wsdl:part name="return" type="intf:Conversion"/>
  </wsdl:message>

  <wsdl:message name="convertRequest">
     <wsdl:part name="amount" type="soapenc:string"/>
  </wsdl:message>

  <wsdl:portType name="CurrencyConverter">
     <wsdl:operation name="convert" parameterOrder="amount">
        <wsdl:input name="convertRequest" message="intf:convertRequest"/>
        <wsdl:output name="convertResponse" message="intf:convertResponse"/>
     </wsdl:operation>
  </wsdl:portType>

  <wsdl:binding name="CurrencyConverterSoapBinding"
             type="intf:CurrencyConverter">
     <wsdlsoap:binding style="rpc"
                    transport="http://schemas.xmlsoap.org/soap/http"/>
     <wsdl:operation name="convert">
        <wsdlsoap:operation soapAction=""/>
        <wsdl:input name="convertRequest">
           <wsdlsoap:body
               use="encoded"
               encodingStyle="http://schemas.xmlsoap.org/soap/encoding/"
               namespace="urn:converters"/>
        </wsdl:input>
        <wsdl:output name="convertResponse">
           <wsdlsoap:body
```

LISTING 25.5 Continued

```
                use="encoded"
                encodingStyle="http://schemas.xmlsoap.org/soap/encoding/"
                namespace="urn:converters"/>
          </wsdl:output>
       </wsdl:operation>
   </wsdl:binding>

   <wsdl:service name="CurrencyConverterService">
      <wsdl:port name="CurrencyConverter"
              binding="intf:CurrencyConverterSoapBinding">
         <wsdlsoap:address
              location="http://localhost:8080/axis/services/CurrencyConverter"/>
      </wsdl:port>
   </wsdl:service>
</wsdl:definitions>
```

CAUTION

When generating a WSDL file, make sure you use different package names for the prototype Web service classes and the `Java2WSDL` generated classes. If you use the same package name, you may overwrite your original prototype files or deploy the wrong class files to the Tomcat server.

Once you have the WSDL file for the Web service, you must generate the server-side skeleton and helper files using the WSDL2Java tool. The following command generates both the server-side and client-side implementation files (you will need to include the Axis JAR files in your `CLASSPATH` to run the `WSDL2Java` application):

```
java org.apache.axis.wsdl.WSDL2Java -s -d Session CurrencyConverter.wsdl
```

The `-s` option tells `WSDL2Java` to generate the server-side skeleton and implementation files, and the `-d Session` flag adds server support for client sessions to the generated skeleton files. You cannot stop `WSDL2Java` from generating the client-side files.

NOTE

The `WSDl2Java -d Session` (note the capital `S`) option adds session support to the server-side skeleton files. The client will still need to enable session support in order to involve the Web service in client-side sessions. This is discussed in the following section, "Developing the Client-Side Components."

The generated files are placed in a subdirectory with the same name as the package name defined in the WSDL file (in this case the `converters` directory).

The server-side Java files generated by `WSDL2Java -s` are

File	Description
`Conversion.java`	An implementation of the Conversion JavaBean compatible with the Axis bean serializer mechanism
`CurrencyConverter.java`	An interface definition for the Web service
`CurrencyConverterSoapBindingImpl.java`	A template class containing a no-operation implementation of the Web service
`ParseException.java`	A wrapper class that wraps the `java.text.ParseException` (thrown by the server) inside an `org.apache.axis.AxisFault` exception

In addition to the Java classes, `WSDL2Java` also generates the following Axis Web Service Deployment Descriptor (WSDD) files:

- `deploy.wsdd`
- `undeploy.wsdd`

These two files are used by the Axis `AdminClient` tool to deploy and undeploy an Axis Web Service. The `deploy.wsdd` file contains a definition of the Web service that enables Axis to associate the Web service URL with the `CurrencyConverterSoapBindingImpl` class that provides the Web service.

With the exception of the implementation of the service, the `WSDL2Java` tool has generated all of the files you need for your Web service.

To implement the service, you should take the generated `CurrencyConverterSoapBindingImpl.java` template file and add suitable code to define your service. Listing 25.6 shows the completed Currency Converter service (the code in bold has been added to the generated template).

LISTING 25.6 Currency Converter Web Service: `CurrencyConverterSoapBindingImpl.java`

```
package converters;

public class CurrencyConverterSoapBindingImpl
implements converters.CurrencyConverter {
```

LISTING 25.6 Continued

```
    public converters.Conversion convert(java.lang.String in0)
    throws java.rmi.RemoteException, converters.ParseException {
        if (bean == null)
            loadBean();
        try {
            bean.setAmount(in0);
            Conversion conv = new Conversion();
            conv.setAmount(bean.getAmount());
            conv.setConvertedAmount(bean.getConvertedAmount());
            return conv;
        }
        catch (java.text.ParseException ex) {
            throw new converters.ParseException();
        }
    }

    private ConverterBean bean;

    private void loadBean()    throws java.rmi.RemoteException {
        try {
            bean = new ConverterBean();
        }
        catch (java.sql.SQLException ex) {
            throw new java.rmi.RemoteException ("Converter bean failure", ex);
        }
        catch (javax.naming.NamingException ex) {
            throw new java.rmi.RemoteException ("Converter bean failure", ex);
        }
    }

}
```

In Listing 25.6, the `convert()` method must create a `ConverterBean` object if one does not already exist and then use this bean to do the conversion. The results of the conversion are encapsulated in the `Conversion` object that is returned to the client. The `converters.ConverterBean` class is the same as the one used in the simple JWS example in the section "A Simple Java Web Service."

Because the generated WSDD file requested server-side support for client sessions, multiple calls to this Web service from one client will reuse the same `CurrencyConverter` object rather than create a new one for each call.

CAUTION

The `WSDL2Java` utility will not overwrite an existing `SoapBindingImpl.java` file in the target directory. If you have written your implementation class and at some future point use `WSDL2Java` to regenerate the server-side skeleton files, you will not overwrite your existing implementation. Conversely, if you change the Web service functionality and regenerate the skeleton files, you will need to rename your old implementation file to create the new implementation template.

One additional point to note in Listing 25.6 is the use of Exception Layering design pattern (or idiom) to catch and then throw different exceptions from within the service. The generated `converters.ParseException` class is used to represent a `java.text.ParseException`, and a `java.rmi.RemoteException` is used to represent the other types of exception that can occur. This approach to exception handling is necessary because the exceptions thrown by an Axis Web Service method must either be a `RemoteException` or a subclass of `org.apache.axis.AxisFault`.

In Listing 25.6, an error in parsing the currency amount is treated as a fault with the client's request and is reported back to the client. However, an error with the underlying JNDI naming service or JDBC database is a server-side problem that is not dependent on the client request. The different nature of these two error conditions is reflected in the strategy of throwing two different exceptions back to the client. One form of error can be corrected by the client by resubmitting valid data, but the other cannot be corrected by the client.

After you have added the required functionality to the Web service implementation class, you can deploy your service. Compile the server-side Java files required for your service and deploy the application as follows:

1. Copy the following generated class files to *<CATALINA_HOME>*`/webapps/axis/WEB-INF/classes`:

   ```
   converters/CurrencyConverterSoapBindingImpl.class
   converters/CurrencyConverterSoapBindingImpl$1.class
   converters/CurrencyConverterSoapBindingImpl$ConversionImpl.class
   converters/CurrencyConverter.class
   converters/Conversion.class
   converters/ParseException.class
   ```

2. Ensure the following helper JavaBean classes are included in *<CATALINA_HOME>*`/webapps/axis/WEB-INF/classes`:

   ```
   converters/ConverterBean.class
   converters/ConverterBean$CurrencyFormat.class
   ```

3. Ensure the `jdbc/conversion` data source is defined in *<CATALINA_HOME>*`/conf/server.xml` as described in the section "Developing a Web Service."

4. Register your Web service using the Axis `AdminClient` tool as follows. Ensure Tomcat is running and enter the following command to register the `CurrencyConverter` example WSDD file in the `converters` subdirectory:

   ```
   java org.apache.axis.client.AdminClient converters/deploy.wsdd
   ```

CAUTION

You must be running the `axis` Web application to register a Web service, and all of the Web service class files must be deployed to the `axis` Web application.

You have now deployed and registered your Web service with Axis. You can test your service by retrieving the WSDL document available by browsing the URL `http://localhost:8080/axis/services/CurrencyConverter`. After you have published your Web service, you can develop a client that uses it.

Developing the Client-Side Components

Developing the client-side program for the `CurrencyConverter` Web service follows the same process used for the simple example previously described in the section "Developing a Web Service Client."

You have already generated the client-side Java helper files using the `WSDL2Java` command when you generated the server-side files. The client requires the following Java classes from the `converters` subdirectory:

- `Conversion.java`
- `CurrencyConverter.java`
- `CurrencyConverterService.java`
- `CurrencyConverterServiceLocator.java`
- `CurrencyConverterSoapBindingStub.java`
- `ParseException.java`

Listing 25.7 shows a JSP that uses the `CurrencyConverter` client-side classes to access the Web service.

LISTING 25.7 Using the Currency Converter Web Service with `convert.jsp`

```
<%@ page import="converters.*" %>
<% String amount = request.getParameter("amount"); %>
<HTML>
  <HEAD>
    <TITLE>Currency Converter Client</TITLE>
  </HEAD>
  <BODY>
    <H1>Currency Converter Client</H1>
    <FORM>
      <P>Amount to convert:
          <INPUT TYPE='text' NAME='amount'></P>
      <P><INPUT TYPE='submit' VALUE='Submit'></P>
    </FORM>
    <%     if (amount!=null && amount.length()>0) { %>
      <H2>
        <%
          try {
            CurrencyConverterService service =
                new CurrencyConverterServiceLocator();
            CurrencyConverter converter = service.getCurrencyConverter();
            ((CurrencyConverterSoapBindingStub)converter).
➥ setMaintainSession(true);
            Conversion results = converter.convert(amount);
            out.print(results.getAmount());
            out.print(" = ");
            out.print(results.getConvertedAmount());
          }
          catch (converters.ParseException ex) {
            out.print("<FONT COLOR='red'>Invalid number: "+amount+"</FONT>");
          }
        %>
      </H2>
    <% } %>
    <P><A HREF='<%=response.encodeURL("homepage")%>'>Return to home page</A></P>
  </BODY>
</HTML>
```

As with the previous Web service client example, this one uses the helper classes to locate the `CurrencyConverter` Web service using the following statements:

```
CurrencyConverterService service = new CurrencyConverterServiceLocator();
CurrencyConverter converter = service.getCurrencyConverter();
```

This client example must also inform the service that it requires the server to be involved with the client's session. The client does this by calling the `setMaintainSession()` method on the `org.apache.axis.client.Stub` superclass of the `CurrencyConverterSoapBindingStub` class as follows:

```
((CurrencyConverterSoapBindingStub)converter).setMaintainSession(true);
```

To deploy this client in a Web application called `web-services`, you will need to

1. Copy `convert.jsp` to `<CATALINA_HOME>/web-services`.
2. Copy the following compiled helper class files to `<CATALINA_HOME>/web-services/WEB-INF/classes`:

```
simple/CurrencyConverter.class
simple/CurrencyConverterService.class
simple/CurrencyConverterServiceLocator.class
simple/CurrencyConverterSoapBindingStub.class
simple/ParseException.class
```

3. Ensure your client Web application has access to the Axis JAR files. If you are deploying the Web application to the same server as the Web service, the Axis JAR files are already accessible as they are stored in `<CATALINA_HOME>/shared/lib`. If you are running the client on a different Web server to Axis, you will need to either include the Axis JAR files in the application's `WEB-INF/lib` directory or add them to `<CATALINA_HOME>/shared/lib`.

You can now run the Web service client by accessing `http://localhost:8080/web-services/convert.jsp`.

Congratulations—you have now written and deployed a Web service and client that participate in client-side HTTP sessions.

Summary

Web services are the natural marriage of Web-based resources with client/server applications. A Web service is an application server that is accessed through a URL. The following standards are used to ensure compatibility between Web service clients and servers developed using different technologies:

- Simple Object Access Protocol (SOAP) combines XML and Multipurpose Internet Mail Extensions (MIME) to provide a standard for transporting data messages over different transport mechanisms.
- Universal Description, Discovery, and Integration (UDDI) defines the standard for organizing, registering, and accessing information about Web services.

- Web Services Description Language (WSDL) uses XML to describe operations, data types, and bindings for Web services.

Web service clients and servers are written using simple method calls and method definitions. Client-side stub classes and server-side skeleton classes generated from the Web service definition (its WSDL document) are used to exchange data over the HTTP network connection.

The Apache Axis project (a successor to the Apache SOAP project) is an open source implementation of a Web service container and supporting utilities.

PART IV
Appendixes

IN THIS PART

A

Apache Software License, Version 1.1

Redistribution and use in source and binary forms, with or without modification, are permitted provided that the following conditions are met:

1. Redistributions of source code must retain the above copyright notice, this list of conditions and the following disclaimer.

2. Redistributions in binary form must reproduce the above copyright notice, this list of conditions and the following disclaimer in the documentation and/or other materials provided with the distribution.

3. The end-user documentation included with the redistribution, if any, must include the following acknowledgment:

   "This product includes software developed by the Apache Software Foundation (`http://www.apache.org/`)."

   Alternately, this acknowledgment may appear in the software itself, if and wherever such third-party acknowledgments normally appear.

4. The names "Apache" and "Apache Software Foundation" must not be used to endorse or promote products derived from this software without prior written permission. For written permission, please contact `apache@apache.org`.

5. Products derived from this software may not be called "Apache", nor may "Apache" appear in their name, without prior written permission of the Apache Software Foundation.

This software consists of voluntary contributions made by many individuals on behalf of the Apache Software Foundation. For more information on the Apache Software Foundation, please see `<http://www.apache.org/>`.

Portions of this software are based upon public domain software originally written at the National Center for Supercomputing Applications, University of Illinois, Urbana-Champaign.

B

Template web.xml File

Listing B.1 contains a web.xml deployment descriptor showing the nested structure of all the deployment descriptor elements discussed in the chapters of this book. Additional elements not discussed in the book have been omitted from this template.

In the following template, the textual leaf elements have been left blank except for the following conditions:

- A question mark (?) is used to mark an optional text element.
- A fixed set of values is listed in the body of the element when the element value is constrained to one of those values.

Optional nested elements that contain subelements are not indicated in the template, but in most cases, you can infer which are the optional elements from the optional nature of the functionality they represent (such as <context-param> in <web-app>).

Where there are alternative structures for an element (such as <servlet>, which can reference a <servlet-class> or a <jsp-file>), all element structures are indicated. The first form is shown with all possible nested tags, whereas subsequent variations show only the mandatory nested elements.

You should refer to the relevant chapters of this book or to the DTD in the servlet specification 2.3 for more information on the use of the individual deployment descriptor elements.

LISTING B.1 web.xml Deployment Descriptor Template

```
<!DOCTYPE
  web-app PUBLIC
  "-//Sun Microsystems, Inc.//DTD Web Application 2.2//EN"
  "http://java.sun.com/j2ee/dtds/web-app_2_2.dtd" >

<web-app>
  <display-name> ? </display-name>
  <description>  ? </description>

  <context-param>
    <param-name>   </param-name>
    <param-value>  </param-value>
  </context-param>

  <filter>
    <filter-name>    </filter-name>
    <display-name> ? </display-name>
    <description>  ? </description>
    <filter-class>   </filter-class>
    <init-param>
      <param-name>  </param-name>
      <param-value> </param-value>
    </init-param>
  </filter>

  <filter-mapping>
    <filter-name>  </filter-name>
    <url-pattern>  </url-pattern>
  <filter-mapping>

  <filter-mapping>
    <filter-name>  </filter-name>
    <servlet-name> </servlet-name>
  <filter-mapping>

  <listener>
    <listener-class> </listener-class>
  </listener>

  <servlet>
    <servlet-name>   </servlet-name>
```

LISTING B.1 Continued

```
    <display-name> ? </display-name>
    <description>  ? </description>
    <servlet-class>  </servlet-class>
    <init-param>
      <param-name>  </param-name>
      <param-value> </param-value>
    </init-param>
    <load-on-startup> true | false </load-on-startup>
    <security-role-ref>
      <description> ? </description>
      <role-name>     </role-name>
      <role-link>     </role-link>
    </security-role-ref>
  </servlet>
  <servlet>
    <servlet-name>  </servlet-name>
    <jsp-file>      </jsp-file>
  </servlet>

  <servlet-mapping>
    <servlet-name> </servlet-name>
    <url-pattern>  </url-pattern>
  </servlet-mapping>

  <session-config>
    <session-timeout> </session-timeout>
  </session-config>

  <welcome-file-list>
    <welcome-file> </welcome-file>
  </welcome-file-list>

  <error-page>
    <error-code> </error-code>
    <location>   </location>
  </error-page>
  <error-page>
    <exception-type> </exception-type>
    <location>       </location>
  </error-page>
```

LISTING B.1 Continued

```
<taglib>
  <taglib-uri>      </taglib-uri>
  <taglib-location> </taglib-location>
</taglib>

<resource-ref>
  <description> ? </description>
  <res-ref-name>  </res-ref-name>
  <res-type>      </res-type>
  <res-auth> Application | Container </res-auth>
  <res-sharing-scope> Shareable | Unshareable </res-sharing-scope>

<security-constraint>
  <display-name> ? </display-name>
  <web-resource-collection>
    <web-resource-name>  </web-resource-name>
    <description> ?      </description>
    <url-pattern>        </url-pattern>
    <http-method> GET | POST | ... </http-method>
  </web-resource-collection>
  <auth-constraint>
    <description> ? </description>
    <role-name>     </role-name>
  </auth-constraint>
  <user-data-constraint>
    <description> ? </description>
    <transport-guarantee> NONE | INTEGERAL | CONFIDENTIAL </transport-guarantee>
  </user-data-constraint>
</security-constraint>

<login-config>
  <auth-method> BASIC | DIGEST | FORM | CLIENT-CERT </auth-method>
  <realm-name> </realm-name>
  <form-login-config>
    <form-login-page> </form-login-page>
    <form-error-page> </form-error-page>
  </form-login-config>
</login-config>
```

LISTING B.1 Continued

```
  <security-role>
    <description> ? </description>
    <role-name>     </role-name>
  </security-role>

</web-app>
```

Index

A

D

E

F

G

H

I

J-K

L

M

N

O

P-Q

R

T

U

V

W

X-Z

Content Master
www.contentmaster.com

Content Master is one of the world's leading technical authoring and consultancy organisations, working with key software vendors to provide leading-edge content to technical audiences. This content, combined with our business knowledge helps enable business decision makers, developers and IT Professionals to keep abreast of new initiatives, helping them build innovative enterprise solutions.

We also offer educational and content consultancy, identifying the most effective strategies for the development and deployment of materials. Our unique approach encompasses technical, business and educational requirements. This ensures that developed content not only offers the right level of specialist knowledge but that it addresses commercial requirements and is structured in the most effective way. This covers a range of media, including web, print and CD.

Other Content Master books:

Sams Teach Yourself J2EE in 21 Days
ISBN: 0-672-32384-2

Tomcat Kick Start
ISBN: 0-672-32439-3

JavaServer Pages 2.0 Unleashed
ISBN: 0-672-32438-5

Content Master

Tortworth House
Tortworth
Wotton-under-Edge
Gloucestershire
GL12 8HQ
http://www.contentmaster.com
Call +44 1454 269222

Content Master has worked with customers to develop strategies to address:

- Internal and external web sites
- Internal systems and business documentation
- Internal and external training materials
- Content development strategies
- Training business strategies

Our other core products and skills include the following;

- Books for publication: Working with the major publishing houses, we author books aimed at the technical and business decision maker audiences
- Content creation:
  - White papers
  - Case studies
  - Blueprints
  - Website Content
  - Deployment guides
  - Software development kits
  - Best practice documentation
  - Business Decision Maker seminars
  - Sales and marketing collateral
- Courseware: we write classroom based and multi-media training courses for leading software companies, usually under the brand of the commissioning vendor
- Resource: we regularly provide the following to our partners:
  - Program managers
  - Technical writers
  - Subject matter experts
  - Testing facilities and resource
  - Editors
  - Instructional designers
  - Consultants